KEENE PUBLIC LIBRARY

D1396979

AUG 2 4 2015

"…Face to Face *is a much-needed, neuroscience-based and well-practiced guide for parents, counselors and all adults who care deeply about the critical and positive development of the youth of our nation. I applaud the authors' clear guidance and essential focus on the positive 'Touchstones' of strong and continuous relational experiences, multiple and rich social connections, mindfulness and reflective skill development, empathic and authentic conversations, and intentional activities and interactions with others. Although these resiliency building blocks are frequently at odds with the fast-moving and disconnected daily lives of youth and families,* Face to Face *provides creative solutions through realistic activities to ensure future well-being and resiliency for every youth. This is a must-read for all parents, professionals and those connected with youth as a step-by-step commitment to strengthening families, youth, our communities and our future human capital."*

DAVID W. WILLIS, MD, FAAP, Pediatrician and founder of the Children's Development Health Institute

"Face to Face *knocks it out of the park as an indispensable guide to safe navigation of families and kids in the digital world. Every parent and caring adult must have this resource!"*

DIANA STERLING, Author of *The Parent as Coach Approach* and founder of The Academy for Family Coach Training

"This book is a vital resource for all parents, educators, health care providers and those who work with, or live in proximity to, children. Jam packed with wisdom, resources, and creative ideas, Face to Face *provides a complete tool kit for facilitating childhoods that are rich with embodied experience, healthy relationships, and hearty cognitive and emotional development. With topics ranging from the impact of technology to how gender influences a child's development to the development of resilience, the authors have gleaned the best resources available and put them in one place for easy accessibility. I will be gifting this book to everyone I know who is important in the life of a child."*

DOREEN DODGEN-MAGEE, PsyD, Psychologist and nationally known speaker focusing on the importance of intentionality regarding media and technology engagement

"Never before have young people had access to the world in its uncensored enormity. Bravo to the Family Empowerment group for writing and compiling such relevant and practical information. This guide is an essential tool of navigation for all involved in the lives of our youth."

NICOLE JON CARROLL, MSW, LCSW, Founder and director of Stand for Courage

"In my 25 years working with children and families, the digital revolution has been the most significant change to the family landscape. Many parents are at a loss as to how to respond… In Face to Face, *parents will find help clarifying their values and expectations regarding media and their families.*

HOWARD HITON, MS, LPC, Counselor and co-author of *BAM! Boys Advocacy and Mentoring*

j 004.67
MASAR

"The team at Family Empowerment Network brings excellent background and insight to this new work, Face to Face. The discussion guide is thoroughly grounded in research. It's also chock full of effective, practical strategies to address kids' social issues in a positive and proactive manner."

> **NANCY WILLARD**, Founder of Embrace Civility in the Digital Age and author of *Cyber Savvy, Cyberbullying,* and *Be a Friend-Lend a Hand*

"This book can change your family's world! It's filled with information and research on the impact screens have on kids' brains—and, ultimately, their lives. Plus, the fact that Face to Face is set-up as a discussion guide takes it to the next level in facilitating proactive, positive cultural change around childhood and screens. It's a must-have in every American home."

> **SUSAN WELLMAN**, Founder of The Ophelia Project

"My whole professional career has been about supporting youth and their families to connect and thrive. And now here is a book with inspiring touchstones that can guide parents on their journey to nurture empathetic, resilient children and teens."

> **BETH HOSSFELD**, LMFT, Co-Founder of One Circle Foundation, curriculum and trainings for strengths-based, gender-responsive circle models for youth, adults, and families

"Are you looking for a book that can offer a springboard into a host of fascinating parenting issues? Are discussions with other parents about social and emotional learning your interest? If so, then you've found your book. This timely volume offers a miniature encyclopedia of the important issues facing parents today. Problems such as eating disorders, anxiety, emotional bonding, digital technology, forming friendships, organized sports, and a host of other relevant and important challenges facing the modern parent are addressed by experts in the field. Dip in, find your interests, and enjoy!"

> **ELIZABETH ENGLANDER**, PhD, Director of the Massachusetts Aggression Reduction Center and Professor of Psychology at Bridgewater State University

"We've seen more and more teachers and students engaging to address the serious problem of bullying. But we need parents to be empowered to find meaningful ways to participate in the effort as well. Face to Face is a critical new resource that makes it easy for any adult who loves young people to do just that. I will be sharing this important new resource whenever I can!"

> **DEBRA CHASNOFF**, Award-winning producer and president of GroundSpark

Face to Face

Cultivating Kids' Social Lives in Today's Digital World

Kathy Masarie MD
Kathy Keller Jones MA
Jody Bellant Scheer MD
Cassandra Dickson MA
Ruth Matinko-Wald MA
Monique Terner MEd

Family Empowerment Network®

Copyright ©2014 Family Empowerment Network®
No part of this book may be used or reproduced without written permission. All rights reserved.

See the Permission List at the back for articles whose permission must be obtained separately. For permission to reproduce any material in this parenting guide not in the Permission List, please send your request to:

Family Empowerment Network®
6663 SW Beaverton-Hillsdale Hwy., PMB 158, Portland, OR 97225
info@family-empower.com   www.family-empower.com

Library of Congress Control Number: 2013949452
ISBN 978-0-9819504-4-0
Printed in the United States of America

Contents

Contents: Articles

Foreward

Stan Davis

Co-researcher, Youth Voice Project
Author of *Schools Where Everyone Belongs* and
Empowering Bystanders in Bullying Prevention
Stopbullyingnow.com

There are a lot of books about raising children. Just now I searched for the word "parenting" in the catalog of a major online book seller and found listings for more than 80,000 different books. Anyone who reads more than a few of these books will find that the advice varies widely from book to book. What are parents to do? I suggest we think about the many *different* goals parents might have for their children. What are *your* most important goals in parenting?

In the 1950s, when I was a child, many parents would have listed good manners, obedience, hard work, and self-control as their primary goals for developing children. In the 1980s, when I was raising children of my own, many parents would instead have described their primary goals for their children as creativity, self-expression, and high self-esteem. These two sets of goals led us to quite different methods of parenting. In 2013 I am part of the family team raising my young granddaughter. Based on our rapidly increasing knowledge about child development, what should our goals be in raising children in this changing Digital Age?

We could focus on raising obedient, conforming children, who do what they are told to do. In doing this, we could lean heavily on praise, rewards, and punishments. We could tell them that we are proud of them when they do what we want, then tell them that we are disappointed or hurt when they do not do what we want. Parenting approaches based on these goals can help youth learn to follow rules, to meet social expectations, and to work hard to please others. On the other hand, we know from the research of Edward Deci and others that young people who comply with rules *just* to obtain praise or rewards are likely to lack internal motivation and may follow life-paths that are not the best for them, just to please significant others in their lives. In addition, today's youth have many other digital voices competing with us to tell them what to do. It is more important than ever that our youth be able to think critically for themselves instead of just doing what they are told. This book will help you teach young people to think for themselves–to immunize your kids against peer pressure and media pressure.

We could raise children who follow their own individual paths, who focus on self expression. We can help each young person see him- or her-self as unique and special. Such parenting approaches based primarily on building self-esteem may maximize unearned praise and avoid rules, frustrations, and negative feedback. Parenting approaches based on these goals can help youth feel pride in themselves. On the other hand, we now know from the research of Carol Dweck and other developmental psychologists that people who think of themselves as smart or talented or "gifted" when they succeed are likely to avoid challenges and become helpless when they experience setbacks or disappointments in life. We also have a body of research about the unintended negative effects of the self-esteem movement–research by Baumeister and others–which shows us that unearned praise can lead to a *reduction* in effort and in a reduction in caring for others. There is a fine line between self-esteem and narcissism. In contrast to that approach, methods in this book will help you to raise children who value themselves *and* who can work hard, who can work toward goals, and who know the value of service to others.

What, then, can our goals be in raising children? I propose that we work toward five interlinked goals:

- Internal motivation for growth
- Self-control
- Empathy
- Self-efficacy
- Resiliency

Internal Motivation for Growth

At present (in the summer of 2013), our granddaughter is almost a year and a half old. We have watched her learn to crawl, sit up, and walk. We are watching her learn to use language to tell us what she needs and wants. She is listening and watching while we read to her, and repeating words from books. She is learning, in spectacularly messy ways, to feed herself. There is something striking about her quest for mastery: She expresses joy when she can do something she couldn't do when she was younger. In a video we made when she was learning to pull herself up to stand, her effort is obvious. She concentrates her whole being into her arms and legs. Then there is a moment where she is standing. In that moment, her whole face is taken over with a smile. Our unconditional love supports her internal motivation for learning. We want *her* to keep being excited about growth and learning instead of focusing on whether she is pleasing *us* when she accomplishes something. When she realizes that she has mastered something, she feels joy. As she grows, we plan to help her make that connection more and more consciously by helping her realize what strategies or actions helped her learn or accomplish something. We will also help her notice how she feels about that learning or accomplishment. You will learn more about effective and ineffective praise in this book.

Self-control

Self-control has two meanings, which are both important in child-rearing. First, youth need to learn to delay gratification, to think about their actions before doing them, and to avoid acting aggressively when they feel anger or frustration. This is the *control* part of this phrase. Spending time with our granddaughter reminds me that waiting is difficult for the very young and has to be learned. Second, youth need to learn to direct their own actions instead of being directed by others. This is the *self* part of the phrase, and it is especially important in the Digital Age. We can help youth learn self-control by teaching them to wait to get what they want. When they have used self-control, we can help them see how they controlled themselves. We can help them see that things got better when they avoided hitting, or did their homework even if they didn't want to, or kept mean words to themselves. Self-control can be developed over time. We help youth to make their own decisions when we talk with them about the choices they have made, what happened after they made those choices, and how they feel about those outcomes.

Empathy

Most human beings are hard-wired to feel empathy. We experience others' sadness or anger or joy almost as if it were our own. Young babies often laugh when others are laughing, for example. We can nurture that innate sense of empathy as children grow, helping them see that others' needs are important and that helping others feels good. Key to that development is a family environment that models valuing others, in which people help each other, and in which people serve people outside the family. We can also help young people to be emotionally literate–that is, to have and use a wide range of words to describe emotions and to have a sense of how to respond to their own and others' emotions. You will learn strategies for promoting empathy in this book.

Self-efficacy

Many of us who were converts to the self-esteem movement in the 1970s now wish that we had instead put the same effort into building young peoples' sense of *efficacy*. Youth with self-efficacy see that their actions make a difference, and that they have the power—through those actions—to do good things. This shift from a focus on self-esteem to self-efficacy leads us to shift from praise to objective feedback about how a child accomplished something. You will learn more about effective use of feedback in this book. Focusing on children's strategies and on the outcome of those strategies helps youth see that they have the power to make their own, and others', lives better. That sense of efficacy builds authentic self-confidence and independence.

Resiliency

As a grandparent, I would like to be able to guarantee my grandchild a life free of negative events. As a person in my 60s, I know that this will not come to pass. People will break her heart. She will set goals and not meet them. Some bad things will happen to her. We want our children to be able to go on—to bounce back—when bad things happen. The keys to resiliency are interwoven with all the goals described above. When youth see that their successes were caused by their choices and strategies, they are more likely to see their failures as things they can change. When youth have unconditional love and connection with others, they are less hurt by failure and loss. Resiliency is a crucial product, then, of all these other goals.

I want to end this foreword with a few principles for raising autonomous, caring, resilient youth. Throughout this book, you will find strategies to extend these principles into our day-to-day parenting behavior. What are your core principles in raising your children? Here are mine:

- Provide unconditional love and nurturing.
- Help youth maintain their own inherent internal motivation for growth.
- Help youth see and understand the outcomes of their own positive (and negative) actions.
- Help youth develop skills as problem solvers.
- Model caring and respect and expect youth to show respect to other people.
- Set and enforce loving limits to help youth learn self-control.
- Help youth learn to be good friends to themselves and others and know how to work together even with people they don't like.

I recommend this book highly. It will help you set goals. It will help you help children learn to think for themselves and help them care for others. This book will help you make and protect family time while it supports you in helping youth navigate their digital lives outside the family. This book will help you raise *resilient* youth, who can overcome stressful events, and to find ways to protect young people from problems they cannot deal with themselves.

In this book you will meet many diverse writers who have thought deeply about what children and teens need. You will also find useful discussion questions to help you and other parents think through these ideas for yourselves, and choose your own path through the landscape of modern parenting.

Stan Davis
Wayne, Maine
August, 2013

Acknowledgements

On behalf of our writing team, I am honored to pen the acknowledgements for this labor of love that has a very long history. In fact, *Face to Face: Cultivating Kids' Social Lives in the Digital World* has its roots in a parent discussion guide created a decade ago through the non-profit organization, Full Esteem Ahead, founded by Dr. Kathy Masarie.

We had just released the first edition of *Raising Our Daughters* in 2004, as more research was becoming available about peer mistreatment (aka bullying). So, with the help of a diverse group of volunteers, we wrote and compiled *Kids' Social Lives and Peer Aggression*. The book had a short life as a spiral-bound volume copied at the local Postal Annex. When Full Esteem Ahead closed its doors, *Kids' Social Lives and Peer Aggression* died with it.

When Dr. Masarie reopened her business as Family Empowerment Network in 2009, she began by rewriting and publishing updated editions of *Raising Our Daughters* and *Raising Our Sons*, supported by co-authors Kathy and Jody, and spreading the word nationally about using our guides to network with other parents and build supportive communities. That left revisiting *Kids' Social Lives and Bullying*, if we were going to support parents and educators with a tool to help them to understand and deal with the perils of peer mistreatment.

The effort was truly a collaborative one. Our six authors represent various backgrounds and expertise. We worked diligently to reach consensus throughout the process, striving to always keep in mind our goal of providing parents and educators with a book that would empower them to raise competent, compassionate children.

Although we tried to incorporate some of the work from the 2004 volume—acknowledging all the work and dedication that went into that first, comprehensive guide—it quickly became apparent to our team that a lot had changed in the last decade and there was so much more to address regarding kids' social lives than just bullying. Given the predominance of media and screen technology in our Digital Age, American families now have a whole new set of challenges we had not dreamed about in 2004! Furthermore, with the burgeoning science of Interpersonal Neurobiology, we also now know so much more about how our brains work and what that means for child development and, ultimately, parenting.

In the early phase of our two-year endeavor to write this book, a number of volunteers assisted us with the initial steering and helped us to review recent literature. To those individuals, we are grateful: Debbie Schuster, Rose Wolfe, and Kate Grant. Glenda Montgomery also stepped up and provided a huge assist with our resiliency chapter. For that we are indebted! Once we had a first draft, we piloted the guide with two groups, one facilitated by Kathy Keller Jones, and the other, by Monique Terner. Kathy's group included Beth Azar, Vicki Bruno, Mary Frazel, Jennifer Freda-Cowie, Heidi McNamee, Erin Morris, and Diana Stickler. Monique's group was composed of Janet Creasy, Alison Jakel, Berdine Jordan, Jean Knahahara, Susan Maginn, Nora Mahmoud, and Luciana Proaño. Their input was invaluable in pointing out areas where parents wanted more information, more research, or more ideas. We can't thank them enough for their time and careful attention to providing us with detailed, honest feedback. The book would not be what it is without their insightful comments.

We also would like to extend a heartfelt "thank you" to those talented, creative individuals who made this book easy to use and easy on the eye:

Cover, touchstones, and graphic design concept: Machele Brass (www.brassdesign.net)
Interior graphic design and layout: Rachel Wald
Cover photograph: Maya Scheer
Cover models: Zesean Ali, Jacqueline Lute, Monnie Spears-Rogers, Shannon Tran, Sydney Tran, and Tyler Thomas

A round of applause also goes to Alana Orzol, who supported us in managing the details of forms, resources, and permissions as our calm, able administrative assistant, and to Julia McLeod, who reviewed the manuscript as our content editor and whose spot-on remarks actually changed the scope of our book. In addition, all the parents whose stories we include deserve a tip of the hat; through sharing your real-life experiences, others will learn what may or may not work for them. (Note: Those stories in the guide without a byline belong to one of the authors or is a story we were asked to keep anonymous. All the stories are true.)

Finally, we thank the many contributors to *Face to Face* who have generously shared their work, words, and ideas—especially Stan Davis. All of you have made our discussion guide a compendium of the latest research, tools, and tips for fostering empathy, connection, and resilience. As adults working in child advocacy in one way or another, each one of you is a shining star, making the world a better place for our children.

Ruth Matinko-Wald
Co-Author, Editor, and Production Coordinator
for *Face to Face: Cultivating Kids' Social Lives in Today's Digital World*

Exploring Values and the Lay of the Land

1
2
3
4
5
6
7
8

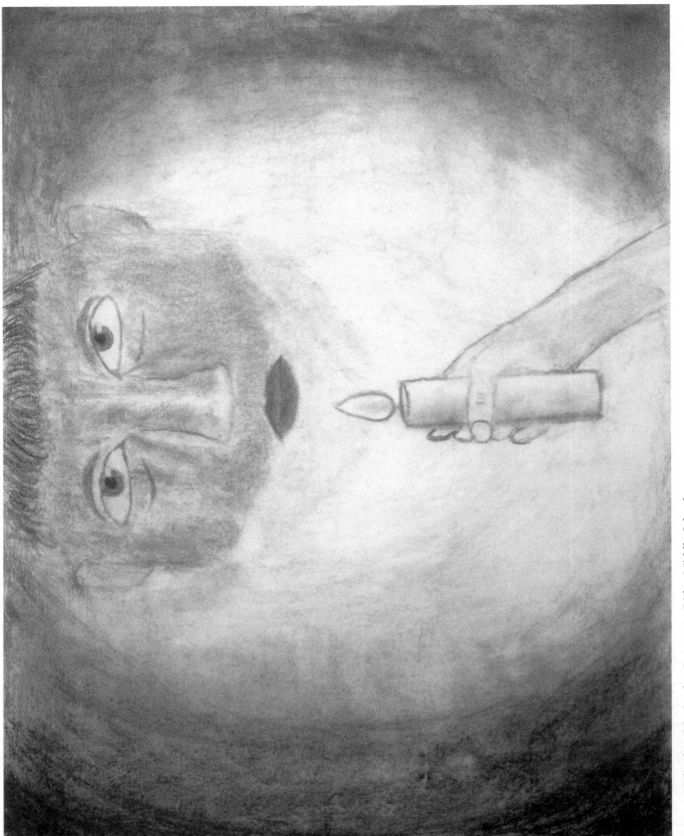

Danny Walinsky, 7th Grader, Rosemont Ridge Middle School

chapter one

Exploring Values
and the Lay of the Land

*"Blessed is the influence of one true,
loving soul on another."* – George Eliot

Raising children is like an odyssey, full of wonders and woes, triumphs and trials. As parents, counselors, grandparents, and other caring adults, we lovingly strive to support our children to become competent, caring, and responsible adults with fulfilling relationships, and our job is not always easy. We live in a world heavily guided by media and technology, with "screens" increasingly competing for our time and attention. But fostering face-to-face relationships continues to be the surest path to family happiness, vital friendships, individual fulfillment, and a caring society. To ensure that the significant value of face-to-face relationships is not lost, this guidebook advocates for mindfulness, learning, and networking with others. We invite you to join us as we work to cultivate healthy kids' social lives in today's Digital Age.

All children long for the gifts of significance, love, and belonging. As parents and loving caregivers, we hold the key to these gifts–to ensuring that children thrive. What is this key? Fortunately, new research in neuroscience offers us the answer: connection. We now know for certain that it is in each other's voices and faces and in our own pauses and reflections that we find and build our best human selves. Neuroscience research also reaffirms what we instinctively know is the way to connection and, ultimately, healthy human development: face-to-face relationships and real-time experiences.

For countless generations, families and communities have been building connection, empathy, and safe havens for their children. These sacred elements are the foundations of our social lives and can grow into resilience, success, and strong social and emotional skills. Yet today's parents are in new terrain as they struggle to maintain the integrity of the family, its values, and practices in the Digital Age. It goes without saying that technology provides many wondrous conveniences and opportunities in our everyday lives, but we also might consider what we risk compromising in this new landscape if we are not mindful.

Face to Face: Cultivating Kids' Social Lives in Today's Digital World is a discussion guide that:

- Is authored by a team of pediatricians, counselors, educators, and parents
- Focuses on fostering empathy, connection, and resilience
- Offers tools and tips for connecting deeply with kids
- Addresses healthy friendships as well as peer mistreatment
- Advocates for parent-to-parent networking
- Leads to long-term change by building stronger families and communities

This book can easily be used by individuals and couples who wish to explore parenting issues. It also can be used as a guidebook for self-led discussion groups of caring adults who wish to share experiences, build community, and expand the village within which they are raising their children.

© 2014 FAMILY EMPOWERMENT NETWORK™ ALL RIGHTS RESERVED.

Raising children has always been one of life's most demanding and rewarding endeavors—and it also has always been about balancing acts, creativity, and finding support in our communities. Indeed, the idea that parents alone cannot provide everything needed for children to thrive dates back millennia to a world of many small, isolated villages where people quickly learned that a supportive network of caring, connected community members can help children to grow optimally and to succeed. It really does take a village to raise a child!

What happens to the nurturing village model, however, when a digital revolution arrives? If face-to-face relationships matter most to our kids' development, how do we continue to cultivate and model interpersonal relationships at home and in the community in an age of instant gratification, airbrushing, and distancing screen technologies? Do entertaining- or productivity-enhancing devices afford us family time, joy, and fulfillment? As screen time increases for everyone in the family, including potentially its youngest members, do we look to our devices for the rewarding feelings we used to provide naturally for each other? In a world of beeping devices, how do we find and claim the quiet solitude and the reflective space that also are integral to balanced human development?

EMBRACE THE CHALLENGE

When it comes to embracing the Digital Age, our children—who are digital natives—are growing up with screens as everyday tools. Nonetheless, now knowing that human brains are optimally wired by interpersonal experiences, nurturing face-to-face relationships must remain our first priority.

Certainly, humans have had to successfully adapt to many new technologies in the past, from the printing press to the automobile. A clear difference with this social revolution, however, is that no other new technology has wielded such direct and intimate influence on a child's developing brain. When the pull of a new technology is so powerfully seductive, how do we help our child to balance screen time with his development into a whole and healthy self?

Granted, parents have always been responsible for creating a loving, supportive, and empowering home environment for their children, but we see the emergence of a critical new role for parents to play in the Digital Age: If our goal is to raise connected, resilient, successful, and empathic children, we must deeply connect with our children and make sure that, at each developmental stage, they have enough time in the real world and enough face-to-face practice to hone vital life skills.

This guidebook is meant to offer support as you embrace this dual challenge of connecting with your children and learning how to creatively adapt to the Digital Age. We begin with the idea of taking the time to identify what matters the most. When we slow down and take the time, we naturally tap into our parental wisdom and connect with our deepest values. Embracing these values will support us in wisely parenting a child of any age.

> *Our deepest wish is that children experience significance, love, and belonging at home in connection with their families, and that over time this connection flowers into a life well-lived within the greater community.*

Taking the time to delineate clearly our most deeply held values empowers us to intentionally structure personal, family, and community time in a way that encourages face-to-face interactions and supports everyone's well-being. Consciously choosing to take the time to reflect on how we are actually living our values allows us to balance our own lives and model this balance for our families. Warning: Mindfully living your family values requires attention and vigilence. Sometimes the most cherished principles and values are overwhelmed by the logistics

ALL RIGHTS RESERVED. © 2014 FAMILY EMPOWERMENT NETWORK™

of a busy, everyday life. Humor and forgiveness are key ingredients for embracing the effort and enjoying the journey.

GUIDEBOOK OVERVIEW

The goal of this guidebook is to offer an overview of current ideas and research in the fields of child development, brain science, and parenting that can help to inform our choices. We particularly admire the work of the following experts and share their research and perspectives throughout this guidebook for your consideration and learning: **Brené Brown, Stan Davis, Carol Dweck, Elizabeth Englander, Ellen Galinsky, Clifford Nass, Jane Nelsen, Charisse Nixon, Kim John Payne, Bruce Perry, Marshall Rosenberg, Daniel Siegel, Rachel Simmons, Michael Thompson, Sherry Turkle, and Rosalind Wiseman.** You will find their books and many others listed in our **"Resources"** section. Our ultimate hope is that you will find meaning in the work of these researchers and weave their insights into your everyday life as you raise happy, strong, thriving children.

One powerful way to utilize this guidebook is by using it as a curriculum for a discussion group with a partner,

friends, other parents, or co-workers. We cannot stress enough the power of connection and networking! By participating in a discussion group about the book, you will find allies, gain wisdom, and create community for your whole family.

Finally, we acknowledge that some of life's biggest challenges and most difficult conflicts stem from a lack of understanding of the diversity in our world and the myriad differing points of view. With this in mind, we have written *Face to Face* fully aware that we, as authors, are products of our own upbringings and regional biases and that we may not adequately represent all backgrounds. Nonetheless, we hope what we offer can be valuable to diverse populations. We encourage you to use the book as a springboard for discussion with others, especially people of different backgrounds. Our intention is that the guidebook will provoke thought and stimulate questions about parenting issues that cross cultural boundaries.

TOUCHSTONES

Sometimes we feel lost, are unsure of ourselves as parents, and long for guidance. It can happen to anyone. For that reason, throughout the book we share six "touchstones" which represent what research shows to be important for healthy and authentic living:

Cultivate Empathy

Stay Connected

Create Safe Havens

Walk the Talk

Take the Time

Play/Create

In Ancient Greece, a touchstone was a tool of guidance, the stone used to determine the value of other precious stones. Used here, our touchstones can empower you

© 2014 FAMILY EMPOWERMENT NETWORK™ ALL RIGHTS RESERVED.

to create a nurturing home and to build bridges to safe havens in your greater community. Safe havens support both a strong sense of connection to family and community as well as offer a foundation for individuation as children navigate the stages of their lives.

We will elaborate on the touchstones in more detail in Chapter 2, and you will find them scattered through the guidebook. They can help to ground you when you are making decisions and can add clarity to the many complex situations that can arise during the course of parenting.

CHAPTER HIGHLIGHTS

Chapter 1: Introduction

This introductory chapter with its Circle Question, discussion questions, and exercises is intended to orient you, to help you break the ice with co-participants if you are in a book group, and to encourage you to explore your values and priorities.

Chapter 2: Parenting Touchstones

A child's first relationship, that with his parents or guardian, lays the critical template for a child's ability to engage with the world. In essence, a child's sense of belonging, connection, empathy, self-worth, and resilience starts here. In this chapter, we explore our six touchstones in depth and delve into how they can guide parents through the phases of kids' social and emotional development. We also remind parents that parenting with mindfulness paves the path for a caring society and bestows lifelong gifts to our children.

Chapter 3: Outside Influences

Being aware of how the forces outside the family can potentially influence our children and ourselves can help to inform our parenting. To that end, this chapter explores consumerism, lookism, gender stereotyping, and digital technology overuse—all of which can overwhelm our lives unless we take active steps to counteract them.

Vigilance about toxic outside influences can help parents to establish safe boundaries for their children so everyone can enjoy the wonder of our world.

Chapter 4: Friendship and Social Groups

Here we explore how kids develop friendships–from connection in the home to the challenges of navigating social groups at school. Our goal is to help you to become aware of how you can encourage and support children's flourishing friendships. We also take a look at the special challenges faced by minority groups.

Chapter 5: Peer Mistreatment

This chapter provides an overview of the basic tools needed to understand childhood peer mistreatment, also called "bullying." Our focus is on whether behavior is acceptable or not, rather than on whether a child is a bully or not. We propose that empathy is the most important skill for helping everyone–those who mistreat others, those who are targets, and those who are witnesses. Learning about peer mistreatment can help parents deal with this ubiquitous and difficult childhood experience.

Chapter 6: Fostering Resilience

In the face of negative influences and challenging social dynamics, how do we raise children to be strong and resilient? This chapter explores key strategies–including being brave enough to let our kids fail, allowing them to gradually hone their skills for dealing with the inevitable ups and downs of life. We also examine how overparenting, fear, perfectionism, scarcity, and shame can undermine our efforts in helping children to become their best selves.

Chapter 7: Courage to Act

Using the touchstones as guideposts, this chapter challenges you to summon the courage to act to positively impact your family. We explore how communities might foster healthy friendships, resilience, and safe havens for our youth. And we ask the question: What actions could you take that would improve the empathy, compassion, and joy in your wider world?

ALL RIGHTS RESERVED. © 2014 FAMILY EMPOWERMENT NETWORK™

HOW TO USE EACH CHAPTER

Each chapter starts with an overview of topics related to various aspects of kids' social lives. We supplement the overviews with related articles and conclude with discussion questions, suggestions on how to take action, and further resources. The articles feature a range of information, research, and opinions exploring topics in detail. Some readers may choose to skip an article or two, based upon personal interests and concerns.

Our questions and activities are meant to challenge you to tap into your own wisdom, values, and opinions. We encourage you to use the **"Circle Question"** page formally in a group or informally with your partner or a friend. You might even talk about what you learn with your children, perhaps during a family meeting. Sharing openly and honestly with others builds strong connections and will go a long way toward affirming your values and strengthening your personal support system.

If you are using this guidebook within the framework of a discussion group, you will want to refer to the **"Guidelines for Discussion Groups"** at the end of the book. These Guidelines, for example, suggest that each meeting last approximately 1.5 hours and that the first 20 minutes of each meeting be devoted to everyone taking turns answering the Circle Question, so everyone has a chance to share.

––––––––––––––––––––

GETTING STARTED

When it comes to the all-important work of living your values, you ultimately will create your own blueprint. Every family will have its own path. Determining your path will be easier if your individual and family values are well defined and understood–and if you make an effort to align your actions with your values. This takes time and courage and may require facing off against prevailing cultural currents and pressures.

To remind you about being mindful of and living your values, we follow this introduction with three suggested activities. The first activity, entitled **"The Rocks and the Jar: Figuring Out What Matters Most in Your Life,"** illustrates how becoming aware of your own priorities can help you to determine how to structure your time. It is also a great activity to enjoy with your partner and/or your children. If you are using *Face to Face* with a discussion group, you could read "The Rocks and the Jar" aloud, spend some time writing out your answers to the questions that follow, and then share your answers.

The second exercise is **"Values Clarification for Families: Exploring Values with Your Children."** A multitude of ways exist to use this exercise. We hope you will come up with something that will serve as a reminder of the family values you want to nurture and prioritize in your daily life, decisions, and relationships.

Finally, we conclude with **"Values Clarification: Exploring Your Personal Values."** This will help you to consciously clarify the values you hold most dear. You will be able to consider if your time is spent actively supporting your highest values. You will recognize where our culture is either nurturing or undermining your parental goals. Ultimately, we hope you will have the courage to take the brave steps needed to choose how you and your children will interact in today's Digital Age.

––––––––––––––––––––

ENJOY THE JOURNEY!

You have all the wisdom and love necessary to bring out your child's most wonderful, authentic self. Gather your courage, trust your instincts, and enjoy the journey!

© 2014 FAMILY EMPOWERMENT NETWORK™ ALL RIGHTS RESERVED.

The Rocks and Jar Exercise:
Figuring Out What Matters Most in Your Life

The importance of taking the time to discern our values is illustrated by the following story of "The Rocks and the Jar." To illustrate the story, here is a YouTube version (www.youtube.com/watch?v=q1as4DNOy3s) featuring author Stephen Covey. Watch the video or read the story and answer the questions that follow.

Alternatively, you may choose to be creative and design your own jar at home, or you might want to discuss the idea of the rocks and the jar with your children and have them identify six or seven "big rocks" to include in the jar (or bucket) they create. This can even be done in a drawing, with construction paper, or with rocks, pebbles, and sand. Be creative and display your rocks and the jar(s) as a reminder of prioritizing what's truly valued in your family.

THE ROCKS AND THE JAR (ANON.)

A philosophy teacher stood before his class and had some items in front of him. When class began, he wordlessly picked up a one-gallon wide-mouthed mason jar and proceeded to fill it with fist-sized rocks right to the top. He then asked the students, "Is the jar full?

They agreed that it was. "Really?" he asked. "Let's see."

So the teacher then picked up a box of pebbles and poured them into the jar. He shook the jar lightly. The pebbles, of course, rolled into the open areas between the rocks. The students laughed. The teacher smiled benevolently and asked again, "Is the jar full?"

The class was catching on quickly. "Probably not," one of them answered.

"Very good!" he replied. The teacher then picked up a box of sand and poured it into the jar. Of course, the sand filled up all the spaces between the rocks and the pebbles. When he was finished, he once again asked, "Is this jar full yet?"

"No!" the class shouted.

"Excellent!" he replied.

He then grabbed a pitcher of water and poured it in until the jar was filled to the brim. Once again, looking intently into the eyes of each student, he asked, "What is the point of this demonstration?"

One eager beaver raised his hand and said, "The point is, no matter how full your life is, if you try really hard, you can always fit some more things into it!"

 ALL RIGHTS RESERVED. © 2014 FAMILY EMPOWERMENT NETWORK™

"Aha, that's very good!" the teacher replied. "But let us look a bit deeper."

He reached for a second empty mason jar and filled it full of sand. Now none of the big rocks nor the pebbles would fit! Then he waited for the students to analyze the two jars, the piles of rocks, pebbles, and sand.

"I want you to recognize that these jars are your life," said the teacher. "The rocks are the important things: your family, your partner, your health, your children—anything that is so important to you that if it were lost, you would be nearly destroyed. The pebbles are the other things in life that matter, but on a smaller scale. The pebbles represent things like your job, your house, your car. The sand and water are everything else. The small stuff. This demonstration teaches us a higher truth: If you don't put the big rocks in first, the things that really matter, you will never fit them in at all!"

Now take some time to ponder the following questions:

What are the six or seven "big rocks" in your own life? _____

_____

_____

How do the "big rocks" in your jar compare to those in your partner's "jar"? _____

_____

_____

How about those in your child(ren)'s "jar(s)"? _____

_____

_____

What gets in the way of you and your family living your "big rocks" daily? _____

_____

_____

List two things you can do to ensure you and your family live your "big rocks" daily. _____

_____

_____

© 2014 FAMILY EMPOWERMENT NETWORK™ ALL RIGHTS RESERVED.

Values Clarification For Families:
Exploring Values With Your Children

Children as young as four may be capable of naming what is truly in their hearts—and the process can be powerful. By clarifying their values, children can learn to understand cause and effect and to see themselves as capable and independent human beings. A myriad of ways exist to use a Values Clarification exercise within families. You might have each family member who can read look over the values noted on the cards (on the opposite page) and choose at least one value that is important to him or her. Because young children might not be able to understand the meaning of some of the words, we have included some defining questions to ask them as an example of how you might help them to identify their values. Once the values are chosen, cut the cards, decorate them, and tape them to a plant pot, a mirror, a pet's water bowl, or other prominent place in your home. Alternatively, cut the cards out first and sort through the words. Then choose one, two, etc., per person. Perhaps the card(s) can be tucked into your child's lunchbox. Or, if you agree on certain family values during a family meeting, you could have everyone in the family decorate a stone with the word of a particular value and then place all the stones in a basket to remind everyone of the commitment to your family's priorities.

One of our co-authors shares her story of how she utilized values clarification with her children:

When my kids were younger, I wanted to find ways for the three of them to develop positive friendships with their peers and also with other families. It became clear that it was important for us to identify some core values for our own family first, which would help us to decide how we wanted to spend our time, energy, and resources.

We all sat down and read through a list of values. Each of us identified four values which were most important to us, and we talked about them. Through discussion, we then narrowed the values down to eight of them (two for each of us) and labeled four notecards with two values each. Once the cards were decorated, we went to the store and each of us selected a small plant for which to care. At home, we taped the card on the plant pot, and the plant became a symbol for the values on the card.

Everyone agreed to take responsiblity for "caring" for the values on his plant. By caring for the plants on a daily basis, we were all reminded of what we had decided was most important to our family. When we got too busy, it was easy to see that we needed to slow down and care for those values again.

Inspired by the example to the left, explore together with your family the values lists and/or cards and create your own "values" plants, posters, or other symbols. Be prepared to talk about the values and provide examples to your children.

The exercise can then be used as a springboard for discussion with your children about what a particular value looks like when someone is following that value. You might follow up the talk with role playing to practice particular values or even point out to your child when you see him using the value later. The activities will remind everyone of the values your family wants to nurture and prioritize in your daily lives, decisions, and relationships.

 ALL RIGHTS RESERVED. © 2014 FAMILY EMPOWERMENT NETWORK™

CONNECTION Do you want to be close to others/your loved ones?	**ACCEPTANCE**	**SAFETY** Do you want to know that you're going to be OK?
TRUST	**COURAGE**	**ADVENTURE**
AUTHENTICITY Do you want to share what's in your heart?	**CONSISTENCY** Do you want people to do what they say they'll do?	**CONTRIBUTION** Would you like to be able to help?
RESPONSIBILITY	**HUMOR**	**FORGIVENESS**
LEARNING/GROWING	**CHOICE**	**GRATITUDE**
CREATIVITY Do you like making something from your own imagination?	**PEACEFULNESS** Do you like being quiet and calm?	**FUN/PLAYFULNESS** Do you just want to do what you feel like doing?
LOVE	**HAPPINESS**	**KINDNESS**
ORDERLINESS Do you want to find things easily?	**RESPECT** Do you want to know that you and your opinions matter?	**PARTICIPATION** Do you want to be a part of what's going on?
COOPERATION Do you want everyone to work together as a team?	**FRIENDSHIP** Do you want to spend time with your friends?	**HONESTY** Do you want to trust that people say what is true for them?

Values Clarification:
Exploring Your Personal Values

Quality of life is influenced by the extent to which we honor our personal values. Listed below are some common values that can help you to narrow down and identify your top seven (or more or less). You can use these words (or decide on your own) for meditation/consideration. Check those that feel particularly important to you. Then narrow down and circle your top ones. Make cards of the words and post them on your bathroom mirror or refrigerator, to stay connected to them. Use them to help drive your decision-making on how you want to spend your life energy.

__ACCEPTANCE	__EXERCISE	__LEARNING/GROWTH	__SECURITY
__ACCOUNTABILITY	__FAIRNESS	__LEISURE TIME	__SELF EXPRESSION
__ADVENTURE	__FAITH	__LOVE	__SELF-WORTH
__AUTHENTICITY	__FAMILY	__LOYALTY	__SENSUALITY
__AUTONOMY	__FINANCE STABILITY	__MASTERY	__SERENITY
__BALANCE	__FLEXIBILITY	__MEANINGFUL WORK	__SERVICE
__BEAUTY	__FOCUS	__MOVEMENT	__SIMPLICITY
__BELONGING	__FORGIVENESS	__NATURE	__SINCERITY
__CALM	__FREEDOM	__OPENNESS	__SOLITUDE
__CARING	__FRIENDSHIP	__ORDERLINESS	__SPACE
__CHOICE	__FUN	__ORIGINALITY	__SPIRITUALITY
__CHALLENGE	__GENEROSITY	__OWNERSHIP	__SPONTANEITY
__CLARITY	__GRACE	__PARTNERSHIP	__STABILITY
__COLLABORATION	__GRATITUDE	__PATIENCE	__STATUS
__COMFORT	__HARMONY	__PASSION	__STEWARDSHIP
__COMMITMENT	__HAPPINESS	__PEACEFULNESS	__STIMULATION
__COMMUNITY	__HEALTH	__PERSEVERANCE	__STRENGTH
__COMPASSION	__HONESTY	__PERSONAL GROWTH	__SUPPORT
__COMPETENCE	__HOPE	__PHYSICAL HEALTH	__TENDERNESS
__CONNECTION	__HUMOR	__PLAYFULNESS	__THOUGHTFULNESS
__CONTRIBUTION	__IMAGINATION	__PRIVACY	__TOUCH
__COOPERATION	__INDEPENDENCE	__PROFESSIONALISM	__TRUST
__COURAGE	__INGENUITY	__PROSPERITY	__TRUTH
__CREATIVITY	__INNER PEACE	__RECOGNITION	__UNDERSTANDING
__CURIOSITY	__INSPIRATION	__REFLECTION	__UNIQUENESS
__DEPENDABILITY	__INTEGRITY	__RELATIONSHIP	__VISION
__DIVERSITY	__INTIMACY	__RESILIENCE	__VITALITY
__EASE	__INTUITION	__RESPECT	__VULNERABILITY
__EFFICIENCY	__JOY	__RESPONSIBILITY	__WISDOM
__EMPATHY	__JUSTICE	__RISK TAKING	__WONDER
__EMPOWERMENT	__LAUGHTER	__ROMANCE	
__EXCITEMENT	__LEADERSHIP	__SAFETY	

ALL RIGHTS RESERVED. © 2014 FAMILY EMPOWERMENT NETWORK™

circle question

What gifts do your children bring to the world?

POSSIBLE DISCUSSION QUESTIONS

1) Think of a time you felt deeply connected to your children. Describe the experience and how it made you feel.

2) As a parent, what are some of the concerns you have about your children? What are your frustrations and challenges? What are your joys?

3) What did you learn about the "big rocks" in your life?

4) What are your top three personal values and how do you live these values?

5) What are your top three family values and how can you focus more time and energy on them?

PUTTING IT INTO PRACTICE

• Place the following in a frame and use a dry erase marker to fill in the blank each day/week, as inspired: "I love you because _____."

• Living your big rocks and values takes time and energy. If you think of your life's energy as a finite bucket, consider what drains your bucket and what fills it.

• After examining your family values, consider drafting a family mission statement, a concise declaration of how your family wants to "show up" in the world.

PUTTING IT TOGETHER–YOUR VERSION

Write down a few ideas you have been inspired to implement after reading/discussing this chapter:

_____

_____

_____

_____

_____

© 2014 FAMILY EMPOWERMENT NETWORK™ ALL RIGHTS RESERVED.

Parenting Touchstones: Friendship Begins at Home

1
2
3
4
5
6
7
8

Liana Hochhalter, 8th Grade, Rosemont Ridge Middle School

chapter two

Parenting Touchstones: Friendship Begins at Home

"Our stories of worthiness–of being enough–begin in our first families. The narrative certainly doesn't end there, but what we learn about ourselves and how we learn to engage with the world as children sets the course that either will require us to spend a significant part of our life fighting to reclaim our self worth or will give us hope, courage, and resilience for our journey." – Brené Brown, *Daring Greatly*

There is no perfect parenting and no one right way to parent. Furthermore, we are parenting during the busiest decades of our lives, in a culture that does not necessarily support us in the process, and, when media and technology, for better and for worse, threaten to reconfigure the traditional family experience. As parents, most of us struggle at times with feelings of guilt or inadequacy. The days of laissez-faire parenting in a safe and socially coherent world seem lost to the past, and the pressure to be a super parent, coupled with the stressors of the Digital Age, is unprecedented.

Take heart! The very baseline of your loving presence, even when you do not know how to proceed, can make a critical difference for your child for decades, even generations, to come. Regardless of where you are in your parenting journey, it is never too late to connect. Developing connection is the key to the ultimate gifts of significance, love, and belonging as you will see in the article, **"Significance and Belonging."** Your relationship with your child carries a blueprint that can influence your child's capacity for healthy friendships and resilience. In this sense, friendship begins at home.

In this chapter, we offer some ideas we have uncovered in our research about what matters most in being a compassionate and aware parent. Yet, every single parent-child relationship is unique and evolves over time, so your parenting approach will be your own. As a start, spend a moment reflecting on the way you were parented: What felt right to you and what was problematic?

Each of us enters the realm of parenting with his or her own parenting inheritance, the experiences which we had as a child with our own parents. If we are fortunate, we can recall our formative years with gratitude toward our

Parenting presents us with great challenges but offers incredible rewards. Truly, the work we do as parents paves the path for a caring society and bestows life-long gifts to our children.

In this chapter, we present six "touchstones" you can return to again and again as grounding themes during your parenting journey:

- Cultivate Empathy
- Create Safe Havens
- Stay Connected
- Take the Time
- Play/Create
- Walk the Talk

We offer these touchstones as ways to cultivate maturity, share the magic of empathy, and create the unparalleled well-being that flows from time spent together. The skills of friendship are first learned and modeled in the home, where parents make all the difference!

© 2014 FAMILY EMPOWERMENT NETWORK™ ALL RIGHTS RESERVED.

own parents. This is a gift. Many of us may have to dig a little deeper to find the blessings that have come from the relationships we had in our families of origin. Even the most problematic parenting inheritance can offer opportunities for valuable learning. What is most important, however, is to remember that we can *choose* what we pass along to our own children. Mindfully choosing how we care for and guide our children is an ongoing process. One of the keys to cultivating this process is being flexible and forgiving with ourselves, our partners, and our children.

In reflecting upon how you were parented, consider that, for many of us growing up in America, our parents possibly had a somewhat easier time parenting than we do; they did not feel an urgency to protect their children from the larger culture. In fact, they were quite sure the culture—and even the iconic family-hour TV—was teaching what parents were trying to teach. Former generations of parents also were aided by the fact that they were not afraid to let their kids play outside all day or roam the neighborhood. In short, stereotypical American cultural values and social norms generally reinforced the parenting practices of our parents' and grandparents' generations. One exception to this trend, however, is families who immigrate to the United States, because they have the added challenge of integrating their cultural norms with American culture.

In general, parents today may feel fearful and demoralized as they find their influence and role diminished by a culture whose reach extends into the heart of the family, touching territory that was traditionally off-limits. There may be pressure on children in elementary school, for example, to dress and act like adolescents and adults. Advertisers actually have a name for this phenomenon: the acronym **KGOY** (Kids are Getting Older, Younger). A signature dilemma in this new cultural wilderness is that parents may experience a double bind in which they feel pressured to let their children grow up too fast, while

they actually long to stay connected to their children and to protect them from the developmentally inappropriate aspects of our consumer society.

So, what's a parent to do? Our children come to us ready to love and to learn; our little ones are wide open for our guidance. Where do we look for guidance? How do we help our children to flourish? Our fast-paced American way of life encourages a parenting approach that focuses great quantities of energy on pregnancy, childbirth, and early childhood, but then loses steam when kids reach kindergarten. With our limited time, we often want quick answers even in complex situations. Sometimes this results in a tendency to fast forward our children's lives, yet human development cannot be rushed. Familiarizing ourselves with the concepts of child development can help us to parent wisely.

> *"How you make sense of your childhood experience has a profound effect on how you parent your own children."*
>
> – Daniel Siegel

There are many good parenting books and classes available to us today that have some core concepts in common and encourage us to be proactive in our parenting. They take the best of the *structure* of the adult-centered approach to parenting (e.g., high expectations, predictable routines and rituals, consistency, clear rules) and combine these with the *nurture and warmth* of a more child-centered approach (e.g., warm emotional tone, empathy, listening, concern for feelings and needs.) Our research supports this middle ground, which cultivates an approach that combines both positive structure *and* nurture. In other words, parents can aim to provide and teach a way of life with warmth, empathy, and freedom within a framework of order and clear expectations. This structure-plus-nurture approach helps us to avoid getting stuck in the extremes, where we may be tempted to cut loose a defiant 12-year-old child with an overly permissive "I-give-up" mentality. Or, at the other extreme, we may find ourselves "helicoptering" our college-aged children by calling their professors to advocate for grades. Our parenting gradually adapts and changes as our chil-

ALL RIGHTS RESERVED. © 2014 FAMILY EMPOWERMENT NETWORK™

dren grow. This means we continually strive to tailor our behavior to the distinct developmental changes and individual characteristics of the child we know so well. One place to start is with an understanding of the different stages of childhood. The following metric, inspired by Rudolph Steiner, is a way of looking at an individual's first 21 years. Notice how the parent role grows and changes as the child matures through the three stages: Hands (Will), Heart (Feeling), and Head (Thinking). In turn, the child's social-emotional learning (SEL)–which we now know is as important to life-long success as their intellectual abilities–grows from basic self-control and manners to understanding his or her own feelings and needs, to being able to integrate these abilities in making wise and compassionate decisions.

1. Hands: Directing the Will –
Parent as Governor

The first seven years are the age when children learn how to develop and direct their will, which is an important first component of emotional intelligence. When parents adopt the kind but firm role of a "Governor," children more readily learn self control. By "Governor," we mean a parent who is unconditionally loving yet also able to follow through calmly. In this role, parents learn to read their children empathetically; they teach a vocabulary for feelings and needs, the manners to communicate them, and how to act pro-socially. This is the beginning of the slow process of socializing our children. Parents and children need a considerable amount of shared time in order to teach and learn life skills and allow children to practice them with their own Hands.

2. Heart: Developing the Feelings –
Parent as Gardener

Around age seven, children develop the ability to hold their feelings and another person's in mind at the same time. Therefore, in these middle years between seven through 13, children are ideally developing the Heart side of their emotional intelligence. Although at times parents are still the Governor, now they take on an additional role of the "Gardener," as they cultivate the child's ability to understand his or her own feelings and needs, and to consider the feelings and needs of others. Parents are a listening heart for their children as they navigate these middle years of friendship; they must increasingly step back when appropriate and allow children to find their own way in their friendship landscape. Parents continue to play a protective role when it comes to media and games that desensitize children to real feelings and face-to-face interactions. Family conversation and experiences become an important source of information and values for the developing child, as he learns to understand the Golden Rule and the importance of helping others.

3. Head: Guiding Thought –
Parent as Guide

Between 14 and 18 and beyond, adolescents build on the first two stages and develop the thinking part of their personality. The prefrontal cortex is not fully formed until the mid-twenties, however, so it behooves parents to increase their role as their child's "Guide" at this stage. As a Guide, the parent shepherds the teen through the process of making wise choices, gradually giving more and more freedom as the teen shows she is ready. As a means to respect the growing maturity of the teen, negotiation and forging joint agreements become a much greater part of the parent-child interaction now. Nevertheless, maintaining clear expectations is also necessary–that the teen be a conscientious, contributing member of the family and, ultimately, the community. It can be a bumpy road and sometimes "messy," as the teen pushes the edges of these boundaries. Naturally, the teen who accepts limits (the Will) and understands his/her own feelings and considers the feelings of others (the Heart), will make much wiser decisions than a teen who has not mastered the earlier skills.

Granted, the parent shifts back to the roles of Governor and Gardener at times during this period, especially with younger teens, but, for the most part, the parent focuses on guiding. In this new role, parents must work hard to stay connected to their teen and love him for who he is and who he is becoming. Truth be told, although teens

© 2014 FAMILY EMPOWERMENT NETWORK™ ALL RIGHTS RESERVED.

are forming their "second family" of trusted friends, they still need to be connected to their first family and also need support in connecting to the greater community through school, activities, work, and volunteering.

With all the parenting information available, many of us feel the pressure to be the perfect parent. This is impossible. With practice and support, however, parents *can* move toward feeling confident and comfortable in their parenting, especially if they are open-minded, life-long learners. Support networks are especially important if we find ourselves parenting alone. The work of parenting is highly creative and one of life's great privileges. It can be the very best of times—and the most demanding. Certainly, parenting keeps our brain cells stimulated!

To help you remain grounded and intentional in your parenting, we offer six touchstones you can turn to for support and reassurance: **Cultivate Empathy, Create Safe Havens, Stay Connected, Take the Time, Play/Create,** and **Walk the Talk**. Living with these touchstones can bring well-being, resiliency, and satisfying social connections for all of us. Practicing them on a daily basis can nourish and fortify not only your children, but also your family as a whole. In this way, you grow as your children grow, and you grow together as a family.

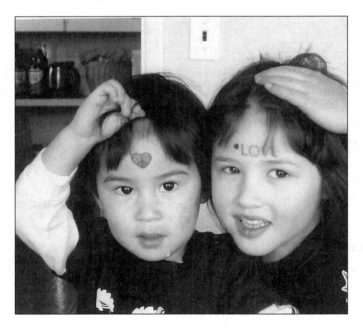

CULTIVATE EMPATHY

"When relationships between parent and child are attuned, a child is able to feel . . . connected and loved. The child's internal world is seen with clarity by the parent, and the parent comes to resonate with the child's state. This is attunement. Over time, this attuned communication enables the child to develop the regulatory circuits in the brain . . . that give the individual a source of resilience as he or she grows." – Daniel Siegel, *The Mindful Brain*

Empathy is the ability to stand in another person's shoes; to understand that other people have their own perspective, feelings, and thoughts; and to vicariously experience those feelings. This ability and understanding drives relationships and is critical to developing healthy social lives.

How does one learn or develop empathy? The roots of empathy take hold early on. With the arrival of a child, parents experience astounding growth in the development of their own capacity to feel and respond to the needs of another person. With their strengthened empathy "muscle," parents lay the all-important groundwork for their children to develop empathy.

We are fortunate to live in a time when there is a wealth of new information about how our brains affect our relationships. Researchers have found that the human brain needs social experience and secure responsive relationships to develop its potential. It is our brain's extraordinary mirror neuron system that enables us to read and respond to the behavioral intentions and emotional states of others. We share the latest in the field of neuroscience in our article, **"The Brain Revolution."**

Surprisingly, the foundation for the ability to empathize with others *and* the ability to handle stress originate in the infant-parent relationship. It is a dynamic interplay and dance: As the parent lovingly responds to a baby's needs, empathy is bestowed and modeled, comfort is restored, and trust is born. For example, when a mother and a baby are approached by new faces, the baby may feel stressed. He turns to his mother for reassurance, and

ALL RIGHTS RESERVED. © 2014 FAMILY EMPOWERMENT NETWORK™

the comforting "it's okay" attention of the mother calms the baby and teaches him how to regulate his stress. In a circular way, when the mother gives this empathetic attention to her child, she is flooded with the comforting hormone oxytocin, which, in turn, helps her to regulate her stress, as well as to facilitate her ability to empathize. What is best in our humanity has its roots in this remarkable parent-child dance.

The Roots of Empathy program (www.rootsofempathy.org), outlined in *Roots of Empathy: Changing the World Child by Child* by Mary Gordon, strikingly highlights this beautiful and critical dynamic of early call and response in their innovative instruction in which school children learn about empathy by observing attuned mothers and their babies:

> *The sixth graders of an inner-city Toronto school are part of the Roots of Empathy program founded by Mary Gordon. They are circled around a six-month-old baby, Sophia, and her mother, Mary. "When we use little babies as teachers," Gordon says, "it is not just the babies we are watching. We're watching the baby in tandem with the parent. I believe that successful people develop empathy from receiving or witnessing empathy"* (Perry and Szalavitz, *Born for Love*, p. 10). *Because being in a sixth-grade classroom is a new situation for baby Sophia, she perceives it as a stressor and alertly watches her mother for cues. Mary's smile relaxes her and assures her the situation is safe and that she can interact with the older children. In essence, Mary is Sophia's external stress regulator. Sophia smiles back, and Mary feels joy, too.*

Truly, the initial bonding process between parent(s) and child, which occurs in the first few years, carries a blueprint for an individual's capacity for healthy, lifelong connection and resilience. When there is secure attachment, the parent is available, responsive, and perceptive.

Breastfeeding, for example, although not always possible, can be a natural (yet learned) and miraculous way of enhancing the attachment process.

Children who are not securely attached as babies and toddlers may need extra support as they grow, especially when it comes to feeling loved for who they are, handling stress, developing empathy, or becoming a good friend. The child may learn to avoid closeness and emotional connection or feel anxious and uncertain about whether he can depend on people. She might also have trouble regulating her emotions. Parents who experienced insecure attachment in their own childhoods have a wonderful opportunity to change this dynamic through the way they interact with their own children, if they take the time to learn about secure attachment.

As children grow older, parents can continue to teach, model, and share self-soothing techniques, letting children experience small, manageable doses of stress along the way to build their resilience. This is an important, ongoing effort, because a highly stressed child or adult is rarely able to show empathy or be a good friend. This demanding and exhausting work, navigating your child's stress and your own, with empathy, is at the heart of parenting. Empathy can enhance all our relationships, including the one with ourselves, for a lifetime.

> *"Stable, safe relationships and rich learning experiences are key to brain development."*
> – Dr. Jack Shonkoff of Harvard University's Center on the Developing Child

Other activities and behaviors that can promote the development of empathy in our children, ourselves, and our families include talking about how someone else might feel; role-playing and perspective-taking; supporting stressed, sick, or elderly friends and family members; practicing random acts of kindness; sponsoring a needy child; practicing appreciation; fostering a shelter animal; mentoring; giving money or food to people on the street; or engaging in community service. It is also our time together, talking about life, listening deeply to each

© 2014 FAMILY EMPOWERMENT NETWORK™ ALL RIGHTS RESERVED.

other's thoughts, and adopting the Golden Rule (treat others as you would like them to treat you) as a family standard, that encourages the development of empathy in our children.

One particularly important way we develop empathy is through reading, especially fiction, according to a recent study conducted through the New School for Social Research. To explain, noted scholar Charlene Spretnak says: "Reading in one's formative years correlates with increased empathy, interpersonal perceptions, and social skills. The reader is drawn beyond… limited life experience to understand more about the lives of other people, from the inside of characters' minds" (Spretnak, *Relational Reality*, pp. 50, 237). In essence, seeing life through others' eyes while reading carries over into real social situations. Sadly, children (and adults) who spend too much time on screens (except for Kindles, Nooks, etc.) often give up reading for pleasure and miss out on this "empathy exercise."

TAKE THE TIME

The Power of Shared Reading

Reading as a lifelong habit can open our minds and our hearts. It can help us to develop empathy. In fact, throughout our lives, books bind us to each other—and to ourselves. The very form and shape of a book, so beautifully scaled to our human need—with a spine like us and with pages to "leaf" through—makes it a perfect companion and one worth sharing. Here are some ideas for fostering the joy and warmth of empathy that comes from shared reading:

- Curl up with a book with your children at your side.
- Encourage independent readers to curl up beside you while they read.
- Older kids can read to their younger siblings and/or to residents at a retirement home.
- Tape your child reading aloud and give it as a gift to a grandparent who lives far away.
- Read to dogs, a practice popular in libraries across the country as part of their early literacy programs.

Reading aloud is a deeply satisfying experience that creates a sense of bonding and belonging in the family—no matter the age. So, keep reading together, even after your children are as tall as you!

while reading, using a calm and soothing voice, caregivers actually engage children in ways which promote their general sense of well-being, which contributes to a sense of secure attachment and attunement between caregiver and child.

Many things affect the development of empathy. For example, shame inhibits empathy. Also, living over-busy lives with high stress, too much screen time, and little transition time between events creates an environment detrimental to the cultivation of empathy. Empathy requires enough space and time in our lives to tap in to our inner wisdom.

Even the way we talk to our children sets the stage for empathy. Paying attention to the words you use with your children, especially during conflict, is one effective way for improving the connection and empathy

In truth, encouraging our children to read is one of the most important things we do as a parent—but the medium can be part of the message. As the e-book market continues to expand, it's important to consider how reading is different when we use a screen instead of a printed book and that parents of young children might still want to choose the timeless pleasure of reading paper books with their children. When you and your young child read together, with your child turning the pages, you aren't just reading a story or building literacy. When fully present you experience in your home. An invaluable tool worth learning to help you in this matter is non-violent communication (www.cnvc.org), based on the work of Marshall Rosenberg. This communication strategy enables you to live peacefully by focusing on underlying values and needs rather than focusing on whether the behavior is right or wrong. Inbal Kashtan's article on **"Parenting for Peace"** provides an overview of compassionate or non-violent communication and how conflict can offer opportunities for fostering empathy.

ALL RIGHTS RESERVED. © 2014 FAMILY EMPOWERMENT NETWORK™

As evidence of how empathy may be endangered, a 2009 meta-analysis by the University of Michigan revealed that levels of empathy in American adolescents have been decreasing dramatically. The meta-analysis examined 72 studies involving close to 14,000 college students to determine how their empathy levels changed over the last several decades. Students in 2009 scored 40% lower in interpersonal sensitivity than their counterparts 20 or 30 years ago, 48% lower in empathic concern, and 34% lower in perspective taking! The change since the year 2000 showed the most precipitous drop (Spretnak, *Relational Reality*, pp. 41, 234).

These striking changes in adolescents' ability to empathize serve as a powerful reminder that the brain's development depends on how we nourish it. New research tells us that it is important to think of children's brains as "under construction." This is particularly important with regard to the teen brain, which is in an active process of pruning neurons not being used. How we use our time and our experiences directly structures the architecture of our brains—at every age. Neuroscientists commonly explain this with the watchwords, "Use it or lose it."

A first step for parents may be a careful and compassionate examination of family life as it is. Often we may find the family needs more time together for sharing life's tasks and pleasures. Once the family regains some uninterrupted time, empathy flows more naturally. Consider a Family Empathy Project such as helping an elderly neighbor, including a child in need in some family activities, creating postcards for distant friends and family, or helping the homeless in some small way. Create a Family Mission statement with empathy at its core. Model being considerate of others and teach your children to contribute to the family and to take responsibility for themselves. Over and over, practice empathy, talk about it, and seek out real, relational experiences for yourself and your children that will foster the gift of empathy.

EMPATHY

Fostering the Gift of Empathy

- Practice self-care and stress reduction together, so all family members are in a better position to be empathetic and to solve problems.

- Alternate active days with calm ones. Constant activity–even if packed with enrichment–can be stressful, and stress diminishes our ability to empathize.

- Recognize and honor that mistakes, conflict, and process are critical components of learning. Everyone makes mistakes. No one is perfect. Growth unfolds over time. When we handle mistakes (ours and theirs) with empathy and a solution-oriented approach, our children learn to take responsibility and to see themselves as problem solvers.

- Work to dismantle shame. Whereas guilt correlates to behavior ("I did something bad"), shame diminishes the self ("I am bad"). Shame can be crippling: It severs connection, kindles rage, and can lead to self-destructive or violent behavior. We all carry shame, but as parents it is vital to avoid using shame to discipline our children. When we can model vulnerability instead, we can defuse shame's power and allow empathy to bloom in shame's place. For inspiration on this topic, read Brené Brown's book, *Daring Greatly: How the Courage to Be Vulnerable Transforms the Way We Live, Love, Parent, and Lead*, or watch her very popular TED talks on vulnerability and shame at http://www.ted.com/talks/brene_brown_on_vulnerability.html and http://www.ted.com/talks/brene_brown_listening_to_shame.html

- Listen carefully and patiently to children's voices and stories–and they will learn to do the same with you, their friends, and, years later, with their own children. Sometimes just listening with empathy can resolve a problem; when our perspective is understood or we understand a friend's perspective–when we listen with our heart–the road to a solution often becomes clear.

- Teach your children to be flexible in their problem solving.

© 2014 FAMILY EMPOWERMENT NETWORK™ ALL RIGHTS RESERVED.

CREATE SAFE HAVENS: A CALL TO HOME

"Children need to know that theirs is a good world. They need to feel that, sheltered by those they love, they are where they should be. They have a place, in a time, and a world full of hope and promise."
– Kim John Payne, *Simplicity Parenting*

Home is the emotional hub of our lives, and, more than ever, our homes need to be safe havens for our children and for ourselves. Ideally, home can be a sanctuary from the confusion and the complexity "out there" that threaten to shorten childhood and frazzle adolescence.

So what does home as a "safe haven" look like? As imperfect as our homes–and relationships–may be, we can still strive to create a home filled with love and permeated with shared experience, deep and ordinary. It starts with unconditional love and acceptance for each member of the family. Our children need a sense of predictability, safety, coziness, and companionship in their homes. Don't we all?

SAFE HAVENS

Think of your most treasured memories of your home and grandparents' homes: watching thunderstorms together, playing a family card game, making popcorn and reading aloud by the fire, making special treats, holding hands with Grandma. How can you create conditions where your children can enjoy the simple pleasures of life?

Another vital ingredient for the creation of a safe haven is play, the powerful tool through which children learn to understand themselves and the world. Our family rituals–from lighting candles to colorful celebrations–are the sacred means through which our families bond and symbolically express our deepest values.

As you imagine your home and your home life, consider that sometimes creating a safe haven lies not in addition, but in subtraction. Children do not learn through "too much, too fast, too soon," as noted educator and author of *Simplicity Parenting*, Kim John Payne tells us. Rather, the extraordinary power of less can be used to raise calmer, happier, more secure kids.

Payne's philosophy of Simplicity Parenting inspires us to simplify our homes and reduce the amount of stuff in them. He encourages us to protect our children from the stress of excess as well as from the increasingly stress-producing and violent content of much of our media and video games. Payne reminds us that our home life can provide "pressure valves" for stress, and that health-promoting connection often comes in the pauses between activities. For example, pressure values can include naps, blowing off steam (respectfully), free play, reading, bike riding, listening to and/or playing music, dancing, playing board/card games, knitting, building model airplanes, gardening, being in nature, and the list goes on.

Ideally, home is a place where we can reduce our stress and feel a sense of well-being. As mentioned earlier, stressed children and adults are less likely to use empathy to solve problems, and this affects relationships as well as contentedness. Payne calls this stress "soul fever." He suggests that, by spending more down time in one's home, one can "heal" and be refreshed. This "down time" can be playing, working, or exercising together, which ultimately reduces stress and returns one to a sense of shared ease. Animals also help us to relax, to give love, and to feel loved. If you are fortunate enough to have pets in your family, you know how positive their presence can be!

Your home also can be enriched by extended family members, family friends, and their children. These can become your family's "village," the people with whom you and your children "belong." This creates a wider safe haven than just your immediate home. Then, as your children grow and invite their friends home or on family outings, more and more people become a part of your nurturing village, your safe haven.

 ALL RIGHTS RESERVED. © 2014 FAMILY EMPOWERMENT NETWORK™

Of particular importance to a child's healthy development are grandparents. Grandparents often are still connected to a simpler and less technology-driven way of life and can share this quality with grandchildren, as well as provide parents some respite and support. The experience of a grandparent's unconditional love is one of life's most profound emotional assets. As such, it is well worth developing positive relationships with your parents in order to offer this opportunity to your children.

Safe havens begin at home and ideally home will always be a safe haven, but as children grow they need our support in creating additional safe havens out in the community, where they can be themselves on their own. Our healthiest teens are connected to both home and to the greater community, in a myriad of ways. Through their involvement in work, volunteering, hobbies, after-school clubs, and supervised youth activities, their perspective expands, their face-to-face skills evolve, they get connected to other healthy teens, and they find adult mentors. Teens with community connections tend to have a much broader focus than worrying about their popularity, since they are busy fostering relationships, finding themselves, and exploring their passions.

STAY CONNECTED

"We are psychologically, emotionally, cognitively, and spiritually hardwired for connection, love, and belonging. Connection, along with love and belonging, two expressions of connection, is why we are here and it is what gives purpose and meaning to our lives."
– Brené Brown, *Daring Greatly*

An ultimate parenting goal is to have a healthy parent-child relationship throughout our lives. Although we may tailor our overall parenting strategy throughout the various development stages as needed to achieve this goal, one consistently sure key is connection. It's important to note that connection and autonomy can and should work hand in hand. In fact, research shows that teens who navigate adolescence most successfully are the ones who are connected to family ("Protecting Adolescents from Harm," *Journal of the American Medical Assn.*, Sept. 1997, v. 278, n. 10, pp. 823-32). At the heart of connection is being truly present. A child's deep sense that he can count on you to be there for him is perhaps what is most profound. When you practice being present, everyone thrives.

In the first few years of their lives, our children do important work. They bond with their parents and siblings; learn communication skills, self control, and how to manage the little stresses of life; as well as develop imagination and creativity. As they get a little older, they help out at home, make friends, learn manners, and develop the ability to focus and push through difficult tasks. In other words, they realize what full engagement feels like— at home, in the classroom, and with friends.

CONNECTION

Into this world, I love to receive my grand-children
Who leave behind their iPhones, iPads, video games, TV.
They are plunged into a world of intimacy
With nature, with themselves, with me. – Lizanne Ryan

For this complicated work to be accomplished, parents need time with their child to teach, model, and reinforce specific skills, habits, and behaviors. Shared time and connection–quantity matters as well as quality–truly is the glue that builds strong kids and strong families. There are many ways to share time, of course, and every family has different priorities, but it often consists of just hanging out together or of kids tagging along with their parents.

Another sure way to nurture connection at home is to preserve and protect the ritual of family meals. Research over decades underscores the astonishing benefits of families eating together, yet many things threaten this simple gathering. Do not surrender it! In the busyness of our

© 2014 FAMILY EMPOWERMENT NETWORK™ ALL RIGHTS RESERVED.

modern, consumer-driven world, we either defend our family time or we lose it. When we eat dinner together regularly (at least five times per week), as in all family rituals, the family's group culture is created and maintained. In addition, during meals family life can be enhanced by the sense of order, the emotional bonding, the sense of being part of a larger whole, and a modeling of family values and communication. For specific research-proven benefits of eating together, see "The Importance of Family Dinners IV" by the National Center on Addiction and Substance Abuse at www.casacolumbia.org.

TAKE THE TIME

Enhancing Connection through Family Meals

- Protect family meals from the interruptions of phones and screens.
- Involve children in some part of the preparation of the meal, e.g. planning, shopping, cooking, setting table.
- Include a symbolic start to the meal (e.g., ring a bell, light candles, moment of silence, song, blessing, or holding hands).
- Emphasize the togetherness rather than what and how the children are eating.
- Share "favorite things" that happened today, something each person is grateful for, or one thing you struggled with and would do differently.
- Discuss ideas and play verbal games to promote the art of conversation.
- Read aloud while other family members are cleaning up (switch roles); involve everyone in the clean up.
- Change mealtimes to fit your schedule (e.g., have dinner in the late afternoon and dessert in the evening after extra-curricular activities).
- If you can't be together for dinner, have breakfast as your family meal.
- Enhance your family's connection to fresh food and community by buying local, seasonal food directly from a farmer. Perhaps join a CSA (Community Supported Agriculture).

The key ingredients of family meals involve gathering together without distractions and having face-to-face interactions. Of course, families with very young children may only be approximating this ideal while they teach the basic skills of sitting and staying at the table for 15 to 20 minutes. Over time, however, family meals can be an opportunity to share the "best and worst" thing that happened that day and to learn to listen to others. Telling and creating family stories also can take place during meals and greatly enriches our children's language and concept development while creating community. All of this requires having a family standard that requires everyone to have all digital devices including smart phones turned off and out of sight!

Becoming organized enough to share regular meals can be a challenge, but it is worth the effort and can include every member of the family. One large blended family organized eating together in the following way: The father cooked breakfast every morning and oversaw the bagged lunch preparation. Each week an older and younger team (parent and child or older child and younger child) signed up to be in charge of each dinner, which included planning the menu in advance, listing and shopping for the items needed, cooking, and cleaning up. In another family, the kids prepare the table 10 minutes before the meal is ready and everyone pitches in on the cleanup.

Without saying a word, parents can model a healthy relationship to food during family meals. Although the companionship at family dinners is more important than the quality of the food, families with frequent meals together often expose children to natural and homemade foods and, therefore, the entire family is less likely to become overweight. When we snack or eat meals individually, we are more likely to eat lower quality, highly processed, and less nutritious foods. For several ideas on how to enhance connection through family meals, check out the box on the left.

ALL RIGHTS RESERVED. © 2014 FAMILY EMPOWERMENT NETWORK™

No substitute exists for the wellness and fulfillment available to us when we are genuinely together. Like eating together, family rituals and routine–morning, bedtime, bath time, family meetings, family fun, periodic one-on-one time with a parent, holiday rituals, yearly camping events, and family reunions–all sow the seeds for lifelong, secure, joyful, healthful connection and trust. Taking the time to mindfully focus upon and practice these rituals and routines can be invaluable.

CONNECTION

If you want suggestions for how to connect, check out these colorful posters: **"150 Ways to Show Kids You Care"** and **"50 Ways to Help Your Whole Family Thrive."**

www.searchinstitutestore.org/category_s/129.htm

Boundaries are also an important part of family life and help us to have peaceful, respectful, and safe interactions. Most children crave order, and without it, they can feel lost and insecure. Boundaries also protect connection, and this is especially true in the area of technology.

In this light, you may want to re-evaluate periodically the role technology plays in your family life. Certainly, there are ways in which technology can enhance family experience. For example, we might look forward to cuddling together on the couch for family movie night or a weekly TV show. Skype and iChat can bring the familiar voices and faces of grandparents or other far-away loved ones directly into the home. Distant friends and relatives can stay in touch via email. Parents and kids can enjoy and benefit from building brain skills together at an educational website, and Wii and other games can offer fitness and fun for the whole family. But beyond experiences during which family members are participating in shared digital activities, parents must carefully consider boundaries and limits that will protect the family's well-being.

Psychologist Doreen Dodgen-Magee provides a great overview of the neurological, interpersonal, and personal impact of being "plugged in" in her thought-provoking article, **"The Key to Surviving the Negative Impact of Digital Technology? Moderation."** We also offer you some strategies that are working for other families in today's Digital Age in **"Tips for Maintaining Digital Sanity and Protecting Your Family."** Or, your family can create its own unique ways of having uninterrupted time together and establishing a climate where family time, play, hobbies, and face-to-face activities have priority. The good habits that you establish for your children and yourself around how we interact with others, use technology, and sleep peacefully will serve you and them throughout your lifetimes.

In short, technology often can draw us away from real experience and from the face-to-face intimacy for which we are so intricately designed, posing a special threat to the healthy development of young people and our connection to them. Parents need to consider the prospect that children who are allowed to grow up online may not develop the vital social and emotional skills they need to succeed and to fulfill their human potential. You will learn more about the potential negative influence of digital technology on child development in the next chapter as well.

> *"Rituals are the lenses through which we see our emotional connection to each other, to a culture, and to a higher power. They are symbolic expressions of our most sacred values."*
>
> –Becky Bailey, *I Love You Rituals*

TAKE THE TIME

How did you experience time as a child? Studies show that when children are chronically overscheduled and pushed beyond their developmentally appropriate limits, stress and anxiety often ensue. Of course, children should be challenged

© 2014 FAMILY EMPOWERMENT NETWORK™ ALL RIGHTS RESERVED.

and encouraged to excel. But when it feels as if every moment of the day is tracked and accounted for on an omnipresent stopwatch, it is probably time to make a change: to slow down and simplify.

It may not be popular to simplify, when so much of life these days is driven by competition, perfectionism, and enrichment opportunities, but the rewards are well worth it. Payne's book *Simplicity Parenting* provides the best road map we know: "The process of simplification removes some of the major stressors of daily life, reducing swollen expectations and sensory irritants. It closes down the 'red alert' or triage approach to daily life, so parents can restore a more natural balance, one where the 'everyday' has a place, and time expands" (p. 215).

> ## 🌱 TAKE THE TIME
>
> - Cook together. Bake simple bread. Invent a new popsicle. Try a new recipe.
>
> - Plant some seeds. Build a window box, a container, a garden.
>
> - Play games: new ones and old favorites. Play catch. Try Settlers of Catan (your children will beat you). Start an epic puzzle.
>
> - Reconnect with the natural rhythms of nature. Go on a walk. Bike to the park. Play with your pets. Buy a moon calendar and stargaze. Revisit your own childhood moments, with your child. Watch the clouds go by….

Why is it so hard these days to "take the time"? The many recently minted phrases we use to talk about time reveal a new relationship in which families are experiencing time as increasingly pressured and fragmented. We talk about "down time," "quality time," "family time," "time poverty," and "real time." No one, it seems, has enough time. Many parents also are tired much of the time and find it challenging to just be present for their children. For inspiration about letting go of the messages that we aren't good parents if we don't have our kids in multiple activities all the time, see **"The Busyness Epidemic."**

Over busy, over scheduled, and over tired, we yearn for a more satisfying experience of time. The best things in life–childhood, friendship, healing, falling in love, creating a masterpiece–take time. Every culture has its enduring proverbs and stories about the importance of "taking the time." Human development cannot be rushed! Yet, that is what our fast-paced society is doing today: All too often, we are pushing our children to grow up too quickly.

When a model driven by efficiency, productivity, and competition becomes the template for contemporary domestic life and family affairs, one of the biggest losses is in relationships.

Our overly busy lives are also encroaching upon our sleep time. For people of all ages, good sleep and the right amount of sleep matters to academic performance, emotional stability, ability to focus, and even maintaining proper weight (*Nurture Shock* by Po Bronson and Ashley Merryman, 2009, p. 31). For an overview of the importance of sleep and how sleep deprivation affects our children's lives–and ours–see **"Give Your Family a Gift: Sleep."**

A recent study by the Centers for Disease Control found that 30% of American workers sleep less than six hours per night; stress contributes to 50% of all illness in the United States; and many Americans are overworked (even as many are unemployed). Current policy with regard to family leave, sick leave, and paid vacation time reveals our national bias for an ideology of overworking–and of being overly identified with our work–that can undermine the powerfully vital work of parenting, citizenship, and wellness. And this attitude that narrowly equates all "work" with busyness, stress, and productivity has trickled down to our children.

When we "take the time," we reclaim two ordinary emotions with extraordinary benefits: anticipation and bore-

ALL RIGHTS RESERVED. © 2014 FAMILY EMPOWERMENT NETWORK™

dom. Some of our fondest childhood feelings and memories relate to anticipation. Often they are connected to simple yet sensory-rich details: the season's first snowfall, the smell of holiday baking, the delivery of a letter, or the opening of a pool in summertime. Remember the yearning, imagining, rehearsing, and patience that were ingredients of your own childhood anticipation? Anticipation builds character, furnishes deep pleasure, and primes us to savor experience. With anticipation, time slowly burnishes itself and is elongated. We want this experience for our children, where time is undivided.

The same is also true for boredom. Take the time to teach your children to have a good attitude toward boredom, to realize it is what naturally happens for a few moments before you figure out what you're going to do next. While it may not be desirable in large doses, boredom is not to be feared or avoided (at least not when it occurs within an environment that is, overall, secure and stimulating). In fact, boredom can bear positive fruit, as it often precedes spark, creativity, and inspiration. It also provides the mental time and space necessary to experience silence, solitude, and the skill of introspection. When they work through boredom, without turning to technology, our children learn to find fulfillment by looking inside themselves.

Families who are trying to reduce screen time may be particularly challenged with the boredom issue. The more prevalent screens have been in a child's life, the longer the phase will last between when the screens are turned off and creativity begins. Learning a new habit takes time. During this "void" phase, parents need to be prepared to shore themselves up for the complaining and push back that will undoubtedly occur. Good parenting does not always mean comfortable parenting!

Another simple yet critically important way to put balance back into the lives of our children is to take the

> *"Activity without down time is like a plant without roots— ultimately, unsustainable."*
> – Kim John Payne, *Simplicity Parenting*

TAKE THE TIME

I wonder how many children in the Digital Age never learn how to whistle? I was out for a walk through the crunchy leaves today with my dog, Zeus, and was delighted to turn a corner to find a father and daughter out for a stroll. The dad was whistling. I realized I hadn't heard random whistling in a really long time and was reminded of my father, a fabulous whistler. It brought back wonderful memories of long evenings out on our porch, listening to the calls of whippoorwills, singing, and my dad teaching us his whistling techniques.

time to enjoy nature. Nature makes kids whole again. Spending time outdoors can build their intelligence and fortify their souls. It can boost physical and psychological well-being. And for everyone–kids and adults alike–it protects against the effects of stress.

When kids spend time in nature, they get to do, naturally, all of their favorite things: explore, play, problem solve, challenge themselves, and imagine. You do not have to go very far from home for kids to experience nature in a profound way. As Richard Louv says in his book *Last Child In the Woods*, "The dugout in the weeds or leaves beneath a backyard willow, the rivulet of a seasonal creek, even the ditch between the front yard and the road–all of these places are entire universes to a young child" (p. 170). Whether they're in a grove of old-growth trees or a vacant lot, when our kids experience the wonder and sense of kinship that spending time outdoors provides, they slow down and find their centered selves. So do we.

We all want to live in a world where we have ample time, enough time to actually be present in our moments: the ordinary ones as well as the precious ones. No one wants to inhabit a world where third graders don't have time to learn to tell time or tie their shoes. For these simple

© 2014 FAMILY EMPOWERMENT NETWORK™ ALL RIGHTS RESERVED.

yet complicated tasks to be accomplished, parents need peaceful, unrushed time with their child to teach, model, follow through, and celebrate together. We also need time to relax and reflect together. We cannot raise a child capable of reflection if that child never sees us in reflection. If we don't take the time—right now—not only will we not remember our best of times, but we also risk losing what's best in ourselves.

PLAY/CREATE

"You can discover more about a person in an hour of play than in a year of conversation." – Plato

Think back: Do you remember a sensation of timelessness and deep satisfaction from your own childhood playtime? Play is a child's medium for flow. And flow is the magical, elusive, psychological state where we are completely and blissfully immersed in an activity that is intrinsically rewarding.

This notion can be especially important to parents in an era where so much digital game playing and increasingly classroom learning involves external compensation. Pure play, the kind that kids intuitively seek out and creatively enact, not only builds crucial lifelong skills and capacities, but it also deepens a child's experience of internally rewarding behavior. Even more importantly, individuation is occurring when kids play. Truly, a child's very self is being chiseled and defined during an epic game of capture the flag or a meditative half hour in the sand box!

Given the sophisticated value of real play, it is helpful to resist the temptation to use play as a "reward" or an activity second to other more organized or academic challenges, such as homework. Play is a right, not a privilege. Many parents give up too early on play by discouraging free play or over scheduling—even though research shows that play is essential to optimal human development and paramount as a medium of mastering academic learning, resiliency and connection (Wenner, "The Serious

PLAY/CREATE

Free Play:
- Promotes brain development
- Builds social skills
- Relieves stress
- Enhances creativity

Need for Play," *Scientific American Mind*, February/March 2009, pp. 21–29). So, instead of phasing out play, play more! Jumpstart random, joyful play in your household, and watch a tide of increased ease roll in.

In previous generations, a more organic model of play meant that children orchestrated play for themselves. Free play happened in all the unstructured time of those days; kids made sure it did. Now, just when parents are feeling the crunch of less time, they find themselves in the often demanding role of facilitator for their children's play time. Play has become extra work for parents—such as the added chore of scheduling and facilitating play dates. Fear, too, plays a role as parents keep their children indoors more in response to the media's relentless messaging about child endangerment. According to William Doherty in *Overscheduled Kids, Unconnected Families: The Research Evidence,* "Children today spend half as much time playing freely outdoors as they did in the early 1980s." If we sincerely wish for our children to flourish in the great arenas of life—socially, emotionally, and cognitively—play may be the most important and untapped ingredient in their lives. The developmental child psychologist Jean Piaget famously said, "Every nutrient for structuring a worldview can be furnished through play."

Sadly, many kids lack the time and space to play. Changing social structures mean that more parents are working, and working longer hours. School choice, a positive force in many ways, also has interfered with spontaneous after-school and neighborhood play. And, as we have discussed, the advent of the Digital Age means that many family members—kids and adults alike—are more

ALL RIGHTS RESERVED. © 2014 FAMILY EMPOWERMENT NETWORK™

distracted and more likely to be "playing" separately on personal devices than with each other or with friends. In some families, electronic play, in fact, is replacing real play, and electronic play is vastly different from the kid-driven, spontaneous play we are biologically evolved to seek out. Digital play does not provide the abundant benefits of real, face-to-face play because it is scripted, socially isolating, and screen based. Real play brings kids together in a way that builds creativity, social skills, problem-solving skills, trust, and intelligences of all kinds. "We are built to play and built through play," as Stuart Brown, author of *Play: How It Shapes the Brain, Opens the Imagination, and Invigorates the Soul*, says (p. 47).

The consequences of missing out on real play may be more dire than we would care to believe. Scholarly research on play has found that an absence of play may be leading to the rise of anxiety, depression, and problems of attention and self control (Gray, "The Decline of Play and the Rise of Psychopathology in Children and Adolescents," *American Journal of Play*, v. 3, n. 4, Spring 2011). Play deprivation is also correlated with juvenile violence (Frost & Jacobs, "Play Deprivation: A Factor in Juvenile Violence," *Dimensions of Early Childhood*, Spring 1995, v. 23, n. 3).

WALK THE TALK

Embracing the Low-tech Life

Our bright, spirited seven- and ten-year-old boys are full of energy, creativity and humor. They have friends, participate in sports, enjoy the outdoors, and they don't use a computer, laptop, hand-held games or cell phones in any of their daily activities. Occasionally, the boys are curious about a video game or Internet time, and we reply with a "less is more" approach. We point out the fantastic privileges that our low-tech life offers and embrace those marvels, rather than feel like our life is diminished by not having the latest, greatest gadget. Card games, board games, and crafts sub in for computer games. Our home is filled with all types of music. Play-dates are exclusively "face time" not "screen time." Communication with their friends isn't limited or restricted; it just has to happen on our land line phone. Once in a great while, as part of a research project, we'l explore a website together, and we share family movie night once a week.

This lifestyle choice began during their infancy when our children seemed so complete simply as human beings. They've grown, but they still don't need an electronic gadget to be any more whole, nor do they need expensive gizmos in order to interact with the real, tactile world. Childhood is such a short portion of their life, we feel compelled to preserve their right to an authentic childhood and make it as memorable as possible. Our boys have their vast adult years to utilize digital media if they choose to do so (and, yes, all of us 30-somethings quickly became tech-savvy and so will they!) As they move into their adult lives, they'll engage in digital media with the awareness that what exists on the screen are just bits, pixels, data, and algorithms that represent aspects of the world they've already touched, smelled, tasted and seen with their whole selves. — Berdine Jordan, Writer and mother of two sons

So, reclaim the simple bounty of play. Give it its proper, sovereign place in kids' lives, along with their other passions and hobbies. Play is a multiple skill-building activity for which children don't need instruction… and they <u>want</u> to practice! Try thinking of play as being as necessary as sleep or good nutrition; prioritize and pattern it in the same dedicated manner. Trust that the goodness that flows from this basic human activity will endow your child with a protective resilience in adulthood. This richly complex part of childhood acts as a garden for our humanity: Critical components of creativity, civility, and empathy are all born here.

Creativity is not only a natural human process; it is one of life's most enjoyable and meaningful pleasures. Whether we are doodling, composing a symphony, or fashioning a valentine, when we create we are in harmony with our generative universe. Parents of young children, toddlers and preschoolers especially, are surrounded by a nearly perpetual bounty of creative gifts and moments that their children bring forth. Over time, however, the "Look what I made!" years begin to fade, and creativity slowly,

© 2014 FAMILY EMPOWERMENT NETWORK™ ALL RIGHTS RESERVED.

mysteriously leaks away. A recent study at the College of William & Mary discovered that creativity in young children (grades K-6) in America is in serious decline since 1990 (Hee Kim, "The Creativity Crisis," *Creativity Research Journal*, v. 23, n. 4, Nov. 2011). And by the time kids graduate from high school, only 5% identify themselves as "creative." In adulthood, many of us long to reconnect to our original sense of creativity.

Creativity humanizes our children and helps them to grow. They first experience creativity through free expression and play during unstructured time. As they age, children begin to benefit from instruction in music, dance, painting, and other arts. These creative pursuits can give them a lifelong means for expressing themselves, feeling balanced, and reducing stress. In addition, the creative arts also build intelligence and foster academic success. As Stuart Brown says, "The arts are indicators of emotional intelligence, but they also produce emotional intelligence" (*Play*, p. 168).

PLAY/CREATE

"Every child is born an artist. The problem is to remain an artist once we grow up." – Picasso

We have all heard of the well-established link between math and musical abilities, but music may empower our children in ways we are only just beginning to understand. As R.R. Konrad notes, "Music enhances the process of learning. The systems [it nourishes]—which include our integrated sensory, attention, cognitive, emotional, and motor capacities—are shown to be the driving forces behind all other learning" (Konrad, *Empathy, Arts and Social Studies*). Indeed, our culture has recently begun to acknowledge that creativity may be the most crucial attribute that young people will bring to their future professions and to the world at large. Sir Ken Robinson, author of *Out of Our Minds: Learning to Be Creative*, captures this insight in his famous TED talk, which can be found online at http://www.ted.com/talks/ken_robinson_says_schools_kill_creativity.html. An entertaining, animated version of Robinson's "Changing Education

Paradigms" talk is also a must-watch at http://www.thersa.org/events/rsaanimate/animate/rsa-animate-changing-paradigms.

What can we do to protect the conditions and attitudes that nurture lifelong creativity? Brown says that play and creativity are interwoven, and that the impulse to create art is a result of the play impulse (*Play*, p. 61). Restoring genuine play to our children's lives, and intentionally valuing it for the treasured behavior it truly is, will undoubtedly help to keep creativity flowing and vital. Consider how much time your family spends on arts-related activities, compared to athletics, for example. Do you notice an art deficit?

Another key condition for nurturing creativity, at home and at school, is by allowing for process, by creating an environment—whether in the kitchen making cookies or in the classroom making a mural—where kids feel comfortable taking risks and failing. When we relax the boundaries and eschew perfectionism, creativity blooms. For more on the value of creativity as well as ideas on using arts and crafts to have fun and bond as a family, see the article **"Cultivating Creativity."**

WALK THE TALK

"A positive family culture can provide children with a strong framework for moving out into the world and finding their own way. Our role as parents is to come to know what we most deeply value, and to embody that as best we can in our own lives and in our parenting." – Jon Kabat-Zinn, *Everyday Blessings*

Walk our talk—so easy to say and so hard to do—yet this is the one touchstone that can make all of the difference for our children. Will we do this perfectly? No. But we can give them the gift of growing and learning as they grow.

ALL RIGHTS RESERVED. © 2014 FAMILY EMPOWERMENT NETWORK™

WALK THE TALK

Explore these thoughts with your family:

- How do we talk about and treat our partners, friends, and family members?
- How do we communicate about people and ideas with whom we disagree?
- How do we act and what do we do when we are stressed?
- How do we interface with technology? Is it clear that family comes first?
- What do we do when we are angry?
- What do we do when we are clearly in the wrong?
- How do we apologize or make amends?

Walk the Talk is not only about modeling. It's also about creating a family that lives and models its values. Every member of the family learns to walk the talk at his/her own developmental level. For example, when five friends show up to play with your 12-year-old son and some of those boys don't follow his family's rules, does he have the inner strength to say, "If you don't follow the rules, you'll have to go home"? In an ideal world, a family can be a safe haven in which we mutually reinforce a set of values that we have defined and believe in, a set of values that can guide and inspire all the family members. Teaching family values also can be fun, as we discussed in the "Values Exercises for Families" in Chapter 1. One family had a special jar in which kids placed a nickel (a quarter for adults) when someone found himself or herself saying a word that was on the agreed-upon "don't-say-it" list. The family value for communicating respectfully was quickly reestablished.

Also keep in mind the power of our mirror neurons; our children internalize what we do and say. This is why the challenge of walking our talk is so important.

An adult son told his mother that the most important thing he learned at home was to be respectful and have honor, and that, sadly, he saw that this was missing for many of his peers. He said that he had learned these values from his father. When his mother remarked that she did not ever remember his father explicitly talking about that, her son replied, "He didn't; he just was that way."

"Don't worry that children never listen to you; worry that they are always watching you."

–Robert Fulghum, *All I Really Need to Know I Learned in Kindergarten*

What are your family values? When you live by your family values, the combination of modeling, teaching, and spending time together will gradually nurture the character of your children. Also remember that teaching when children are not in trouble is much more fruitful than talking and talking (lecturing) about misbehavior. Parents who provide clear boundaries and promptly follow through on them rather than over negotiate in the first 12 years of their child's life are more likely to have children who are able to Walk the Talk of the family values. This is not to say that children won't push up against these family values as they grow in independence. As children become full adolescents, gradually increasing negotiation is one way to show respect for the new brain power of the teen.

What will your children say about what they have learned about life from your actions? Without realizing it, our own behavior sometimes teaches the exact opposite of what we are trying to teach. How are you modeling technology use? Do you answer your cell phone when your child is telling you something important to him? Is it clear to your child that the real world is more important to you than the virtual world?

One important way to help everyone to Walk the Talk is to create a ritual of having family meetings. As soon as all members of a family can sit for a half an hour, family meetings can be used to reinforce the concept that every-

© 2014 FAMILY EMPOWERMENT NETWORK™ ALL RIGHTS RESERVED.

one's needs matter and to clarify family values and rules. An important part of the family meeting is planning fun activities to do as a family or to do with family friends. Family meetings also can increase a sense of security and belonging in your family through previewing the schedule for the week and choosing weekly chores. (Be sure to keep meetings short and have popcorn, dessert, or games when the meeting concludes.) Ideally, any of your children could rattle off to a visitor, "This is how we do things in our family" or "This is what we believe in our family."

IN CONCLUSION

Parents make all the difference. Our children's early experiences with connection, empathy, and kindness plant the seeds of a caring society. There has never been a more confusing moment to be a parent, given the cultural cross-currents created by the mixed signals of a digital, consumerist society. But simple truths can still prevail: Being present, and being genuinely together, promotes wellness and fulfillment. Play is deep nourishment. Face-to-face, real experience is the balm against the itch and emptiness that too much busyness, technology, and consumerism can inflict.

Have faith in the process–the slow, sometimes messy unfolding of human development. Resist the temptation to pursue the perfect; honor the ordinary instead. With courage, keeping the touchstones in mind, and a sense of humor, we can pass on the values, hopes, and dreams of our precious stories, our deep humanity.

ALL RIGHTS RESERVED. © 2014 FAMILY EMPOWERMENT NETWORK™

What have you intentionally preserved from your parents' parenting? What are you doing differently?

POSSIBLE DISCUSSION QUESTIONS

1) Recall and share one or two Golden Moments, those quintessential best memories, from your childhood.
2) What has come naturally to you in your parenting?
3) What are your greatest parenting fears?
4) Describe what you do to take care of yourself physically, mentally and emotionally? Is there an area you would like to improve?
5) When is it hard for you to "walk the talk"?
6) How do you feel about the amount of quality time for connection that you, your partner/spouse, your children, grandparents, etc., have together?
7) Describe the "rhythm" of your family life. What feeling/pace do your kids experience when they enter through the door after a long day at school?
8) Is your home a "safe haven" for your kids? Other people's kids? Is it a place kids feels accepted just the way they are? What more can you do to create such a feeling?
9) How does your family decompress and have fun at home, in the community, and in nature?
10) Discuss the role digital technology plays in your home and in your family life.

PUTTING IT INTO PRACTICE

- Take some time to envision your ideal week. How would work, homework, extracurricular activities, unstructured play and fun, creativity, etc., balance out? How does this ideal compare to your reality?
- Draw a rectangle on a piece of paper. Imagine it is your "tank." Write inside the rectangle what "fuel" you need to keep your tank full. Alone time? Time in nature? Sleep? Good food? Quality time with your partner/kids? Now draw lines coming out of the bottom of the rectangle and write on the lines what "drains" your tank. Nagging? Rushing in the morning? Commuting? Tight shoes? Complaining? After doing this exercise, ask yourself, "How am I doing on taking care of myself–on keeping my tank full–so I can show up as the parent I want to be?"
- Pick an activity you enjoy doing with each of your children, an activity that offers each of you a sense of connection, and turn that activity into a habit or ritual you engage in even if your schedules are busy with other activities.

PUTTING IT TOGETHER–YOUR VERSION

Write down a few ideas you have been inspired to implement in your own life after reading/discussing this chapter.

_____

_____

_____

© 2014 FAMILY EMPOWERMENT NETWORK™ ALL RIGHTS RESERVED.

Significance and Belonging

By Glenda Montgomery

based on and inspired by the work of Jane Nelsen *et al* of Positive Discipline

Our kids long for the knowledge that their lives matter to those around them. They need to know that they belong, that they have a place in which they make a difference. In generations past, children's contributions were essential to the survival of the family as a whole. They milked cows, did laundry, helped plant and harvest, churned butter, cooked, fed horses, or were employed outside of the home. Through this work they became skilled, competent, and important contributors to their family's ability to survive and thrive.

At that time, we didn't fully understand how crucial these feelings of belonging and significance were to healthy development and emotional health. With the work of Alfred Adler, Jane Nelsen, Dan Siegel, Bruce Perry, Brené Brown and many others, we now understand that what once seemed like unfair treatment of children actually fostered the opportunity to develop a sense of capability and confidence and allowed children to feel solidly significant within their worlds. Now, in a world where a children's contributions don't really mean much to our survival, it is up to us to use our understanding of our children's deep need to be competent, capable beings and create ways in which we can teach them skills and encourage them to use their skills in ways that they perceive are useful to those around them.

Connection is a human necessity. Through connection, children develop secure attachment. This attachment is necessary for healthy brain growth and emotional well-being. Yet, in our busy world, our attention is drawn to other things. Phones, iPods, computers, and TVs often take the focus of parents and children alike. Even if kids *seem* okay with a lot of non-connecting activities, the feeling of belonging is such a basic human need that kids start to act out when they don't have enough of it.

Though they crave *deep connection*, they will settle for *attention;* they don't have the experience yet to understand the difference. You will start to see attention-getting behavior ranging from constant interrupting, to inappropriate acting out, to refusal to comply or insisting you do things for them that they already know how to do. Power struggles start to crop up, and the intensity serves a purpose: It takes *two* to power struggle and the "locked in" nature of it at least satisfies some of that need for connection, even if it is in a contorted kind of way. As parents, we have much to do, and we shouldn't always be focused on our children; however, we can't ignore their need for connection. So, how do we help to ensure that this need is fulfilled?

There are many ways to foster connection and provide opportunities for our kids to contribute meaningfully, but, unlike in the past, when the hardships of survival assured our kids an important role, today we need to create these opportunities. Our awareness of the importance of this is the first step. We have to force ourselves to be less competent and begin to rely on our kids more. We need to train them for jobs around and in the house, beginning at preschool age, so that they can see _themselves_ how competent they are. Then we need to find ways to rely on their special talents, drawing these out to serve our family or the community as a whole. Volunteer work by kids fulfills this need to matter and is very worthwhile to organize with your family.

Note, however, that connection requires vigilance. Refuse to talk on the cell phone in the car when the kids are there. A simple, "Hey, I am driving in the car with the kids now; I'll call you back" sends the message to your children that you want to be with them and they are worth the time. When you go for walks with your kids, stay open to them. Lately, I have seen mothers walking young children with their earphones in and their iPods on. What message do the children receive then? Regular, defined time spent together doing whatever the child wants to do allows you to begin to develop play, a language, jokes, and habits that connect the two of you and are unique to you as a pair. Spending time just "being," rather than time running errands and getting things done, also sends a strong message of connection. Slowing down, challenging yourself to look into your child's eyes as you talk together, spending time at your child's level, all of these develop a sense of belonging. When children feel the nurturing, sun-like warmth of belonging and have faith in themselves as capable of making a difference in the world around them, what we see is positive behavior. When they are unsure of these, we see misbehavior as they seek to get that feeling any way they can. It is our job as parents to help them find a path to the "light" by making it a priority to find ways to foster feelings of connection and significance in their lives.

Glenda Montgomery is a Positive Discipline lead trainer as well as the mother of a daughter and son.

ALL RIGHTS RESERVED. © 2014 FAMILY EMPOWERMENT NETWORK™

The Brain Revolution

By Kathy Keller Jones, MA

Knowledge about the human brain has radically grown and changed in the last few decades. Here is a quick overview that can help you to understand yourself and others, as well as influence how your child's brain grows.

The brain is the top-most part of a human's extensive nervous system, which is distributed throughout the body. (We also have "gut wisdom" and "heart wisdom.") Experience shapes the brain by causing neurons to fire as ions throughout more than two million miles of neuronal fibers; the human brain, in fact, is thought to be the most complex thing in the universe (Siegel, *Parenting from the Inside Out*, p. 33).

Every brain is wired differently, yet humans have evolved to have three brains in our head (Medina, *Brain Rules*, p. 47). Over the course of our evolution, humans started with a "lizard brain" (brainstem) to keep us breathing and safe; then added a "mammalian brain" (limbic system or "Downstairs Brain") to help us feel, nurture our young, and remember; and finally topped those with the "human brain," known as the cortex (or "Upstairs Brain"). The cortex not only facilitates speech and all of our senses, but it also controls our higher order and analytical thinking such as self control and decision making. Our brains are remarkably adaptable. Our goal as humans is to get the different parts of the brain to work together so we not only meet our needs for survival but also have emotional balance and insight.

The part of the brain that makes us different from other mammals is the Prefrontal Cortex (PFC), the "third eye." The PFC affects seven critical functions (Siegel, *The Mindful Brain*, p. 42):
1. Body regulation such as putting on the brakes
2. Attuned communication–coordinating the input of another's mind with one's own
3. Emotional balance
4. Response flexibility–pausing before acting
5. Empathy–the empathic imagination of what might be going on inside someone else
6. Insight or self-knowing awareness
7. Fear modulation

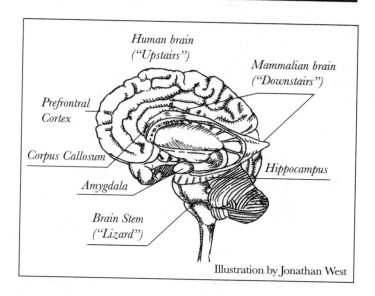

Human brain ("Upstairs")

Mammalian brain ("Downstairs")

Prefrontal Cortex

Corpus Callosum

Amygdala

Hippocampus

Brain Stem ("Lizard")

Illustration by Jonathan West

These functions do not mature until approximately age 25, which is why we must sometimes act as the prefrontal cortex of our children and teens. This part of the brain can continue to grow throughout the life span. Dan Siegel calls the attitude most conducive to optimum brain growth "COAL": Curiosity, Openness, Acceptance, and Loving kindness.

We are designed to never stop learning and exploring, and exercise improves cognition (Medina, *Brain Rules*). Our brain is like a muscle, which grows as we practice. As the neuro-scientists say, "Neurons that fire together, wire together." The more we do something, the stronger this part of our brain becomes. For example, when we teach our children good habits (and model them ourselves), this becomes part of their brain structure. The more we and our children live balanced, active lives--where we are moving and out of doors (much like our prehistoric ancestors)–the happier and sharper our brains will be.

Neuroplasticity: Our brains are much more malleable than we imagined a generation or two ago. For better and for worse, our brains change based on our experiences and how we attend to our experiences. "While you can learn when you divide your attention,

© 2014 Family Empowerment Network™ All Rights Reserved.

divided attention doesn't lead to abiding change in your brain maps" (Doidge, *The Brain That Changes Itself*, p. 68). That is, anything we practice intently will develop a region of our brains. For example, if we regularly play violent video games and interact with Internet porn, we can change our brain in counterproductive ways. On the contrary, if we mindfully explore positive endeavors, our brain can change for the good.

The human brain needs social experience and secure, responsive relationships to develop its potential. The new field of Interpersonal Neurobiology (IPNB) is based on this concept, that human development is interpersonal. Growing up in an empathetic, attuned environment where people treat each other well sets the stage for all family members to thrive. The way this works is that through mirror neurons we read and respond to the behavioral intentions and emotional states of others. This enables us to not only imitate people but also actually come to understand their feelings–to empathize.

The development of a person's social and emotional intelligence is greatly affected by experiences during childhood, adolescence, and young adulthood. Practicing social and emotional skills, including the ability to empathize and incrementally handle stress, begins in a child's initial attachments. In truth, early attachment to family creates a template for future relationships. Then, during adolescence and young adulthood, individuals hone their face-to-face social skills and, through practice, develop social/emotional intelligence. The principle "Use it or lose it" strongly correlates with adolescent brain growth.

Male and female brains tend to have different strengths due to the influence of sex-related hormones that flood the brain. fMRI scans show that the differences between male and female brains are complex and widespread. The brain centers for language and hearing are larger in women's brains, giving them a greater ability to observe emotions in others and to remember the details of emotional events. Men have a larger brain space devoted to sexual drive, action, and protection, as well as to spatial understanding (Brizendine, *The Female Brain* and *The Male Brain*).

Stressed brains don't learn the same way (Medina, *Brain Rules*, p. 195). Stress impacts people of all ages and interferes with flexibility, learning, and memory. Implicit memories of stressful events can even interfere with our functioning, albeit at a later time. As parents, therefore, we can work to reduce stress and increase enjoyable family time in order to positively influence implicit and explicit memories of childhood. See Daniel Siegel and Mary Hartzell's book *Parenting from the Inside Out: How a Deeper Self-Understanding Can Help You Raise Children Who Thrive* (2004).

Certain kinds of learning affect the brain in general rather than specific ways. When it comes to the Prefrontal Cortex, mindfulness training, such as meditation, strengthens the entire Prefrontal Cortex for both children and adults (Siegel, *The Mindful Brain*, p.103-4) and give us happier and healthier lives. See *10 Mindful Minutes* by Goldie Hawn and Wendy Holden (2011), who also developed the MindUP™ school curriculum designed to strengthen children's minds and to foster more empathy and compassion within relationships.

As a PFC aid, Paul Merzenich developed an online "game" called *Fast ForWord*, which is a kind of cerebral cross-training for children with attentional issues or autism (Doidge, *The Brain That Changes Itself*, p. 70-75). Even cursive handwriting and memorizing poems can be used as tools to encourage improvements in children's speaking, writing, and reading (Barbara Arrowsmith in Doidge's *The Brain That Changes Itself*, pp. 38, 39). Music lessons also can improve general intellectual abilities (see the work of E.G. Schellenberg).

Understanding the brain and developing a vocabulary to talk about the brain can be invaluable to our parenting. Dan Siegel's book *The Whole Brain Child: 12 Revolutionary Strategies to Nurture Your Child's Developing Mind* teaches us about:

* Integrating the right and left sides of the brain
* Integrating the Upstairs Brain (the cortex) with the Downstairs Brain; exercise the Upstairs Brain by teaching sound decision making, self control, self understanding, empathy, and morality *and* moving the body to avoid "losing the mind"
* When the Upstairs Brain (the cortex) and the Downstairs Brain (limbic system) do not work together, we call this "flipping our lid."
* How to integrate the memory so we can use it productively in our lives rather than having memories remain wordlessly stuck in our feelings and bodies

ALL RIGHTS RESERVED. © 2014 FAMILY EMPOWERMENT NETWORK™

Parenting for Peace

By Inbal Kashstan

When my son was four years old he asked me to read a book about castles that he had picked up at the library. He picked the book because he loves the Eyewitness series and was methodically going through as many of those books as we could find, irrespective of their subject matter. I didn't like this one. It depicted not only castles but also knights, armor and weapons of all kinds used in battles in centuries past.

I am not ready for weapons. One of the things I enjoy about my son not going to preschool and not watching TV is that his exposure to violence has been extremely limited. He has never said the word "gun" or played pretend violent games–yet. He doesn't know about war and people purposely hurting one another–yet. But here was the castle book, and he wanted to read it.

I am not trying to shield my son from the reality of violence and suffering in the world–but I am in a (privileged) position to choose, often, how and when these realities enter our lives. I read him some of the book, with numerous editorials. But when he asked to read the book again a few days later, I found myself saying that I feel a lot of sadness about people being violent with one another because I believe human beings can find peaceful ways to solve their conflicts.

Questions, of course, ensued. In response to one of my son's questions, I shared with him that my sadness was related not only to the past, when there were knights and castles, but to the present as well: people in the area where I grew up, Israelis and Palestinians, are also fighting. "Why are they fighting?" my son asked. "Because they both want the same piece of land and they haven't

figured out how to talk about it," I replied. "I'll teach them!" he volunteered. "What will you teach them?" I asked. "I'll teach them that they can each have some of the land, they can share," he replied easily. "The only problem," he continued, "is that I don't know how to find them."

I felt a mixture of joy and grief at his words. How wondrous to hear from my son–and from so many children–a desire to contribute to the world and a trust in the possibility of solving conflicts peacefully. Yet how apt his words were–"I don't know where to find them." How do we find the hearts of "enemies" so we can reach them with a message of peace? How do we find our own hearts and open them to those whose actions we object to profoundly?

This search for our own and others' hearts is at the core of my hope for peace has been the greatest influence on my parenting, including the decision to practice attachment parenting when my son was a baby. It has also led me to teach a process called Nonviolent Communication (developed by Dr. Marshall Rosenberg and taught around the world). I lead workshops for parents, couples, teachers, social change activists, and others who want to connect more deeply with themselves and with others and who want to contribute more effectively to mutual understanding, safety and peace in families, schools, organizations, and in the wider world.

My experience convinces me that what happens in our families both mirrors and contributes to what happens in our societies. Just as "enemies" fail to see each other's humanity, so we, too, at times fail to relate with others,

© 2014 FAMILY EMPOWERMENT NETWORK™ ALL RIGHTS RESERVED.

even loved ones, with compassion. Probably the primary challenge most parents tell me about is that though they yearn for peace and harmony in their families, they find themselves getting angry with their children more often and more quickly than they would like. Because the problem-solving model we follow so often relies on threat of consequences or promise of reward, it's almost guaranteed that anger will crop up regularly. For what children learn from this model is not cooperation, harmony and mutual respect; it's more often the hard lesson of domination: that whoever has more power gets to have his or her way, and that those who have less power can only submit or rebel. And so we continue the cycle of domination that is leading human beings close to self-destruction.

What alternative do we have? As parents, we have a remarkable opportunity to empower our children with life skills for connecting with others, resolving conflicts, and contributing to peace. Key to learning these skills is our conception of what human beings are like. Nonviolent Communication teaches that all human beings have the same deep needs, and that people can connect with one another when they understand and empathize with each other's needs.

Our conflicts arise not because we have different needs but because we have different strategies for how to meet our needs. It is on the strategy level that we argue, fight, or go to war, especially when we deem someone else's strategy a block to our own ability to meet our needs. Yet Nonviolent Communication suggests that behind every strategy, however ineffective, tragic, violent or abhorrent to us, is an attempt to meet a need. This notion turns on its head the dichotomy of "good guys" and "bad guys" and focuses our attention on the human being behind every action. When we understand the needs that motivate our own and others' behavior, we have no enemies. With our tremendous resources and creativity, we can and—I hope—we will find new strategies for meeting all our needs.

We can teach our children about making peace by understanding, reflecting, and nurturing their ability to meet their needs while we also understand, express and attend to our own. One of the needs human beings have is for autonomy, for the ability to make decisions about things that affect us. This leads us on a path of self-interest and a search for confidence and power. Yet if we nurture this need in our children to the exclusion of others, it can be difficult for us to get our own needs met. Thankfully, our need for autonomy is balanced by another shared human need, for contribution to others. This need leads us on a path of consideration, care and generosity to others. NVC enables us to look at both needs (and many others) and find a way to balance them with each other so that we recognize our need to give, to consider others and contribute to them, as an autonomous choice. When giving is done freely, out of mutual care and respect, it does not conflict with autonomy and choice but rather complements them.

From this perspective, parents may find that we don't need punishments or rewards in parenting our children—we can instead invite our children to contribute to meeting our needs just as we invite ourselves to contribute to meeting theirs: with joy and willingness instead of guilt, shame, fear of punishment or desire for reward. This is not permissive parenting—it is parenting deeply committed to meeting the needs of both parents and children through a focus on connection and mutual respect.

Transforming parenting is hugely challenging in the context of the daily, overwhelming reality of parenting. Yet this transformation enables a profound depth of connection and trust among family members. Perhaps more poignantly for me, choosing to parent this way gives me hope for peace for our world—perhaps for our children's generation, perhaps for future generations, when human beings have learned to speak the language of compassion.

ALL RIGHTS RESERVED. © 2014 FAMILY EMPOWERMENT NETWORK™

As the world enters our home and my son's exposure to life's realities grows, I hope he will sustain these lessons and carry them into his own life. I hope he will know that the path to peace is most effectively followed not by rewarding the "good" guys and punishing the "bad" ones, but by striving to find strategies that will meet people's needs–not just our own, but everyone's. I hope he will have the confidence and trust in his own peaceful resources and in human beings' capacity for peace. I hope he remembers that we can find other people's hearts by seeing their humanity.

Copyright © Inbal Kashtan. A version of this article appeared in Parenting From Your Heart, *by Inbal Kashtan, and also was published in* Paths of Learning *(Spring 2003) and* California Home Schooler *(Oct. 2002).*

THE STEPS OF NVC

Expressing Ourselves: NVC includes stating our observations, feelings, needs, and requests.

Step 1—Observations: Descriptions of what is seen or heard without added interpretations. For example, instead of "She's having a temper tantrum," say "She is lying on the floor crying and kicking."

Step 2—Feelings: Our emotions rather than our story or thoughts about what others are doing. For example, instead of "I feel like you're irresponsible," which includes an interpretation of another's behavior say "I feel worried." See [feelings lists] for an inventory of feeling words.

Step 3—Needs: Feelings are caused by needs, which are universal and ongoing and not dependent on the actions of particular individuals. State your need rather than the other person's actions as the cause; for example, "I feel annoyed because I need support" rather than "I feel annoyed because you didn't do the dishes." See [needs list] for an inventory of needs.

Step 4—Requests: Doable, immediate, and stated in positive action language (what you want instead of what you don't want); for example, "Would you be willing to come back tonight at the time we've agreed?" rather than "Would you make sure not to be late again?" By definition, when we make requests we are open to hearing a "No," taking it as an opportunity for further dialogue.

Example of NVC Statement:

Original statement: "You're irresponsible! You made me so worried when you didn't get home on time! If you come home late again, you'll be grounded."

NVC statement: "When you came home at midnight after agreeing to come home at 10 p.m., I felt so worried because I need peace of mind about your safety. Would you be willing to spend time right now coming up with a plan that will give you the autonomy you want and also help me feel more peaceful?"

Empathizing with Others:
In NVC, we empathize with others by guessing their feelings and needs: "Are you feeling ____ because you need ____?" Instead of trying to "get it right," we aim to understand. In the example above, the teen's response may be, "No!" The parent can then switch from expression to listening with empathy: "Are you feeling annoyed because you need your ability to choose how to spend your time to be trusted?" From here, the dialogue can continue with empathy and expression until both people's needs for connection and understanding are met.

Copyright © Inbal Kashtan. Excerpted from Parenting From Your Heart, *by Inbal Kashtan and also published in* Mothering, *Jan./Feb. 2002.*

Inbal Kashtan is the author of Parenting from Your Heart: Sharing the Gifts of Compassion, Connection, and Choice, *and numerous articles about parenting with NVC. She also has a CD,* Connected Parenting: Nonviolent Communication in Family Life. *Both are available at www.nonviolentcommunication.net. Some of her videos about parenting with NVC can be found on YouTube, and more can be found at www.nvctraining.com. For more information on Nonviolent Communication, see www.cnvc.org and www.nvctraining.com. All rights reserved.*

Feelings and Needs Inventories

Needs Inventory:

"A need is life seeking expression within us." Marshall Rosenberg, PhD

Autonomy
To choose one's dreams, goals, & values
To choose one's plan for fulfilling one's dreams, goals, & values
Freedom
Choice
Independence
Space
Spontaneity

Connection
Acceptance
Affection
Appreciation
Belonging
Closeness
Community
Consideration
Emotional Safety
Inclusion
Inspiration
Interdependence
Intimacy
Love
Reassurance
Respect
Self-love
Support
Sympathy
Trust
Understanding
Warmth

Physical Nurturance
Air
Food
Exercise
Movement
Physical Safety
Rest/sleep
Sexual expression
Shelter
Touch
Water

Meaning
Awareness
Celebration of life
Challenge
Clarity
Competence
Consciousness
Contribution
Creativity
Discovery
Efficacy
Effectiveness
Growth
Learning
Making a contribution
Making a difference
Mourning
Participation
Purpose
Self-expression
Stimulation
Understanding

Celebration
Gratitude
To celebrate the creation of life and dreams fulfilled.
To celebrate losses: loved one, dreams, etc. (mourning)

Integrity/Honesty
Authenticity
Creativity
Honesty
Presence
Self-worth

Play and Recreation
Exercise
Fun
Humor
Joy
Laughter

Spiritual Communion
Beauty
Communion
Ease
Empathy
Equality
Harmony
Inspiration
Order
Peace
Unconditional Love

Feelings Inventory:
How We Are Likely to Feel When Our Needs ARE Being Met:

Adventurous	Compassionate	Enthusiastic	Invigorated	Reassured
Affectionate	Composed	Fascinated	Involved	Rejuvenated
Alive	Confident	Free	Intrigued	Relaxed
Amazed	Contented	Friendly	Joyous	Satisfied
Animated	Curious	Fulfilled	Lively	Secure
Appreciated	Dazzled	Glad	Loving	Serene
Aroused	Delighted	Glowing	Moved	Stimulated
Astonished	Eager	Grateful	Optimistic	Tender
Blissful	Ecstatic	Gratified	Overjoyed	Tickled
Calm	Elated	Happy	Peaceful	Thankful
Carefree	Empowered	Helpful	Pleased	Upbeat
Cheerful	Encouraged	Hopeful	Proud	Wonderful
Comfortable	Energetic	Inspired	Radiant	etc...

Feelings Inventory:
How We Are Likely to Feel When Our Needs AREN'T Being Met:

Afraid	Depressed	Flustered	Lethargic	Repulsed
Aggravated	Despairing	Forlorn	Listless	Resentful
Agitated	Detached	Fragile	Livid	Sad
Alarmed	Devastated	Frazzled	Lonely	Scared
Alienated	Disappointed	Frightened	Mad	Self-conscious
Aloof	Disconnected	Frustrated	Mean	Shocked
Ambivalent	Discouraged	Furious	Miserable	Sorrowful
Anguished	Disengaged	Gloomy	Morose	Startled
Angry	Disgusted	Guilty	Mortified	Surprised
Annoyed	Dismayed	Harried	Mystified	Suspicious
Anxious	Distaste	Heartbroken	Nervous	Tepid
Apathetic	Distracted	Heavy	Nostalgic	Terrified
Ashamed	Distressed	Helpless	Numb	Torn
Baffled	Disturbed	Hopeless	Outraged	Troubled
Bewildered	Downhearted	Horrible	Overwhelmed	Uncomfortable
Bitter	Dull	Hostile	Pained	Uneasy
Bored	Edgy	Hurt	Panicky	Unhappy
Brokenhearted	Embarrassed	Impatient	Passive	Unsteady
Burned out	Embittered	Indifferent	Perplexed	Upset
Concerned	Envious	Insecure	Pessimistic	Vulnerable
Confused	Exasperated	Irate	Puzzled	Wary
Dazed	Fatigued	Irritated	Rattled	Weary
Dejected	Fearful	Jealous	Reluctant	Worried
Depleted	Fidgety	Lazy	Remorseful	etc...

Adapted by Kathy Masarie and Jody Bellant Scheer from Nonviolent Communication by Marshall Rosenburg, PhD, the Center for Nonviolent Communication www.cnvc.org.

The Key to Surviving the Negative Impact of Digital Technology? Moderation

By Doreen Dodgen-Magee, PsyD

The "M word." Moderation. Those of us who live in the West don't utter this word very often. Neither do we practice it. It just isn't part of the 21st century American lexicon of language or practice. We seem to favor consumption, amassment, and more.

Several years ago researchers believed that Americans had hit a ceiling in terms of screen time, finding that we spent an average of 6.5 hours "plugged in." Now, however, when multi-use is controlled for, it appears that we spend almost 11 hours a day interacting with technology (Rideout, V.J, Foehr, U.G, and Roberts, D.F, 2010). The tendency to under-report plugged in time (Webroot Software, 2007) along with the fact that this statistic does not include pre-school and early elementary aged children's interaction with computer chip enabled toys (think teething toys that vibrate and light up and the new popular "tablet like" early readers for young kids), there is a strong chance that this number may actually be an underestimation of our average daily screen time.

Some will say "So what? All this technology is making our kids smarter, enabling them to fit in with their peers, and preparing them for an adult world where screens dominate." The reality is, however, that this hyper-adaptation to technology as a primary point of engagement and use of time is costing our children.

The literature suggests that as time plugged in increases, family talk time and social practice opportunities decline (Shklovski, Kraut, and Rainie, 2004), grades drop (Kirkorian, H.L, Wartella, E.A., and Anderson, D.R, 2008), and impulse control, ability to delay gratification, and emotional regulation skills wane (Roberts, D.F, Foehr, U.G, Rideout, V.J, Brodie, M, 1999). Distractibility increases (Schmidt, M.E and Vandewater, E.A, 2009). It appears that full scale adoption of technology's "bene-fits" might cost more than we can afford.

History tells a similar story in other venues. Browse Life magazine from the late 1950's and early 1960's and you'll find glossy, highly stylized ads for convenience foods. Intended to be an accompaniment to our meals we bought fully into the claims of health and speed made by the convenience food industry and gobbled up the sodium laden, nutritionally weakened, time saving goods as main course faire. The result, 20 years later, was a generation whose taste leaned toward processed over fresh, fast over slow, and who was dealing with hypertension, obesity, and high cholesterol in record numbers. The FDA intervened with a food pyramid but our cultural habits were firmly in place and our convenience food dependence remains an issue today. A similar story can be told with tobacco. We all know how our efforts to cut back on cigarette consumption have gone.

It's a universal truth: habits are hard to break and, as a culture, we are highly habituated to our dependence on technology. Screens surround us. From the grocery store where televisions play for us while we wait in line, to the classroom where computers are a must, to our bedrooms where mini internet enabled computers called smart phones do everything from play our movies to control our thermostats to wake us up in the morning, we are rarely out of range of technology. Our habits are in place and are impacting the way in which our children think, relate, and develop a sense of self.

Neurological Impact

A healthy brain is one that shows evidence of stimulation and resulting wiring in both hemispheres and in all regions. Complexity is key. Given that the brain "wires together where it fires together," a diverse and evocative set of experiences lead to healthy neurological function for

© 2014 FAMILY EMPOWERMENT NETWORK™ ALL RIGHTS RESERVED.

children. The converse is also true. When children limit their involvement in the world to one or two domains of experience, the brain's wiring becomes less complex and cognitive flexibility is sacrificed. If we rely on our brains less to retain and recall information or if we provide them with only screen forms of stimulation we sacrifice complexity (Seigel D.J, Bryson, T.P, 2011). Further, with screens and digital engagement leading to a reduction in social practice and talk time (Webroot Software, 2007), the regions of the brain related to emotional regulation, interpersonal communication, and executive function may suffer. By the time we have hard science to support these hypotheses, it will be late in the game for an entire generation of screen dependent digital natives.

Impact on the Development of Self

Before children can struggle with self esteem they must develop a sense of self. Formed by bumping up against ones own strengths, weaknesses, limitations, and capabilities, a sense of self grows out of a person's beliefs about who they are and what they most deeply value. It is also the foundation upon which relational abilities rest and serves as a kind of true north for choices, behaviors, and attitudes. Skills such as self control, an ability to delay gratification, resilience, and empathy emerge from a sturdy sense of self.

When a significant portion of time is spent in cyber spaces it is easy for an individual to develop what the psychological community refers to as an external locus of control as opposed to a grounded sense of self. In basic terms this means that the outside world becomes the primary reference point for determining how to feel about ones' self and also from which to receive stimulation, soothing, and direction. An external locus of control can over-ride an individual's true north and lead them to

become passively dependent upon external sources, as opposed to internally chosen values and knowledge, for guidance and direction.

Relational Impact

Relationships are important for both healthy brain function and contented living. The skills necessary for navigating conflict, intimacy, and varied kinds of connections are important for success in the both the internal and external world. Communication is the currency of relationship. As an increasing proportion of relationships occur in cyber spheres, a marked shift in communication is occurring. Impulsively typed, instantly received messages are replacing face to face and voice to voice communication, omitting the important information that non verbal cues provide and the forethought and discernment that less "distanced" (by time, space, physical proximity) communiques require. Further, technology provides an "out" in every relational situation. If a conversation is deemed boring, difficult, unwanted, there is another conversation happening somewhere else that can be engaged in instantly. Finally, social networking's emphasis on quantity over quality and appearance over authenticity sets children up to compare and amass rather than work toward authenticity and genuinely sustainable friendship.

Moving from Habit to Health

While most people have inklings that an over dependence upon technology might not be healthy, the strength of the habits around its use keep change from occurring. Just as it's easier to heat up a nutritionally compromised can of soup, disregarding the niggling fact that it isn't nearly as good for us as home made, we go right on texting, Facebooking, and video gaming away even though we imagine we're losing something important along the way.

ALL RIGHTS RESERVED. © 2014 FAMILY EMPOWERMENT NETWORK™

The truth is, it is easier to establish healthy norms than to break bad habits. Note: easier, not easy. If norm-setting, forethought, and planning were a breeze, every family would establish clear, wisely discerned guidelines about technology use long before children interacted with it in the first place. They would take time to anticipate where the sticky spots and pitfalls might arise and establish boundaries up front to anticipate them. Since most families are working from evolved habits, however, two processes are required to move toward health. One, habits must be broken and two, new norms put in place. This is no small task.

To break habits families must be willing to first assess their level of dependence upon technology. Honest data regarding time spent, content, and transparency regarding both, must be accumulated. From there, conscious and deliberate discernment must occur regarding how current use may be affecting relational, intra-personal, and neurological function for each family member. Assessment and discernment can then lead to action, which is where norms can be laid down to help guide technology use in directions that will enhance health rather than rob it.

Moderation is a powerful helper in this process. Technology is here to stay and is not, in and of itself, evil. As parents help children engage in use that is moderate and part of a complex set of activities available to them, they are helping their children learn the important lessons of self control and self regulation. Teaching children the concept of budgeting and good stewardship of time, money, and energy in the arena of their technology use helps them everywhere. Providing them with limits and requiring them to respect them is similarly important. Just as giving a child his life-time allowance in one lump sum on his 6th birthday would rob the parent the opportunity to teach money management and self care skills, so does providing them unlimited access to technology with no limits or opportunities to develop prowess and responsibility and earn more opportunities steal important teaching.

In order to break the over-use habit families must find ways of supporting children specifically in the areas where technology has taken over. If a child's only friends are on Facebook, yanking it away might do more harm than help. Setting up the environment, however, with opportunities for success in real time, face to face, voice to voice encounters supports skill development as well as motivation for building real time connections. Other real life opportunities that are targeted to a child's unique temperament and style must present themselves in order to provide muses worthy, in a child's mind, of moderating technology. Driving a slick track car instead of playing racing games, watching a live performance of Hamlet in place of a violent movie, playing a complex strategy board game in place of a video game, taking a hip hop class rather than watching hours of dance videos online are all examples of making the physical world as compelling as the digital one. Requiring phones to be left in a basket at the door of a party is a way of helping them encounter the people they're actually with as opposed to those they merely have access to.

In support of giving children every opportunity to thrive, the concept of moderation is key. Moderation creates space where indulgence once fit. When applied in a world overly plugged in it provides a break from screens long enough to develop grounded selves, complexly wired brains, and relationships that are messy, real, deep, flavorful, and born out of the investment of time . . . just like homemade soup.

Dr. Doreen Dodgen-Magee is a psychologist maintaining a private practice and national speaking docket. Her blog (doreendm.blogspot.com) and frequent journal articles highlight the importance of intentionality regarding media and technology engagement. Her most important role is that of mom to Connor and Kaija and auntie to Ethan and Ella.

Resources

Kirkorian, H.L., Wartella, E.A., & Anderson, D.R. (2008). "The Future of Children." *Children and Electronic Media*, 18 (1), 39-61.

Rideout, V.J., Foehr, U.G., and Roberts, D.F. (2010). "Generation M2: Media in the Lives of 8- to 18- Year Olds." A Kaiser Family Foundation Study. http://www.kff.org/entmedia/upload/8010.pdf

Roberts, D.F., Foehr, U.G., Rideout, V.J., Brodie, M. (1999). *Kids and Media @ the New Millennium: A Comprehensive National Analysis.* Darby, PA: Diane Publishing Co.

Seigel, D.J. and Bryson, T.P. (2011). *The Whole-Brain Child: 12 Revolutionary Strategies to Nurture Your Child's Developing Mind*, NY: Delacorte Press.

Schmidt, M.E. & Vandewater, E.A. (2008). "Media and Attention, Cognition, and School Achievement." *Children and Electronic Media*, 18 (1), 63-85.

Shklovski, I, Kraut, R, & Rainie, L. (2004). The Internet and Social Participation: Contrasting Cross-Sectional and Longitudinal Analyses. *JCMC, 10* (1), Article 1.

Webroot Software. (2007). State of Internet Security. Q207 Focus, Protecting Children Online. http://www.webroot.com/pdf/Webroot_SoIS_Q0207.pdf

© 2014 FAMILY EMPOWERMENT NETWORK™ ALL RIGHTS RESERVED.

Tips for Maintaining Digital Sanity and Protecting your Family

By Kathy Keller Jones, MA

One of our vital roles as parents is to help our children have balanced lives. We do this by cultivating healthy habits that leave time for real-time experiences and time for the family to connect.

Developing healthy habits is easier than breaking bad habits later. In the case of digital technology, this means creating family agreements about electronic use. This can be pioneering work for us, as we adults struggle with the allure of digital devices as much as children do. Here are some ideas for maintaining digital sanity that have worked for other caring, proactive families:

MAKE SURE YOUR FAMILY HAS DIGITAL-FREE TIME TOGETHER.

Don't let smart phone rings and beeps interrupt face-to-face engagement, especially with your children. Your time with them is precious.

• **Turn off cell phones and other hand-held devices during meals and when out with friends and family.** Better yet, set up a basket at your front door to drop off phones upon entry or leave them in the car when you go out to dinner!

• **Don't let TV and computer screens be focal points in your home.** Also, be sure to turn them off during dinner, when they are not being used, or when you are not at home.

• **Be mindful of the placement of screens in your home.** Some families have a separate room for TV and computer use. It's easier for parents to supervise TV watching, computer use, and gaming if the computer is in a common area of the home. Consider having laptops for homework because you can collect them when homework is done.

• **Designate technology-free sanctuaries in your home** (except for homework time for older children). It's more peaceful to have areas of the house where there are no screens–and this leads to opportunities for other kinds of activities such as board games, creative activities, ping pong, etc.

• **Commit to a "digital Sabbath" one evening or day of the week.** This is when a family turns off or stores all electronic devices and relaxes or has fun together.

• **Pull the plug.** Consider turning off your wireless connection nightly, about an hour before bedtime.

• **Get out in nature and the real world together and leave technology behind.** Teens, in particular, need to decompress from the social pressures of their lives and discover that their friends will still be there when they return.

• **Pool your best family ideas (include all family members) to create new and original rituals in and around the encroachment of electronics.** Problem solve together; support each other. Have faith that good things result from good habits and connections.

LIMIT TIME SPENT WITH ELECTRONICS.

Explore your family's values and establish routines that allow you and each member to honor and live those values. Because time spent with electronics can be a black hole and keep you from living your values, limiting screen time is a good place to start.

• **Avoid the use of technology as an electronic babysitter.** Set up your home so there are clear limits and readily available non-media activities such as an arts and crafts table, dress-up supplies, sand, hobbies, books, games, journaling,

ALL RIGHTS RESERVED. © 2014 FAMILY EMPOWERMENT NETWORK™

music, physical activities in and out, bikes, forts in the backyard…. If your child says he/she is bored, don't worry; boredom often leads to creativity and initiative!

• **Keep screens out of kids' and teens' bedrooms.** As a group, kids with screens in their rooms spend more time on screens, read less, and do not do as well academically (Kaiser Family Foundation Study, 2004).

• **Limit the amount of time children can use screens for fun to an hour or less total on school days.** Turn off screens in your home when they are not in use. Some families do not allow TV, recreational digital use, or video games on school days; some allow no electronic entertainment at all except for a weekly movie night; and some dramatically reduce digital entertainment during the summer. John Medina, author of *Brain Rules for Baby*, had his school-aged sons purchase weekend digital time for Wii and educational games with hours they read during the week.

• **If you are going to allow video games, recognize the addictive nature of gaming and make sure the games being played in your home fit with your family values.** Substitute sports, creative activities, and strategy games for violent games. Teens still need time limits for game use. They might experience violent games at friends' houses, but they will not associate them with home and self in the same way.

• **Practice "appointment" TV.** Use the latest technology to record worthwhile shows and watch them at appointed times. Teach the skill of muting commercials and turning the TV off when the show or game is done.

• **Set and honor limits for your own computer-use time,** and your kids will complain less when you set limits for them.

PROTECT GOOD SLEEP HABITS.

Using social media and the Internet can creep into sleep time, yet good sleep matters to academic performance, emotional stability, ability to focus, and maintaining general health (*Nurture Shock* by Po Bronson and Ashley Merryman, 2009, p. 31). It makes sense, then, to set limits around technology use in relation to bedtime.

• **Collect all devices and put them in the "dog house"/basket at least a half an hour before bedtime.** Cell phone or Internet access after bedtime is an invitation for creating counterproductive habits and welcoming "drama."

• **Create a buffer zone between the time technology is shut down and bedtime.** Allow time to read, talk, and decompress. Safeguard this important transition time; honor the sacredness of the night.

• **Help your teens to figure out how to get their work done without staying up late on a regular basis.** Getting up early is often a better alternative.

DELAY THE INTRODUCTION OF PHONES, TEXTING, AND SOCIAL NETWORKING FOR AS LONG AS POSSIBLE.

• **Delay the introduction of phones and especially texting for tweens and teens.** Phones rarely make your child safer, but they do expose them to overwhelming distractions and interfere with family connection. Also, overuse of texting can interfere with your child's ability to self regulate, attend to tasks, relax in the moment, etc.

• **If possible, have a graduated introduction to cell phones.** If you feel your child must have a phone, start with a basic phone *without* texting, then add texting a year or two later based on good academic performance and maturity. Only introduce smartphones when your teen can use the Internet and video games wisely. Some families allow smartphone use only on weekends.

• **Come to an agreement around cell phone/ texting use** and designate times when all devices are turned off, e.g., dinner and bedtime and other family activities.

© 2014 FAMILY EMPOWERMENT NETWORK™ ALL RIGHTS RESERVED.

- **Consider purchasing parental controls from your cell phone company** (usually around $5 per month.)

- **Limit texting and/or social networking** by letting your tween socialize on-line for no more than one-half hour/day; otherwise, silence the device and put it out of sight.

- **Delay the use of Facebook and other social media as long as possible.** If you need backup, read *Talking Back to Facebook* by John Steyer, 2012.

- **Develop a contract around the use of social media** and make its use contingent on following family rules. Phones and social media are a privilege, not a right. Encourage teens to develop their own values statements around digital media and use agreements.

TALK TO YOUR TEEN BOYS ABOUT THE ADDICTIVE NATURE OF ONLINE PORNOGRAPHY.

See Norman Doidge's book, *The Brain that Changes Itself,* pp. 102–112, and Chapter 3 of *Face to Face.*

TAKE CARE OF YOURSELF.

Make sure you have the time you need away from your children to feel balanced, so you are less likely to use electronics for babysitting. If you work at home, do your best to find strategies to keep work separate from regular family life. Some families create a separate room where family members go to do their digital work.

Recommendations for Children's Cell Phone Use

	"Basic Phones"	**Texting**	**Smart Phones/ devices**
Elementary School	No cell phones unless needed for safety; basic phones only	No	Supervised and limited use of Internet-ready hand devices* e.g., FaceTime with grandparents
Middle School	Delay if possible. Can introduce phone use based on being a conscientious student/family member Can be limited to weekends Phones collected before bedtime	Texting at limited times only, e.g., weekends only or after homework is done Purchase parental controls or block texting	Delay use until high school if possible or have clear agreements and limits around the use of smart phones and Internet-ready held devices.
First Half of High School	Phone use based on being conscientious student/family member Phones collected before bedtime	Texting based on being a conscientious student/family member and no overdoing Agreements about not texting at home in the kitchen/dining area or in the car	OK to introduce with maturity May offer teen the opportunity to pay for the upgrade from basic to smart

* Parents of preadolescents who have smartphones are encouraged to purchase and use parental controls from their service providers and to establish a clear contract with their children.

ALL RIGHTS RESERVED. © 2014 FAMILY EMPOWERMENT NETWORK™

The Busyness Epidemic

By Kathy Keller Jones, MA, Kathy Masarie, MD, and Cassandra Dickson, MA

These days, when any adult is asked, "How are you?" the answer is almost universally "I am so busy!" Somehow, in this land of opportunity and abundance, we have accepted (chosen) busyness as the American way of life. We seem to have morphed from "human beings" to "human doers." When did we fall into the "busy trap?"

It crept up on us slowly. All those appliances of the 1950s that people predicted would lead to oodles of free, relaxing time instead led to more to do in our bigger, better houses. With faxes, computers, Internet, and cell phones, we reply 24/7 instead of just 9 to 5. And, then, before we can take a breath, the reply comes back demanding more!

One tool we try to use to "get it all done" is multi-tasking. In truth, multi-tasking is not even possible with thinking-intensive tasks. All we really do is rapidly move from one task to another. Between each task, however, is transition time which cannot be skipped and which is extremely draining. Eventually, we just shut down, like a computer with too many windows open. Oh, if we could only upload some more gigabytes into our memory!

Then there is the addiction to work, the presumption that, if "work" demands something, it is more important than hanging out and connecting with our spouse or our children. Plus, being a busy mom came to mean "I am a good mom," whether I work in the home or outside the home.

While we may thrive on busyness for a while–there are so many good things to do–eventually we begin to feel stressed and overwhelmed. Overdone, busyness robs us of depth, presence, memory, sleep, exercise, and often the ability to parent the way we truly want: calmly and mindfully. When busyness trickles down to our children, we find ourselves pushing them to keep up, or nudging them into sports or academic stardom before they are ready. The pressure on families to be busy, and to accept busyness as an indicator of achievement and future success, has never been more intense.

While it can feel good to "get things done," busyness, like anything else, can become addictive. Some of us even use "busy" as a way to stay numb and avoid dealing with deeper struggles and conflicts. New research also shows that the relentless pursuit of efficiency may be overrated. For the research and insight into what brain science tells us about the detrimental effects of busyness, check out John Medina's book, *Brain Rules*. In the book, Medina shares ideas that can transform our daily lives.

The Take the Time touchstone reminds us of the value of unstructured time–for ourselves, our children, and our families. Deep connection with friends and family takes time. Research in neuroscience is affirming the importance of "down time" for the brain to function optimally. It's also easy to forget that kids don't need to be busy to learn and grow up healthy. On the contrary, unstructured play is a rich resource for developing creativity, mastering skills, and relieving stress. When we take the time to value free time in our children's lives, we are protecting childhood itself, and the lifelong joys that come with it: adventure, wonder, laughter, and meaning.

Simple Steps for Slowing Down

When you are asked, "How are you doing?" do not reply "busy" and then list all you are doing to justify it. Instead respond, "Great!" and list all the things going well in your life, all those things for which you are grateful.

Say "no" more often, not only to others respectfully, but to yourself. Model this for your children. Talk about it.

Grab some free time by limiting and scheduling your own screen time.

Live in the present moment, which is the only one you have control over.

Put in support structures and rituals for connection and slowing down.

© 2014 FAMILY EMPOWERMENT NETWORK™ ALL RIGHTS RESERVED.

Give Your Family a Gift: Sleep

By Kathy Masarie, MD

Most of us know the numbers: Babies need anywhere from 10.5-18 hours of sleep; pre-schoolers, anywhere from 11-15 hours; 6-9 year-olds, from 10-11 hours; and adolescents, from 8.5-9.5 hours. The question is: Do we safeguard sleep, especially given the encroachment of digital devices in our lives?

Teens are an espcially vulnerable group and have struggled with getting enough sleep for decades. Their natural circadian rhythm is like having an internal clock of 25 hours. Every night, their biologic drive is to stay up an hour later, exacerbated by insane school demands and the screen time which is so rampant in their lives. What is different today is that teens have no role models for healthy sleep habits. Their parents are as sleep-deprived as they are.

Case study: Me. But I had a major wake-up call when I read Martha Beck's article on burnout called "Stay Cool" (*Oprah*, Nov., 2011). Her "Chill Principle 2: Sleep As If Your Life Depends on It" struck a chord. She says, "Some people feel superior when they work around the clock. This is like proudly pouring Tabasco sauce in your eyes. Sleep makes you smarter, better-looking, and more creative. It can add years to your life. It does more to improve long-term quality of life than money, fancy vacations, or hot sex. Not giving high priority to sleep is frankly, insane." She goes on to say, "Ignore these minimums and eventually your body will eventually end up lying still anyway–in your bed, a hospital, or the morgue. You choose." Whoa. OK! I am listening now.

We live in a culture moving faster than the "speed of life." Even slowing down isn't slow enough. Sleep is the first to go and the last to come back. We think it gives us that buffer to fit everything in a day, especially after we finally get those little darlings to bed. But the bottom line is: Sleep deprivation is detrimental, leading to reduced immunity, poor performance, poor learning, and poor driving!

Because a child's brain is still developing, and so much of that neural growth and pruning happens while they're sleeping, a deprivation of even one hour can have consequences. A Tel Aviv University study confirms this assertion, proving a performance gap with even one hour less sleep. The book *NurtureShock* by Po Bronson and Ashley Merryman highlights the results of similar studies in its chapter, "The Lost Hour." Bronson and Merryman also delve into the neuroscience of what happens to our children's brains if they are sleep deprived.

A view of sleep that really speaks to me comes from Kim John Payne. In his book, *Simplicity Parenting*, Payne talks about going to bed as a trust process in "letting go of your day" and says this process begins during the day with "pressure valves." For babies, a pressure valve can be nap time. For older kids, it may be a foot rub with those deep, sharing talks at bedtime. It might be a prayer or moment of silence at dinnertime as a candle is lit. Or it might be time set aside for mindful meditation such as the "square breathing" that my third-grade teacher friend does several times a day: Deep breath in 1-2, hold 3-4, breath out 5-6, hold 7-8 for one minute.

The sure-fire test if you or your kids are getting enough sleep is how you all get out of bed in the morning. If it is a knock-down, frantic fight with your kids, check out *Snooze… or Lose: 10 "No War" Ways to Improve Your Teen's Sleep Habits* by Dr. Helene Emsellem. For a "Green Time for Sleep Time" report from the National Wildlife Federation, detailing how time spent outdoors improves sleep, visit www.nwf.org.

The very best gift we can give our families is our full, wonderful selves. When we get enough sleep, we are rested and resourceful and can handle whatever crabbiness the world throws at us. Then, we just might have the reserves to support our kids to get the sleep they need and have time for a little self-care, too.

Reprinted from Nov. 2011 Family Empowerment Network's "emPower Monthly."

ALL RIGHTS RESERVED. © 2014 FAMILY EMPOWERMENT NETWORK™

Cultivating Creativity

By Kathy Masarie, MD

Want to help prepare your child for a satisfying future? Support him to tap into his creative side! That's right, pull out the paint brush, sewing needle, guitar, clay, fabric, pipe cleaners. . . . Exercising the right brain will do wonders for maximizing brain flexibility and adaptability. Plus, creating art with your kids is fun and connecting.

When I look back on my education, art is what I remember most fondly: the teepees, the catacombs, a bull-fighting ring, and the life-size, *papier-mache* lady sitting with a cup of tea. My high school art class was where I could be me, where I could explore and experiment without judgment.

Today, in many schools, the arts and creativity are relegated to the bottom of the education hierarchy–the first to go with budget or time crunches–with math, science, and literacy on top. Of course, these are important. The problem is with the extreme focus on testing or learning for testing in the "heavy" subjects, which are more left-brain focused, leaving the right brain and the rest of the body in the dust.

Creativity expert Sir Ken Robinson, author of *Out of Our Minds: Learning to Be Creative* (2011), says, "schools are killing our kids' creativity." Sir Ken Robinson champions radical rethinking of our school systems to cultivate creativity and acknowledge multiple types of intelligence. And he has good reason. Our world is rapidly changing, and companies must adapt fast with new products and services. IBM surveyed 3,000 CEOs about challenges facing today's businesses. Promoting creativity topped the survey as the major priority for CEOs.

My favorite "Sir Ken" story is of a fidgety, "underperforming" eight-year-old. When Gillian visited a physician on the recommendation of administrators who planned to move her to Special Education classes, the physician asked to talk privately to her mom, turned on the radio, and left Gillian alone. Peeking in the room, the physician and her mom saw Gillian dancing. The physician prescribed, "Send her to dancing school," and the rest is history. The girl, Gillian Lynne, went on to dance professionally and choreograph world-renowned musicals such as *Phantom of the Opera* and *Cats*. Today, this same girl would probably be put on Ritalin and told to "stuff" her desire to move.

Who knows exactly what skills your kindergartner will need in 25 years? All we know for sure is, he will need to be creative and rapidly adaptable to thrive–at home, at school, and in the workplace. You can make a difference by making creativity a priority in your family and encouraging your child to exercise both sides of the brain! We must educate our children's whole being for the future they face.

One of the best ways to practice and strengthen our innovative, creative muscle is to spend time doing art. Being flexible and "going with the flow" is the only way art works. In *The Creative Family: How to Encourage Imagination and Nurture Family Connections*, Amanda Blake Soule not only shares many wonderful projects, but she also showcases the power of family art. She notes that creativity in your everyday home life can be the gravitational field that pulls your family inward and closer. Think how fun and connecting a family drawing time would be or a family puppet show or a family hoe-down with everyone playing musical instruments, singing, and dancing! Creative living and the arts also can connect us to others, locally and globally. For example, one classroom of third graders participated in the Zimbabwean Artist Project, writing and illustrating stories in the African tradition. Their art was hung in a gallery side-by-side with illustrated stories from Zimbabwean women who sell their artwork as a major source of income.

Some of my favorite project ideas from *The Creative Family* include:

- **Banging Wall:** Hang a clothesline and hang pots from it. Give each child a wooden spoon.
- **Homemade Book:** Kids write and illustrate a story on 8 ½" x 11" paper folded in half. Poke holes for the seam and tie with dental floss. Make a cardboard cover and decorate it. Glue first and last page to hold book in place.
- **Fairy Furniture:** Go for a walk, gather natural items, and, with a glue gun, make chairs, beds, houses, forts…
- **Making pants or shorts** from Dad's old shirts connects kids to Dad every day they wear them.
- **Gather fabric** of all sizes, textures, and colors. Your kids will invent with it for years to come.

The big lesson for parents here is to find an artistic outlet to practice being free and creative, and for providing a framework to remove the critics and the rules that get in our children's way of doing anything and everything. It is in this place of freedom that we and our children can feel fully alive and let our imaginations soar.

Excerpted from Aug. 2011 Family Empowerment Network's "emPower Monthly."

© 2014 FAMILY EMPOWERMENT NETWORK™ ALL RIGHTS RESERVED.

Related Resources for Further Exploration

BRAIN SCIENCE RELATED TO PARENTING

Brain Rules for Baby: How to Raise a Smart and Happy Child from 0 to 5 (2011) and *Brain Rules: 12 Principles for Surviving and Thriving at Work, Home, and School* by John Medina, PhD (2009). Seattle, WA: Pear Press.

Brainstorm: The Power and Purpose of the Teenage Brain by Daniel Siegel, MD. NY: Tarcher, 2014.

The Brain that Changes Itself: Stories of Personal Triumph from the Frontiers of Brain Science by Norman Doidge, MD. NY: Penguin Books, 2007.

The Mindful Brain: Reflection and Attunement in the Cultivation of Well-Being by Daniel Siegel, MD. NY: W.W. Norton & Co., 2007.

The Neurobiology of "We": How Relationships, the Mind, and the Brain Interact to Shape Who We Are by Daniel Siegel, MD. (CD – 2008). www.drdansiegel.com

The Whole-Brain Child: 12 Revolutionary Strategies to Nurture Your Child's Developing Mind by Daniel Siegel, MD, and Tina Payne Bryson, PhD. NY: Bantam, 2012.

EMPATHY AND SOCIAL/EMOTIONAL LEARNING

Born for Love: Why Empathy is Essential—and Endangered by Maia Szalavitz and Bruce Perry, MD, PhD. NY: William Morrow, 2010.

Emotional Intelligence: Why It Can Matter More Than IQ (rev. 2007) and *Social Intelligence: The New Science of Human Relationships* (rev. 2005) by Daniel Goleman. NY: Bantam.

Roots of Empathy: Changing the World Child by Child by Mary Gordon. Ontario, Canada: Thomas Allen Publishers, 2005.

PLAY, CREATIVITY, AND THE IMPORTANCE OF BEING OUTDOORS

The Art of Roughhousing: Good Old-Fashioned Horseplay and Why Every Kid Needs It by Anthony DeBenedet, MD, and Lawrence Cohen, PhD. Philadelphia, PA: Quirk Books, 2011.

Flow: The Psychology of Optimal Experience by Mihaly Csikszentmihalyi. NY: Harper, 2008.

Last Child in the Woods: Saving Our Children from Nature-Deficit Disorder by Richard Louv. NY: Algonquin Books, 2008.

ALL RIGHTS RESERVED. © 2014 FAMILY EMPOWERMENT NETWORK™

Out of Our Minds: Learning to Be Creative by Sir Ken Robinson. 2nd Ed. MN: Capstone, 2011.

Play: How It Shapes the Brain, Opens the Imagination, and Invigorates the Soul by Stuart Brown and Christopher Vaughan. NY: Avery Trade, 2010.

Playful Parenting by Lawrence Cohen, PhD. NY: Ballantine Press, 2002.

The Power of Play: Learning What Comes Naturally by David Elkind. Cambridge, MA: Da Capo Press, 2007.

Rules of the Red Rubber Ball: Find and Sustain Your Life's Work (2005) and ***What's Your Red Rubber Ball?! Discover Your Inspiration and Chase It for a Lifetime*** (2008) by Kevin Carroll. NY: ESPN.

Film. ***Play Again.*** Dir. Tonje Hessen Schei. Ground Productions, 2010. http://playagainfilm.com

PARENTING IN GENERAL

Everyday Blessings: The Inner Work of Mindful Parenting by Myla and Jon Kabat-Zinn. NY: Hyperion, 1997.

The Parent as Coach Approach by Diana Sterling. Baltimore, MD: White Oak Publishing, 2008.

Parenting from the Inside Out: How a Deeper Self-Understanding Can Help You Raise Children Who Thrive by Daniel Siegel, MD, and Mary Hartzell, MEd. NY: Tarcher Publishing, 2004, revised.

Positive Discipline by Jane Nelsen, EdD. 4th ed. NY: Ballantine Books, 2006.

Positive Discipline for Teenagers by Jane Nelsen, EdD. 3rd ed. NY: Three Rivers Press, 2012.

Raising Our Daughters: The Ultimate Parenting Guide for Healthy Girls and Thriving Families by Kathy Masarie, MD, Kathy Keller Jones, MA, and Jody Bellant Scheer, MD. Portland, OR: Family Empowerment Network, 2009.

Raising Our Sons: The Ultimate Parenting Guide for Healthy Boys and Strong Families by Kathy Masarie, MD, Kathy Keller Jones, MA, and Jody Bellant Scheer, MD. Portland, OR: Family Empowerment Network, 2009.

Simplicity Parenting: Using the Extraordinary Power of Less to Raise Calmer, Happier, More Secure Kids by Kim John Payne and Lisa M. Ross. NY: Ballantine Books, 2010.

Outside Influences

Kara Tucker, 8th Grade, Rosemont Ridge Middle School

chapter three
Outside Influences

"Children are like wet cement.
Whatever falls on them makes an impression."
– Haim Ginott, *Between Parent and Child*

We are not parenting in a vacuum, and our children are not making friends in a vacuum. Powerful outside influences–good, bad, and some ugly–can affect both us and our children. The more we are conscious of these influences, the better we can mindfully support our children as they learn to navigate their social worlds.

As you will recall learning in the last chapter, groundbreaking brain research during the last few decades has confirmed the impact of outside influences on our social and emotional well-being. To recap, our brain is wired to mirror or copy and reflect the expressions of others. If a child's experiences or outside influences are positive and healthy, he most likely will thrive, grow to be hardy and strong, and develop high levels of emotional and social intelligence–a predictor of happiness. Unfortunately, our mirror neurons also make us vulnerable to being affected by and to imitating messages we see in our consumer, media-driven world–messages that can be damaging to our well-being.

In essence, we must ask ourselves, "What happens if a child's experiences are negative or toxic?" Growing up in an environment where kids are pushed early to competition rather than cooperation, where wearing the "right" clothes matters more than being yourself, where "everyone" plays games on their smartphones rather than playing outside can lead to a population of unhealthy, disconnected, unhappy children.

As parents and caring adults, how can we help youngsters to develop positive attributes and, consequently, enjoy healthy social dynamics? And when must we step up to protect them from unhealthy outside influences?

OUTSIDE INFLUENCES WITH NEGATIVE IMPACT

In this chapter, we will explore a few of the destructive outside forces that can potentially influence our children and cause them to develop unhealthy behaviors which may impact their neurological, relational, and emotional

It is within the arms of our family that we hopefully first experience belonging and a sense of significance, where we develop ways to solve problems, learn how to express feelings, and come to understand our place in the world. Eventually, as we grow up, we are exposed to life outside our first family; and the sights, sounds, joys, and pressures of this outside world further shape our identity and impact how we connect with others.

In this chapter, we will explore three aspects of American culture today and examine how they influence our children and us:

- Consumerism and Lookism
- Gender Stereotyping
- Digital Technology Overuse

Then we will discuss the positive outside influences that can be instrumental in raising healthy, hardy children.

It is up to us as parents and caring adults to be aware of what is toxic in our culture and to be vigilant about nurturing resiliency in our children despite inevitable exposure to negative outside influences. More importantly, it is our responsibility to be proactive about introducing our children to the wonder and awe of our world and encouraging their full and active participation in it.

© 2014 FAMILY EMPOWERMENT NETWORK™ ALL RIGHTS RESERVED.

lives. We direct attention to these negative forces so that parents and other caring adults are aware of them and can be proactive about standing up for and modeling pro-social values that promote healthy development. Doing so often feels counter-cultural and takes courage, but our children will benefit in the long term.

And, it is not only our own kids who will benefit if we take the time to work toward a healthy culture. All kids—those in our neighborhoods, schools, and places of worship—need the active support of the adults in their communities. This support can come from people like you, the involved parents, aunts, uncles, grandparents, teachers, counselors—all the caring adults—who refuse to be discouraged. By working together, we can protect our children from toxic influences and create resources and support systems that truly encourage all children to develop into competent and caring adults.

> *"It takes considerable courage to recognize where our culture has gotten off base, and to take action in support of your own family and parenting values."*
>
> – Kim John Payne

CONSUMERISM AND LOOKISM

"Talk to your daughter before the beauty industry does."
– Dove Campaign for Real Beauty advertisement

Where do children learn their values and develop a vision of their futures? What do they "mirror"? That all depends! Too many American children learn their values from TV, movies, music, the Internet, and video games—and then they mimic what they have learned. While we may work to provide our kids with positive messages, the reach and impact of the media on their lives is profound. For an in-depth (and shocking) look at our consumerist culture and its effect on our children, read Juliet Schor's *Born to Buy: The Commercialized Child and the New Consumer Culture* or Susan Thomas' *Buy, Buy Baby: How Consumer Culture Manipulates Parents and Harms Young Minds*. As highlighted in these books, marketing firms have become more and more sophisticated in the last few decades, and

advertising aimed at children has become commonplace. We now accept as normal some things that would have been considered criminal 30 years ago.

From a very early age, children are exposed to a barrage of advertisements telling them they need to buy certain toys, eat a specific brand of cereal, and wear the "right" brand of clothes so they look and feel "cool." Then the nagging begins, and we work longer hours to pay for the stuff our kids say they need. One of the really sad things about "cool" is that it implies that, without a certain product or look, a kid will never be popular, independent, good-looking enough, or successful. Advertising, in general, is geared to make us dissatisfied with the lives we have, convincing us that buying is good and will make us happy.

For example, consider commercials for alcohol, especially during televised sporting events. Advertisements convince young men that alcohol will make them cool and allow them to get the girl. We all know this isn't true, yet the media message is so pervasive that many people regard drinking as a normal part of growing up for boys as well as girls. It isn't. Underage drinking is dangerous. Period. People who begin drinking early in life (especially before age 15) run a greater risk for developing serious alcohol problems, for risky sexual behavior, and for poor academic performance. The cost to society is high due to alcohol-involved motor vehicle crashes, homicides, suicides, and other injuries ("Underage Drinking," National Institute on Alcohol Abuse and Alcoholism; http://pubs.niaaa.nih.gov/publications/AA67/AA67.htm).

By getting the message of "buying or doing ____ will make you cool" over and over again, and having it reinforced through peer pressure, kids are encouraged to become obsessed with drinking, material things, and their appearance. For teen boys, for example, being "macho" and "buff" and having a chiseled "six-pack" can become

ALL RIGHTS RESERVED. © 2014 FAMILY EMPOWERMENT NETWORK™

an obsession that eventually can lead to excessive working out, taking steroids, and even eating disorders. Only a decade ago, clinicians thought that only five percent of anorexics were male. Today's estimates suggest the number is closer to 20 percent and rising (Penn, "20% of Anorexics Are Men," *GQ*, Sept. 2012). Another image marketed to our sons is the crude, loud, obnoxious characters being popularized in movies such as *Wedding Crashers* and *Superbad*.

Where girls are concerned, the prevailing marketing message is that a girl must be skinny and that she is primarily a sexual object, eye-candy for others. Sexuality in the media, in fact, is often equated with power and liberation, and the age to exhibit sexuality is being pushed on younger and younger girls. Consider, for example, that clothing retail giants market push-up bra swimsuits to eight-year-olds. A 2007 report by a task force of the American Psychological Association that examined the sexualization of girls in today's culture provided additional shocking examples: thongs for seven- to ten-year-old girls, "sexy cat" or "sexy witch" Halloween costumes, cartoon characters with cleavage, dolls with fishnet stockings and tube tops, real toddlers with spray-on tans and cosmetically enhanced smiles in beauty pageants, and the list goes on.

The cost of an overly consumerist, sexualized culture focused on appearance and toys is high—promoting a world in which nothing matters except looks, popularity, power, and material gain. Statistics over the last few years bear out the negative impact of our consumerist culture.

CHECK OUT THESE RESOURCES

For an in-depth look at the dark side of the pretty and pink culture confronting our girls at every turn as they grow into adults, check out Peggy Orenstein's book, ***Cinderella Ate My Daughter: Dispatches from the Front Lines of the New Girlie-Girl Culture.*** Another great resource is the film ***Miss Representation*** (90 min; www.missrepresentation.org), which is available for sale as well as for community screenings. Written and directed by Jennifer Siebel Newsom, the film challenges the media's limited and often disparaging portrayals of women and girls. Both Orenstein and Newsom were inspired to raise red flags when their daughters were born and they were worried about how they could raise their girls to be hardy and thrive in a culture saturated with sexualization and the degradation of women.

One landmark study found that just three minutes spent looking at a fashion magazine caused 70% of grown women to feel depressed, guilty, and shameful of their bodies (Heinberg & Thompson, "Body and Televised Images of Thinness and Attractiveness," *Journal of Social and Clinical Psychology*, 1995, pp. 325-338). Another survey of fifth- through 12th-grade girls found that those who frequently read fashion magazines, compared to less frequent readers, were twice as likely to have dieted and three times as likely to have initiated an exercise program solely for the purpose of losing weight (Morris & Katzman, "The Impact of the Media on Eating Disorders in Children and Adolescents," *Pediatrics and Child Health*, Sept. 2003). The survey also revealed that, whereas 42% of first- through third-grade girls wish to be thinner, a staggering 80% of them have dieted by the time they reach the age of ten. Research further suggests that dieting often plays a key role in triggering eating disorders, which affect five to ten million American girls and women, including girls of surprisingly young ages. Cosmetic surgery to perfect their noses or augment their breasts is yet another extreme measure some young women (and women of all ages) take in an attempt to achieve the unrealistic beauty ideal relentlessly portrayed by the media.

How is all this affecting the long-term mental health of our children? The numbers do not look good. The American Association of Pediatrics, for example, reports that as many as one in 13 adolescents experience symptoms of depression (AAP Web site at http://

© 2014 FAMILY EMPOWERMENT NETWORK™ ALL RIGHTS RESERVED.

www.healthychildren.org/English/health-issues/conditions/emotional-problems/pages/Depression.aspx). The extent to which consumerism plays a key role in the escalating mental health problems of our children is not precisely clear, but we as parents cannot afford to wait for conclusive results before doing something. For ideas on how to stand up to corporate America and protect your children from "lookism" and "cool" marketing, check out the ideas listed in the Take the Time box. It is never too late to develop media literacy and to take a stand on the positive power of personal integrity and the beauty of authentic selfhood.

TAKE THE TIME

Teach Your Kids to Be Media Literate

- First, educate yourself about the power and effects of media. Check out www.commonsensemedia.org or www.commercialfreechildhood.org for research, insight, and regular updates.

- Know what your kids are watching, reading, and listening to; watch, read, and listen with them as often as possible and deconstruct the messages with them. Show and tell them about the lies of racism, sexism, machoism, etc. Talk with them about the gratuitous violence in TV programs and movies.

- Advocate for media literacy programs in schools.

- Plan and implement media literacy programs through neighborhood and community programs such as scouting.

- Walk the talk: Don't fall prey to the media messages about looks, products, and power. Advocate for authenticity.

GENDER STEREOTYPING

"To be nobody but yourself—in a world which is doing its best, night and day, to make you everybody else—means to fight the hardest battle which any human being can fight, and never stop fighting." – ee cummings

If we're not careful, children may be learning their values from the media. They also may find advertising, TV, movies, magazines, and the Web reinforcing detrimental social norms about what it means to be a boy or girl, a man or woman. Think about the first question everyone asks a new mother or father: Did you have a boy or a girl? If the response is "boy," then, from the get-go, cultural stereotypes influence how we treat that child and what behavior we expect. In truth, the toys and clothes we buy them, the books we read to them or they read on their own, the media messages with which they are bombarded in the grocery stores, the malls, the doctors' waiting rooms, etc. (unless we're hyper vigilant and monitor them), and the activities to which we expose them all impact the development of their gender identities.

The Boy Code

From a very early age, most boys are driven to be stereotypically masculine: tough, athletic, and non-communicative. They are taught through social norms and the media to hide emotions such as pain, sadness, love, shame, and loneliness. Instead, they are directed to be macho, aggressive, in charge, and to not make mistakes. Sadly, as boys move through adolescence, their feelings often get funneled into one acceptable feeling: anger. And a simultaneous mission of "manliness" teaches them another unhealthy message: never cry.

An exercise to illustrate how prevalent gender stereotypes are in American culture is described in our "**Girl or Boy in the Box Activity.**" The exercise is designed for the tweens/teens/young adults in your life. The boxes represent what American media say about what it means to be male or female in our culture today. You can do this activity with your partner, friends, or even a child over

ALL RIGHTS RESERVED. © 2014 FAMILY EMPOWERMENT NETWORK™

10 years of age. The experience will be enlightening! Once you see for yourself how limiting the Boy Box/ Code is, for example, you can then work on providing your son with a counterpoint so he does not get trapped in the box.

Some boys will work hard to maintain the Boy Code and let other boys know in kind—or mean—ways when they are not conforming to the norms. Even young boys who do not conform are teased, or worse. As boys enter adolescence, if they try to step outside the box, they are often pressured back inside with verbal assaults or even by physical abuse—which can come from their peers, girls, and even the adults in their lives. Why, as a culture, do we blindly accept this cruel social norm and the devastating costs? Shouldn't we really want our boys to be able to be themselves—in all their imperfect, sad, lovable, vulnerable, embarrassed, goofy, frustrated glory?

In his book *Guyland: The Perilous World Where Boys Become Men*, sociologist Michael Kimmel details the pressure on boys to accept and conform to the Boy Code as they grow up. These "rules" of male behavior, he notes, undermine the most desirable qualities for young men—integrity, courage, and connection—and, instead, leave them emotionally impaired and often unable to find and

take their place in the adult world. Kimmel shows how three cultural dynamics–entitlement, silence, and protection–work to keep violent behavior at the center of "guyland." He proposes that it is a fear of shame, of not being masculine enough in the eyes of other males (or females), that perpetuates the devastating cycle of gender policing and aggressive behavior. Further, he challenges his readers to make a collective effort to change these social norms, nothing short of creating a new model of masculinity. And he posits that we can plant the seeds for this new model by recommitting to having parents remain an important part of the process of boys becoming adults.

CONNECTION

Tips for Raising Our Sons

- Encourage boys to express themselves openly and honestly through loving acceptance at every age.

- Respect the cultural pressure to appear strong at all times and make it safe to open up his heart to you.

- Get boys talking by engaging them in "action talk" (i.e., while they're playing, shooting hoops, working on hobbies, riding in the car, etc.).

- Plan opportunities for your sons to exercise their empathy muscles through volunteering in the community, especially with younger kids or older adults.

- When a boy is upset, give him space until he's ready to talk. Women tend to want to jump in right away.

- Boys do better talking about important, sensitive topics in one-on-one conversations (shame-free zones) rather than with "witnesses."

© 2014 FAMILY EMPOWERMENT NETWORK™ ALL RIGHTS RESERVED.

Here is how parents can make a difference. In order to be authentic and truly himself, every single young man needs respectful affection from the adults around him. Our desire for closeness with boys, however, is often at odds with our perceived need to toughen up our boys so they will not be vulnerable in a world that expects them to be macho. Instead of giving in to the belief that "boys will be boys" and all that implies, we need to remind ourselves that they need our support in figuring out how to be themselves in spite of the media messages and the Boy Code. One of the most impactful ways we can do this is by providing them with positive role models, caring mentors, and growth opportunities such as summer work, volunteering, and traveling abroad, rather than allowing them to look to the streets, to TV, or to the movies to learn what it takes to be a man. Plus, having an ongoing dialogue with boys about how they view themselves on the inside and encouraging and rewarding them for focusing on both their internal and external selves are great places to start. For further reading on raising sons, check out the **"Related Resources for Further Exploration"** at the end of this chapter.

What About Girls?

American social norms and the media expect girls to be stereotypically feminine–thin, submissive, sexy–and these characteristics form the basis of the Girl Box. To the extent that a girl gets stuck in the box, she feels she must hide her true personality and intelligence with the ultimate goal of being popular with the boys. Girls who are different (e.g., too forward, too opinionated, wear unstylish clothes, are overweight, struggle with acne, identify themselves as lesbian, etc.), who don't care what other people think, or who do their own thing despite disapproving public opinion are at risk for being taunted or worse. If girls hide their true selves to fit in, they ultimately experience a loss of connection to themselves and others and suppress their own feelings, joy, and passion. The disconnection between the true self and the public self often results in hurtful aggression against self (eating disorders, cutting, self-embedding, depression, etc.) and/or against others (bullying, girl fighting, etc.). Read **"Body Image and Eating Disorders"** for an up-close look at this frightening issue.

Because many teen girls also like to be pleasers and achievers, when it comes to sexual behavior, they may feel they are damned if they do ("slut") and damned if they don't ("prude"). This confusion sometimes causes them to split their identity into the "good girl by day" and the "bad girl by night." The "bad girl by night" may dress provocatively and drink to be "cool," which lowers her inhibitions and allows her to engage in sex and other risky behavior. Sometimes girls continue drinking, lacking inhibition, and "splitting" into their 20s, trying to work through the confusion of expectations in our culture. We must help them to see that what they are

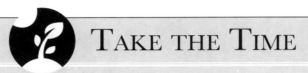

TAKE THE TIME

Tips for Raising Our Daughters

- Empower her to be daring–to embrace physical, mental, and emotional courage. Treat her as the strong being she is.

- Teach her to see beyond the ideals of "perfect" beauty and to celebrate her beautiful self.

- Encourage her to use her body for physical challenges and accomplishments such as sports and connecting with the outdoors rather than as an ornament as promoted by the media.

- Encourage her to revel in her uniqueness and find her own voice.

- Support her to be honest with herself and others–even when it seems risky.

- Find good, solid role models in literature and life for her to emulate.

ALL RIGHTS RESERVED. © 2014 FAMILY EMPOWERMENT NETWORK™

doing is unhealthy and to encourage them to develop their own voices and become their authentic selves.

A great resource for a closer examination of today's girl culture is the work of Rachel Simmons (www.rachelsimmons.com), author of the national bestseller *Odd Girl Out* as well as *The Curse of the Good Girl: Raising Authentic Girls with Courage and Confidence*. In *Odd Girl Out*, Simmons captures what may go on socially when a girl does not fit in. In *The Curse of the Good Girl*, she argues that the version of selfhood which girls are pressured to embrace–the nice, polite, modest, and selfless "good girl"–is an identity so narrowly defined that it is unachievable and sharply curtails the power and potential of girls. She further posits that, when girls fail to live up to these empty expectations, they become paralyzed by self-criticism, which stunts their personal growth. A list of other resources about raising our daughters, including the groundbreaking book *Reviving Ophelia: Saving the Selves of Adolescent Girls* by Mary Pipher, can be found at the end of this chapter.

Finding ways to support our girls to be assertive and strong should be one of our principal goals as parents and caring adults. What we would hope for our daughters is that they could grow up to be independent and empowered–free from the media lies that looks and getting a guy are the most important values for women. We want them to know that, if they want romance, they can get it by being themselves. Truly, we want our daughters to be able to be nice *and* powerful, to be loving *and* assertive, to be wise *and* humble, etc. Would that each girl be encouraged to be her best authentic self and that she find trusted friends with whom she could be that best authentic self!

Lesbian Gay Bi-sexual Transgender Questioning (LGBTQ) Youth

As we discuss gender stereotyping, it is critically important to address stereotyping based on sexual orientation and on transgender issues. Although America has made some progress in the last quarter century with the passage of anti-discrimination legislation, many Americans,

TEACHING TOLERANCE

"Teaching Tolerance" is a great project of the Southern Poverty Law Center. As one of the nation's leading providers of anti-bias education resources, they reach hundreds of thousands of educators and millions of students annually through their award-winning *Teaching Tolerance* magazine, multimedia teaching kits, online curricula, professional development resources such as their "Teaching Diverse Students Initiative," and special projects such as "Mix It Up at Lunch Day." This activity involves kids breaking up cliques in the lunch room by re-combining and re-mingling where people sit. All their materials are provided to educators at no cost.

www.splcenter.org/what-we-do/teaching-tolerance

adults and kids alike, still suffer on a day-to-day basis from stereotyping and outright harassment based on sexual orientation or transgender prejudice. Gay slander, for example, is used commonly in our society against anything disliked or undesirable, highlighting the devaluing of anything associated with being gay. For example, unless they are taught otherwise, middle-school boys often refer to anything they don't like, such as homework, as "gay." For more information, see "Lesbian, Gay, Bisexual and Transgender Youth Issues," from SIECUS Report, Vol. 29, No. 4, April/May 2001. Reprinted by the Sexuality Information and Education Council, on its website: www.siecus.org/pubs/factfact0013.html.

Perhaps most noteworthy as a resource related to this all-important issue is the work of award-winning film director and producer Debra Chasnoff. Chasnoff has made changing the social norms related to gender stereotyping her life's work. One of her latest documentaries is *Straightlaced–How Gender's Got Us All Tied Up*. The stories she shares in *Straightlaced* and some of her other films offer a window for understanding social dynamics

© 2014 FAMILY EMPOWERMENT NETWORK™ ALL RIGHTS RESERVED.

related to gender inequality, homophobia, and racial bias. They also provide models for expanded conversation, increased understanding, creativity, collaboration, ally-building, and empowerment. To host a screening of *Straightlaced* in your school, community program, or parent meeting and/or for ordering the curriculum guide that can ensure the screening has the greatest possible impact, go to www.groundspark.org. Also check out the article **"Straightlaced: How Gender's Got Us All Tied Up"** that supplements this chapter; it provides a great overview of the gender issues plaguing our children today.

Healthy Sexuality

Given all the conversation about unhealthy sexuality in our culture, let's consider briefly what healthy sexuality looks like. It helps to remember that sexuality and its exploration is a natural and powerful expression of being human, from early childhood on. Let your kids know it is okay to feel sexual and it is okay not to feel sexual; that everyone has his/her own individual path when it comes to sexuality; and that we experience sexuality on different levels (our personal sexuality and the sexuality we share with others).

Remind them that becoming comfortable with sexuality is a process that takes time, even a lifetime, and that the process can be rocky: We all get our hearts broken and at times feel confused, even remorseful. It is important your children know they can always come to you if they want a shoulder to lean on.

As you anticipate heart-to-heart conversations with your children about sexual relationships, think about the big messages you might like to communicate to them such as mutual consent, safety (from pregnancy, disease, and being taken advantage of), or the ability to communicate with a partner in a way that results in respectful consideration of each person's needs and desires. Following are some words of wisdom about sexuality you may choose to pass on to your children:

Tips for Healthy Sexuality

- Friendships hold up much longer than romance in adolescence, so find friends you can trust of both genders.
- Take your time. There are 100 sweet steps between someone liking you and having sex.
- If you are dating, choose someone who respects you and listens to you. Prioritize inner beauty, not outer looks.
- Terminate a relationship if a person tries to control you or put you down.
- Work on your own personal authority so you are able to say "No" for anything that isn't right for you at the time. Sometimes, what we really want is closeness, but we end up having sex.
- Know that alcohol use can make you vulnerable to unwanted sexual experiences, because inebriated people typically lose their ability to make good choices or stand up for themselves.
- Try to delay having sex until you are physically and mentally mature and, ideally, feel committed to the other person.
- Know where and how to get effective birth control for yourself and your friends. A condom is essential, but, with the average rate of pregnancies with condom use being around 15%, a condom is not enough. (Pratima Sharma, "How Reliable are Condoms for Contraception?" www.onlymyhealth.com)
- If you do decide to have sex, make sure you are going to be physically and emotionally safe.

These are concepts you can share with your children over the years–and especially during adolescence. Although teens have a developmental need to find their own way, they need the security of family expectations and help in handling complicated situations. They need us to be open-minded, attentive, and provide a listening heart, even when they may not want to talk about their relationships. During those times, they may be open to using other resources such as Elsbeth Martindale's "Things

ALL RIGHTS RESERVED. © 2014 FAMILY EMPOWERMENT NETWORK™

to Know Before You Say 'Go': Powerful Questions to Ask Before You Give Your Heart Away," which comes in both card form and as an app (www.couragetobloom.com). You also might find helpful the comprehensive sexual education curriculum offered and utilized by the Unitarian Universalist Association. Called OWLs (Our Whole Lives), this outstanding program is available for six age groups and helps participants make informed and responsible decisions about their sexual health and behavior (http://www.uua.org/re/owl).

DIGITAL TECHNOLOGY OVERUSE

"We may think of our kids' online, mobile, and technological activities as their 'digital lives.' But to them, their plugged-in, networked world is life. It's displacing and replacing the real, physical world of interaction and communication that's always been the core human experience." – James P. Steyer, *Talking Back to Facebook: The Common Sense Guide to Raising Kids in the Digital Age*

Technology and social media have the potential for educational enhancement and allow kids as well as adults to connect with friends, family, and others with shared interests–all good stuff. But what starts out innocently enough can turn into a beast. It begins with a little TV here or there while making dinner, a cell phone to stay safe, a few video games so friends will come over to play, computer learning modules to help our kids do better in school, and dabbling in Facebook, Snapchat, or Instagram to stay connected to friends. Then, step-by-step, you may find yourself allowing digital technology to play a huge role in your family's life.

Left unchecked, overuse eventually can put one at risk for attention, learning, and behavioral problems (Amanda Gardner, "Kids' TV Time Linked to School Woes, Bad Habits," www.Health.com, May 3, 2010). And outright abuse of digital technology can potentially lead to life-devastating problems such as video game addiction. In addition, the level of media violence that permeates modern screen technologies (as well as some music) can be psychologically damaging to children. In effect:

- Media violence encourages children to act more aggressively.
- Media violence encourages attitudes that are distorted, fearful, and pessimistic.
- Media violence desensitizes children to real-life violence.
- Desensitized children are more likely to be aggressive than children who are not desensitized.
- Desensitization interferes with a child's capacity for empathy.

This leaves parents with the onerous task of trying to protect their children from the effects of media violence and wondering how to do this. For a look into how media violence affects our children, see **"Media Violence and Its Effect on Children."** The second chapters of both *Raising Our Daughters* and *Raising Our Sons*, books by Family Empowerment Network (www.family-empower.com), also have helpful information on this issue.

Another of the big downsides of digital technology is the myriad of things we miss out on because of screen time. Having an average of 7.5+ hours of screen time per day in the lives of children (eight to 18-year-olds) leaves little time for much else: There is less time or motivation for playing outside, picking up a musical instrument, concentrating on homework, reading books, going for walks, helping with family chores, or riding bikes. The resulting me-centered lifestyle can lead to social isolation, weight issues, health complications, and so much more (Kaiser Family Foundation Study, "Generation M2: Media in the Lives of 8- to 18-Year-Olds," 2010). For a synopsis of an eye-opening documentary that addresses the impact of children's increasing screen time, check out Meg Merrill's article, **"Play Again: Reconnecting Children to Nature,"** at the end of this overview. In her article, she encourages us specifically to examine screen technology in relation to our dwindling engagement with nature.

© 2014 FAMILY EMPOWERMENT NETWORK™ ALL RIGHTS RESERVED.

SAFE HAVENS

Technology and Our Youngest Children

We all thrive with face-to-face time, but this is particularly true for babies and young children who need real-life relationships and lots of play time for optimal brain development. Unfortunately, according to the Campaign for a Commercial-Free Childhood (CCFC):

- On any given day, 64% of babies between one and two watch TV and videos for an average of slightly over two hours, despite the American Academy of Pediatrics' recommendation for no screen time for children under two.
- In 2011 there were three million downloads just of Fisher Price apps for infants and toddlers.
- Estimates of how much time preschoolers spend on average with screen media range from 2.2 hours to 4.6 hours per day.

Dr. Dimitri Christakis of the University of Washington researches the impact of screens on children ages 0-5. His research results show that the quantity as well as the quality of media exposure for our youngest children directly influences attentional problems in school and throughout life. For example, he notes that prolonged exposure to the rapid image changes of most kids' TV programs and movies during a child's critical period of brain development preconditions the mind to expect high levels of stimulation. In other words, that exposure causes real life to be too slow and too boring, and, in essence, that child is conditioned to a reality that doesn't exist in real life. To learn more about Dr. Christakis' work, check out his TEDxRainier talk at http://tedx-rainier.com/2/speaker_christakis.asp. During this talk, Christakis elaborates on the correlation of hours of TV per day for children under age three leading to an increase in attention deficits.

To help educators and parents make informed decisions about using screen technologies with young children, CCFC created *Facing the Screen Dilemma: Young Children, Technology and Early Education* with the Alliance for Childhood and Teachers Resisting Unhealthy Children's Entertainment (TRUCE). This publication can be downloaded for free at http://commercialfreechildhood.org/screendilemma.

Perhaps the most significant area of loss, with regard to spending so much time using digital technology, is in real experiences with other people face-to-face, shoulder-to-shoulder—in just being present with each other. So much precious family and face-to-face time has been taken over by time spent on screens: watching television, texting, video gaming, Facebooking, Internet shopping, Web browsing, Tweeting, Instagramming, Snapchatting, Pinteresting, or checking out the latest YouTube videos. These technologically based activities can become a black hole!

Face-to-face time is vanishing, and our culture is changing! As parents and caring adults, we need to re-evaluate our priorities and re-focus our attention. A great reference for understanding the importance of face-to-face communication is *Born for Love: Why Empathy is Essential and Endangered* by Maia Szalavitz and Dr. Bruce D. Perry. In their book, Szalavitz and Perry talk about the origins of human civilization and make a compelling case for the importance of connection and empathy. They also explicitly state that healthy emotional development takes practice. Just as muscles atrophy if they are not exercised, the emotion-processing parts of the brain need to be regularly stimulated by face-to-face interaction to remain effective.

Without sufficient practice observing, trying out, and experiencing true emotions such as empathy, love, and frustration, kids are often less equipped to navigate the social world. Their expectations, too, might be unrealistic, because social media—with all of us airbrushing our own lives—magnifies a perfect world where there's no room for sharing the frailties and foibles of the human condition. Consider the tragedy of the psychological diagnosis "Facebook envy" (people tracking other people's activities and number of friends with jealousy). Or think about the sad ease of getting rid of someone on a video game or unfriending someone on Facebook, compared to the stickiness of the challenge (and satisfaction) of facing and resolving a disagreement with a friend.

ALL RIGHTS RESERVED. © 2014 FAMILY EMPOWERMENT NETWORK™

Even dating is on the decline, because we are turning ever more to machines to fulfill our biochemical needs. For insight on this subject, watch psychologist Sherry Turkle's TED talk at http://www.ted.com/talks/sherry_turkle_alone_together.html or check out her book, *Alone Together: Why We Expect More from Technology and Less from Each Other*, or her article, "The Flight from Conversation," that appeared in the April 21, 2012, edition of the *New York Times*.

The long-term effect of overuse of social media, video gaming, texting, and the like is now the subject of a lot of research–and the results of that research are sobering. According to Stanford sociologist Clifford Nass, "Tween girls who are heavy users of online social interaction feel less 'normal' than girls who use online social media less frequently" (Nass, "The Keyboard and the Damage Done," *Pacific Standard*, May/June 2012, p. 23). His research also indicates that those girls who use more social media derive fewer positive feelings from interacting with friends, they have more friends whom their parents think are a bad influence, and they get less sleep, which is associated with negative mood and irritability. What does Nass' research show is the one positive predictor of healthy emotional interactions and feelings of social success? Surprise! Lots of face-to-face communication! Although his research has been with tween girls, other research metes out similar results for all audiences. A great resource for this material is *Talking Back to Facebook: The Common Sense Guide to Raising Kids in the Digital Age* by James P. Steyer, founder of Common Sense Media (www.commonsensemedia.org). The book offers a blend of advice and anecdotes addressing what Steyer calls "RAP," the major pitfalls relating to kids' use of media and technology: Relationship issues, Attention/addiction problems, and the lack of Privacy. His practical approach gives parents tools to help filter content, preserve good relationships with their children, and make common sense, value-driven judgments for kids of all ages.

Suggested Parent Guidelines for Technology Use

1. Discourage all media use for children younger than two. This includes protecting youngsters from exposure to television being on in a room even when the show is intended for adults (American Academy of Pediatrics, "Media Use by Children Younger Than 2 Years," *Pediatrics*, Oct., 17, 2011. http://pediatrics.aappublications.org/content/early/2011/10/12/peds.2011-1753).

2. Limit children ages 2-12 to no more than two hours per day (one hour or less on school days) of total screen time, including phones and devices that have apps. Screen engagement should be limited to high-quality, age-appropriate movies, TV shows, or electronic games. Some parents limit games to ½-hour per day. They set the timer on the iPad and let the child play agreed-upon games until the time runs out.

3. Become knowledgeable about the power and effects of digital influences, and educate your children. If you watch TV/movies and play electronic games, do so together and discuss controversial, violent, or unreal situations. Also, ask the question: Do the shows/games/activities fit the values of our home?

4. Wait until your child is responsible enough to make good choices before buying him/her a cell phone and start with a basic phone without texting. When you do introduce texting, we recommend you get parental controls so you can regulate what times kids are allowed to text. Check out Common Sense Media's advice for parents regarding cell phones by going to www.commonsensemedia.org/advice-for-parents/cell-phone-tips or refer back to our suggested guidelines in **"Tips for Maintaining Digital Sanity and Protecting Your Family"** that appeared in Chapter 2.

© 2014 FAMILY EMPOWERMENT NETWORK™ ALL RIGHTS RESERVED.

5. Delay the use of Facebook and other social media as long as possible. Many social media sites are not meant for kids under age 13. Consider drawing up an agreement with your tween/teen for the use of smartphones and social media. Some ideas to consider include: representing yourself truthfully, posting only things you would be comfortable with Grandma seeing, and never using social media to be mean to another person. If your child has a say in the agreement, then he/she may more likely adhere to it. A sample agreement can be found at http://www.search-institute.org/system/files/facebook_contract.doc, or check out writer Janell Burley Hofmann's creative approach to the idea at http://www.huffingtonpost.com/janell-burley-hofmann/iphone-contract-from-your-mom_b_2372493.html.

6. Be mindful when allowing video games in your home. Video games can introduce a whole new set of challenges in a home, depending upon the values illusttrated in the games. Too many games present sexist, homophobic, and racist viewpoints. Some promote gratuitous violence. Establishing a gaming contract with your child(ren) in a good idea. For a sample contract and an insightful examination of video gaming (and what your child may be exposed to if he is playing in multi-player games with unknown players with the chat function on), see Chapter 10 of Rosalind Wiseman's book *Masterminds & Wingmen*.

7. Supervise your children's online activities for safety. Safety must be a life-long priority. We cannot slack off. Stress that online activity creates a digital "tattoo" that may follow them as they apply for college scholarships or employment. Kids live in the now and do not think ahead. Great online resources include www.commercial-freechildhood.org, www.commonsensemedia.org, the Massachusetts Aggression Reduction Center at www.bridgew.edu/marc, and Embrace Civility in the Digital Age at www.embracecivility.org.

Research shows that screen use can be very addictive and even rewire our brains. Young people who spend a lot of time online can lose their motivation to head out of the house in search of adventure, friends, relationships, and work. Adolescence and young adulthood is a time for building our social skills. What happens to those boys who are online during most of this critical period for developing the emotion-processing parts of their brain? How can they become good workers, friends, or lovers if they have not practiced social and emotional skills but, instead, have spent all their time in the over-stimulating world of virtual war and virtual sex? For teen boys and those in their early twenties who identify as gamers, the computer has become frighteningly satisfying as they get drips of "feel-good" hormone chemicals with each computer chime because of the brain's anticipation of a "reward." And, then, it's like eating one chocolate chip: They want more dopamine and more of its effects.

One particularly addictive aspect of online activity is pornography (Doidge, *The Brain that Changes Itself*, p. 106). Males are biologically driven to be aroused by visual images, but, over time, people using pornography become more and more dependent on it and seek higher and higher levels of stimulation, which in today's online pornography means that violence and sex become mixed together. Normally, the human brain has very separate brain maps for violence and sex, but repeated exposure to pornography causes our malleable brains to rewire.

Stanford psychologist Philip Zimbardo delves into this frightening phenomenon in his book, *The Demise of Guys: Why Boys Are Struggling and What We Can Do About It*. He points out that boys start watching pornography as young as age 10, and that the average American high school boy spends two hours each week watching porn. He says that video games and pornography can lead to "arousal addictions, where the attraction is in the novelty, the variety, or the surprise factor of the content. Sameness is soon habituated; newness heightens excitement. . . . The consequences could be dramatic: The excessive use of video games and online porn in pursuit of the next thing is creating a generation of risk-averse

ALL RIGHTS RESERVED. © 2014 FAMILY EMPOWERMENT NETWORK™

guys who are unable (and unwilling) to navigate the complexities and risks inherent to real-life relationships, school, and employment" (Zimbardo and Duncan, "The Demise of Guys: How Video Games and Porn are Ruining a Generation," CNNHealth, http://www.cnn.com/2012/05/23/health/living-well/demise-of-guys/index.html).

To further underscore the consequences of pornography addiction, a 2011 study by Italian urologist Carlo Foresta showed that, over time, pornography addiction can lead to erectile dysfunction. This is a dramatic example of how technology can rewire our brains and cause devastating consequences. Combined with messages from the media, pornography also impacts the ability of males to see and respect females as equals, which ultimately undermines the healthy development of satisfying relationships with the opposite sex. For further exploration of this important topic, check out Gary Wilson's TED talk on the Great Porn Experiment at www.yourbrainonporn.com or Zimbardo's TED talk at www.demiseofguys.com.

As sad and frightening as this reality is for our sons, what does it say for our daughters who also are affected by porn addiction, as their boyfriends want them to dress and act like porn queens? Being their real, normal selves isn't stimulating enough! And, what does it mean for the future of relationships and for the future of families?

The bottom line is that we must talk to our sons. They must understand the biology behind their actions in order to make choices that promote their healthy sexual and emotional development as young men. And we must talk to our daughters, to assure them they are equal to men and to encourage them to seek out young men who will treat them with the dignity and respect they deserve. For guidance, see Dr. Marty Klein's blog post at http://sexualintelligence.wordpress.com/2013/09/05/time-to-talk-to-your-kids-about-porn. For an examination of Internet addiction, see **"Avoiding the Addictive Potential of Internet Use"** by Hilarie Cash, PhD.

© 2014 FAMILY EMPOWERMENT NETWORK™ ALL RIGHTS RESERVED.

TAKE THE TIME

What Our High-Energy Eight- to 12-year-old Kids Really Need

Many eight- to 12-year-old boys and some girls this age pressure parents to allow them to play video games, which takes up time they might be doing other activities. Step back and consider what our kids really need to have in their everyday lives, in addition to academics:

- Vigorous play and activity; time to practice physical skills in their own way
- Outlets for their exuberance and ingenuity
- Adventure and challenges
- Imaginative play (e.g., forts, treehouses, etc.)
- Healthy ways to compete in interactive games of skill
- Time outdoors
- Tagging along with adults they respect and seeing how things are done
- Hanging out with friends and figuring out how to keep the play going
- Wrestling, drawing, and other healthy ways to express an interest in combat
- Meaningful ways of helping
- Skill building of all kinds
- Art and music that expresses their inner thoughts
- Lots of little reinforcing interactions with the adults in their lives, so they know they are loved for who they are
- Rest and recharge
- Time to read and see how other people handle situations
- Instruction on the safe use of tools
- Opportunity to practice social skills and understand feelings and needs
- Enough freedom to make mistakes and then learn to make amends

Not surprisingly, video games fulfill some of the needs of this age group for challenge, competition, and games of skill. But their presence in kids' lives (especially if it is more than a half hour per day) disregards their real needs and cuts into their time for autonomy, connection, and skill building. The situation also sets parents up for constant arguments about time on games, rather than satisfying connection, and often results in grumpy children who haven't had enough physical activity and have difficulty transitioning from games to real life.

HEALTHY OUTSIDE INFLUENCES: A BLUEPRINT FOR RAISING HEALTHY, HARDY CHILDREN

"Children become moral beings not through didactic lectures or harsh discipline but through countless daily conversations and encounters, stories and lessons, in which habits of honesty, kindness, responsibility, tolerance and courage are steadily, painstakingly instilled by wise and attentive adults."
– Robert Coles, *The Moral Intelligence of Children*

Why are our children spending so much time with digital technology any way? How did we let this happen? Parents want the best for their kids. We invest a lot of time and energy in their futures. Then, in the blink of an eye–perhaps because we have evolved to seek out the new–we undermine it all by having unregulated access to the Internet through smartphones, allowing kids to be on screens more than they are spending time with their family or even at school, or by allowing them to play video games that are directly opposed to family values.

What can we do about it? Refer back to Doreen Dodgen-Magee's thought-provoking article, **"The Key to Surviving the Negative Impact of Digital Technology? Moderation"** and to our **"Tips for Maintaining Digital Sanity and Protecting Your Family"** in Chapter 2 for some suggestions on how you might help to create a more balanced life for your children. For even more ideas, at the end of this chapter we've included recommendations from expert Nancy Willard in the article, **"Screen Savvy Parents: Embracing Civility in a Digital Age."**

We all need to figure out how to live in the digital world without letting it overwhelm our waking and sleeping hours, our close relationships, our social skills, and the development of our inner lives and deepest values. Outside influences such as the digital world can be particularly overwhelming to kids. While it may be a heroic effort, today's parents bear the unique responsibility of pioneering new patterns and practices around technology in order to realize their hopes and dreams for their

---

A MINDFUL APPROACH TO TECHNOLOGY USE

Ben's parents had planned to raise him without video games. When he was 12 years old, however, he came to his parents to let them know that he had nothing to talk to his friends about because he didn't play video games. He and his parents then explored finding an innovative game about which they could all feel okay and decided on Minecraft. They told Ben they would decide about limits for the game by the weekend and, until then, he could play as much as he liked. After several days, he found himself exhausted and behind in his life--which was a problem because he was an athlete who spent a lot of time on his sport as well as academics. They agreed upon time limits and prerequisites (homework, outdoor time, chores) for weekdays and weekends, as well as an all-electronics-off rule an hour before bedtime. Ben played on the family computer, which made it easier to enforce rules. Ben greatly enjoyed playing Minecraft with one or two friends, while chatting on FaceTime simultaneously. Occasionally, he and his sister, who otherwise had no interest in games, would create a beautiful masterpiece together. Ben was able to live a balanced life even with the addition of gaming, although his parents had to be particularly careful to make sure he continued reading for pleasure. All in all, it has been a successful experience for the family.

---

families. There is no one way to do this. We need to be creative. One young mom has chosen one room in her home as the screen room, where she works, so her children see screens as tools for work rather than entertainment. In general, the key is to consciously make choices regarding technology. If you choose to position media as an aspect of your children's balanced daily diet, don't let them over-consume, and be sure what they do consume is healthy for their overall development.

One way to guide our children through the negative outside influences rampant in our culture is through the lens of the **"40 Developmental Assets."** These are an inspired and clinically proven blueprint, developed by the Search Institute (www.search-institute.org), that we can use to strengthen our families and our children.

ALL RIGHTS RESERVED. © 2014 FAMILY EMPOWERMENT NETWORK™

They comprise 40 socialization experiences that support health-promoting behaviors and decrease risky behaviors across gender, racial, economic, and cultural lines.

The "assets," which you can find described in more detail and listed in a chart at the end of this overview, are grouped into 20 External and 20 Internal Assets. The External Assets include the categories of Support, Empowerment, Boundaries and Expectations, and Constructive Use of Time, whereas the Internal Assets comprise the categories of Commitment to Learning, Positive Values, Social Competencies, and Positive Identity.

Among the External Assets are:
- Family support
- Caring neighborhood
- Parent involvement in school
- Safety
- Having clear boundaries at home and school
- Positive role models
- Creative activities

Examples of the Internal Assets are:
- Reading for pleasure
- Valuing integrity, honesty, responsibility, and restraint
- Having the skills to resist negative peer pressure
- Being optimistic about the future

Research shows that the Developmental Assets are cumulative: As the number of assets in a child's life increases, so does that child's sense of well-being. Research also indicates that the more assets children report having, the more likely they are to maintain good health, to value diversity, and to report high levels of leadership and success in school. Most importantly, the assets also help to inoculate youth against high-risk behaviors: The more assets a young person has, the less likely he/she is to make harmful or unhealthy choices regarding alcohol, drugs, violence, and sexual activity. Sadly, even though most people will recognize the importance of the 40 assets, the vast majority of our nation's youth possess less

---

AWESOME ORGANIZATION

Looking for things to do when you reclaim family time? Check out the **Campaign for a Commercial-Free Childhood's "101 Screen-Free Activities"** at the end of the chapter. This list is just a sampling of the great free resources offered by CCFC via their website at www.commercialfreechildhood.org. Look up this organization–which annually sponsors the National Screen-Free Week and the annual TOADY award for worst toy of the year–and sign up for their monthly newsletter.

---

than one half of them in their lives. In fact, only 8% have 30 or more assets, according to the Search Institute.

To learn more about the Developmental Assets, go to the Search Institute's website at www.search-institute.org. The organization has a plethora of resources for parents, schools, and communities, including charts of the Developmental Assets targeted to specific ages including ages 3-5, 5-9, 8-12, and 12-18. The charts also are available in Spanish. In addition, this venerable research institution has identified key qualities that help families be strong. Their list of **"Family Assets"** can be found after this overview. Every chapter of Family Empowerment Network's *Raising Our Daughters* and *Raising Our Sons* books also shares ideas on how to build assets. Check them out!

In truth, it is up to parents to choose the virtues (assets) their family will hold most dear as their Family Code and to ensure their family's activities follow suit, especially when it comes to the cultural influences of consumerism, lookism, stereotyping, and digital technology overuse. One way to guarantee you are doing this is by asking yourself, "When my child is an adult, what values do I want him to hold, what kind of person do I want him to be, and how will this activity help him to get there?" If the means serves the end, you're on a great path!

© 2014 FAMILY EMPOWERMENT NETWORK™ ALL RIGHTS RESERVED.

40 Developmental Assets

By Search Institute, from *The Asset Approach: Giving Kids What They Need to Succeed*

Search Institute has identified the following building blocks of healthy development that help young people grow up healthy, caring, and responsible. Percentages of young people who experience each asset represent almost 150,000 6th- to 12th-grade youth surveyed in 213 towns and cities in the United States.

Asset Type		Asset Name and Definition	
Support	1.	**Family support** – Family life provides high levels of love and support.	68%
	2.	**Positive family communication** – Young person and her or his parent(s) communicate positively, and young person is willing to seek advice and counsel from parent(s).	28%
	3.	**Other adult relationships** – Young person receives support from three or more nonparent adults.	43%
	4.	**Caring neighborhood** – Young person experiences caring neighbors.	37%
	5.	**Caring school climate** – School provides a caring, encouraging environment.	29%
	6.	**Parent involvement in schooling** – Parent(s) are actively involved in helping young person succeed in school.	29%
Empowerment	7.	**Community values youth** – Young person perceives that adults in the community value youth.	22%
	8.	**Youth as resources** – Young people are given useful roles in the community.	26%
	9.	**Service to others** – Young person serves in the community one hour or more per week.	48%
	10.	**Safety** – Young person feels safe at home, school, and in the neighborhood.	51%
Boundaries and Expectations	11.	**Family boundaries** – Family has clear rules and consequences and monitors the young person's whereabouts.	46%
	12.	**School boundaries** – School provides clear rules and consequences.	52%
	13.	**Neighborhood boundaries** – Neighbors take responsibility for monitoring young people's behavior.	47%
	14.	**Adult role models** – Parent(s) and other adults model positive, responsible behavior.	27%
	15.	**Positive peer influence** – Young person's best friends model responsible behavior.	63%
	16.	**High expectations** – Both parent(s) and teachers encourage the young person to do well.	48%
Constructive Use of Time	17.	**Creative activities** – Young person spends three or more hours per week in lessons or practice in music, theater, or other arts.	21%
	18.	**Youth programs** – Young person spends three or more hours per week in sports, clubs, or organizations at school and/or in the community.	57%
	19.	**Religious community** – Young person spends one or more hours per week in activities in religious instruction.	58%
	20.	**Time at home** – Young person is out with friends "with nothing special to do" two or fewer nights per week.	51%
Commitment to Learning	21.	**Achievement motivation** – Young person is motivated to do well in school.	65%
	22.	**School engagement** – Young person is actively engaged in learning.	55%
	23.	**Homework** – Young person reports doing at least one hour of homework every day.	47%
	24.	**Bonding to school** – Young person cares about her or his school.	52%
	25.	**Reading for pleasure** – Young person reads for pleasure three or more hours per week.	22%
Positive Values	26.	**Caring** – Young person places high value on helping other people.	50%
	27.	**Equality and social justice** – Young person places high value on promoting equality and reducing hunger and poverty.	52%
	28.	**Integrity** – Young person acts on convictions and stands up for her or his beliefs.	68%
	29.	**Honesty** – Young person "tells the truth even when it is not easy."	66%
	30.	**Responsibility** – Young person accepts and takes personal responsibility.	63%
	31.	**Restraint** – Young person believes it is important not to be sexually active or to use alcohol or other drugs.	45%
Social Competencies	32.	**Planning and decision making** – Young person knows how to plan ahead and make choices.	29%
	33.	**Interpersonal competence** – Young person has empathy, sensitivity, and friendship skills.	45%
	34.	**Cultural competence** – Young person has knowledge of and comfort with people of different cultural/racial/ ethnic backgrounds.	43%
	35.	**Resistance skills** – Young person can resist negative peer pressure and dangerous situations.	41%
	36.	**Peaceful conflict resolution** – Young person seeks to resolve conflict nonviolently.	40%
Positive Identity	37.	**Personal power** – Young person feels he or she has control over "things that happen to me."	42%
	38.	**Self-esteem** – Young person reports having a high self-esteem.	48%
	39.	**Sense of purpose** – Young person reports that "my life has a purpose."	57%
	40.	**Positive view of personal future** – Young person is optimistic about her or his personal future.	72%

EXTERNAL ASSETS

INTERNAL ASSETS

The list of **40 Developmental Assets®** is reprinted with permission. Copyright © 1997, 2006 Search Institute®. All rights reserved. No other use is permitted without prior permission from Search Institute, 615 First Avenue NE, Minneapolis, MN 55413; www.search-institute.org.

circle question

Try doing the "Girl in the Box" & "Boy in the Box" as a group and discuss how gender stereotyping affects your life, your partner's, your child's.

POSSIBLE DISCUSSION QUESTIONS

1) Look through the 40 Developmental Assets and the Family Assets. Which assets do your children and family have and which ones are you still working on? The overarching message of the Search Institute is to connect with kids–all kids. Share ideas about making connections with other people's children.

2) What are the negative outside influences in your life? How are they affecting you and your family? What do you do to minimize their impact?

3) How does consumerism affect your family? How do you help your children to understand the powerful subversive influence of media messages? How do you help your kids to connect buying things with needing to work to earn the money to pay for things?

4) How much time does each member of your family devote to TV, movies, video games, and social networking online? Is the use of digital technology influencing connection with family, friends, or the greater community?

5) How can you influence the media to stop producing sexualized, violent movies, TV shows, and video games?

6) What are you doing to teach your children about healthy sexuality?

7) Do you know children (or adults) who struggle with harassment because of their sexual or gender orientation? If so, what can you do to help them find safe havens and to support them in their self discovery and attainment of authenticity? How do you communicate with your children about these issues?

8) What are biases and stereotypes (racial, cultural, etc.) that impact you and/or your family? Identify them, discuss them within the group, and explore what might be done to address them.

9) When do you find it challenging to walk the talk for your children regarding media, consumerism, and bias?

PUTTING IT INTO PRACTICE

- Subscribe to New Moon Girls' newsletter at www.daughters.com for more ways to support our girls.
- Spread the word on the importance of no screens for children under two and keeping screens out of bedrooms.
- Lead the charge on organizing a school or community Screen Turn-Off Week.
- Buy the PBS "Frontline" special, "Merchants of Cool: A Report on the Creators and Marketers of Popular Culture for Teenagers" for your school library and facilitate a screening of it for other parents.

PUTTING IT TOGETHER–YOUR VERSION

Write down a few ideas you have been inspired to implement in your own life after reading/discussing this chapter.

_____

_____

_____

© 2014 FAMILY EMPOWERMENT NETWORK™ ALL RIGHTS RESERVED.

Girl or Boy in the Box Activity

This exercise can be used with adults and girls/boys from 4th grade and up. It helps participants to see the messages we receive from the media about what it means to be a girl or boy in our culture—which ultimately limits full and active participation in the world.

1. Draw a box. If you are doing the exercise about girls, write "Girls" at the top. If you are doing it about boys, write "Boys" at the top.

2. Brainstorm as a group all the things you associate with acting or looking like a girl/boy. Write these words and phrases inside the box.

3. On one side of the box, as you are brainstorming, note how others act to reinforce the traits and try to keep a girl/boy "in the box." These actions can include phys-ical and verbal mistreatment, shaming, shunning, gossip, exclusion, name-calling, etc.

4. On the other side of the box, as you are brainstorming, list the thoughts a boy/girl might have within his/her own head to reinforce his/her own attempts to stay in the box. If you are having trouble thinking of examples, fill in the following blanks: "If I don't act like … (a lady, a stud, etc.), I won't …(get a guy, have friends, be popular, etc.)," or "I can't . . . (be smart, take risks, sweat, have zits, be fat, act loud and crazy, etc.), because that isn't like a girl/guy," or "In order to fit in, I'll have to . . . (fill in the blank), even if I don't feel like it."

5. Once participants understand what it means to be a girl or boy "in the box," brainstorm how they can achieve authenticity.

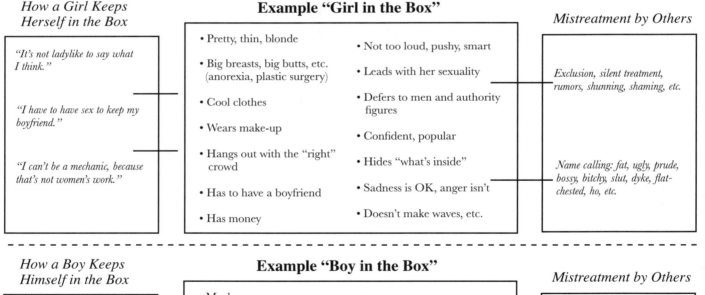

How a Girl Keeps Herself in the Box

"It's not ladylike to say what I think."

"I have to have sex to keep my boyfriend."

"I can't be a mechanic, because that's not women's work."

Example "Girl in the Box"

- Pretty, thin, blonde
- Big breasts, big butts, etc. (anorexia, plastic surgery)
- Cool clothes
- Wears make-up
- Hangs out with the "right" crowd
- Has to have a boyfriend
- Has money

- Not too loud, pushy, smart
- Leads with her sexuality
- Defers to men and authority figures
- Confident, popular
- Hides "what's inside"
- Sadness is OK, anger isn't
- Doesn't make waves, etc.

Mistreatment by Others

Exclusion, silent treatment, rumors, shunning, shaming, etc.

Name calling: fat, ugly, prude, bossy, bitchy, slut, dyke, flat-chested, ho, etc.

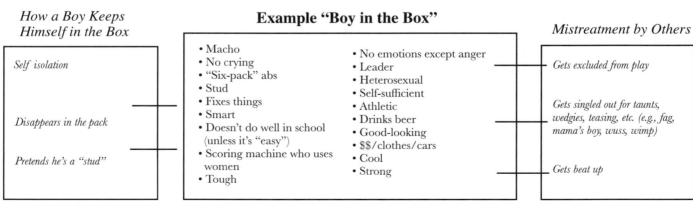

How a Boy Keeps Himself in the Box

Self isolation

Disappears in the pack

Pretends he's a "stud"

Example "Boy in the Box"

- Macho
- No crying
- "Six-pack" abs
- Stud
- Fixes things
- Smart
- Doesn't do well in school (unless it's "easy")
- Scoring machine who uses women
- Tough

- No emotions except anger
- Leader
- Heterosexual
- Self-sufficient
- Athletic
- Drinks beer
- Good-looking
- $$/clothes/cars
- Cool
- Strong

Mistreatment by Others

Gets excluded from play

Gets singled out for taunts, wedgies, teasing, etc. (e.g., fag, mama's boy, wuss, wimp)

Gets beat up

ALL RIGHTS RESERVED. © 2014 FAMILY EMPOWERMENT NETWORK™

Girls' Body Image and Eating Disorders

By Kathy Keller Jones, MA

Anorexia and bulimia are serious issues. They affect over one million American women a year, 5-15% of whom eventually die as a result. Up to one-half of the others never fully regain their health after the ravages of starvation weaken their bodies. Anorexia and bulimia are eating disorders that overwhelmingly affect high-achieving adolescent girls and young women. Anorexia involves starving oneself even to the point of multi-organ failure. The results may include (but aren't limited to) infertility, heart failure, immune system dysfunction, sleep disturbances, gastrointestinal atrophy, and death. Bulimia is characterized by a pattern of overeating, then purging via self-induced vomiting or laxatives. Both eating disorders are characterized by a girl's preoccupation with thinness and are exacerbated by the images of unrealistically thin women in the popular media. As well, anorexics and bulimics are commonly people-pleasers who expect nothing less than perfection from themselves and who are extremely sensitive to rejection and outside expectations. Psychological issues of control, separation, and independence also play a role in these eating disorders. Control over food intake becomes a central theme in these girls' lives that separates them from feeling or dealing with other difficult issues facing them.

Prevention of anorexia and bulimia best starts long before girls start thinking of themselves as fat, which now commonly occurs at around ages 9 or 10 regardless of body build. Some prevention strategies include:

• Starting early, teach your daughter about healthy eating habits and demonstrate them in your home.

• Avoid using the giving or withholding of food as a reward or punishment. Encourage a positive approach toward food as sustenance, not as a substitute for love, support, or comfort.

• Make peace with your own body and set a good example with your own diet and exercise patterns. Cultivate a "you're-just-right-the-way-you-are" attitude rather than perfectionism.

• Love your daughter unconditionally. Protect her from any family teasing and criticism about her body.

• To the extent possible, let your teen daughter's weight and eating habits be her own business. If your daughter asks for your help losing weight, teach her how small changes in her eating and exercise will bring gradual, positive changes. If anorexia or bulimia is suspected, however, your family should immediately seek outside help.

• Encourage fathers to have warm, close, respectful relationships with their daughters, especially as they enter puberty.

• Girls learn early that society values women's bodies, not their minds. When you criticize or make fun of other women's appearances, you feed into this. Instead, make positive comments about other women in front of your daughters. Accepting women who don't meet your physical ideals and acknowledging the women in your life for their many-faceted talents other than physical beauty can make a huge impression on your own daughters.

• Recognize and be sensitive to your daughter's possible self consciousness and concerns about breast size. Even in early adolescence, girls are aware of the unhealthy media pressure to have large breasts. Think plastic surgery/implants.

• Our girls get heavy exposure to models, whose bodies are 24% underweight. Give them plenty of access to accurate information about real women's bodies and take the opportunity to discuss with them issues around body image and eating disorders.

• Explain to your daughter the difference between image and true substance and encourage her to pursue the latter, even though it takes more effort. When girls and young women feel valued and admired for who they are and what they do, they may be helped to stop obsessing about how they look. The best place for this to happen is in the home.

For more information about eating disorders and treatment, check out the National Eating Disorders Assn. at http://www.nationaleatingdisorders.org/get-facts-eating-disorders or any of the following resources:

The Body Betrayed: A Deeper Understanding of Women, Eating Disorders, and Treatment by Kathryn J. Zerbe

"Eating Disorders Impact Adolescents." Ch. 64 of the *Adolescent Health Sourcebook* edited by Joyce Brennfleck Shannon

Reviving Ophelia: Saving the Selves of Our Adolescent Girls by Mary Pipher

Surviving an Eating Disorder: Strategies for Family and Friends by Michele Siegel, Judith Brisman & Margot Weinshel

Things Will Be Different for My Daughter by Mindy Bingham, Sandy Stryker & Susan Allstetter Neufeldt

© 2014 FAMILY EMPOWERMENT NETWORK™ ALL RIGHTS RESERVED.

Straightlaced:
How Gender's Got Us All Tied Up
By Debra Chasnoff

This article appears as the "Background for Teachers and Facilitators" in the Curriculum Guide that accompanies the film, Straightlaced: How Gender's Got Us All Tied Up. *It is here reprinted by permission of GroundSpark (www.groundspark.org) and film director Debra Chasnoff. The film is available for screenings as a tool to:*

- *Support teens to better navigate the pressures caused by gender expectations and negative attitudes about LGBTQ people;*

- *Expand understanding of how gender experiences connect with other dimensions of identity—including race, ethnicity, and class;*

- *Inspire youth and adults to become allies and advocates to break down the biases that divide us; and*

- *Create environments where all young people can be their best, fullest selves.*

Gender pressures and expectations are everywhere, and they limit all youth from being their fullest, truest selves. As the stories in *Straightlaced* show us, young people are constantly bombarded by messages about how they are supposed to be as girls and boys, men and women. These expectations—sometimes contradictory—come from family, friends, culture, school, and the media. They influence students' decisions about what to wear, how to carry themselves, and what hobbies to pursue. They also shape young people's feelings about basic issues in their lives: how to navigate the world of relationships and sexuality, how deeply to engage in school, how they feel about themselves, and what expectations to hold

for their future. All youth are limited by gender pressures, both those who fit traditional norms and, perhaps especially powerfully, those who don't.

Gender expectations exist across cultures and are expressed differently in different contexts. Our feelings about gender and sexuality are profoundly shaped by the cultures we live in. Every community—ethnic, racial, religious, regional, linguistic, socioeconomic—has deeply held attitudes and traditions about gender, rooted in shared values, beliefs, and history. Young people internalize these traditions as they grow up. Every group also has questions and struggles about gender and sexuality. Some gender norms and values are shared across cultures, while others are culturally specific. In thinking about *Straightlaced*, it is important to be mindful of all this and to find ways to help students simultaneously respect and *critically engage* their own cultures. It is also important to recognize that many youth struggle to navigate two or more different sets of gender expectations—because they come from culturally mixed backgrounds and/or because there are differences between their home cultures and the dominant culture.

We all have multiple dimensions to our identities. Young people's experiences of gender are intimately connected to their experiences of race, class, culture, sexual orientation, nationality, religion, language, and ability/disability. There is no generic "female" or "male" expe-

 ALL RIGHTS RESERVED. © 2014 FAMILY EMPOWERMENT NETWORK™

rience; instead, we walk through the world with more complex identities–as an African-American boy or an Asian-American girl, a middle-class lesbian, or a straight guy whose family is on welfare, an immigrant Latino or a U.S.-born white teen questioning her gender identity. Sometimes people may feel that certain dimensions of themselves are more primary than others. Other times, the dimensions may all feel equally important. And all of these dimensions of identity exist within a larger context of power and privilege. Throughout our lives, our multiple identities affect the way we think and feel about gender and sexuality–the pressures and limitations we face, and also our hopes and opportunities.

Gender stereotypes often intersect with stereotypes based on other dimensions of identity. Consider, for example, the way society constructs images of female beauty. As some of the youth in *Straightlaced* note, these images not only reflect stereotypical ideas about gender and body type–"You're supposed to be curvaceous, with big boobs, a big butt, and a skinny little waist"–but also reflect racial stereotypes: beauty is "blond and blue-eyed." Women's beauty is also highly sexualized. Images of women tend to present them as objects of male attraction and, therefore, as symbols of heterosexuality. Male stereotypes also often involve stereotypes about race and sexual orientation, as when a boy who likes the arts is called "feminine" and then presumed to be gay, or when a guy who wears tight clothes is considered both "unmanly" and "un-Mexican."

Rigid gender expectations are frequently held in place by both anti-gay attitudes and a devaluation of female experience. In most middle and high schools today, those who don't act enough like their gender risk being labeled gay, and then ostracized, harassed, or tormented. This is true not only for youth who truly *are* gay or lesbian but also for those who are not.

Because of the enormous social stigma around lesbian, gay, bisexual, and transgender sexuality, the mere threat of being thought to be gay is often enough to keep students following rigid gender rules. This limits all young people's dreams and opportunities. Young men face additional challenges because most people, sometimes unconsciously, see females as less valuable than males. If guys show any characteristics traditionally associated with girls and women–such as sensitivity, emotion, or a nurturing spirit–they are frequently considered weak and are ridiculed–either through gender-related taunts ("Don't be such a girl!") or through a combination of gender insults, homophobic remarks, and racist comments. To avoid being judged as less powerful, guys will often limit their options by adhering to strict codes of masculinity. For girls, the devaluation of women puts them in a different kind of bind. Like boys, they are pushed to follow strict gender codes by the pressure to avoid homophobic harassment But then, by following traditional "feminine" expectations, girls may end up finding themselves stuck in a box with less social power, rather than more.

Our society is organized around a simple *binary*–male vs. female–idea of gender. However, this idea does not do justice to the complexity of young people's lives. One of the deepest and most powerful aspects of traditional gender socialization in our society is the way most of us are taught to understand gender as an "either-or" phenomenon: You're either *male* or *female, masculine* or *feminine*. We are taught to believe that gender comes in two neat boxes, with clear edges and strict rules, and that things outside the boxes are scary, strange, or just plain "wrong." As many of the stories in *Straightlaced* teach us, however, young people's identities do not always fit into traditional boxes. Some youth talk about having both strongly masculine and strongly feminine qualities or being somewhere in the middle on a gender "spectrum." Others express the feeling that, although their bodies fall in one category (male

© 2014 FAMILY EMPOWERMENT NETWORK™ ALL RIGHTS RESERVED.

or female), their true identities fall in the other. Still more challenge the categories entirely, noting a desire to move, not just among genders, but "beyond gender" altogether. To be inclusive of all students' experiences, we need to learn to think beyond a binary understanding of gender and embrace all of these complexities. To say: There are lots of different ways to be a guy or girl, and all of them are OK. And also to say: Not everyone feels like they fit into the box of "male" or "female," and that's OK.

Gender codes and stereotypes take a heavy toll on individuals. Dealing with gender pressures is hard. And the stakes are high. Whether or not young people fit traditional expectations, they may struggle with a range of challenges. Their attempts to conform may cut them off from important parts of themselves—or from their friends, family members, and cultures or communities. They may suffer health problems, such as eating disorders, steroid side effects, and depression. Pressures not to seem too intelligent, along with lowered academic expectations for many girls and many students of color, can mean limited school success and career options. And trying to live up to stereotypes about sex and sexuality can lead to teen pregnancy, sexually transmitted infections, and dating or relationship violence. Youth who don't fit traditional norms also may experience bullying or violence in school or in their communities, and girls in particular are often vulnerable to sexual harassment. In some cases, gender-related pressures and challenges—sometimes compounded by racial or other biases—become so great that young people turn to drugs and alcohol, cutting, or even suicide. These dynamics affect all youth, but not in the same ways. The impacts often differ by gender, gender conformity, sexual orientation, race, culture, nationality, religion, and so on.

Gender expectations and related stereotypes help to maintain larger systems of power and inequality. Along with their impacts on young people's personal lives, gender roles and stereotypes also have important societal results. By weaving through social attitudes, policies, and institutional practices, stereotypes help to maintain systems that give power and privilege to men over women, heterosexual over LGBTQ people, white communities over communities of color, U.S.-born people over immigrants, and those with greater socioeconomic status over those with less. For instance, a belief that men are smarter than women can lead to limited academic and professional opportunities for women, reduced skills, lower-level jobs, less economic power and

less political power—all of which then turn around and feed back into a sense that women are less capable than men. In another example, stereotypes of young black males as "violent" often contribute to a lack of respect in schools, disproportionate school discipline and dropout rates, disproportionate incarceration, lower economic prospects, and a perpetuation of poverty and racial fear in some communities. In these and many other ways, gender stereotypes support the status quo of power.

We all have the capacity—and the responsibility—to create climates of respect, inclusion and equity. A key message of *Straightlaced* is that, although there are many ways gender pressures limit young people's lives, adults and youth alike also have much room for creativity, self-expression, and expansive change. Building an inclusive and equitable climate takes dialogue and support, along with both personal and systemic transformation. It requires an effort from everyone—students, educators, administrators, program leaders, parents/guardians, and community members. But change is possible, and there are lots of ways, large and small, that each of us can make a difference.

To learn how you can host a screening of Straightlaced: How Gender's Got Us All Tied Up *(or another GroundSpark film) at your school or in your community, email screenings@ groundspark.org. GroundSpark's Respect for All Project facilitates the development of inclusive, bias-free schools and communities by providing media resources, support, and training to youth, educators, and service providers.*

ALL RIGHTS RESERVED. © 2014 FAMILY EMPOWERMENT NETWORK™

Media Violence and Its Effects on Children

By Jody Bellant Scheer, MD, and Monique Terner, MEd

My children were ages three and five and on a vacation when they accidentally witnessed a violent death for the first time. They were upset and traumatized. They peppered me with questions about this homicide for well over a year, asking for explanations about why a policeman would chase and gun down another man. My children's fears and nightmares were easier to calm than my own, for I recognized in my own children an innocence and a lack of familiarity with homicidal violence that was virtually missing in their peers–because, by conscious choice, my husband and I had raised our children without TV.

Watching the anguish my children suffered after one inadvertent exposure to graphic TV violence confirms what studies have shown: The level of media violence that permeates modern screen technologies can be psychologically damaging to children and portrays a world that is much more violent and fearful than actual reality. – Jody Bellant Scheer, Pediatrician and mother

Concern about media violence is not new. Elizabeth Thoman, from the Center for Media Literacy, summarized the need for American society to move from blame to action around escalating media violence in her testimony before the U.S. Senate Commerce Committee 20 years ago. She posed this question: "What is the long-term impact on our national psyche when millions of children, in their formative years, grow up decade after decade bombarded with very powerful visual and verbal messages demonstrating violence as the preferred way to solve problems and normalizing fear and violence as the way things are?" ("TV Violence," Thoman) According to the American Psychological Association, the answer to Thoman's question is this: Exposure to media violence has at least four long-term negative effects on children:

- Aggressiveness and antisocial behaviors;
- Increased fear of being or becoming a victim;
- Increased desensitization to violence and to victims of violence; and
- Increased appetite for more and more violence in entertainment and real life ("Violence and Youth," Common Sense Media).

The effects of media violence also are compounded by the overuse of screen media in children, which has been shown to have detrimental effects on learning, socialization, cognitive performance, and attention spans. The average American young child (0-23 months of age) spends two hours in front of a screen each day ("Zero to Eight," Common Sense Media), while the average 8-18-year-old spends seven hours each day with screen media ("Media and Violence," Common Sense Media). While it is true that not all children and their parents are consciously choosing to view media violence, the average child entering kindergarten has already seen approximately 8,000 murders and 100,000 assorted other acts of violence and destruction on television (Nat'l. Inst. on Media and the Family). While efforts have been made to inform parents about movies and video games that contain content inappropriate for young children, children often unintentionally view violent images online and in both printed and online advertisements. These viewings have been linked to an increase of aggressive thoughts in children (*Science Daily*). To paraphrase a statement by former FCC Chairman Nicholas Johnson, "All television (and screen media) is educational. The question is, what does it teach?" (Nat'l. Inst. on Media and the Family)

Violence in the media is so pervasive, a simple family gathering to watch the Super Bowl may result in young children viewing advertisements glamorizing violence and the sexualization of women (*Science Daily*). In fact, our nation's citizens have become so used to viewing violence in the media that it takes more graphic and more realistic levels of violent images to maintain viewer interest and habits. This desensitization trickles down to affect what society deems "appropriate viewing" for even our youngest children. For example, two-thirds of Hollywood's movies released in 2001 were rated "R", and 80% of these were actively marketed to children under 17 (Media Educ. Foundation). As well, prime time adult broadcasting now averages 3-5 violent acts per hour, while Saturday morning cartoons contain 20-25 violent acts per hour, and a popular cartoon geared for

© 2014 FAMILY EMPOWERMENT NETWORK™ ALL RIGHTS RESERVED.

toddlers and preschoolers, "Power Rangers," averages an astonishing 200 violent acts per hour (Grossman and DeGaetano).

Although video game and movie producers use labels with maturity ratings or v-chips to help parents identify which media has violent content, often even media rated highly for young children have scenes depicting violence. Additionally, many younger children may have access to mature-rated games and movies at home through older siblings or parents who play, or at friends' homes. Parents are rightly concerned about the long-term effects of exposing their children's young and vulnerable minds to such acts of media violence, which are portrayed as normal and acceptable forms of fun and entertainment.

Parents and educators are faced with a growing concern about the effects of media violence on young children's social and emotional development, learning, attention spans, and relationships. It is now well known that there are negative long-term effects of exposure to widespread media violence, especially in young children. This leaves parents with the onerous task of trying to protect their children from the effects of media violence and wondering how to do this.

When children do have access to violent media, including music with mature lyrics, video games, movies, television programs, and books based on these shows and games, children have a tendency to act out what they see, and educators and parents alike are noticing the influences. The American Academy of Pediatrics Committee Position Paper on Media Violence concludes from over 1000 studies that the link between media violence and increased aggressive behaviors in children is confirmed ("Some Things You Should Know About Media Violence and Media Literacy").

Marketing violent media to children adds another level of complexity to modern life. Marketing to parents with young children may begin with selling products to advertise mature-rated games. A quick search on Amazon.com will find baby clothes sporting "ads" for popular video games such as Halo and Warcraft. Parents of young toddlers and preschoolers may find their children playing with action figures from those same mature-rated video games. Favorite toy makers such as Mega Blocks market action figures from mature-rated games to children as young as six years of age, encouraging young children to play out violent story lines of the game.

The video gaming world carefully studies and uses multiple psychological reinforcements to encourage the habitual and addictive use of their games for entertainment, and to link violence with feelings of excitement. Home and arcade games are designed with the following addictive elements: players experience feelings of mastery and control while playing the game; levels of play are exactly calibrated to the player's ability level, thereby ensuring feelings of success; immediate and continual reinforcements are used to encourage habitual play; and players experience gaming as a way to escape life and to be immersed in a constructed reality under their own complete control (Grossman and DeGaetano). These elements might not be so concerning if it weren't for the widespread pattern these games have of linking personal experiences of fun and excitement to acts of graphic and realistic murder, violence, misogyny, and racism.

"The mind is like a filing cabinet. Everything you see and do goes into that filing cabinet. And when something happens to you, you go to that file."
– Shooting victim who was asked if there were a relationship between TV violence and young people

The marketing and development of "first person shooter" games allows players–with keyboard, joystick or laser-activated guns–to participate more realistically in computer or video fantasy games, and, in many cases, to simulate killing for pleasure. Lt. Col. David Grossman, a West Point psychology and military science professor, outlines in his book, *Stop Teaching Our Kids to Kill*, that first person shooter video games marketed to kids are the very same tools used by the military to teach soldiers to kill. These games use a powerful form of stimulus-response training (called operant conditioning) to train users to perform under stressful conditions. Flight simulators use such measures to train pilots to respond reflexively to disasters during flight, while military and law enforcement agencies use first person shooter video games to train their recruits to kill. The result of putting these games into the widespread hands of children, without any complementary disciplinary training such as soldiers and law enforcement officers receive, is that our children are being trained to use guns to reflexively kill with uncanny accuracy, little cognitive involvement, and minimal remorse.

Other common and popular video games create fantasy

ALL RIGHTS RESERVED. © 2014 FAMILY EMPOWERMENT NETWORK™

environments that help foster sexism and racism. Some use images and music to intensify sexual arousal just before finding and killing scantily clad, busty, over-sexualized women–justifying the killing because these women are prostitutes (Grossman and DeGaetano). Likewise, many of these games link inner cities, dark colors, and dark-skinned human targets with evil ("Game Over," Media Educ. Foundation). The fact that these games are interactive, elevating children from passive viewers of media violence into the position of active participants should send shock waves of concern through our nation. Unfortunately, these games are highly addictive, readily available, and enormously profitable.

A final area of recent concern is the virtually unstudied effects of exposure to online violence that is easily accessed by youths in the privacy of their own smartphone or computer. Woefully missing is research exploring how online violence affects kids, though it is beginning to crop up in unusual places. Sexual addiction counselors note that pornography addiction and sexual dysfunction are affecting an increasing number of young and adult men. Psychologists also report drastic increases in Internet and gaming addictions, where individuals' use of online gaming or interactive technology interferes with their ability to function in the real world.

The good news is that, in a world in which violent media content is pervasive and children are susceptible to its effects, parents are the best mediators of their children's viewing. Parents can very effectively limit their child's exposure to violent media at home, as well as mitigate the untoward effects of media violence ("TV Violence," Josephson). Family media literacy is a valuable and critical tool for mediating media violence. Developing family media literacy involves taking an active role in reducing the amount of violent media watched as an entire family, locating and appreciating alternative entertainment that is not violent, learning skills to mitigate and talk about

the impact of violent images that their children see or hear, and expressing informed opinions to policy makers, the media industry, and to one another in public forums ("TV Violence," Thoman).

Creating the kind of world that we want our children to live in is a parents' biggest challenge, but a worthy and rewarding one. Our vision is of a future where our children see the world as a welcoming place, where they continue to be disturbed and outraged by violence, and where they see conflict resolution modeled for them using diplomacy and compassion.

Resources
"Game Over: Gender, Race, and Violence in Video Games." 2000 video exposé by Media Educ. Foundation at www.mediaed.org

"Government and Industry Responses to Media Violence." An online article by Media Smarts, Canada's center for digital and media literacy. http://mediasmarts.ca/violence/government-and-industry-responses-media-violence

"Media and Violence: An Analysis of Current Research." A Common Sense Media Research Brief, Common Sense Media, Feb. 13, 2013. www.commonsensemedia.org

Media Education Foundation, 60 Masonic St., Northampton, MA 01060. www.mediaed.org

"Media Violence: The Children Are Watching." A guide for parents and teachers published by Canada's Society for Safe & Caring Schools and Communities. (1999; rev. 2006). http://safeandcaring.files.wordpress.com/2012/07/media-violence-web-version.pdf National Institute on Media and the Family. 606 24th Ave. S., Ste. 606, Minneapolis, MN www.mediafamily.org

"Some Things You Should Know About Media Violence and Media Literacy." Statement of the American Academy of Pediatrics Committee on Communications. www.aap.org

Stop Teaching Our Kids To Kill by Lt. Col. David Grossman and Gloria DeGaetano. NY: Crown Publishers, 1999.

"Study on Effects of TV Ad Violence on Kids Has Super Bowl Implications," excerpt based on materials provided by Iowa State University. *Science Daily*, 2011. www.sciencedaily.com/releases/2011/02/110205141720.htm

"Television Violence: A Review of the Effects on Children of Different Ages," by Wendy L. Josephson, Ph.D. Dept. of Canadian Heritage, February 1995. Child and Family Canada Media Awareness Network. www.cfc-efc.ca.

"TRUCE Action Guides." TRUCE 2010. www.truceteachers.org

"TV Violence: It's Time to Break the Circle of Blame," summary of testimony to the U.S. Senate Commerce Committee, July 12, 1995, by Elizabeth Thoman, Center for Media Literacy, Los Angeles, 3101 Ocean Park Boulevard, Ste. 200, Santa Monica, CA www.medialit.org.

"Violence on TV." Canadian policies, responsibilities, etc., regarding TV violence by Canadian Radio-television and Telecommunications Commission. www.crtc.gc.ca/eng/info_sht/b317.htm

"Zero to Eight: Children's Media Use in America." A Common Sense Media Research Study, Common Sense Media, 2011. www.commonsensemedia.org

---

Take Action

For further exploration on the topic of media violence and its effects on children, check out the following organizations and their resources:

Campaign for a Commercial Free Childhood
www.commercialfreechildhood.org

Common Sense Media www.commonsensemedia.org

TRUCE (Teachers Resisting Unhealthy Children's Entertainment) www.truceteachers.org

© 2014 FAMILY EMPOWERMENT NETWORK™ ALL RIGHTS RESERVED.

Play Again:

Reconnecting Children to Nature

By Meg Merrill, producer of the movie *Play Again*

About six years ago, Norwegian film director Tonje Schei mentioned an idea for a new film about children, technology, and nature. As a social worker with an interest in these issues, I enthusiastically asked, "What can I do to help?" "Produce it," she replied. "Okay," I said on the spot, and promptly went home to Google "film production."

Play Again is a documentary that addresses the issue of children's increasing screen time and their decreasing time in the natural world. It encourages us to examine our relationships with both screen technology and nature. We have been fortunate enough to show the film all over the world, and the issues it raises are resonating deeply with audiences. We are happy to be part of the growing movement to reconnect children to nature.

During the production of the film, I interviewed Bill McKibben, author and founder of 350.org, and asked him what the most important difference is between what media teaches kids and what nature teaches them. He said, "Media teaches kids 'I am the center of the universe. It's all about me.' Nature teaches them that they are just a small part of a much bigger picture." It is this contrast in values that I believe is at the heart of the sustainability movement today and what fuels my commitment to this film.

One generation from now, most people in the U.S. will have spent more time in the virtual world than in nature. New media technologies have improved our lives in countless ways. Information now appears with a click. Overseas friends are part of our daily lives. And even Grandma loves Wii. But what are we missing when we are behind screens? And how will this impact our children, our society, and, eventually, our planet?

For many people, especially children, screens have become the *de facto* medium by which the greater world is experienced. A virtual world of digitally transmitted pictures, voices, and scenarios has become more real to this generation than the world of sun, water, air, and living organisms, including fellow humans.

Average American children now spend over seven hours in front of screens each day, not including school time. They can recognize hundreds of corporate logos but fewer than 10 plants in their own backyards. They are almost completely disconnected from the world that, over millions of years, shaped human beings–the natural world.

The long-term consequences of this experiment on human development remain to be seen, but the stakes couldn't be higher. By most accounts, this generation will face multiple crises–environmental, economic, and social. Will this screen world–and its bevy of virtual experiences–adequately prepare these "digital natives" to address the problems they'll face?

There is much to learn from the experts and youth featured in *Play Again* as well as from the parents, teachers,

ALL RIGHTS RESERVED. © 2014 FAMILY EMPOWERMENT NETWORK™

and students who see the film each month. Here are a few tips to consider as we prepare today's youth for the exciting challenges that lay ahead:

1. Decrease screen time; increase green time. Allow kids to develop a personal relationship with nature, through free play and exploration. Making this a daily priority is an important contribution to your child's well-being and to society. As Charles Jordon, quoting John Muir, says in *Play Again*, "What they do not know, they will not protect, and what they do not protect, they will lose."

2. Be a role model. It sounds simple, but it is a struggle for many of us. Turn off the laptop and the phone and get outside. Eat dinner on the porch, take a walk, draw birds, collect leaves. Breathe. Think. Reflect. Connect. Talk to your kids about how it feels.

3. Be an advocate. Be a champion for safe, natural play areas and equal access to urban greenspace. As schools move toward technology, encourage them to consider their role in connecting students to nature. Time in nature increases concentration and memory while decreasing symptoms of ADHD and depression, all of which has an impact on learning.

4. Be proactive. Instead of watching kids play video games all morning while your resentment boils, plan ahead. Create a neighborhood scavenger hunt, invite friends to go hiking, sign up for a camp that encourages free play outdoors. When kids are used to being entertained by screens, we have to work a little harder.

5. Give youth a voice. Have meaningful conversations with your kids about media, screen time, and nature connection. Ask good questions and listen to their answers. Try to respect kids' competence in the virtual world while providing ample opportunities in the natural world.

6. Encourage both environmental education and nature connection. Kids of all ages need the time and space to connect with nature and each other. As they grow older, they also benefit from more formal environmental education. Both experiences will empower them to solve the many local and global environmental challenges we face today.

Most importantly, enjoy the natural world and the part you play in it.

Play Again (2010) is a multi award-winning film about the consequences of a childhood removed from nature. Watch the trailer and find resources at PlayAgainFilm.com or facebook.com/PlayAgainFilm.

© 2014 FAMILY EMPOWERMENT NETWORK™ ALL RIGHTS RESERVED.

Avoiding the Addictive Potential of Internet Use

By Hilarie Cash, PhD

In our modern age of digital media, it's easy for parents to succumb to children's wishes for more and more access to their computers and the Internet. Why not give in? The answer has to do with a child's brain development and how it is influenced by the use of screen technology. Bottom line: A child's development is influenced by his or her use of screen technology. When the use is excessive, the impact can be profound, negative, and could lead to addiction.

Statistics tell us that 1 in 11 youth (ages 8 to 18) is addicted to texting, Facebook, video games, and/or pornography. In the college age population, that number stands between 13 and 19%! In South Korea and China, the problem is growing so rapidly that those governments have declared Internet Addiction as their #1 public health threat.

When considering addiction, we usually think of drugs, alcohol, sex, and gambling. But Internet addiction? Let's look at how it starts. In all of us, powerful neuro-chemicals (dopamine, endorphins, etc.) are released when we experience any type or pleasure. Receptors in the brain and elsewhere in the body pick up the chemicals and make us feel good or "high." When we "fall in love," are doing an exciting sport, or playing with our friends, for example, we are high on these neuro-chemicals.

In moderation, these highs can be great and are healthy. But when these highs occur too often and are "over the top"—as can happen with drinking, taking drugs, gambling, texting, viewing porn, video gaming, etc.—that's when addiction takes hold. At a breaking point, the brain withdraws neuro-receptors in an effort to restore balance, which is called "tolerance." Then we no longer get the high from the same level of activity or chemical use. To get any pleasure, we need more of the activity or substance. If we go without, we go into withdrawal, which can be both physiological as well as psychological (irritability, restlessness, poor concentration, increased anxiety and depression, etc.).

Once an addiction takes hold, the addict continues to chase highs or tries to avoid withdrawal. This, in turn, leads to obsession and engaging in the behavior in spite of negative consequences. The pleasure pathway, now overused, becomes highly sensitive and responsive to cues that trigger cravings for the drug or behavior. For example, if you've become addicted to Farmville or World of Warcraft, then merely sitting in front of a computer or opening up the Internet on a smart phone can trigger the release of neuro-chemicals that make you crave engagement in those games. These cravings are very strong and tend to override our rational brain. Thus, even though you may have recognized that your video game play or other Internet use is harming your life in some way, resisting the urge to do it anyway can be very difficult. Afterward, the addict feels remorse, shame, and regret, because the rational mind functions again. This is the classic pattern in all addictions, whether chemical or behavioral.

As an example of how far some people will go, consider a bright young man who went to college and felt like a little fish in a big pond. Rather than dealing with his anxiety directly, he distracted himself from his emotions (fear) by playing video games. Eventually, he became so obsessed with Everquest that this great student, strong athlete, and socially popular kid stopped going to classes, rarely emerged from his room, lost his Ivy League scholarship, and flunked out of school. Next, he married his high school sweetheart and found a job in the computer industry. Although he promised his wife he would stop gaming, he failed and went to extraordinary lengths to game in secret, pretending to go to work. Eventually, he made up stories about going to work even after he had been fired, paying their bills with credit cards. For months he kept up the charade, driving them into deep debt. His shame grew until he felt suicidal and finally confessed to his wife who found him help through the ReSTART: Internet Addiction Recovery Program near Seattle.

> Check out **"No Time to Think: How Technology Is Shaping Human Behavior,"** a documentary film by Road Trip Productions that explores our obsessions and addictions to new emerging technologies and devices. www.notimetothink.net

ALL RIGHTS RESERVED. © 2014 FAMILY EMPOWERMENT NETWORK™

How to Prevent Internet Addiction

With Internet-enabled devices more and more accessible to younger and younger children, the threat of addiction starting at younger ages is very real. So, if you are going to allow your child access to computers, the Internet, or video games, there are some guidelines which, if followed, can allow your child to develop a healthy relationship to digital media.

1. Don't let your child use a computer or video games before the age of 7. This delay gives the child a "human-focused start to life" (Payne, *Simplicity Parenting*, p. 168) and a chance to develop self-control and social relationships before he/she starts gaming. This will allow your child to fully engage his/her natural inclinations toward creative play, curiosity, sociability, and physical activity. Allowing children at young ages to spend time captivated by a digital screen can interrupt natural development and set them up for a lifetime of underperformance and poor self-esteem. It can also set the stage for digital addiction.

2. Limit the amount of time your child is playing video games or using Internet-enabled devices for personal pleasure: less than 1 hour for elementary school children, 2 hours for middle schoolers, and 3 hours for high schoolers. Make sure your child understands that the privilege of using such powerful media lasts only as long as he/she demonstrates age-appropriate maturity and the ability to follow your rules. If the child fails, you should then withdraw the privilege ("unplug") for an extended period of time, allowing maturation to proceed to the point that she or he can comply.

3. Avoid playing Internet games and chatting online with strangers. When and if you allow your child to play video games, limit him/her to casual games played alone, with others in the home, or, once the child is a responsible and mature older teen, over the Internet only with good friends. The rewards and sense of obligation that occur when playing with others greatly increases the risk of addiction. Also, the content of conversation among unknown Internet players is often highly inappropriate and, especially for girls, predatory.

4. Screen what comes into your home. Make sure you are comfortable with the digital content, whether it is a video game or the sites visited by your child. Use software to screen out porn and track where your child goes on the Internet. Let your child know the computer is not a private space, that you are supervising computer use, and that, if privacy is what

he/she wants, phones and face-to-face get-togethers allow for those private conversations.

5. Your child's first phone? Make it a "dumb" one, not a smart phone with access to the Internet. Also, limit texting until your child is in high school and demonstrating a high level of maturity both at home and with academic work. Texting is highly distracting, interfering with a person's ability to focus as needed on school, driving, sleep, and social interactions. If the child falters once she/he acquires a smart phone, that phone goes away.

6. Do NOT feel guilty because your child is unhappy when you enforce rules. She or he will get over it and still love you.

7. Don't worry that by limiting your child's access to digital technology you are being a bad parent. Quite the contrary! You are helping your child to learn to lead a balanced life! Research has demonstrated that teens who grow up without computers are able to use digital technology with as much skill as their "digital native" peers within months of use.

8. Model what you preach. If you want to raise a child who lives a well-balanced life, then you need to model that. You cannot expect your child to use digital media moderately if you, yourself, are constantly on your smart phone, tablet, laptop, or the home computer.

9. Avoid using screens to babysit your children or keep them distracted. Invest your time in your children. Our kids need us–our attention, our insistence on the rules, our consistency, our wisdom, our love. Don't let a screen come between you. Get out and enjoy real life. There's no app for that!

10. If you do see the signs of Internet addiction in your child, check out the guidance offered in our book, *Video Games & Your Kids*, on our website at www.netaddictionrecovery.com, and on the website of Zone'in Programs (www.zonein.ca), founded by *Virtual Child* author Cris Rowan. If this does not work, find a counselor who "gets it" and make a plan for intervention.

Hilarie Cash, PhD, LMHC, is the co-founder of the Digital Center for Technology Sustainability and the ReSTART Internet Addiction Recovery Program in Fall City, WA. She is a psychotherapist, speaker, teacher, and co-author of Video Games & Your Kids. *For more information about the ReSTART program, see http://www.netaddictionrecovery.com.*

© 2014 FAMILY EMPOWERMENT NETWORK™ ALL RIGHTS RESERVED.

Screen Savvy Parents:
Embracing Civility in a Digital Age
By Nancy Willard, MS, JD

Digital Parenting Research Insight

Several research studies are helpful in understanding the issue of effective digital parenting. These studies ground their analysis of the impact of parenting styles on Dr. Baumrind's seminal work on parenting styles.

- Authoritative—actively involved in a positive manner
- Authoritarian—actively involved but in a negative manner
- Indulgent—positively involved but not active
- Neglectful—negatively involved and not active

Research that examined the relationship between parenting styles and online teen behaviors found that the children of parents who adopted an authoritative parenting approach demonstrated fewer online risk behaviors. Another study that investigated cyberbullying incidents found that those teens who had parents who used an authoritative parenting style were less emotionally distressed and better able to respond effectively to these incidents.

A Place to Start . . . with the Power of the Positive Comment

One of the most important strategies to recommend to parents is reliance on this specific technique: Every time they interact with their children in relation to using digital technologies, parents should be mindful of the need to make one positive statement per interaction about their children's activities—or more if they are so inclined. This is classic operant conditioning. From the child's per-

spective, interactions with a parent related to the use of digital technologies will "feel good." Thus, the child will be more inclined to want to share aspects of his or her digital life with a parent.

Filtering & Monitoring Technologies: The Good and the Bad

We all know that companies currently are pushing parents, out of fear, to install filtering and monitoring technologies. Some family safety features are offered through computer operating systems and browsers; others can be purchased as software or as a service by companies; and some are provided on interactive gaming consoles. (Note: Some companies provide monitoring for free, but they are market profiling children's personal communications.)

If a parent chooses to utilize filtering or monitoring technologies, the child should know that everything he or she does online is open to parental review. Such digital safety features can allow parents to limit their child's access to selected sites, control who can communicate privately, manage time spent online, and review the history file.

Although these safety features and devices can be somewhat useful in creating a "fenced play yard" for young children, parents of tweens and teens should never expect the filtering and monitoring technologies to work for their kids. To understand the futility, simply conduct an Internet search on the phrase "bypass Internet filter"! Also, monitoring technologies can encourage passive reliance on a technology quick fix.

ALL RIGHTS RESERVED. © 2014 FAMILY EMPOWERMENT NETWORK™

General Guidance for Parents

The following guidelines are appropriate for parents of children, tweens, and teens:

- **Appreciate your child's online activities.** Show interest in your child's online friends. Help your child learn to make positive choices in accord with your family's values, and comment positively every time you notice that they have done something that reflects these positive values.

- **Never overreact if your child reports an online concern.** You want your child to feel comfortable reporting online concerns. Your first comment when your child reports a negative situation should be positive. Your next comment must indicate a commitment to a partnership in response to the situation.

- **Use logical consequences.** If your child engages in any risky, inappropriate, or harmful behavior, impose a logical consequence that will focus your child's attention on why this action has caused or could cause harm to him or to someone else. Require that your child remedy any harm.

- **Pay attention to possible red flags.** Red flags include appearing emotionally upset during or after use, disturbed relationships with family members or friends, spending too much time online, engaging in excessively secretive behavior when using digital technologies, and making subtle comments about online concerns. If any red flags are evident, pay closer attention and carefully try to engage your child in discussion.

- **Encourage personal responsibility.** Encourage your child to help others directly or to report to you or another responsible adult if she witnesses someone being harmed or at risk online.

- **Maintain computer security.** Make sure you have implemented appropriate security against malware, use a spam blocker, block pop-up ads, and use safe search features. Never allow peer-to-peer (P2P) software, as this can lead to accidental access of pornography and is a significant source of malware that can result in identity theft.

- **Educate yourself on issues of profiling and advertising.** Read the privacy policies. Pay attention to the strategies sites use to obtain your child's demographic and interest information and the various ways in which sites advertise, including targeted banner ads, ads integrated into games, and sites that ask children to sign up to receive ads or send ads to their friends. When you recognize these profiling or advertising techniques, point them out to your child to increase his understanding. Take advantage of the emerging ability to restrict the ability of sites to track use for profiling.

Regarding Younger Kids & Tweens

When children are young, it is the parents' responsibility to make sure their Internet use is in a safe online environment and that they engage in safe communications. Children who still believe in the tooth fairy cannot be expected to protect themselves online. To them, the Internet is more of a "magic box." By third grade, young kids can begin to grasp essential concepts about how the Internet functions, which provides the ability for them to take on more personal responsibility for good decision making. By middle school, many tweens will want to jump into environments and activities with teens. This shift needs to be made carefully, based, in part, on an understanding of the child's social-emotional maturity. These are strategies parents can use with elementary school kids and tweens:

- Create a "fenced play yard" for your younger child online. Limit your child's access to sites you have selected as appropriate. As your child grows, make decisions together about additional sites that are appropriate.

- Make sure you personally know everyone your child is able to communicate with through e-mail, texting, and any other form of personal communications. Limit communication with strangers to general areas of safe, moderated children's sites.

- Keep your family computer in a public place in your house, so you can remain engaged in what your child is doing.

- If you provide a cell phone for your child or tween, implement the safety and security features provided by the company.

- If you choose to allow your child to participate in a social networking environment, select a safe site designed for children and tweens, not teens.

© 2014 FAMILY EMPOWERMENT NETWORK™ ALL RIGHTS RESERVED.

• It is best not to allow your child to register on social networking sites for users over the age of 13. If you do allow this, go through all privacy settings to make sure that only accepted friends can see your child's profile. Have your child's login password. Insist that your child only establish friendship links with people she knows and trusts, and review all friends to make sure this is the case. Advise your child that you will regularly review his profile, and, if any material is posted that is not safe or not in accord with your family's values, you will place restrictions on his or her use.

• Help your child create a safe and fun username that does not disclose personal details, as well as a safe password. Make sure your child knows to never disclose his or her password to anyone other than you. Use your e-mail address for any site registrations.

Regarding Teens

• Implement the use of cell phone safety and security features, if you have any concerns about your child's responsible use. Otherwise, discuss issues of responsible use including texting and creation of potentially damaging images of self or others. Make sure your child turns off his cell phone when going to bed. If there are any problems associated with this, make sure her cell phone remains outside of the bedroom at night.

• When your child sets up a social networking profile, jointly go through all privacy settings to make sure that only accepted friends can see this profile. Insist initially that your child only establish friendship links with people he knows face-to-face and trusts. As your child gains experience, allow the establishment of friendship links with people your child's friends know face-to-face and people they meet online through safe online activities. Jointly review the profile of any person whom your child does not know face-to-face to evaluate this person's values, standards, and choice of friends.

• Either have your child's login password (best approach when they are starting) or create your own profile and friend your child, so that you can regularly review what is happening on your child's profile, including materials posted and friends added. Advise your child that you will regularly review her profile, and if any material is posted that is not safe or not in accord with your family's values, you will place restrictions on her use.

• Keep your computer in a public area until your child is older and has demonstrated making positive choices.

• Pay attention to what your child is doing online, but balance your supervision with your child's emerging legitimate interests in personal privacy. Positive interactions will encourage your child to share. At this age, if your child feels you are overly intrusive, he could easily find a way to go behind your back. In a few short years, your child will be out of your home. It is necessary for her to independently make safe and responsible decisions, which requires practice in doing so.

Resources

Baumrind, D. (1991). "The influence of parenting style on adolescent competence and substance use." *Journal of Early Adolescence*, 11, 56-95.

Rosen, L. D., Cheever, N. A., & Carrier, L. M. (2008). "The association of parenting style and child age with parental limit setting and adolescent MySpace behavior." *Journal of Applied Developmental Psychology*, 29, 459-471.

Hay, C. & Meldrum, R. (2010). "Bullying, victimization and adolescent self-harm: Testing hypotheses from general strain theory." *Journal of Youth and Adolescence*, 39(5), 446-459.

Reprinted with permission from Nancy Willard © 2007. Willard is the author of Cyber-Safe Kids, Cyber-Savvy Teens *(2007, Jossey-Bass),* Cyberbullying and Cyberthreats *(2007, Research Press), and* Cyber Savvy: Embracing Digital Safety and Civility *(2011, Corwin Press). She also is the founder of Embracing Digital Youth (program of the Center for Safe and Responsible Internet Use), which promotes positive approaches that will best ensure that all young people become cyber savvy. For more information, check out: http://embracecivility.org or info@embracecivility.org*

Family Assets

By Search Institute, from *The Asset Approach: Giving Kids What They Need to Succeed*

Search Institute® has identified the following key qualities that help all kinds of families be strong. When families have more of these research-based assets, the teens and adults in the family do better in life.

Nurturing Relationships

- **Positive communication**—Family members listen attentively and speak in respectful ways.
- **Affection**—Family members regularly show warmth to each other.
- **Emotional openness**—Family members can be themselves and are comfortable sharing their feelings.
- **Support for sparks**—Family members encourage each other in pursuing their talents and interests.

Establishing Routines

- **Family meals**—Family members eat meals together most days in a typical week.
- **Shared activities**—Family members regularly spend time doing everyday activities together.
- **Meaningful traditions**—Holidays, rituals, and celebrations are part of family life.
- **Dependability**—Family members know what to expect from one another day-to-day.

Maintaining Expectations

- **Openness about tough topics**—Family members openly discuss sensitive issues, such as sex and substance use.
- **Fair rules**—Family rules and consequences are reasonable.
- **Defined boundaries**—The family sets limits on what young people can do and how they spend their time.
- **Clear expectations**—The family openly articulates its expectations for young people.
- **Contributions to family**—Family members help meet each other's needs and share in getting things done.

Adapting to Challenges

- **Management of daily commitments**—Family members effectively navigate competing activities and expectations at home, school, and work.
- **Adaptability**—The family adapts well when faced with changes.
- **Problem solving**—Family members work together to solve problems and deal with challenges.
- **Democratic decision making**—Family members have a say in decisions that affect the family.

Connecting to Community

- **Neighborhood cohesion**—Neighbors look out for one another.
- **Relationships with others**—Family members feel close to teachers, coaches, and others in the community.
- **Enriching activities**—Family members participate in programs and activities that deepen their lives.
- **Supportive resources**—Family members have people and places in the community they can turn to for help.

For information on the research behind the family assets, visit www.search-institute.org/familyassets

For practical ways to build assets in your family, visit www.ParentFurther.com/familyassets

This page may be reproduced for educational, noncommercial uses only. Copyright © 2012 by Search Institute, 615 First Avenue N.E., Suite 125, Minneapolis, MN 55413; 800-888-7828; www.search-institute.org. All rights reserved. Search Institute® and ParentFurther® are registered trademarks of Search Institute.

101 Screen-Free Activities - Turn off the screen and ...

At Home
1. Listen to the radio.
2. Write an article or story.
3. Paint a picture, a mural, or a room.
4. Write to the President, your Representative or Senator.
5. Read a book. Read to someone else.
6. Learn to change the oil or a tire on a car. Fix something.
7. Write a letter to a friend or relative.
8. Make cookies, bread, or jam and share with a neighbor.
9. Read magazines or newspapers. Swap them with friends.
10. Go through your closets and donate items to Goodwill, the Salvation Army, or a local rummage sale. Have a garage sale.
11. Start a diary/journal.
12. Play cards.
13. Make crafts to give as gifts. Try a new craft.
14. Do a crossword puzzle.
15. Save money! Cancel your cable TV!
16. Learn about a different culture. Have an international dinner.
17. Teach a child some of your favorite childhood games.
18. Study sign-language.
19. Write a letter to your favorite author.
20. Cook dinner with friends or family.
21. Make cards for holidays or birthdays.
22. Play chess, bridge, or checkers.
23. Play charades.
24. Have a cup of coffee and a conversation.
25. Repair or refinish a piece of furniture.
26. Make a wooden flowerbox.
27. Wake up early and make pancakes.
28. Read a favorite poem.

Outdoors
29. Learn about native trees and flowers in your area.
30. Plan a picnic or barbeque.
31. Go bird watching. Learn the names of local birds.
32. Walk the dog. Wash the dog.
33. Plant a garden. Work in your garden.
34. Take a nature hike.
35. Feed fish or birds.
36. Watch the night sky through binoculars; identify different constellations. Observe the moon.
37. Learn to use a compass.
38. Take photographs and then organize them into an album.
39. Do yard work.
40. Go camping.
41. Take an early morning walk.
42. Climb a tree.
43. Watch a sunset; watch the sunrise with a friend.

Around Town
44. Attend a community concert. Listen to a local band.
45. Visit the library. Borrow some books.
46. Visit a local bookstore.
47. Visit the zoo.
48. Visit the countryside or town. Travel by bus or train.
49. Attend a religious service.
50. Walk to work or school.
51. Attend a live sports event.
52. Look for treasures at a yard sale.
53. Try out for a play. Attend a play.
54. Collect recycling and drop it off at a recycling center.
55. Learn to play a musical instrument.
56. Go to a museum.

On the Move
57. Go roller skating or ice skating.
58. Go swimming. Join a community swim team.
59. Start a community group that walks, runs, or bikes.
60. Organize a game of touch football, baseball, or softball in the local park.
61. Go for a bicycle ride.
62. Learn yoga.
63. Play soccer, softball, or volleyball.
64. Play Frisbee.
65. Work out.
66. Go dancing. Take a dance class.

In Your Community
67. Organize a community clean-up or volunteer for charity.
68. Become a tutor.
69. Join a choir. Sing!
70. Start a bowling league.
71. Visit and get to know your neighbors.
72. Start a fiction or public policy book group.

With the Kids
73. Make paper bag costumes and have a parade.
74. Design a poster for the TVTN/ Hearthsong contest.
75. Discover your local community center or local park activities.
76. Blow bubbles.
77. Mark and color in Screen-Turnoff Week on the calendar.
78. Build a fort in the living room and camp out for one night.
79. Research your family history and draw a family tree.
80. Invent a new game and teach it to your friends and family.
81. Make a sign to tape across the TV during Screen-Turnoff Week.
82. Play hopscotch, hide & seek, or freeze-tag.
83. Organize a neighborhood scavenger hunt.
84. Play board games with family and friends.
85. Clean up or redecorate your room.
86. Make puppets out of old clean socks and have a puppet show.
87. Write a play with friends. Perform it at a nursing home.
88. Construct a kite. Fly it.
89. Go on a family trip or historical excursion.
90. In the snow, go sledding or make a snowman.
91. Create a collage out of pictures from old magazines.
92. Shoot hoops with friends. Play a round of H.O.R.S.E.
93. Make a friendship bracelet.
94. Draw pictures of members of your family.
95. Tell stories around a campfire.
96. Plan a slumber party.
97. Bake cakes or cookies and invite friends for a tea party.
98. Construct a miniature boat and float it on water.
99. Write a letter to your grandparents. Make a special card.
100. Create sidewalk art with chalk.
101. Everyone!!! Have a huge party to celebrate Screen-Free Week!

Reprinted by permission of the Campaign for a Commercial-Free Childhood. For other handouts and great resources, go to www.commercialfreechildhood.org

Related Resources for Further Exploration

BIAS

"Why White Parents Don't Talk About Race," Chapter 3 in *NurtureShock: New Thinking About Children* by Po Bronson and Ashley Merryman. NY: Twelve, 2009.

Organization and films: *GroundSpark.* This organization creates visionary films and dynamic educational campaigns that move individuals and communities to take action for a more just world. www.groundspark.org

Organization and program: *Stand for Courage.* An organization that works with youth to provide celebrity recognition for individuals who stand up for one another and themselves. www.standforcourage.org

BOYS

Boys Adrift: The Five Factors Driving the Growing Epidemic of Unmotivated Boys and Underachieving Young Men by Leonard Sax, MD, PhD. NY: Basic Books, 2007.

The Demise of Guys: Why Boys are Struggling and What We Can Do About It by Philip Zimbardo, PhD, and Nikita Duncan. TED Conferences: 2012.

Guyland: The Perilous World Where Boys Become Men (Understanding the Critical Years Between 16 and 26) by Michael Kimmel. NY: Harper, 2008.

It's a Boy: Your Son's Development from Birth to Age 18 by Michael Thompson, PhD, and Teresa Barker. NY: Ballantine Books, 2009.

The Male Brain: A Breakthrough Understanding of How Men and Boys Think by Louann Brizendine, MD. NY: Three Rivers Press, 2010.

Masterminds & Wingmen: Helping Our Boys Cope with Schoolyard Power, Locker-Room Tests, Girlfriends, and the New Rules of Boy World by Rosalind Wiseman. NY: Random House, 2013.

Raising Boys: Why Boys are Different–and How to Help Them Become Happy and Well-Balanced Men by Steve Biddulph. NY: Celestial Arts, rev. 2008.

Raising Cain: Protecting the Emotional Life of Boys by Dan Kindlon, PhD, and Michael Thompson, PhD. NY: Ballantine Books, 2000.

Raising Our Sons: The Ultimate Parenting Guide for Healthy Boys and Strong Families by Kathy Masarie, MD, Jody Bellant Scheer, MD, and Kathy Keller Jones, MA. Portland, OR: Family Empowerment Network, 2009.

© 2014 FAMILY EMPOWERMENT NETWORK™ ALL RIGHTS RESERVED.

Real Boys: Rescuing Our Sons from the Myths of Boyhood (1998), ***Real Boys' Voices*** (2001), and ***Real Boys' Workbook: The Definitive Guide to Understanding Boys*** (2001) by William Pollack, PhD. NY: Owl Books.

The Way of Boys: Raising Healthy Boys in a Challenging and Complex World by Anthony Rao, PhD, and Michelle Seaton. NY: HarperCollins, 2009.

Book and support group for boys: ***BAM! Boys Advocacy and Mentoring:*** A Leader's Guide to Facilitating Strengths-Based Groups for Boys by Howard Hiton, MS, Stephen Grant, LCSW, and Peter Mortolla, PhD. NY: Routledge: 2007. www.bamgroups.com

DVD: ***"What About Boys? Connecting with Our Sons"*** with Kathy Masarie, MD. 2010. www.family-empower.com

Organization/support group for boys: ***The Council for Boys and Young Men***: The Council is a strengths-based group approach to promote boys' and young men's safe and healthy passage through pre-teen and adolescent years. www.onecirclefoundation.org

Video: ***Tough Guise: Violence, Media and the Crisis in Masculinity.*** Produced by Media Educational Foundation, 1999.

CONSUMERISM AND LOOKISM

The Adonis Complex: How to Identify, Treat, Prevent Body Obsession in Men and Boys by Harrison Pope, MD, Katharine Phillips, MD, and Roberto Olivardia. NY: Free Press, 2002.

Born to Buy: The Commercialized Child and the New Consumer Culture by Juliet Schor. NY: Scribner, 2004.

Buy, Buy Baby: How Consumer Culture Manipulates Parents and Harms Young Minds by Susan Gregory Thomas. Boston: Houghton Mifflin, 2007.

Cinderella Ate My Daughter: Dispatches from the Front Lines of the New Girlie-Girl Culture by Peggy Orenstein. NY: Harper Collins, 2011.

Consuming Kids: Protecting Our Children from the Onslaught of Marketing & Advertising by Susan Linn. NY: Anchor Books, 2004.

"Report of the APA Task Force on the Sexualization of Girls" by the American Psychological Assn. Task Force on the Sexualization of Girls. Washington, DC: American Psychological Assn., 2007. www.apa.org/pi/wpo/sexualization.html.

Book, CD, & DVD: ***Free to Be You and Me*** created by Marlo Thomas and Friends. 2012 marked the 40th anniversary of this landmark children's book that was turned into an album, CD, a hit TV primetime special of the 1970s and '80s, and a DVD. The inspirational stories, poems, and songs told or sung by celebrities of the day celebrate individuality and challenging stereotypes. They empower children and adults wtih the freedom to be who they want to be and to have compassion and empathy for others who may be different. Available on Amazon.com.

DVD: ***"Merchants of Cool: A Report on the Creators & Marketers of Popular Culture for Teenagers."*** PBS "Frontline" Special. 2001. www.shoppbs.org

 ALL RIGHTS RESERVED. © 2014 FAMILY EMPOWERMENT NETWORK™

Film: *"Miss Representation."* Dir. Jennifer Siebel Newsom. 2011. www.missrepresentation.org

Organization: *Campaign for a Commercial-Free Childhood* www.commercialfreechildhood.org

DIGITAL TECHNOLOGY IMPACT

Alone Together: Why We Expect More from Technology and Less from Each Other by Sherry Turkle, PhD. NY: Basic Books, 2011.

Disconnect: The Truth about Cell Phone Radiation, What the Industry Has Done to Hide It, and How to Protect Your Family by Debra Davis, PhD, MPH. NY: Penguin Group, 2010.

"Is Facebook Making Us Lonely?" by Stephen Marche in *Atlantic Monthly*, May 2012. Available online at http://www.theatlantic.com/magazine/archive/2012/05/is-facebook-making-us-lonely/8930/

"The Keyboard and the Damage Done" by Clifford Nass, PhD, in *Pacific Standard*, May/June 2012, pp. 22-25. Available online as "Is Facebook Stunting Your Child's Growth?" at http://www.psmag.com/culture/is-facebook-stunting-your-childs-growth-40577/

The Shallows: What the Internet is Doing to Our Brains by Nicholas Carr. NY: W.W. Norton & Co., 2010.

Talking Back to Facebook: The Common Sense Guide to Raising Kids in the Digital Age by James P. Steyer. NY: Scribner, 2012.

Unplug Your Kids: A Parent's Guide to Raising Happy, Active, and Well-Adjusted Children in the Digital Age by David Dutwin. Avon, MA: Adams Media, 2009.

Video Games & Your Kids: How Parents Stay in Control by Hilarie Cash, PhD, and Kim McDaniel, MA. Enumclaw, WA: Idyll Arbor Press, 2008.

Virtual Child: The Terrifying Truth About What Technology is Doing to Children by Cris Rowan. 2010.

DVD: *"Growing Up Online."* PBS "Frontline" Special. 2008. www.shoppbs.org

Film: *"No Time to Think."* Dir. Brian Huston and Brian Grubb. Road Trip Productions. 2013. www.notimetothink.net

Organization: *Common Sense Media* www.commonsensemedia.org

GIRLS

The Curse of the Good Girl by Rachel Simmons. NY: Penguin Books, 2010.

Dads and Daughters: How to Inspire, Understand, and Support Your Daughter by Joe Kelly. NY: Three Rivers Press, 2003.

The Female Brain by Louann Brizendine, MD. NY: Broadway Books, 2006.

© 2014 FAMILY EMPOWERMENT NETWORK™ ALL RIGHTS RESERVED.

For All Our Daughters: How Mentoring Helps Young Women and Girls Master the Art of Growing Up by Pegine Echevarria. Worcester, MA: Chandler House Press, 1998.

Growing a Girl: Seven Strategies for Raising a Strong, Spirited Daughter by Barbara Mackoff. NY: Dell, 1996.

The Mother-Daughter Book Club (Harper Perennial, 2007) and *100 Books for Girls to Grow On* (Wm. Morrow, 1998) by Shireen Dodson.

The Mother-Daughter Project: How Mothers and Daughters Can Band Together, Beat the Odds and Thrive Through Adolescence by SuEllen Hamkins, MD, and Renee Schultz, MA. NY: Hudson Street Press, 2007. www.themother-daughterproject.com

Nourishing Your Daughter: Help Your Child Develop a Healthy Relationship with Food and Her Body by Carol Beck, MS. NY: Perigee Trade, 2001.

Raising Our Daughters: The Ultimate Parenting Guide for Healthy Girls and Thriving Families by Kathy Masarie, M., Jody Bellant Scheer, MD, and Kathy Keller Jones, MA. Portland, OR: Family Empowerment Network, 2009.

Reviving Ophelia: Saving the Selves of Adolescent Girls by Mary Pipher. NY: Riverhead Trade, rev. 2005.

DVD: *"Empower Our Girls: Seven Strategies That Work"* with Kathy Masarie, MD. 2010. www.family-empower.com

DVD: *"A Girl's Life with Rachel Simmons."* PBS "Frontline" Special. 2009. www.shoppbs.org

Film: *"Finding Kind."* Dir. Lauren Parsekian. 2011. http://findingkind.indieflix.com/movie/

Organization: *The Dad Man* and *Dads & Daughters*®: Great resource for dads & stepdads. Fathers are a powerful, yet largely untapped resource in our society. On this site, you will learn how men can be better fathers, and how everyone can activate fathers to help enrich and strengthen our families, communities, organizations, workplaces, and schools. www.thedadman.com

Organization: *Girls' Circle*®: Promotes girls' resiliency and connection by equipping group facilitators with skills and resources to hold girls' support groups in their communities. The Girls' Circle Facilitator Activity Guide, Complete Set, Facilitator's Manual, and many other resources are available at www.onecirclefoundation.org.

Organization: *Girls Inc.*®: Inspires all girls to be strong, smart, and bold. Publications include "Know Your Rights: An Action Kit for Girls," "Money Matters: An Economic Literacy Kit for Girls," "In Their Own Words: Young Women Write About Their Lives," "Luann Becomes a Woman," and others available at www.girlsinc.org.

Organization: *Hardy Girls Healthy Women*: Dedicated to the health and well-being of girls and women, so that all girls and women experience equality, independence, and safety in their everyday lives. www.hghw.org

Organization: *New Moon Girls*®: An online community where girls create and share poetry, artwork, videos, and more—all in a fully moderated, educational environment designed to build self-esteem and positive body image. www.newmoon.com (for girls 8-14)

ALL RIGHTS RESERVED. © 2014 FAMILY EMPOWERMENT NETWORK™

Navigating Friendship and Social Groups

1
2
3
4
5
6
7
8

Lee Ogle, Asst. Teacher and Artist

chapter four

Navigating Friendships and Social Groups

"A friend may well be reckoned the masterpiece of nature."
– Ralph Waldo Emerson

We all have a need to belong. From the time we are babies, we belong to a social group. Parents, immediate family, and extended family members help children to develop a sense of security and belonging, while teaching them the social rules and cultural expectations that will influence their future relationships. As children develop their independence, they will experience different types of social expectations and norms. They will draw, however, upon their first experiences at home as a way to check in and determine their comfort levels before moving further out into the world.

Within a loving circle of parents, siblings, and close relatives, a child learns the basics of friendship and how to belong to a group. He practices give and take, enjoys the satisfaction of being close to others, and learns how to control himself and cooperate, be respectful of differences, and empathize. In short, he learns the priceless skills he will use in relationships throughout his lifetime.

As humans, we thrive when our relationships have depth. Indeed, good friends are good for us—as the human brain is primed to connect and through relationships we grow to be ourselves. As neuroscientist Daniel Siegel says in *The Whole-Brain Child* (p. 122), "The 'me' discovers meaning and happiness by joining and belonging to a 'we.'"

Eventually, a child will find himself in situations where he can choose the group(s) to which to belong. Through group experiences, the child learns decision-making skills and how to navigate relationships with others who may share common interests, common values, and views. At other times, kids encounter groups to which they want to belong, but members of those groups may not share core values; these conflicts can provide more opportunities for growth and development in kids' social lives.

This chapter of *Face to Face* deals with developing friendships and navigating social groups. In the first section, "Planting the Seeds of Friendship," we

What are the conditions that support children to become authentically themselves within their social worlds? What causes them to experience challenges and difficulties? What is "normal"? When should adults intervene? Within this context, in this chapter, we will explore friendship in three sections:

Part I: Planting the Seeds of Friendship

Part II: Finding a Place in the Group

Part III: Choosing Healthy, Not Harmful

Empowering you with information, we encourage parents and loving caregivers to be proactive about modeling positive connection for your children and helping them to learn the skills they need to navigate social groups and form lasting friendships.

© 2014 FAMILY EMPOWERMENT NETWORK™ ALL RIGHTS RESERVED.

examine the parents' role in children's friendships, the differences in boys' and girls' friendships, and the developmental stages of kids' social lives. Then, in "Finding a Place in the Group," we look at popularity, social groups, the spectrum of behavior one might expect to see in various groups, and how we can best support our children as they go through the ups and downs of the relationships in their lives. We conclude with a close look at choosing healthy, rather than harmful behavior and relationships. By helping our kids to master the art of connection, we will help them to build lasting friendships that will enrich their lives and satisfy their innate need to belong.

PART I: PLANTING THE SEEDS OF FRIENDSHIP

Friendship Starts at Home

As parents, we create the home base from which our children venture out into a sometimes daunting world. Because our initial caring relationship with our young children becomes a template for their future friendships, being fully engaged with them is one of the single most important ways we can promote their healthy development. Our being responsive and attuned to our child ultimately will give him the confidence and information about how to attune to others and himself.

What happens, however, when a child regularly feels she can't get a parent's attention? How confident will this child feel as she ventures into the world of peers? We may think, "That doesn't happen at my house. We give our child(ren) lots of attention." In our Digital Age, getting parents' attention can be surprisingly difficult. Can we tear ourselves away from our screens or smartphones and really focus on a person? Some children may grow

up believing they are less important than their parents' technology. For example, if Mom picks you up from preschool every day glued to her phone and doesn't really greet you, you might conclude you were less important than her phone. Here's another example:

> **EMPATHY**
>
> Your child's emotional intelligence is equally as important, if not more important, to her lifelong well-being as her academic journey.

Third grader Colin looks forward to wrestling and hanging out with his father each evening. His dad loves him dearly but is also intent on making money on Ebay every evening after work. Colin asks his father to play, and his father replies he will in five minutes, but, 20 minutes later, Dad is still glued to the screen. Colin, meanwhile, feels upset and unimportant because he can't get his father's attention. This carries over into his attitude throughout the next day. Fortunately for Colin, his dad notices what happened and recommits to being available before bedtime and sets a timer when he needs "just five more minutes."

When we slow down our own lives enough to really be present with our children, we set up the ideal conditions for brain development, for connection, and for resiliency. And we plant the seeds for our child's growing ability to create friendships.

In addition to being cognizant of our own relationship with our child, parents also have the responsibility to slowly introduce children to the wider world. The younger the child, the more instrumental we are in facilitating social interactions through neighborhood playdates and family gatherings. As kids transition through develop-

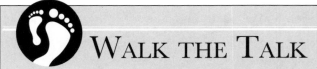

> **WALK THE TALK**
>
> *"What we are teaches the child more than what we say, so we must be what we want our children to become."*
> – Joseph Chilton Pearce, *Teaching Children to Love*

ALL RIGHTS RESERVED. © 2014 FAMILY EMPOWERMENT NETWORK™

mental stages, our role changes. For example, a five-year-old is happy to have us monitor and redirect during a playdate, whereas a 10-year-old may not want us getting involved in the ups and downs of play. She may, however, love a listening ear later when reflecting on her day. During teen years, adolescents worry that adults may get over-involved or over-react, but they still long to have a parent who listens well and understands and has faith in them.

Often a child's temperament informs his friendship experience. We all have temperament differences that determine whether we have more introverted or extroverted personalities. Some of us, therefore, are naturally contented to be with one or two friends, whereas others seek out many friends. In addition, some children will make and keep friends with ease, and they won't need much help from us other than transportation or a listening ear. Other children will need more support creating even a few good connections.

Talk to your children about this continuum of different friendship styles and needs. Share stories from your own childhood to illustrate concepts. As parents, being invested in our children's friendships is normal. We all want our kids to be well liked. Some of us even venture into wanting our kids to be popular. One sure thing is that each child is an individual. What leads someone to be friends with another is sometimes a mystery.

What do you do if your child seems not to have friends? First, note that there is no right number of friends. Some kids will have one or two, and others will have many. If your young child, however, says, "No one will play with me," listen very carefully and allow space for the story to unravel. Often, little kids exaggerate about someone who wouldn't play with them on one particular day, turning the situation into: "I don't have *any* friends." Remind your child that every day is a new day.

If, after further questioning, it seems your child really has no friends, you can support him or her by brainstorming

SAFE HAVENS

In general, children benefit from having a friend or two at school and one or two neighborhood or family friends. If they have more, that's fine, but not necessary. Think quality rather than quantity.

options. For example, you might expose him to new and different environments. A child who doesn't do well in a crowded school might flourish in scouts or a youth group. Another strategy for fostering friendships in young children is by spending time with your friends and their children so the kids grow up like cousins. (Warning: This can backfire.)

Also, consider if your child needs extra support with social skills. Role playing, rehearsing, and direct teaching can be helpful in making friends, especially in today's times when kids are exposed to so much negative modeling. If your young child wants to play with other children but the interactions are repeatedly not going well, we suggest reading **"Making a Plan for Success in Play: Extra Help for Children with Perspective-Taking Difficulties"** by Deanne Nelson and Katie Willis of the Children's Developmental Health Institute. Nelson and Willis offer very specific strategies that can be useful for young children who need specific work with perspective taking and the give-and-take of play.

Helping our children to foster friendships is important work. Through fun times, trials, and tribulations, real friends will make room for your child to become himself, encouraging growth while providing support. You might also enjoy reading and sharing Glenda Montgomery's story below, which illustrates the importance of helping children cultivate their social lives, so they "feel the warmth of significance and belonging":

> *"When I was in seventh grade, we did an experiment at school with plants. We tucked them into the far corners of boxes, shaded them from sunlight by cardboard lids, but left a small opening for light to get in. Those plants twisted and*

© 2014 FAMILY EMPOWERMENT NETWORK™ ALL RIGHTS RESERVED.

contorted and grew toward the light no matter how awkward and difficult it seemed for the plant to do. I was impressed by that experiment and am reminded of it when I think of kids and what drives them. Like plants to the sun, children seek the warmth and well being of feeling that they matter and that they belong. These feelings are so important to them that they are driven to achieve the feelings in any way they can. Like the plants striving toward sunlight, kids aren't always aware of their striving. When they feel the warmth of significance and belonging, they blossom; without it they are off kilter and agitated and will use their behavior to try to elicit those feelings, sometimes in unskilled ways that draw negative attention rather than positive." – Glenda Montgomery, Positive Discipline Instructor and Trainer

Looking at Friendship Developmentally

"Wishing to be friends is quick work, but friendship is a slow ripening fruit." – Aristotle

Being able to make and keep friends is not only natural for our brains but also critical to our well-being, health, and probably to our survival in ancient times. Yet learning to be a good friend is a slow process developed through experience.

As noted in the last section, as parents and caring adults, we can support children in honing their friendship skills even before their preschool years by facilitating social interactions with relatives, neighbors, or the children of close friends. By the time they are ready to take toddler classes, go to library story time, or attend pre-school, children begin to discover the world around them. With the guidance of parents and loving caregivers, they can learn how to transition from their "me"-centered world to an ability to engage in community with other young children and their families. By expressing their needs when they are hungry or if they can't see because someone is sitting in front of them at a puppet show–and by learning how to take turns by waiting for a park swing–young children begin to exercise the skills necessary to navigate social relationships.

Well-known author and psychologist Michael Thompson has extensively studied the evolution of children's friendships and describes their three developmental stages in his book, *Best Friends, Worst Enemies*:

- Ages 3-7: Learning to sustain play
- Ages 8-12: Finding a place in the group
- Ages 13-20: Developing more intimate friendships

MORE PLAY PLEASE

Here are some ways of being pro-active about prioritizing play:

- At home, let children play freely (of course, with light supervision), skin their knees, get bored, learn from the stickiness of life! In doing so, you'll be giving them the opportunity to build a repertoire of positive strategies for facing life's challenges and building healthy relationships.

- Advocate for a minimum of one gym class and three recess breaks/day in school. (Stuart Brown, author of *Play*, says that "adequate recess time leads to increased long-term academic accomplishments.")

- Advocate for no homework weekends and holidays. See Race to Nowhere's "Take the Homework Pledge" web page (www.racetonowhere.com) or Alfie Kohn's book, *The Homework Myth: Why Our Kids Get Too Much of a Bad Thing.*

- Allow your kids to play outside again, to undo the damage we've done with a "stranger danger" approach to personal safety. See the Children and Nature Network (www.childrenandnature.org) and the inspirational film *Play Again* (www.playagainfilm.com).

ALL RIGHTS RESERVED. © 2014 FAMILY EMPOWERMENT NETWORK™

Stage 1–Learning to Sustain Play

Caring friendships outside of the family may begin in infancy, but it is between three and seven years of age when children gradually learn how to sustain play–to make play fun for everyone and to keep play going. Everyone is learning to be a good friend during this time, and every child needs practice.

As parents and loving caregivers, we have a primary role in teaching friendship skills and setting up opportunities for practice. We can focus on sharing and taking turns, not taking things out of other people's hands, being polite, listening to others, controlling one's temper, and problem solving, as well as redirecting when needed. Indeed, the traits that foster friendships are willingness to share, willingness to cooperate, skills in joining the play of another child, and possessing a sense of humor. All of these make establishing friendships much easier and form the basis of our most important life skills. Then, amidst the hubbub and challenge of sustaining the free play that children relish so deeply, they discover how to be a good friend. In essence, learning the give-and-take of reciprocal play is the great developmental achievement of this first stage of friendship. For a special look at the power of play, read **"The Power of Play"** at the end of the chapter.

Stage 2–Finding a Place in the Group

By eight to 12 years of age, children typically begin to enter group settings on their own (e.g., school, church group, dance class, etc.) and to learn social norms and expectations outside their families. Truly, every child needs to have places in the world he belongs and feels accepted for who he is. There often is pressure for that to happen in school; unfortunately, it doesn't for many kids. This is when parents can really help, by finding and connecting their children to groups and safe havens where the kids naturally "fit in."

Some children flourish during this stage, whereas others question their safety and take more time to find friends and feel comfortable. Some of this has to do with the temperament of the child. Extroverted kids easily enjoy being around others, whereas introverted children might prefer more time alone. (Both extroverts and introverts have satisfying social relationships, but extroverts get energy from being with people, whereas introverts get energy from being alone.) As parents and caregivers, our job is to help children find the right balance of social interaction in developmentally appropriate situations.

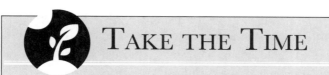

TAKE THE TIME

Help Your Child Navigate Friendship

- Set clear behavioral expectations for your child. Communicate how you expect him to treat others at home and wherever he goes.
- Teach your child to be friendly and fair, to treat others as she would like to be treated.
- Empower your child to stand up for himself–to choose what's "right" rather than what's "cool," to follow his values rather than just go along with others to be "nice."

When in settings where children first try out their own wings, the hope is that each child will receive the needed personal guidance from the teacher, instructor, or caregiver. Because this is not always the case, parents can play the most important role of ensuring that their child be given the individual attention he needs to navigate his new, bigger social world successfully. One way to know if a child's needs are being met in the group environment is by listening to her "stories" when she returns home, paying close attention to her responses to her experiences and not over reacting. Children who have parents or loving caregivers to talk to, share stories with, and receive support from are better able to manage difficult situations

© 2014 FAMILY EMPOWERMENT NETWORK™ ALL RIGHTS RESERVED.

and maintain important relationships. Nurturing relationships truly starts at birth and is a life-long process!

When children are finding a place in the group during these middle years, navigating friendship can be challenging. In addition to maintaining individual friendships, during this stage children have the added job of learning how to handle group dynamics. This requires sufficient cooperation skills and often involves competition, which Michael Thompson calls "measuring up." Friendships can be so complicated in this middle stage, in fact, that our children really benefit from a neighborhood or family friend with whom they can navigate life in a more relaxed way. Michael Thompson refers to these home friendships as the "back roads of life," compared to the "super highways" of groups at school (*Best Friends, Worst Enemies*, pp. 11-12). Although learning group dynamics takes practice and can be challenging, gradually most children do develop a balanced group of friends, at school and at home.

By the end of elementary school, social groups tend to have a very powerful influence on children. For better or for worse, groups begin to set the standards and norms for relationship interactions in the middle years. From our experiences as educators and counselors, we have observed that children whose parents teach the Golden Rule of treating others as you would like to be treated–and who moderate screen time–often have an easier time remaining true to themselves during this period.

As children move into the tween years, they gradually seek out an increasing amount of independence from their parents and caregivers. This process of individuation is an important part of identity formation and a normal part of childhood development. It can, however, create some stress in family relationships simply because kids at this age may want to try something different. As parents, we may not agree with their choice of friends or we may fear that our child may get hurt or be disappointed. We need, however, to allow kids at this age to explore, while maintaining a strong presence for support when needed. Wendy Mogel, in her book *The Blessings of a B Minus*, gives this poignant advice for parents: "Be compassionate and concerned, but not enmeshed."

At this stage, it also may be helpful for caregivers to shift into a new role of "guide." In this role, we mentor, coach, model, and encourage kids to try new things, make new friends, and treat their old friends kindly. We also support them through their achievements as well as through the inevitable hurts and challenges that come along with new experiences.

The only way kids truly learn how to navigate their social worlds is through real-life experience. While often difficult for parents to watch, children will undoubtedly encounter many ups and downs as they develop socially, but we must remember that each child's successes and challenges as a problem solver, negotiator, mediator, and friend will help him to hone invaluable skills. Although parents are always beneficial as loving listeners, if we repeatedly rescue our children during difficulties, the children will not grow from their own successes or failures.

Maintaining a clear perspective on our children's friendships and knowing that they need to have their own personal experiences during this stage is an important aspect of allowing children to individuate. A scenario that can cause us to lose perspective on friendship during

---

IS YOUR CHILD STRUGGLING WITH FRIENDSHIPS?

If your child has difficulty making and maintaining friends, observe to see if he or she is having difficulty with impulsivity, being short-fused, speaking disrespectfully, or exclusivity. For ideas on teaching anger and impulse control, see the article **"Tips for Coping with Anger and Impulsivity: Learning Self Regulation."**

ALL RIGHTS RESERVED. © 2014 FAMILY EMPOWERMENT NETWORK™

this stage is when we allow ourselves to be triggered by our children's experiences. Popularity, for example, may be a trigger for both parents and kids. While we all want our children to be well liked, striving to be popular is an elusive goal that often requires sacrificing who we really are. Also, friendships based on popularity and idealization often do not leave room for the nuanced complexity of true friendship. Remind yourself how irrelevant it is at your current stage of life who was popular in middle school or high school!

Stage 3–Developing More Intimate Friendships

During this third developmental stage, one task of adolescence is to individuate from the "first family" and develop a "second family" made up of trusted friends. Intimate friendships can be vital to a teen's mental

> *"Nature's way for juveniles to achieve maturation . . . is a story of paradox: It is dependence and attachment that foster independence and genuine healthy separation."*
>
> – Charlene Spretnak, *Relational Reality*

health, as close friends (and their families) can help compensate for stresses in a teen's life. True friends keep you in mind and make sure you are safe.

With this shift in autonomy, friendships become more complex for our children, and the benefits and liabilities of groups become an even greater issue. In fact, teen friendship groups, which are often coed, can be a wonderful protective factor–just as they can lead kids into trouble. For example, when kids experience inevitable friendship losses, other friends within the group (along with parents) can play an important supportive role. And when girls and guys start dating, they need to remember to keep their other friendships strong, so they have other friendships to fall back on when needed.

Despite the natural and critically important individuation process, teens also need time at home with family. Family remains the valuable counterpoint to the stress and busyness of their teen culture. Herein lies a paradox: As important as teen friendships are in the healthy development of autonomy, they must not be the substitute for trust-filled caring relationships with adults. This principle is at odds with an idea that has gained currency in our culture recently–that we need to separate from our adolescent kids in order for them to be successful. To the contrary, research shows that the teens most connected to their parents are also the most capable of navigating skillfully the turbulence of this stage of life ("Protecting Adolescents from Harm," *Journal of the American Medical Assn.*, Sept. 1997, Vol. 278, No. 10: pp. 823-32).

Unfortunately, some teens get "lost" and immerse themselves in their "second family" of peers. One way to help ensure that your teen spends time with you and your family is to establish traditions and rituals. The earlier you start the better, and it's never too late. Some examples include:

TOP TEN FRIENDSHIP TIPS

According to a group of teens at a local high school, here are the top ten friendship tips for making and keeping friends—a list you might like to share with your children:

1. Show your friends kindness and respect.
2. Stick up for your friends.
3. Be supportive when your friends need help or advice.
4. Tell the truth (but be kind about it).
5. If you hurt a friend, ask for forgiveness.
6. If a friend hurts you, give forgiveness.
7. If you make a promise, keep it–even if a "better offer" comes along.
8. Put some effort into your friendships, otherwise your friends might feel neglected.
9. Don't try to change your friends; accept them the way they are.
10. Treat your friends the way you want them to treat you (the Golden Rule).

We would add one more thing:
Always be thankful for your true friends.

© 2014 FAMILY EMPOWERMENT NETWORK™ ALL RIGHTS RESERVED.

- Each parent going on a date with each child each week/month. The activity should be something both enjoy such as building a model airplane or a bird house, going putt-putt golfing or on a bike ride, or getting ice cream together.

- Having Family Night once a week or making homemade pizza and playing board games every Friday night.

- Having a habit of stopping activity and cuddling on a comfy couch when your child is distressed and needs to talk.

- Getting teens involved in planning family trips and vacations.

The bottom line is that teens need the security of having an adult (better yet several adults or mentors) who is there for them, someone to help them find their way and understand their lives. Teens who are overly peer-oriented and who lack a simultaneous strong connection to their families (or a friend's or relative's family) are more susceptible to insecurity, emotional hardening, and general aimlessness, as Charlene Spretnak reports in her book, *Relational Reality* (pp. 31-38).

Given the challenges teens face growing up, an important aspect of friendship during this stage is learning to set boundaries for safety. Parents can play a critical role by setting appropriate expectations for teens such as no drinking and driving. Another way parents can help is by teaching Internet, texting, and social networking etiquette and enforcing screen time limits. At times, you have to be your teen's frontal lobe! (Remember, the frontal lobe—which is in development until approximately age 25—has

the executive functioning task of assessing, "Is what I am about to do a safe and good decision?") One mother of several teenagers resorted to turning off the family Internet connection before going to bed. Of course, our long-range goal is that teens learn to set appropriate boundaries for themselves in relation to others–and that they support each other in making healthy decisions. For example, teens need to have a clear understanding of sexual harassment and the importance of learning to say "No," while building clarity about the **"Ingredients of a Healthy Relationship"** (see page 4:20).

So, what can parents do to support their teens in developing healthy friendships and friendship skills? Because teens' social lives flourish in organized supervised activities, parents can help by getting teens involved in activities such as music, youth groups, clubs, sports teams, volunteering, Scouts, or neighborhood work. Other teens may need help making choices on the way to spend their time. Parents can support those kids by discouraging the tendency to spend hour after hour playing video games and surfing the Internet. Agreements about time spent using digital technology can be invaluable! Adolescence is a critical period for learning social skills, and screen time directly interferes with this process. Even text messaging, in the extreme, interferes with the face-to-face time that humans need to develop good social skills. Finally, while we remain connected to them and simultaneously encourage their independence, we can help our children by modeling and encouraging them to live balanced lives. As mentioned in chapters 2 and 3, getting our children actively engaged in the wider world–as well as in the natural world–can be the key to a flourishing life. Revisit Meg Merrill's article, **"Play Again: Reconnecting Children to Nature"** at the end of Chapter 3 for inspiration.

EMPATHY

"Your effectiveness as a parent comes much, much more from what you hear than from what you say."
– Mira Kirshenbaum and Charles Foster,
Parent/Teen Breakthrough, p. 60

ALL RIGHTS RESERVED. © 2014 FAMILY EMPOWERMENT NETWORK™

It is also important to note that parents might find themselves in the position of not liking the friends their kids choose. If that happens, the best defense is a good offense: Find ways to spend time with those friends. Stock your home with good food and provide space and acceptance so they want to hang out with you. This is a great investment in the long run. You might also allow your child to invite friends to family functions and outings, building even more connection with the friend. Eventually, you may start to see what your child sees and actually like the friend(s). Also, if you encourage the kids to hang out at your house, you ultimately may have a good influence on them and be someone they turn to in difficult times.

If you are worried about the negative influence of a particular friend or group of friends, do the same as above and strive to keep communication open with your child. Under some circumstances with younger children, you may choose to restrict play to your house and school. As kids get older, they may need help learning strategies about how to be friendly with a peer who tends to get them in trouble and under what circumstances they can have a good, safe time with that friend.

CONNECTION

The Beauty of Boy-Girl Friendships in Action

With the support of their parents, two nine-year-olds, Maeve and James, are still best friends, after three years, at the end of third grade. Their friendship is not exclusive, and they both have other healthy, same-sex friendships. But it is within their special friendship that the most prized fun occurs: elaborate running games at recess; complex spying activities and code-making; fort-building; extended sessions of talking and laughter; as well as, at their own request, attending each other's recitals and athletic games.

The Tendency toward Gender Differences: The Nature of Boys' and Girls' Friendships

Gender division–boys playing with boys and girls hanging out with girls–starts as early as preschool, intensifies in elementary school, and lasts into adolescence. Children throughout the world go through this latency period and tend to gravitate toward the same sex. Often, this gender segregation makes cross-gender friendships difficult until high school, and the segregation can be exacerbated by media messages and social norms that exaggerate boy/girl differences.

While we recognize and honor that there are always friendships and individuals who do not fit the stereotypes, we are going to offer some generalizations about the nature of boys' and girls' friendships. To begin, we know that, beginning in utero, girl and boy brains develop differently. (See Louann Brizendine's books, *The Male Brain* and *The Female Brain*.) With larger communication centers and emotional memory centers in their brains, girls have a greater ability to read emotional cues. While boys can be taught emotional literacy, testosterone shapes boys' brains to facilitate exploratory behavior, motor control, spatial skills, and rough and tumble play. It is no surprise, therefore, that boys' and girls' friendships, in general, look different.

Girls seem to be relationship oriented from the beginning. They often design their play around talking and socializing in small groups and in pairs, and they have an easier time sharing and cooperating in the early years. In general, they tend to have intimate, one-on-one relationships while functioning within larger groups, and they solidify their friendships by sharing deep secrets. Also, girls are more easily swayed by their friends and need more reassurance from their friends than boys do. They are more driven to find a close friend, whereas boys may be content being part of a team or group. One reason girls focus so much energy on relationships is because they are so good at it; they are often able to cue into what people around them are thinking.

© 2014 FAMILY EMPOWERMENT NETWORK™ ALL RIGHTS RESERVED.

Whereas girls' friendships focus on shared intimacies, boys tend to enjoy more action-oriented play. Most, in general, are content with accomplishments and orient themselves to physical achievement, sports, and instrumental tasks such as building things. They have "side-by-side" relationships with one another, socializing and non-verbally bonding in "packs" via competitive games with set rules. Boys generally prefer structured, active games where they can test their skills against one another. One of the complicating factors in boys' and men's friendships is that, although boys experience the same range of emotions that girls do, starting very young, they are taught to suppress their feelings of vulnerability, rejection, fear, shame, frustration, embarrassment, and sadness. These feelings often get channeled into one acceptable emotion, loosely termed the "emotional funnel" of anger. This anger can lead to fights with friends over misunderstandings that could have been resolved with direct communication and honesty. See Chapter 3 for a discussion of the "Boy in the Box" and the origin of this damaging social norm of anger being the only emotion boys are allowed.

Another interesting difference is that boys tend to readily employ humor and teasing, as they alternate between competition and cooperation. Their place in the social hierarchy or "pecking order," based on physical prowess and size, or being quick-tongued, seems more set than for girls. Boys also are more likely to seek attention by doing risky things or breaking rules or laws. Our sons will have many opportunities, starting before adolescence, to decide whether they are going to follow a friend into trouble or not! As they grow, boys must learn—with the aid of our light-handed guidance—under what circumstances it works to play with various friends. Of course, girls need to know this, too, but they may have a few more years to prepare.

Let us now take a look at boy-girl friendships. Although they are not the norm until adolescence, boy-girl friendships can be important and advantageous, helping kids to glean the positive characteristics of both sexes and provide a healthy template for relationships later in life.

Research suggests that boy-girl friendships, including boy-girl sibling friendships, provide "unique private spaces" (William Pollack, *Real Boys*, p. 203) where the Boy Code (and presumably the Girl Code), has less power and children encounter each other, in play, beyond the reach of gender stereotypes, sex roles, and prevailing cultural mores. When parents can support these rare friendships, they are helping to break down gender expectations and encouraging kids to be their authentic selves.

Handling Conflict with Friends

Normal social play involves conflict: disagreements about what to play, arguments about roles and rules, anger over feeling left out or not being listened to, trying to say what we want without being bossy, and so on. As parents, it helps to remember the normal flux in the evolution of friendship and that conflict is an essential part of friendship, critical for growth and resiliency. Conflict helps kids to learn the important skills of negotiation, problem solving and forgiveness. Because each child has potentially conflicting needs for connection, recognition, and power,

KELSO'S CHOICE

One tried-and-true conflict-management curriculum used in many elementary schools is Kelso's Choice. Created over two decades ago by two elementary school counselors, Barbara Clark and Diane Hipp, **"Kelso's Conflict Management Wheel"** and **"Kelso's Character Wheel"** (samples of which are found on page 4:27) are concrete tools that children can easily remember and understand. The program is based upon the premise that every child can be a peacemaker. It teaches children how to determine the difference between minor problems they can handle and serious problems that require an adult's help. Kelso's Choice posters are adapted for early and later elementary school kids (as the examples at the back of the book show) and are available in Spanish as well.

www.kelsoschoice.com

ALL RIGHTS RESERVED. © 2014 FAMILY EMPOWERMENT NETWORK™

we have to do our best not to be conflict averse and to acknowledge that healthy conflict produces learning.

There may be times when a child loses a friend or has fewer friends and spends more time at home. That is okay. Furthermore, every child will experiment at times with trying on different friendship roles in his attempts to satisfy his needs, even to the point of sometimes mistreating others. It is helpful for us to avoid judging children during these times and to focus instead on the behavior itself. Then we can concentrate on teaching them more effective, kinder ways to get their needs met.

A good place to experiment and practice with friendship roles is at home. Most of us know all too well how often children with siblings play various roles, explore boundaries, and handle—and sometimes solve—conflict. When we look on as parents, it often can be difficult to evaluate the potential for harm in friendship or sibling conflict. Taking time to observe and listen is a best first strategy.

Watching our children go through the ups and downs of friendship can be difficult, yet a wise approach is often to be a "listening heart," as Glenda Montgomery describes in her article **"When Our Kids Fight with Friends."** She reminds us that friendship is a learning experience, that most problems can be solved peacefully, and that things change over time. After all, one of our long-term goals is to have strong, competent children who have relationships they can trust—and they need practice in developing these relationships. There are times, however, when we will have to play a more active role: e.g., sexual harassment, repeated emotional or physical harassment, or cyberbullying. (See Chapter 5 for more information on resolving complex friendship issues.)

TAKE THE TIME

When your child has a fight with a friend, listen attentively and caringly, but empower your child to solve her own problem. Focus on supporting your child rather than rescuing her. Act as though you are your child's consultant, so she feels free to come to you with any friendship problem. Also, watch your baggage here. Although you may hang onto friends forever, your child may move on to new ones frequently. Accept her style.

PART II: FINDING A PLACE IN THE GROUP

The Power of Social Groups

"The strength of the Pack is the Wolf and the strength of the Wolf is the Pack." –Rudyard Kipling

Kids' social groups can support children in their social lives and/or become "exclusive zones" where teasing, relational aggression, and even physical fighting may take place. Some kids are only mildly annoyed by being an "outsider," but others may be excluded to the point of being socially, emotionally, or physically harmed. In those cases, parents must be vocal advocates for their children! We will discuss this in the next chapter: what to do when normal, healthy conflict crosses the line into peer mistreatment.

You can get an idea of the social groups in your child's middle school or high school by asking about the school cafeteria. Every child knows who sits where and at which tables he is welcome—and at which tables he is not welcome. Your child could map these out for you and describe the characteristics of each group. Then he can tell you where he fits in. Ask your son, "How does that feel? What group do you want to be in? Why? Which group do you admire most?" His answers can give you incredible insight into his life and help your child to frame where he fits into the social scene. If your child has acquired strong social skills and is fairly outgoing by nature, he may be comfortable in several different groups ("floater").

A developmental task of tweens/teens is to learn how to function in group settings in addition to having satisfying one-on-one friendships. No matter which group a child

© 2014 FAMILY EMPOWERMENT NETWORK™ ALL RIGHTS RESERVED.

belongs to or wants to belong to, most groups have their unwritten rules that kids have to deal with in order to fit in somewhere. In *Best Friends, Worst Enemies*, Michael Thompson identifies five invisible rules or social norms which affect kids as they navigate the "super highways" of groups:

1. Be like your peers.
2. You must belong to a group.
3. Be in—or be out.
4. Find a place in the social hierarchy.
5. You must play a role.

Children who belong to a minority group—whether by socio-economics, religion, race, ethnicity, or sexual orientation—may face additional challenges in "fitting in." Stigmatization of differences creates added burdens for minority adolescents who are exploring and establishing their own healthy sense of self and their own unique identities. Despite the resiliency of many minority youth, stigmatization may create feelings of isolation and despair, along with loss of hope for the future and an increase in high-risk behaviors and failure in school.

Our article entitled **"Cultural Identity Formation"** describes cultural identity formation as a series of typical stages that minority youth experience. These individuals tend to move from a stage of innocence or denial of differences through stages of questioning, confusion, anger, and minority pride. Some are able to make it to the final stages of cultural identity formation, where one's minority status is positively integrated within the larger cultural context, and self-acceptance and appreciation of diversity emerge. Individuals who do not complete this developmental process of identity synthesis may suffer from persistent feelings of isolation, anger, or guilt, and varying degrees of identity confusion. Parents,

---

"[Here] is the truth about girls and popularity. It is a cut-throat contest into which girls pour boundless energy and anxiety. It is an addiction, a siren call, a prize for which some would pay any price."

– Rachel Simmons in
Odd Girl Speaks Out

---

counselors and teachers who understand these normal developmental patterns of cultural identity formation will be better equipped to appreciate and provide supportive guidance for minority children. This will help to ease the way for these youth at various levels of identity development during their sometimes turbulent path through adolescence.

The Lure of Popularity

Although children are very different in their friendship needs, partially based on temperament, something nearly all children desire is to be one of the "in-kids" or to be "popular." Many of us even think we want popularity for our kids, although we are not sure if it means the same thing to them as it means to us.

It is important to note that popularity does not always have to be negative. At least two types of popularity actually exist: popularity-as-decency ("good" popularity) and popularity-as-dominance ("bad" popularity). Consider the boy or girl who is outgoing, caring, confident, and comfortable with himself, the child who is liked by all and can "float" between various groups. Contrast that child to the "cool" jock who spearheads and gets away with unacceptable behavior such as making fun of others or hazing, or the girl who is the leader of a tight-knit group of girls who wear similar clothes, share closely monitored behaviors, and are unfriendly to "outsiders," often to the point of picking on other girls.

In his book, *The Friendship Factor*, Kenneth Rubin describes popularity as "reputation bestowed upon an individual by one's social peers." Popular boys, for example, are usually perceived by their peers as those who are the best athletes, wear the coolest clothes, and have sassy, tough-guy attitudes, a good sense of humor, and advanced social

ALL RIGHTS RESERVED. © 2014 FAMILY EMPOWERMENT NETWORK™

skills. Popular girls are often described by their peers as attractive, socially competent, fashion savvy, financially well off, and precocious about boys.

Michael Thompson, author of *Best Friends, Worst Enemies*, further explains that the basic rules of gender and popularity are reminiscent of the era of hunters and gatherers: "Alpha" males strut, marking their territory with their physical prowess and dominance like top dogs; "queen bees" flit from one friend to another, dispensing sweet words or stinging barbs, depending on situations and relationship issues. These stereotypical displays of gender behavior begin in preschool, intensify in elementary school, become deeply entrenched by middle school, and, fortunately, begin to dissipate in high school and college. By tenth grade, teens tend to be more comfortable with who they are and spread out into more diverse groups to which they fit in more naturally. Being a part of the "in-crowd" seems to slowly lose its lure.

> *"Next to food and water, friends are the most important part of a girl's existence. Girls will say, 'My friends are my life.' So when [her] friends turn on her, everything about [her] life looms larger. Things that were hard before now seem impossible."*
>
> – Rachel Simmons in *Odd Girl Speaks Out*

"Good" popularity is what we really want for our kids. We want them to be liked for who they are as individuals, with qualities such as friendliness, ability to share, kindness, assertiveness, compassion, etc., as the basis for friendship. Truly, likeability among one's peers, as opposed to dominance over one's peers, is a far more important goal for which to strive; and having a friend or two you can trust and who trusts you is far more important than popularity.

Help your children not to get caught up in seeking "popularity-as-dominance" by de-emphasizing clothes, looks, and possessions. Instead, "walk the talk" and model an emphasis on inward beauty, character, inclusiveness, and values. And, ideally, focus your attention on your child's quality of friendships as opposed to the quantity. Why? Because it only takes just one good friend to carry you through tough social times!

PART III: CHOOSING HEALTHY, NOT HARMFUL

When Healthy Groups Turn into Harmful Cliques

"Nothing seems to threaten the human spirit more than rejection ... and lack of love. Nothing can equal insults to the soul."
– James Garbarino in *Lost Boys: Why Our Sons Turn Violent and How We Can Save Them*

The group experience is a normal and important part of our lives as humans. Teens (and adults), however, ideally need to understand the difference between groups and cliques. This helps everyone to recognize when a group starts to become a clique–when power over others and exclusion start to crowd out inclusion and respect.

What is the difference between groups and cliques? What is your definition of a clique? For the sake of clarity and consistency, we define *group* as a set of people regarded as belonging together because they share something in common such as an interest in the same music or activity. We use the term *clique* to identify groups whom outsiders regard as excluding them. Learning about the rules of and roles within social groups can help you to understand the social world of your children and can be used as a talking point with them to explain how healthy groups can turn into unhealthy, exclusive cliques.

Cliques start out like any groups of boys or girls with common interests, struggles, history, etc., and are often unisex. They become unhealthy when there are qualifiers to belong. Popular girl cliques, for example, might emphasize clothing and looks, and popular boy cliques might emphasize activity and strength. Whereas many kids are content to remain in their own interest groups,

© 2014 FAMILY EMPOWERMENT NETWORK™ ALL RIGHTS RESERVED.

some kids struggle as "wannabes" and will compromise their own values and authenticity to belong to the popular group.

> *When Denise was in seventh grade, the Queen Bee of her clique would decide who they were going to exclude from the group that week. Everyone obeyed for fear they would be left out next if they didn't. As a torn bystander, Denise had difficulty with this dilemma and chose to give up her allegiance to the clique to keep her values. She became part of a less competitive group.*

Hierarchies and competition may lead to uncomfortable situations for children. Cliques of boys may establish a strict pecking order, ranking personality traits such as the boys' performance, size, and sense of humor. Girls may compete for looks, clothing, and the boy. In fact, from an early age, girls often have conflicting emotions of wanting to connect with their girlfriends but also wanting them to look bad in the eyes of the boys from whom they want attention. (See Rosalind Wiseman's articles, **"Girls' Cliques"** and **"Boy Groups"** for more information about social groups.) Below is a story about what this conflict looks like in real life:

> *Megan, an intelligent, extroverted, seventh grader attended a suburban middle school. Although she had been identified as a TAG (Talented and Gifted) student, she struggled to maintain a C average. When asked to discuss her lackluster academic performance, Megan responded that her perpetual goal was to be "popular" since being smart "wasn't cool." "I wanted my friends to like me and I didn't want them to think I was a nerd! I figured I'd start doing my homework in high school," she quipped.*

Sadly, cliques can become extremely destructive, and members can mistreat others inside or outside the clique. This peer mistreatment can take a physical or emotional form. Unlike physical aggression, emotional aggression (also known as relational aggression) is often not black and white, and putting a stop to it can be extremely difficult. Why someone says or does something, for exam-

ple, can be unclear. Often, emotional aggression is even inadvertent. It is normal, for example, for kids and adults to tease each other in friendly ways, for people to confide their feelings and concerns to close friends, and, at times, to exclude others from groups; including everyone every time is not possible! Nonetheless, accidental harm might occur, and we need to be aware of how our behavior may be hurtful to others.

MORE ON SOCIAL GROUPS

For more information about the perils of being popular through dominance–and in-depth information about social groups–read Rosalind Wiseman's **Queen Bees & Wannabes** (2002, 2009), **Queen Bee Moms & King Pin Dads** (with Elizabeth Rapoport, 2006), and **Masterminds & Wingmen** (2013). Wiseman, a parenting educator and author, also created the **Owning Up™ Curriculum: Empowering Adolescents to Confront Social Cruelty, Bullying, and Injustice** (2009), a program that teaches students and educators to take responsibility for unethical behavior. You can find the books and more information on her website: www.rosalindwiseman.com.

The Continuum of Friendly to Harmful Interactions

The continuum of friendly to harmful interactions includes a significant gray zone, where it is unclear if someone may innocently and accidentally have hurt someone or whether she intended to cause another person harm or discomfort. We need to empower children to speak up about how they are feeling and to model how to apologize when they make a mistake and hurt someone's feelings. Consider the following story:

> *"I do believe! I don't care what you say; magic is real and Hogwarts exists!" My son, Chase, would not back down.*

ALL RIGHTS RESERVED. © 2014 FAMILY EMPOWERMENT NETWORK™

The boys laughed at him and reminded him that it was just a pretend story and that he would not be heading to Hogwarts School of Witchcraft and Wizardry when he turned 11.

Chase reported that this scenario had happened a few times in the cafeteria, and I could tell he was upset by it. I've always loved my son's innocence in life and his wholehearted belief in everything magical. It has resulted in many scary "images" in his bedroom and in the basement, but it is such a gift of childhood to believe in magic. I was devastated for him that he was being made fun of for this gift.

I knew this was his "fight" but wished there were something I could do. I assumed the teasing would stop and was shocked when, a month later, after many mornings of his not wanting to go to school, he broke down in tears at bedtime to report that the teasing had not only continued but increased. I also was saddened that his close friends had not said anything to stand up for him. Nonetheless, I found myself reacting more calmly than I expected to the news. I reassured him that he didn't deserve to be treated this way and that his imagination was a special quality in him. I asked Chase what strategies he had tried so far, and he reported that he just stopped saying anything. I let him know that many times this strategy works, but that it sounded as though it was time to try something new.

We brainstormed other strategies and he decided to give another one a try, knowing that he had even more strategies as backups if that one failed. He decided to say something to let the boys know how he was feeling and practiced over and over again saying, "Please stop saying that; it hurts my feelings." When I picked Chase up from school the next day, I asked about how things went at lunchtime. He said that the boys had teased him again, but he told them to stop and that it hurt his feelings. He said they had no idea it hurt his feelings. They stopped teasing him and talked during lunch. The teasing happened one more time, so my son repeated the same thing. That was the end of it. Now lunch is "great."

We celebrated his bravery at home and talked briefly about how wonderful it would be, if he ever saw the same thing happening to someone else, if he could share his strategy. He

was willing to give it a try, so we'll wait and see if he can take that huge step to be an effective bystander.

Tough work for a 10-year-old, but successfully navigating accidental harm can be done with the right support and guidance. And, learning to manage scenarios such as these at an early age can provide invaluable exercise for dealing with even more difficult mistreatment circumstances as children age.

Now, flip the scenario: Acknowledging that you are sometimes in the aggressor seat can be difficult. Sometimes you know you are being mean; sometimes you don't. Perhaps you are a little jealous of someone or want to get back at him, so you add a slight dig to your "friendly" tease. Perhaps you are peeved at someone for something she said, so you don't invite her to a party. Life is complicated, and sometimes the motives for why we do or say things are hidden from even ourselves. We must be open, however, to the fact that we all make mistakes. Owning up to them and apologizing makes all the difference to our friends and to our children who learn from us.

© 2014 FAMILY EMPOWERMENT NETWORK™ ALL RIGHTS RESERVED.

This chart illustrates "accidental harm versus likely harm." When everyone is feeling good and having fun with teasing, it is not a problem. With name-calling and put-downs, the potential for harm is usually obvious. The difficult part lies in the middle. Sometimes, when someone is teasing you, there is some stinging truth to what he is saying and you feel hurt.

	HEALTHY INTERACTION	ACCIDENTAL HARM	LIKELY HARM
TEASING	"Razzing" or "joshing" someone in a friendly way to connect with her	Teasing someone who is a friend, but inadvertently hurting his feelings	Put-downs, name-calling, or taunting to make someone feel bad on purpose or to make your friends laugh
GOSSIP	Sharing stories confidentially between friends; venting privately one-on-one	Venting too openly to too many people; sharing "enticing" secrets; "Don't tell anyone, but . . . "	Spreading gossip or starting a rumor to hurt someone's reputation
EXCLUSION	Inviting people to a birthday party; getting together regularly (sports, youth groups, art, dance, etc.)	Not inviting someone to your party who thought he was your friend; not having enough "room" for all your friends at the party	Forming a group or club or having an event to leave someone out on purpose; interest groups that talk about their activities in front of non-members to make them jealous

Regarding gossip, most people never think of it as a healthy interaction, but, in **"Social Connection and Gossip,"** we explore the importance of sharing our personal stories. Sharing stories (or healthy gossip) keeps track of what your loved ones are up to, helps you with your reputation management, and lets you know who is not playing by the rules.

Used properly, sharing stories can be incredibly connecting and a medium for sharing insights, morals, and values. In fact, through the art of storytelling, many cultures pass on life lessons, wisdom, and history. In American culture, however, the all-powerful media has taken storytelling in a negative direction and to an extreme: Knowing the latest gossip about sports figures and movie stars has become a national pasttime, and, unfortunately, marketing firms use this revered art to convince people to buy things and to act certain ways.

The media has made negative gossiping and secret-telling the American social norm. Talking about other people is so ingrained in all of us that it is hard not to tell others about some spicy thing we hear about a friend or acquaintance. The line gets crossed, however, when we know or suspect we might hurt the other person, when we are sharing private information, when we find ourself venting to numerous people, or when we continually vent without taking any positive action. Here's a quick tip to avoid accidental gossip: Ask yourself if you would say what you are about to tell someone in front of the person about whom you are talking. If you would not, then think twice about saying what you were going to say.

Truly, managing gossip and keeping from hurting others is one of life's difficult challenges. That middle ground

ALL RIGHTS RESERVED. © 2014 FAMILY EMPOWERMENT NETWORK™

where accidental harm can happen is tenuous. When we are angry, it is important to deal directly with the person involved instead of venting. If you do vent, do so only with very close friends you can trust. Once we make the choice to vent with a large group, comments can quickly spread–and turn into rumors. Remember the game "telephone"? When you sit in a group circle, someone whispers something into someone's ear, then that person passes along the whispered words, and, by the time the last person repeats the statement, it is nothing like the original. That's what happens with venting in a group!

If we think managing our own adult venting/gossiping is tough, triple it for our kids–especially our daughters. Rosalind Wiseman, author of *Queen Bees & Wannabes*, put it best: "Gossip is the currency of girls." Information on others is the ultimate power. To keep gossiping in check, we can teach our children how easily venting turns to harm, how to stop rumors, and how not to ever start one.

Exclusion is another behavior that needs a close look. Sometimes, it can actually be a healthy behavior. For example, you don't have room for all the people you know to come to your dinner party, so you limit the number. But you don't pass out invitations in front of people not invited, nor do you talk about how fun your party was in front of them! Your friends understand, because they would do the same.

But exclusion also can be very, very harmful. Exclusive birthday parties are the worst for children. They are the main parties kids get to go to, and, if a child doesn't get invited one year, she has to wait another whole year. Rarely can children invite every child in their class to a birthday party, so parents must teach children to avoid talking about parties at school (and why) and keep invitations out of school. After all, why should we put our kids in a position we would never want to be in as an adult?

One last area to examine is prejudice. Often, conflicts that occur between individuals or groups are born of prejudice. Webster's dictionary defines *prejudice* as "an unfavorable opinion formed beforehand or an irrational dislike of a person or group of people, especially one of a particular religion, ethnicity, nationality, sexual preference, or social status." Many visual differences (i.e., height, weight, skin color, glasses, etc.) can evoke assumptions which often can lead to prejudice. According to Michele Borba, author of *Building Moral Intelligences* and *Parents Do Make a Difference*, "Prejudice is learned!" Our children are not born with prejudices and stereotypes; they pick them up from us. The key is to stop and transform prejudice as soon as it appears.

The Impact on Friendship of the Digital Age

"Without sufficient practice with observing, trying out, and experiencing true emotions such as empathy, love, and frustration, kids are often less equipped to navigate the social world." – Sherry Turkle, author of *Alone Together*, in her February, 2012, TED talk, which can be viewed at http://www.ted.com/talks/sherry_turkle_alone_together.html

Texting, emailing, and social networking are also complicating today's already complicated social interactions. Everyone is exploring how to get the most out of our new technologies, but even adults are just learning how to transfer to this experience the manners and responsiveness we typically have with face-to-face interactions. Texting and emailing, for example, make it way too easy to gossip, start a rumor, or call off a get-together–or a relationship–without having to deal with the other person's reactions.

With digital conversations, we do not receive the feedback–the look on the face, the pause in the conversation–which helps us to understand and empathize with the other's feelings. To complicate matters even more, these technologies follow us everywhere. Why is it that the false urgency of phone beeps and texts seem more important than the friend standing next to us? Finding a way to blend politeness with social technologies can be a useful point of discussion with our tweens/teens–because we are all in the same boat.

© 2014 FAMILY EMPOWERMENT NETWORK™ ALL RIGHTS RESERVED.

With our tweens and teens regularly using electronic communication and social networking, how do we help them to live a balanced life? Everyone needs a daily break from electronic stimulation and relationships. Stanford University's Clifford Nass found that eight- to 12-year-olds who spend most of their waking hours multitasking by switching frantically between, for example, YouTube, Facebook, TV, and text messaging were more likely to develop social problems than youth who were spending less time on electronics. The antidote, naturally, was that they spend more real-life time interacting with people face-to-face, looking at and listening to people. Otherwise, digital natives are missing out on social skills; are less able to interpret emotions, read body language, and facial expressions; or even feel empathy. The imbalance in their lives handicaps their emotional intelligence, which is a critical factor in life success ("Clifford Nass on Tweenage Girls and Multi-tasking," http://www.youtube.com/watch?v=68N0cjgE-L6Y).

Too much multitasking and time on technology not only affects the attentional and social emotional parts of our children's brains, and their family bonding time, but it also affects the development of their sense of self and their stress levels. Caitlin Flanagan, in her book *Girl Land* (pp. 85-86), addresses the upshot of what happens with girls when technology steals away their time for dreaming, thinking, reading, and reflecting: "For generations, a girl alone in her room was understood to be doing important work. . . . The Internet changed all that.

Today's girls leave the hothouse environment of school and peers, retreat to their rooms, and, instead of getting a break from the pressure, they reenter it. The drama of the day continues . . . ." Similar words could be written about our sons.

Tragically, social media are perfect for inflicting not only accidental harm but also purposeful, intentional harm. The less balanced and less emotionally savvy our teens are the more likely they are to get involved in cyber bullying. Teens are often impulsive by nature, and the new technologies give them the ability to do damage to countless people before they realize what they have done. It truly is a different ballgame for teens today; the speed of the timing and the breadth of the people they can reach—and crush—with the push of a button is unprecedented. The impact on the target can be so much more devastating than any teen has had to deal with before the Digital Age. And this threat can keep teens obsessively connected, out of fear that, if they unplug, they cannot do damage control.

The escalation of harm that can occur via digital media suggests that we, as adults, need to step up and set higher standards for our children when it comes to digital technology use. For example, if your children are playing video games, insist that they avoid sexist, racist, and homophobic talk or acting as a "griefer" who intentionally sets out to harass and ruin other people's fun. This is where agreements and contracts around digital use can be very effective. For other tips on parenting our digital natives through online social aggression, check out Nancy Willard's article, **"CyberbullyingNOT: Stopping Online Social Aggression."**

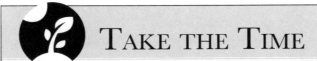

TAKE THE TIME

The Sleep-over: Honoring Kids' Needs

Kids benefit from time for close communication with their friends, and slumber parties traditionally have been one way that can happen. Today, digital games, apps, and/or Instagramming may monopolize this special friend time. When you are planning the evening's activities with your child, consider diplomatically scheduling a time with phones/electronics and a time without. Some families choose to collect hand-held devices/phones, encouraging kids to spend time together without any media distractions at all. An unexpected boon: Parents of your children's friends may be happy to follow suit when overnights are at their homes—and you will have then a coordinated effort to give your children some important downtime.

ALL RIGHTS RESERVED. © 2014 FAMILY EMPOWERMENT NETWORK™

Modeling Acceptance, Respect, and Appreciation

As parents, we provide an invaluable counterpoint to media when we model what it means to be an authentic man or woman and, more broadly, a person with integrity and compassion.

When we can model and teach kids the importance of acceptance, understanding, and appreciation of the differences among all people, we can influence the next generation to be strong, loving, and wise. We can do this by:

1. Focusing on the similarities and traits that make us all human
2. Identifying prejudicial comments and stereotypes in our own lives
3. Refusing to participate in hurtful conversations
4. Modeling respect for all people
5. Putting our children in situations where they get to know people who are different from themselves
6. Being especially proactive about interacting with those who might feel socially isolated

Maintaining satisfying friendships can be particularly challenging for children with disabilities and their parents. Life in a wheelchair or with autism, Downs Syndrome, or blindness/deafness, etc., can deeply impact typical social dynamics. Amy, a mother of three, cried as she expressed what she would like other parents to know about raising a child with a visible medical challenge. Her daughter, Riley, has Spina Bifida, is unable to walk, and spends her days in a wheelchair. Yet Riley's feelings and social needs are the same as every other nine-year-old girl. She wants to do things with her peers but often can get left behind as friends run off to play.

Consider the reflection of the mother of an autistic son: *"We've worked hard to provide Liam with opportunities to foster positive relationships with others and to practice his social skills through a Special Olympics ski team, horseback riding, and ice skating. While these avenues do allow him a fuller life—and we are incredibly grateful to those individuals of these 'mini-communities' who 'include' Liam—his desires for friendship aren't really met. Play dates and birthday parties are generally a one-way street and need to be facilitated, which becomes a barrier because we, as parents, have limited time to devote to orchestrating such activities. Also, while some families do make the effort to reach out to him and find outings and activities that include him, his emotional challenges can make participation difficult, which is a further stress on us as a family—and another barrier to meeting his needs.*

While I'm not trying to be overly negative, in reality, kids with disabilities often feel socially isolated, even when they spend a significant amount of time in a social setting such as school. In fact, social isolation may be one of the biggest concerns parents of children with disabilities have. Perhaps the segregated nature of our society when it comes to people with disabilities contributes to biases and fear of those who seem different. Sadly, most people who aren't directly associated with someone disabled tend to never even question their attitudes and beliefs, or really even give any thought to what life is like for kids like Liam or us, his parents. We can only continue to hope that social change will take place someday which can lead to more acceptance and inclusion of disabled people in mainstream settings." – Angie, Mother of Liam

How do we make this social shift happen? How, as caring adults, do we ensure that all children feel a sense of significance, love, and belonging? How can we and our children be empathic and inclusive of all?

The bottom line is, we need to be proactive and pay attention to what we do and say, to how we treat our neighbors and friends, to how we contribute to building a better world. We need to be mindful of all the children in our lives, where they fit in their social world, whether or not they are happy in that place, and how we might help them navigate to a better place, if needed. We also must empower our children with positive social, emotional, and communication skills that foster empathy and connection. And we must let them practice their face-to-face skill-building, over and over, through all the ups and downs of the natural, human, social rollercoaster.

© 2014 FAMILY EMPOWERMENT NETWORK™ ALL RIGHTS RESERVED.

INGREDIENTS OF A HEALTHY RELATIONSHIP

Self Esteem: People who believe in themselves and their own worth are more able to believe in the worth of others.

Mutual Respect: People in healthy relationships respect each other's opinions, feelings, goals, and decisions–even if they don't always agree with each other.

Trust: People in healthy relationships are honest and open with each other. Trust builds over time and is based on consistent, honest behavior.

Open Communication: People in healthy relationships are not afraid to express their needs, concerns, and feelings. They listen attentively while their friends or partners do the same.

Nonviolence: People in healthy relationships do not hit, threaten, or otherwise scare each other. They do not use words to hurt each other.

Personal Responsibility: People in healthy relationships take responsibility for their own actions and feelings. They do not blame each other for losing one's temper or making a bad decision.

Shared Decision-Making: People in healthy relationships use communication and negotiation to make decisions about their activities. One person does not dominate the decision-making.

Non-Controlling Behavior: People in healthy relationships are not jealous or possessive of each other.

Non-Abuse of Drugs: People in healthy relationships do not pressure each other to use alcohol and other drugs. They do not get high to make the relationship better.

Mutual Friends & Interests: People in healthy relationships continue their own interests and friendships outside their romantic relationships.

Hearing "No!": People in healthy relationships don't pressure or force the other person to have sex or do things they are not comfortable doing.

Reprinted with permission from the Raphael House of Portland.
Originally printed as "A Recipe for Healthy Relationships."
www.raphaelhouse.com

Discuss a difficult friendship issue you have faced with your child or in your own life.
What helped? What didn't help?

POSSIBLE DISCUSSION QUESTIONS

1) What kinds of qualities do you value in a friend? What qualities does your child look for?

2) Talk about the social skills you think are most important. Give examples of how you could teach these to your children. What are your child's strengths and weaknesses regarding social skills?

3) Discuss the importance of kids playing together during free, unstructured time to learn social skills.

4) What strategies do you use to calm down when you get angry or triggered by something or someone? What helps your child to calm down when angry or triggered?

5) What made certain kids popular or "cool" when you were a kid? In what ways are popular kids different today than when you were young? Discuss "good popularity" vs. "bad popularity" and their important differences.

6) Discuss the fine line parents walk when their desire for their kids to have friends pushes over into a "popularity quest" or forces their kids into uncomfortable social situations.

7) Discuss the differences between the groups and the cliques at your child's school.

8) Discuss accidental harm versus intentional harm regarding gossip, exclusion, and teasing. Can you think of a time you or someone else accidently harmed another?

PUTTING IT INTO PRACTICE

- Model being a good friend. Talk with your children about the qualities you love in your friends.

- Get to know your child's friends. Support your child's friendships by adding a few things that will make friends feel more welcome in your home.

- Foster empathy by practicing being empathetic and listening deeply when your child shares stories about conflicts.

- With your older children, map out the groups in their school cafeterias. Talk about the characteristics of each group. Are any of the groups cliques? Who is popular and why? Who's helpful? Who's a class leader? Who wants to be alone a lot?

- When you volunteer in school, closely observe the interactions between students. If you identify kids who are being left out, be friendly and reach out to them.

- Embrace diversity. Find ways to introduce your children to people of different cultures and backgrounds–and foster the relationships.

PUTTING IT TOGETHER–YOUR VERSION

Write down a few ideas you have been inspired to implement in your own life after reading/discussing this chapter.

_____

_____

_____

© 2014 FAMILY EMPOWERMENT NETWORK™ ALL RIGHTS RESERVED.

Making a Plan for Success in Play:

Extra Help for Children with Perspective-Taking Difficulties

By Deanne Nelson, M.S., CCC/SLP and Katie Willis, M.A., CCC/SLP

Playing with peers can be a lot of work and can have a lot of rules: In social interaction, kids must generate play ideas, share the idea(s) with others, initiate play, and sustain the play while maintaining one's presence as a part of the group. All are essential for play success and can be overwhelming and challenging for many children with perspective-taking difficulties.

One great way to help children increase the likelihood of their success in social interactions is to talk with them about aspects of play–in advance of the activity. The discussion can include:

- Describing the activity
- Figuring out what each wants from the activity
- Practicing how to tell an idea or to entice others to like the idea (need to use the most commonly recognized vocabulary)
- Discussing potential problems or barriers
- Planning possible solutions to problems

In addition to helping to increase the likelihood of success in play, using these strategies also increases the child's ability to respond to cues or assistance in the moment.

These strategies are best implemented using paper and pen/pencil to write the information while having the discussion with the child. You might try line drawing the ideas, which will visually support the concepts and show the sequence of the actions that will take place. Having the plan on paper also increases accountability and assists with sustaining an activity for longer periods of time.

When problems occur, you can refer to the plan. It will be a visual reminder of what everyone expects to be happening in the play. You also can point to the plan to offer options for adhering to the plan or for making changes

to the plan. It is important, however, to emphasize that the plan is just a starting point; children can change their minds or come up with different ideas at any point during the play, but they will need to discuss and get agreement on the change in the plan.

PUTTING THE STRATEGY TO WORK

Preparing for Play/Making a Plan

- Choose an activity
- Understand familiar vocabulary and concepts
- Understand roles and rules
- Recognize needed materials
- Decide where to play (e.g., inside/outside, at the table/on the floor, etc.)

You create a plan in order to develop a strong concept of what the child wants so that he/she can initiate and sustain successful play with others. By pre-planning play, you can help the child to increase his/her ability to describe an idea clearly, use concepts and language that peers will respond to readily, and consider ideas that have a greater chance of success. Exploring in advance what others might want out of the activity also increases the likelihood of successful negotiation and compromise, because the choices of negotiation and compromise will have been discussed calmly prior to play rather than in the heat of the moment when conflict occurs.

Anticipating Problems

During the planning stage, you need to ask questions that encourage the child to discuss the activity from various perspectives: his/her own and that of the other child(ren). Then you need to help the child think of problems that might come up–and possible solutions:

- What does it mean? (e.g., Tag means I tap you and you are It.)

ALL RIGHTS RESERVED. © 2014 FAMILY EMPOWERMENT NETWORK™

- What does that look/feel like? (e.g., I just tap soft, not pushing. Then you are It.)
- What will happen? (e.g., If you are It, you have to tap someone to tag them.)
- How will they know? (e.g., I will tap you and say, "Tag. You're It.")

A common area of difficulty for individuals who exhibit challenges in peer-related social interactions is their assumption that, because they shared an idea, everyone has the same concept of the idea. Discussing possible problems will increase the likelihood of using explicit language to describe what many will know and how they will respond instinctively. Talking about the incidentals increases the ability of the child to anticipate and to try to avoid problems.

Planning Possible Solutions

By discussing possible solutions, you help the child to prepare for the flexibility that is needed in social situations. You also help to reinforce choices that impact being a participant of social interaction versus those choices that separate him/her from an activity or groups.

Examples of "What Ifs":

- What if you don't like getting tagged? Then I can just say, "I don't want to play tag," and I will not be part of the game, because being tagged is part of the rules of the game.
- What if you don't want to be It? Then I can just say, "I don't want to be It," and I will not be part of the game, because being It is part of the rules of the game.
- What if your playmate still wants to play? Then she can decide tag is still fun and tag someone else.
- What if I have an idea or a problem? Then I have to tell someone or he will not know and cannot fix it.
- What if your playmate doesn't hear you/or listen to you when you want to tell him about a problem? Then I can say "time out" or "wait" to get his attention to tell him the problem.
- What if your playmate doesn't agree with your idea or chooses not to fix the problem? Then I have to accept his decision or try to convince him to go along with my idea or to fix the problem.

Tips for Initiating the Plan

- Enter play with an idea or purpose.
  - o Enter into the group looking at and acknowledging those with whom you are going to play.
  - o Use initiation phrases such as "I have an idea."
  - o Use language and concepts that entice or encourage others to agree to your ideas.

- Gain peers' attention.
  - o Use peer names or attention-getting phrases for a group such as "Hey, guys…"
  - o Maintain proximity, eye contact, and physical presence to show you are a part of the group but also to be heard and noticed by others.

- Demonstrate consideration of others' ideas as well as your own ideas.
  - o Use language to consider others. e.g., "Johnny, I remember you liked playing tag," or "If I play your game, will you play my game next?"

- Acknowledge the responses of peers to your ideas.
  - o Pause and respond, verbally or nonverbally, to peers.
  - o If they disagree with your idea, consider how you might compromise or negotiate.

Deanne Nelson, MS, CCC/SLP, is a Speech-Language Pathologist with the Children's Developmental Health Institute (www.childrenspdx.org). Katie Willis, MA, CCC/SLP is a Speech-Language Pathologist with the Birth to Three ESD 112 (katie.willis@esd112.org).

© 2014 FAMILY EMPOWERMENT NETWORK™ ALL RIGHTS RESERVED.

The Power of Play

By Cassandra Dickson, MA, and Kathy Keller Jones, MA

"As play is woven into the fabric of social practices, we will dramatically transform our personal health, our relationships, the education we provide our children, and the capacity of our corporations to innovate." – The National Institute for Play

What if you discovered an activity that could strengthen your child's very core, while fostering resilience, creativity, and lifelong vitality? And what if this behavior were free, always available, and your child were already biologically wired to excel at and take great enjoyment from it? Play is the jewel in the crown of childhood. It is what we remember, looking back on our lives, and it's what our children yearn to do, instinctively, on a daily basis.

Play–pure, unstructured play–is essential for healthy human development. Many parents, however, worry that play is "unproductive." Play may be considered a "distraction" that is less valuable than other pursuits. But researchers are proving otherwise: Play has been found to be absolutely crucial for optimal brain development! In his book, *Play: How It Shapes the Brain, Opens the Imagination, and Invigorates the Soul*, Stuart Brown, founder of the National Institute for Play, notes, "The truth is that play seems to be one of the most advanced methods nature has invented to allow a complex brain to create itself" (Brown, *Play*, p. 42).

Take a look at how completely engaged your children are when they play. Marvel, for a moment, at the magic of play: "Everything on the ground is hot lava" or "This restaurant only serves pink food–to fairies." Building forts, climbing trees, molding mud–the games kids make up when they play are landscaping their brains. Even a deceptively simple game that starts with "Let's use this cardboard box" is building synaptic connections.

Play comes from the child's own imagination and is engaged in for the sheer joy of the activity. Although games with set rules are certainly sources of learning

for kids, free play does not have set rules; kids make up the rules as they go along. It's amazing how fast kids can agree on complex rules, terms, and parameters of a game when they are driven to play. Here's a real-life example:

> *Five neighborhood kids quickly invent a game on a trampoline, using a ball. They call it "Evolution." The goal of the game is not to be hit by the ball; when you're hit, you have to "evolve." The game entails bouncing your way up through a ladder of characters: Toxic Blob, Human, Alligator, Horse, Angel, and, ultimately, Zombie. The first one to evolve three times through the whole chain is out.*

Cool! At the heart of this spontaneous neighborhood game is a subtle suggestion of the rich adaptation, intellectual growth, and spontaneous creativity that play has brought to our own human condition.

Truly, playing by one's self is an incredibly valuable skill, a wonderful way to develop resiliency, imagination, and a means for processing the stresses of the day. Children who can play by themselves become adolescents who have an inner life to balance their outer world; we cannot overemphasize the vital role of our inner lives in building character and contentment! Developing a richly layered internal life, and experiencing high-quality introspective states shows again and again how what looks like simple "child's play" is, in fact, providing the very qualities our children need most for life-long wellness and success.

Playing with others–parents, siblings, and peers–is where children's relationships are forged, practiced, and maintained. This last idea holds true for adults as well, as play is not just for kids. It's never too late to embrace play!

Rx PLAY

The Oregon Parks and Recreation Association is asking pediatricians and health insurance companies to prescribe play for children who are struggling with obesity, diabetes, and ADHD. See their website for details and ideas: http://www.oregon.gov/oprd/PLANS/pages/planning_rx_play_prd_admin.aspx.

 ALL RIGHTS RESERVED. © 2014 FAMILY EMPOWERMENT NETWORK™

Tips for Coping with Anger and Impulsivity:

Learning to Self Regulate

By Kathy Masarie, MD

"Real freedom is the ability to pause between stimulus and response and, in that pause, to choose." – Rollo May

Controlling anger and impulsivity are key skills that parents can teach and encourage in their children. While many in our culture never become competent in these pro-social skills, those who do are more likely to experience success, connection, and happiness in their lives. In fact, when people remain in control of themselves in difficult situations, they retain a powerful sense of dignity.

Here are some tips for learning to self regulate and cope with anger and impulsivity:

START AT HOME

Establish a house rule to "Talk only when calm," or remind your child that your house is a "No hit, no hurt home." While exact words might later be forgotten, yelling, hitting and out-of-control behaviors rarely are.

ACKNOWLEDGE ANGER

• **Let your child know that anger is a normal and important feeling,** that its purpose is to act as a signal that her needs are not being met, and that there are healthy ways to manage her anger and have her needs met.

• **Encourage your child to express his anger in words.** Suggest he write a poem, story, or letter–or draw a picture–that describes the anger. Consider tearing up the paper afterwards as a symbolic way to "throw away your anger."

• **Show your child you are listening** by repeating what she has said and expressing some understanding of her feelings. With children, it is important to help them identify and validate their emotions as they are feeling them.

• **Allow your child time and space to cool off.** Encourage "time-outs" as a way to regain self-control, not to punish. During time-outs, children can use reason to work out other ways to handle a situation or communicate their feelings without hurting someone either physically or emotionally.

MODEL COOLNESS

• Parents, your kids are watching! How do you act when you are in a crisis, after a hard day with your patience sagging, or when you think no one is watching?

• Do you follow the same rules you set for your kids? Do you talk only when calm and treat your child with dignity and respect, even when she is misbehaving?

© 2014 FAMILY EMPOWERMENT NETWORK™ ALL RIGHTS RESERVED.

• Have you made a strong commitment to teaching self-control and healthy anger management by example? When angry yourself, do you treat your partner or loved ones in a way you'd like your child to treat you?

• Have you shown your child that you can control your own impulses? Share lessons about how you manage your anger. You might use examples such as, "See, I just stopped myself from shouting at that bad driver." Tell him why you believe it was a wise decision and how glad you are that you paused and chose before reacting.

TEACH "TELLING" SIGNS

• Teach your child to become aware of the **physiological signs** of stress: flushed cheeks, rapid breathing, dry mouth, etc.

• Teach your child to become aware of the **physical signs** of stress: clenched fists, loud voice, hunched shoulders, aggressive stance, etc.

• After learning to recognize the early signs of distress that usually precede loss of control, your child can do something to calm herself down before blowing up. Let her know she can choose not to become enraged.

ENCOURAGE HEALTHY OUTLETS

• Try to help your child to become desensitized to his triggers by convincing himself through **self-talk** that he won't be bothered by them. Teach her to say to herself: "Calm down," "Slow down," "Keep control," "Be Cool," or "Be Calm."

• Teach **relaxation techniques** such as taking deep, slow breaths, contracting and relaxing muscles (such as the fists), or visualizing a calming experience or place.

• **Exercise!** Physical activity helps to expend energy– and anger and aggression create lots of energy. Have kids beat pillows or a punching bag in a designated place. Take an active "time-out"–such as running around the perimeter of the house, throwing nerf balls, or kicking a soccer ball. This helps to dissipate anger along with the desire to seek immediate retaliation.

• **Practice the 1+3+10 Rule:** This is one of the most effective formulas for self-control in both kids and adults, according to Michele Borba, author of N*o More*

Misbehavin': 38 Difficult Behaviors and How to Stop Them. Here's how it works: As soon as you feel you're losing control (when you feel your stress warning signs), do 3 things:

1. Tell yourself inside your head to "Be Calm";
2. Take three deep, slow breaths from your tummy (getting oxygen to the brain helps to calm you down); and
3. Count slowly to 10 inside your head. Putting this together makes 1+3+10–an easy way to stop the tide from anger to outburst.

WHEN ALL ELSE FAILS IN "THE MOMENT"

Distract your child by involving her in something that requires attention and energy.

BE PROACTIVE ABOUT ANGER MANAGEMENT

Work through the following questions/ideas together with your child to help him learn to vent anger nonviolently:

• What makes you really mad?
• When was the last time you were really mad? How did you handle it?
• Brainstorm five nonviolent ways of venting anger.
• What are some of the benefits of anger? How can anger teach you some things about yourself?
• List five ways of venting anger that are hurtful and destructive to yourself or others.
• Role-play a situation that might make your child angry–such as a friend being unfair in a game– and brainstorm some new ideas for handling the situation.
• Practice calming down and figuring out nonviolent ways to vent feelings.

For further exploration, see:
Adolescence, 2001 Spring; 36 (141): pp. 163-70
"Anger" chapter from *Nonviolent Communication* by Marshall Rosenberg (2003)
Building Moral Intelligence: The Seven Essential Virtues that Teach Kids to Do the Right Thing by Michele Borba (2001)
Journal of Psychosomatic Research, 2000 Oct.; 49(4): pp. 247-53
Positive Discipline Solutions A to Z by Jane Nelsen (1999)
No More Misbehavin': 38 Difficult Behaviors and How to Stop Them by Michele Borba (2003)
Raising Nonviolent Children in a Violent World by Michael Obsatz (1998)

 ALL RIGHTS RESERVED. © 2014 FAMILY EMPOWERMENT NETWORK™

DO YOUR BEST

RESPECTFUL
HONEST
CARING
RESPONSIBLE
FAIR

BE A STAR

WWW.KELSOSCHOICE.COM ©2013 CEREBELLUM CORPORATION

DO YOUR BEST!

RESPECTFUL
HONEST
CARING
RESPONSIBLE
FAIR

BE A KELSO STAR

WWW.KELSOSCHOICE.COM ©2013 CEREBELLUM CORPORATION

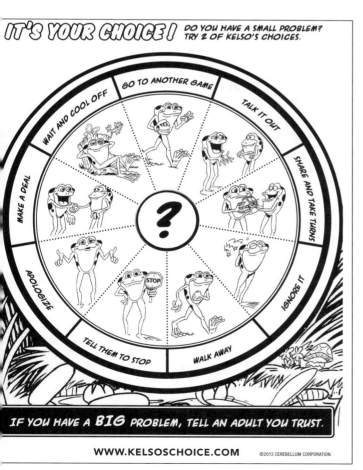

IT'S YOUR CHOICE!
DO YOU HAVE A SMALL PROBLEM? TRY 2 OF KELSO'S CHOICES.

WAIT AND COOL OFF
GO TO ANOTHER GAME
TALK IT OUT
SHARE AND TAKE TURNS
MAKE A DEAL
?
IGNORE IT
APOLOGIZE
TELL THEM TO STOP
WALK AWAY

IF YOU HAVE A **BIG** PROBLEM, TELL AN ADULT YOU TRUST.

WWW.KELSOSCHOICE.COM ©2013 CEREBELLUM CORPORATION

CHOOSE 2
AND DIFFUSE

VERBAL
NONVERBAL
MAKE A DEAL
WAIT & COOL OFF
TELL THEM TO STOP
WALK AWAY
APOLOGIZE
?
GO TO ANOTHER GAME
TALK IT OUT
IGNORE IT

GOTTA SERIOUS PROBLEM?

TELL AN ADULT YOU TRUST

WWW.KELSOSCHOICE.COM ©2013 CEREBELLUM CORPORATION

When Our Kids Fight with Friends

By Glenda Montgomery

One of the most difficult times to be a parent is when we witness our child experiencing the intense emotional pain inherent, at times, in learning to be in human relationships. We all remember the gut-wrenching feeling that accompanies the trauma of fighting with or being rejected by our friends. So, as concerned parents, we will often leap into what I call the "mother bear" mode: bristling, ready to pounce, eager to protect and to rescue. However, as difficult as it is for us, what is most helpful for our children in these times is to allow them to experience the trials, tribulations, and challenges that come along with the joys of friendships. Rather than being a rescuing mother bear, we are more helpful and productive long term if we choose the roles of listening heart, coach, and cheerleader.

As a listening heart, we listen with empathy, identifying with our child's emotions. We refrain from judging the behavior of our own child or of the other child involved. We refrain from treating our children like victims or they will begin to see themselves as victims. We don't explain other points of view at this point; we just listen. This is extremely difficult to do. Unless we listen in this respectful way, however, we risk losing our child's confidence.

As a coach, we can be available to encourage our children. We can help them to brainstorm some potential solutions or action plans. We can describe some ways we might have approached a similar problem when we were little. We can stimulate creative thought and ways of looking at other points of view. We cannot, however, force our child to take our advice. We are *available as needed,* but the creation of plans or any action must come from our child, not from us.

As a cheerleader, we can let our children know we have faith in their ability to confront difficult situations, deal with pain, and be strong enough to withstand rejection. We can celebrate with them when they have successes and let them know that, no matter what, we love them completely and unconditionally. When we listen, encourage and offer faith in our children's abilities, rather than jumping in and making the problem go away, our children learn that:

- They can handle emotional pain and that it eventually does lessen and go away.
- They can deal with rejection, and the whole world does not fall apart.
- They are capable human beings, able to solve friendship problems.
- They can fight with friends and make up with friends.
- They can stand up for themselves.

Their youth is the time for children to learn about themselves and the world of human relationships. They need practice and support. Should your child be the target of peer mistreatment, physical abuse, sexual abuse, or racism, you *would* need to step in and take an active role in getting help, as this trouble is beyond a child's ability to manage. In cases of normal relationship turmoil, however, do choose to be a listening heart, a coach, and a cheerleader. Keep that "mother bear" at bay and then stand back, allowing your children to build their friendship skills, their problem-solving skills, and their faith in themselves.

Glenda Montgomery is a Positive Discipline lead trainer and the mother of a daughter and son.

ALL RIGHTS RESERVED. © 2014 FAMILY EMPOWERMENT NETWORK™

Cultural Identity Formation

By Jody Bellant Scheer, MD

• *Living in suburban Seattle, Cindy is distraught because her American-born middle-school children, Kayla and Jay, consider themselves white, like their father and most of their classmates. She worries that they seem to have no apparent interest in their Chinese heritage. Cindy blames herself for failing her children: She worries that they will never have an appreciation of their mixed racial heritage or of her Singaporean roots.*

• *Clarys is a single African-American mother raising her children in a suburb with excellent schools but few minority students. Her son, Tyrone, is a popular eighth grader who is student body president and one of the school's top-performing academic stars. Clarys recently received a call from her son's school advisor who is worried about Tyrone's future academic success. He is worried because Tyrone only hangs out in the lunchroom with the school's few other young African American students, who tend to idolize sports and music over academics. Clarys is proud of Tyrone and is very confused about whether or not there is anything at all wrong with his choice of friends.*

• *Tom and LeeAnn are the parents of Cybil, a senior in high school who first identified herself as a lesbian in eighth grade. Their family dealt with Cybil's disclosure by seeking help from local support groups, counselors, and administrators at their daughter's school. They have made peace with her sexual orientation and want her to look forward to a hopeful future. They are currently worried, though, because Cybil chooses to spend most of her time involved with gay and lesbian political activism, while distancing herself from family, church, and her heterosexual friends. Tom and LeeAnn are worried that Cybil is harming her future by becoming socially isolated and overly invested in the gay-lesbian agenda.*

Cindy, Clarys, Tom and LeeAnn are suffering a good deal of confusion and concern for the well-being of their children. They are united, however, in wanting to raise their kids, who belong to a minority group, to successfully navigate one of the most important achievements of childhood and adolescence: the establishment of a positive and healthy sense of self.

Parenting in today's world is already complex and difficult enough for most parents, but the job is especially challenging for parents of children who differ in some significant way from the majority culture, which in America means white, Anglo-Saxon, and heterosexual. Learning about the process of forming an identity, especially for kids who belong to minorities, can help parents to support their kids while reducing their own anxieties and confusion.

Social scientists have studied the process of identity formation among minority youngsters in many settings and have identified a series of common stages that these kids tend to go through. Children tend to move from stage to stage in a fluid, non-linear pattern, and individuals can start or stop at any place along the continuum. This six-stage process, known as the theory of Cultural Identity Formation, has been developed by social researchers Cass (1979) and Fontaine and Hammond (1996). It is based on studies of the shared experiences of minority children who move from innocence, or lack of awareness of difference, through intermediate stages of confusion and self-ex-

© 2014 FAMILY EMPOWERMENT NETWORK™ ALL RIGHTS RESERVED.

ploration, to final stages of identity pride and identity integration. Briefly, these stages include:

Stage 1: Identity Confusion: A child moves from innocence, or a lack of awareness of being different from the majority culture, to a phase of confusion and questioning. At this stage, often occurring sometime in early adolescence, kids will often seek information about their race, ethnicity, or sexual orientation from libraries or media sources.

Stage 2: Identity Comparison: A child begins to be aware that he or she is different from others in the majority culture. There is often a lot of questioning, denial, rationalizing, and confusion related to this stage, due to fears of social isolation and/or prejudice. Middle-schoolers who are at this stage may feel especially vulnerable, because of their overwhelming need to belong.

Stage 3: Identity Tolerance: Children begin to claim their minority status at this stage, resolving some of the confusion and turmoil of earlier stages but creating a larger gulf of comparison between themselves and others. Adolescents in this stage may go to great lengths to minimize or hide their differences; alternatively, they may act out and be at higher risk of engaging in risky behaviors. Providing positive minority role models for children at this stage is important, to instill hope for a positive future, and to encourage self acceptance over self hatred.

Stage 4: Identity Acceptance: Children will accept their minority status and look for increased contact with similar peers. Teachers may notice that kids will segregate themselves in the lunchroom with others of the same race, ethnicity, or sexual orientation. Social isolation can become nearly unbearable at this stage, and minority children may be at increased risk of school failure, running away, or involvement in high-risk behaviors. Support groups and counseling can be of great help at this stage.

Stage 5: Identity Pride: Individuals develop a strong identification with their minority group and may devalue the majority culture. This stage can be very difficult for school-aged children, because of their dependency issues and, for some children, a lack of family, school, and/or community support.

Stage 6: Identity Synthesis: One moves from a polarized, "us-versus-them" world view to one that is less rigid and more accepting of differences. A healthy, hopeful view of life as a minority adult begins to emerge. Again, this may be a difficult stage to accomplish for school-aged adolescents and often takes place in early adulthood, if at all.

Kayla, Jay, Tyrone, and Cybil are all minority children who exemplify varying stages of cultural identity formation. Kayla and Jay are at the beginning of the process, Tyrone is in the middle, and Cybil is well into identity pride. All of their responses are normal behaviors seen in children as they journey toward forming an identity within their minority group. Knowing this will greatly ease the burden for the parents and teachers who are seeking to support them.

While children in the majority culture face individuation without the added burden of feeling so different, most minority children are quite resilient, as they encounter these additional challenges. Stigmatization, isolation, and an increase in high-risk behaviors can complicate this normative process for minority children. To thrive, minority children will benefit from the supportive presence of loving parents and well-informed schools and communities.

References

Cass, V. *Journal of Homosexuality*, 4(3), 219-235, 1979.

Fontaine, J.H. & Hammond, N.L. *Adolescence*, 31, 817-830, 1996.

 ALL RIGHTS RESERVED. © 2014 FAMILY EMPOWERMENT NETWORK™

Girls' Cliques

By Rosalind Wiseman

We like to think that girls' cliques are worse today than they used to be, but I know that's not true. While writing *Queen Bees and Wannabes*, I was struck by how universal an experience this seems to be, but it's a universal experience that no one talked about. I had 60- and 30-year-old women follow me around at parties to tell me about clique incidents as if they had just happened yesterday—all the girls' names are still right there. They told me about situations identical to the ones I'm working with right now.

I think this kind of behavior has always been around. It may start a little younger than it used to. Girls are sexualized at a younger age and will deal with these friendship issues at a younger age, too. I see eight-year-old girls, even four-year-old girls, anointing certain friends and excluding others. There are always going to be Queen Bees, even in the poorest schools. But, typically the wealthier a community is, the more of a problem this is.

One thing that is worse today is the way parents behave. I think that today's parents are either micromanaging their kids' lives or they are totally out of the picture, which is equally problematic. Kids in these cases will do anything to create space or get the appropriate attention.

But I fundamentally disagree with some critics who say worrying about clique behavior represents micromanaging kids' social lives. Instead, every time you deal with one of these friendship issues, it's a teaching moment about ethics. It's at these moments that your kids realize what you stand for.

How to Handle It

The whole issue of mean girls touches a nerve with parents, especially with mothers. Women are in such turmoil about how to raise assertive, strong women. Yet in our efforts to raise girls with high self-esteem, we sometimes lose sight of the importance of kindness. In schools I've worked in, I've seen girls with very high self-esteem who are really, really nasty.

As a parent, one of the hardest things to do is to decide how to handle these situations. Should you wade in, do nothing, or stand there and cheerlead behind her but let her fight for herself?

I think that, unless a child is in a very serious situation, you should encourage her to stand up for herself, with her skills in place. By that I mean that parents should affirm their daughter and her courage, and then help her think through how to deal with the situation. Have her write it down, and decide what the most important issue is. The best strategy is usually for a girl to get the child who mistreated her away from the other girls, describe to her what's happening, what she needs to happen differently, and have that child affirm her.

In other words, parents should be their daughter's cheerleader, but not take care of her business. If she can face this, she can face anything. Dealing with a girl who mistreats others will give her practice for someday having to deal with an inappropriate boss.

Setting the Stage for Talk

To let her know it's okay to tell you about clique problems, say something like, "Hey, look, lots of times it's normal to have problems with friendships. If you ever have a problem with that, I'll help you or we can get you an ally, like an aunt or an older friend, to help you." Then you run away. Plant the seed and run away.

Another thing girls are going to encounter at adolescence is what I call the "fruit cup girl," named after a girl who once pretended—in order to impress a boy—to be incapable of opening her fruit cup. We're always going to have to educate girls about this kind of thing. You can't stop your daughter from having those experiences, but you can give her a head's up before it slams her in the face. You could say something like this: "You might see girls act silly and not as smart when around boys, and it might make you feel bad. When that happens, come to me and we'll talk about it. Think about why the girl is doing it and how you feel." Check in with her regularly.

When do kids tell me they will reach out to their parents? The number one time is in the car while the parent is driving. Girls also tell me that, if they try to get alone with their mom, it's usually because they need to talk. Even if they say it isn't a big deal, it is. They need at that moment to check in with her.

© 2014 FAMILY EMPOWERMENT NETWORK™ ALL RIGHTS RESERVED.

One final point about talking with girls: Sometimes parents ask questions that are actually springboards to asserting what they think or feel. They say, "How's it going with Amy?" because they want to say they don't like her. In cases like these, your daughter will shut down. Keep in mind that talking with her is not an opportunity to force-feed her your opinions.

Holding Her Accountable

Unfortunately, it's really the exceptional parent who holds his or her child responsible for bad clique behavior. Recently, I heard of a woman who found out that her daughter was behind all the nastiness going on in the girl's fifth-grade class—the girl was totally the Queen Bee—and this mom believed the principal even though she was shocked. She talked to her kid and withdrew her privileges, which mostly meant taking away her means of communication—texting and e-mail. And that really hurts a girl that age. But sadly, I've found that it's rare for most parents to hold their kids accountable for these unacceptable behaviors.

The hardest work for me is dealing with a Queen Bee girl and a Queen Bee mom. Then I've got two people who don't like me. Those operating from a position of privilege don't like to be told they should change, nor do they believe there really is a problem. It's the kids on the outside who know the most about a school's social hierarchy.

Over and over again I have been struck by parents' inability or unwillingness to apologize to other parents for their kids' behavior. It really hurts parents' relationships with each other at the worst possible time. Kids may start lying to you when they're teens, and, if those parent friendships dry up, you'll be cut off from knowing what's going on, making it harder for you to keep your own girl safe.

The bottom line? Affirm her and hold her accountable. That's my best advice to parents. You don't always have to like your kids; you have to parent them. If you find yourself asking, "Who is this child?" don't feel guilty. If your girl does something mean, she's not necessarily a mean person and you're not a bad parent.

Queen Bees Don't Have It Made

One thing to remind your daughter is that lots of girls in the Alpha group don't want to be there; it's very confining. Most people look at the "it girl" and think she's got it all. I look at her as being stuck in solitary confinement, so tied to stereotypical femininity that she has no choices in life.

What's especially sad is that those girls in the Alpha clique are so vulnerable to early sex, drinking, drugs, and even abuse. That's because they need to keep the Alpha boy for status, even if he's abusive. Often these girls know their lives are a house of cards, which makes them anxious, and so they self medicate.

Girls who are on the outside of the box are much more likely to be successful and authentic. They are not frauds, not always pleasing others. Remind your girl that there are true costs to being popular.

When All Else Fails

Outside activities, such as theater or sports, can be an excellent way to help girls remember that there's life outside junior high or high school. On the other hand, some of the worst cliques I've seen have been in regional soccer teams—the girls and parents both. In fact, any time you have parents inappropriately involved in kids' social status, bad stuff happens.

Changing schools should be the last resort. You want your daughter to know that she can figure this out, and that you're not fighting her battles for her. But if the school turns a blind eye, or even seems to be helping create a bad social environment, you may have to pull her out of school. If she's unable to get her work done, if she's so distracted she can't focus—or if your gut tells you she's really in trouble—trust it, and intercede.

The bottom line is to remember that parents do matter. You might feel rejected over the next few years, but you are essential to your daughter navigating adolescence safely.

Reprinted, with permission, from New Moon Girl Media, Duluth, MN www.newmoon.com

Rosalind Wiseman (http://rosalindwiseman.com) is an internationally known author and educator on children, teens, parenting, education, and social justice. Her books include: Queen Bees & Wannabes: Helping Your Daughter Survive Cliques, Gossip, Boyfriends & Other Realities of Adolescence *(Crown, 2002);* Queen Bee Moms & Kingpin Dads *(Crown, 2006);* Boys, Girls, and Other Hazardous Materials *(Speak, 2011); and* Masterminds & Wingmen: Helping Our Boys Cope with Schoolyard Power, Locker-Room Tests, Girlfriends, and the New Rules of Boy World *(Random House, 2013). Wiseman also has created* Owning Up® *curriculum, a structured program for teaching students to own up and take responsibility—as perpetrators, bystanders, and targets—for unethical behavior. The curriculum is designed for adolescent groups in schools and other settings.*

ALL RIGHTS RESERVED. © 2014 FAMILY EMPOWERMENT NETWORK™

Boy Groups

By Rosalind Wiseman

Excerpted from *Masterminds & Wingmen* (pp. 26, 38-45)

Group dynamics have distinct but unwritten rules. Understanding what those rules are and how they're created is critical to understanding boys' social dynamics. . . . Not every guy reacts to these rules in the same way. Some guys really drink the Kool-Aid. Others openly despise or rebel against the rules. Some guys are in the middle. But one thing is always true. In order for a boy to come into his own, he has to come to grips with how these messages exist inside his head and how they influence what he thinks, says, and does. . . . . [Editor's Note: Ms. Wiseman calls these unwritten messages the "Act-Like-a-Man" Box (ALMB). In Chapter 3 of Face to Face, we discuss and outline the ALMB as the "Boy Box."]

Most guys I talk to believe there's an elite 10 percent who look like they fit into the ALMB the most, followed by the 75 percent who make up the general population and the 10 percent who hang out at the bottom but have a strong group, leaving five percent of kids who, for a variety of reasons, satellite around everyone else from the outer perimeter. Every group has a corresponding girls' group to the point that some are entirely coed, but for the most part there's limited social interaction between these larger groups of boys.

The 10 Percenters

For the top 10 percent, conforming to the ALMB is law. Those in this group aren't individuals, they're pieces of a machine. There are four defining characteristics of this top 10 percent. One, they look like they're good (less important is actually being good) in at least one Boy World sport–football, basketball, soccer, hockey, lacrosse, or water polo (depending on your geographic location). Two, their hair, clothes, walk, swagger, and slang are the same. That look becomes their social uniform. (Think of how they all shave their heads before a game.) Three, their parents are so invested in their sons' status that they allow any "bad boy" behavior from them by supporting it outright, looking the other way, making excuses for it, or denying it altogether. Four–and maybe the most important–these guys have an intense desire to be in, and remain in, that 10 percent group.

The "10 Percenters" are usually identified by seventh grade. By eighth grade, it's absolutely clear to all the other boys in the grade who is in the top 10 percent. While some of the 10 Percenters may have leftover friends who didn't make the cut, the public nature of these friendships will gradually disappear and will only be resurrected by necessity. (Maybe they're related, or their parents are friends and their families socialize, or they have a class with the guy and no other guy in the 10 percent is in the class with him.)

The Majority

While the 10 Percenters feel self-conscious about socializing outside of their tribe, the guys of "the Majority" usually feel that they can hang out with kids in other groups. The 75 percent is made up of different groups of about five to 10 kids each. Regardless of social status, all guys are still subject to the pressure to live up to our culture's standards of masculinity, so the guys in the Majority can be self-conscious–but they don't constantly think about their image in terms of the ALMB, the way the 10 Percent guys above them do. The only time a guy in the Majority intensely cares about his image is when he decides to fight his way into the 10 Percent. The parents of these boys don't tend to invest in their kids' social status or to make intense efforts to steer them into ALMB activities.

The Bottom Rung

Adults often assume that guys on "the Bottom Rung" are miserable, lonely, depressed, and the subject of the most bullying. It's not true. Bullying between boys usually happens when they jockey for power within a group or when someone goes after a kid in the outer Perimeter. . . . Guys on the bottom rung know their low social position, know they can appear odd to others, and don't care as long as they have at least one strong friendship. Many of them believe that, because they aren't even in the running for high social status, they have more dependable friends. That's debatable, but what is true is that the members of the group are usually very connected to each other and don't feel like they have to constantly prove themselves to anyone.

© 2014 FAMILY EMPOWERMENT NETWORK™ ALL RIGHTS RESERVED.

While most boys don't mind being low in the pecking order, most parents either don't believe their son ranks so low or are so unhappy about it that they can't stop interfering in their son's life to improve his social standing. When this happens, a boy may know his parents mean well, but their efforts make him feel that his parents either think he's a loser, don't understand him, or value social standing more than what and who he values. Of course, sometimes the boys themselves are unhappy with their place in the pecking order; if they don't have much luck with girls, for example, they may feel like being "cooler" or more popular would solve the problem. But the last thing even these boys want is to have their parents interfering to help them "be cool" or "get a girlfriend." Nothing will embarrass a boy quite so much as the idea that he needs his parents to get him dates or manage his reputation.

The Outer Perimeter

The Outer Perimeter is made up of guys who are seen by their peers as existing apart from the entire social system. It's populated with anarchists, pranksters, politicians, obsessed single-subject or single-sport high-achievers, and kids seriously lacking in social skills. . . .

A boy can choose to be in the OP because he understands the ALMB (even though he's not going to call it that), sees no value in joining the social system, and has strong friendships outside the school. This kid can be exceptionally good at blending into the background. Other kids don't find him irritating; they just don't know what to make of him and sometimes don't know he's there.

There are also guys in the OP whose position is inflexible. With limited skills in forming and maintaining basic social relationships, they have a really hard time understanding how they come across to others and an equally hard time reading social cues that are obvious to everybody else. These kids are either ignored or targeted for ridicule because they can be so weird to the other kids.

THE MASTERMIND AND HIS MINIONS

Within any one group, most boys have a best friend, a three- to five-boy inner circle core group, and then a few more guys who they associate with as part of their group but who they're not close to—that is, they don't do things one-on-one. Boys have assured me that these roles can be found in every group, regardless of social status. The

boys and I came up with following list to describe these roles. But also give the boys some credit; few of them are walking around obviously and precisely fitting into these roles:

- Mastermind
- Associate
- Bouncer
- Entertainer
- Fly
- Conscience
- Punching Bag
- Champion

This excerpt from Masterminds & Wingmen *presented a picture of how boy groups work in relation to each other. To go deeper and examine the individual roles in the group, read Wiseman's book in its entirety.*

Reprinted with permission from Random House.

Rosalind Wiseman (http://rosalindwiseman.com) is an internationally known author and educator on children, teens, parenting, education, and social justice. Her books include: Queen Bees & Wannabes: Helping Your Daughter Survive Cliques, Gossip, Boyfriends & Other Realities of Adolescence *(Crown, 2002);* Queen Bee Moms & Kingpin Dads *(Crown, 2006);* Boys, Girls, and Other Hazardous Materials *(Speak, 2011); and* Masterminds & Wingmen: Helping Our Boys Cope with Schoolyard Power, Locker-Room Tests, Girlfriends, and the New Rules of Boy World *(Random House, 2013). Wiseman also has created the* Owning Up® *curriculum, a structured program for teaching students to own up and take responsibility–as perpetrators, bystanders, and targets–for unethical behavior. The curriculum is designed for adolescent groups in schools and other settings.*

ALL RIGHTS RESERVED. © 2014 FAMILY EMPOWERMENT NETWORK™

Social Connection, Gossip and Venting

By Kathy Masarie, MD

"There's a fine line between a little dirt and a mudslide."
– Robin Westin, *Psychology Today*

Supporting Your Child

One of your jobs as a parent is to help your children understand gossip and to help them stop gossip that hurts. Be ready for the teachable moments. Consider, for instance, the real-life example of a conversation overheard by a mom:

Her daughter and two of her 14-year-old friends are talking about how another friend dresses. The tone of the conversation is "helpful criticism," but the person being criticized isn't present. The girls are interrupted by a phone call. Finally, getting back to the conversation, one girl says, "Now we can get back to the things we wouldn't talk about if other people were around!" (Apparently, moms aren't other people). After a period of silence, another girl wisely says, "When you put it that way, maybe we shouldn't be talking about this at all."

Whether your child gossips, is a witness, or is a target, your number one job is to listen. If situations are extreme, you will need to take steps to stop the mistreatment. In most cases, some general guidelines will help your child to manage his relationships.

The Gossip

If your child has a tendency to gossip or you simply overhear a conversation like the mom above, asking a few pertinent questions can help open a discussion with your child:

- You seem concerned about (frustrated, etc.) _____ (target). Have you thought about talking to _____ directly?
- How do you think _____ would feel if he/she knew you were talking about this?
- How would you feel if you knew your friends were talking about you in this way?
- Do you have all the facts? Are they important to share with another person?
- You've chosen to tell _____(bystander) this. Can you help me understand why you made that decision?
- Did something happen?
- Are you angry, jealous, or frustrated with _____?
- Are you looking for help?
- Is it important to share this information with another child? Does it affect his/her safety or emotional well-being?
- If you really need to talk about _____ (target) or this situation, who would be the best person to talk to? The person him/herself, a common friend, an anonymous friend, a teacher, or a parent?
- Is it important to share details or could you get by without specifics?

Helping kids understand the importance of respecting privacy, the impact of their behavior, how they may be

© 2014 FAMILY EMPOWERMENT NETWORK™ ALL RIGHTS RESERVED.

perceived, and the potential for hurt is an important part of your job. The challenge is to tell it so they can hear it.

The Bystander/Witness

Even if you believe your child is not a malicious gossip, she most certainly has witnessed it (i.e., she is told directly or inadvertently overhears gossip–or is a recipient of cyber gossip). It is difficult to explain to children that listening to gossip can be just as bad as spreading gossip, particularly if they act on that gossip or spread the gossip further. To listen to gossip is to "be in"; to tell someone to quit gossiping is taking a chance that you will "be out." It is particularly difficult for a child to say, "I don't want to hear that." (Let's face it; it's difficult for an adult to say that.)

Helping your child find ways to counteract or stop gossip, within the bounds of his/her own style and personality, is important. If your child mentions a particular situation, ask him what his role was and how it felt to be in that role. Brainstorm and role play ways that he might stop the gossip or at least not be an audience to it. Anything from "That's interesting… but that's not my experience with her" to "Hmm…I wouldn't want that said about me; would you?" to "If you feel that strongly, you should tell her" are all options. The key is to find something your child feels comfortable with and will do.

The Target

If you suspect your child is the target of gossip, decide the degree of severity. For non-extreme situations, help them:

- Try to figure out why the gossip started (some times getting to the "why" can help in a solution).
- Realize that the gossip is more about the person spreading the gossip than it is about what that person is saying.
- Remain calm, as outward frustration or anger will just aggravate the situation.
- Think about ways to shut the gossip down. (e.g., "Are they saying that about me? I wonder why someone would go to so much trouble to spread this?" or "Have you heard what they are saying about me? Ha!")
- Decide if it makes sense to confront the gossiper. If it does, how should you do it?
- Believe retaliation is not the answer. Experts say retaliation will just keep the gossip going.

Venting

Venting could be considered a type of gossip, but its differentiation lies in the degree of emotion. The *American Heritage Dictionary* describes "venting" as an action, "a forceful expression or utterance . . . by which a person unburdens himself of a strong, pent-up emotion such as anger or grief." While gossip can be based on emotion (jealousy, frustration, anger), venting is always a release–typically a one-sided purging of emotion and personal perspective.

We've all vented–usually in the heat of the moment when something is so outrageous in our eyes that we just have to tell someone. Just like gossip, it can be healthy or it can come back to bite us and others. As a parent, watch how and when you vent around your children. If you do vent (and you will), help your kids to understand what you are doing and be honest if you go overboard.

The following will give you and your kids a litmus test for venting:

- Are you venting to a trusted friend who will not share the information or use it inappropriately?
- Can your friend (to whom you are venting) take the information in context? (e.g., You are mad! You need someone to listen!)
- Will your friend help you figure out what to do with your emotion? (Do you need to confront the person with whom you are angry? Is venting simply enough?)
- Are you simply "letting go" or are you spreading destructive information? Be honest.
- How long have you been venting and to how many people?
- Do you really need to share specifics or would it be enough to say, "This friend really made me mad"?
- Who are you venting about? If it's a close friend, would it be better to talk with her directly?

The bottom line about gossip and venting is that you first have to be the change you want to see. And you have to be realistic; gossip is a part of your kids' lives. It's your job to help them decide how to keep gossip and venting from becoming ugly.

ALL RIGHTS RESERVED. © 2014 FAMILY EMPOWERMENT NETWORK™

CyberbullyingNOT:
Stopping Online Social Aggression
By Nancy Willard, MS, JD

Cyberbullying is using the Internet or cell phones to send hurtful messages or post information to damage the reputation and/or friendships of others.

Types of Cyberbullying
- Flaming. Angry, rude arguments.
- Harassment. Repeatedly sending offensive messages.
- Denigration. "Dissing" someone online by spreading rumors or posting false information.
- Outing and trickery. Disseminating intimate private information or tricking someone into disclosing private information, which is then disseminated.
- Impersonation. Pretending to be someone else and posting material to damage that person's reputation.
- Exclusion. Intentionally excluding someone from an online group.
- Cyberstalking. Creating fear by sending offensive messages and engaging in threatening activity.

How, Who, and Why
- Cyberbullying occurs via texts, emails, Twitter, Facebook messages, Instagrams, Snapchats, websites, blogs, discussion groups, message boards, chat, instant messaging, or via voice on phones.

- A cyberbully may be a person whom the target knows or an online stranger. A cyberbully may be anonymous and enlist the aid of others, including online "friends."
- Cyberbullying may be a continuation of, or in retaliation for, in-school bullying. It may be related to fights about relationships or be based on hate or bias. Some teens think cyberbullying is a fun game.
- People engaging in cyberbullying might think…
  o They are invisible, so they think they can't be punished.
  o No real harm has been caused online.
  o They should have a free speech right to post whatever they want, regardless of the harm.

The Harm
Cyberbullying can cause great emotional harm. The communications can be vicious and occur 24/7. Damaging material can be widely disseminated and impossible to fully remove. Kids are reluctant to tell adults for fear they will be restricted from online activities or the cyberbully will retaliate.

Responsible Management of Internet Use
Keep the computer in a public place and supervise. Find out what public online sites and communities your child uses and review what your child is posting. Emphasize that these are public places!

Prevent Your Child from Cyberbullying
- Make it clear that all Internet use must be in accord with family values of kindness and respect for others.
- Recognize that you can be held financially liable for harm your child causes to another through cyberbullying.
- If your child is being bullied at school, work with the school to stop the bullying and make sure your child knows not to retaliate online.
- If you know your child has cyberbullied others, be very proactive in preventing any continuation.

© 2014 FAMILY EMPOWERMENT NETWORK™ ALL RIGHTS RESERVED.

Prevent Your Child from Becoming a Target
• Make sure your child knows not to post information that could be used maliciously.
• Visit your child's online communities and discuss the values demonstrated by those who participate.
•Bully-proof your child by reinforcing your child's individual strengths and fostering healthy friendships.

Warning Signs
• Sadness or anger during or after Internet use.
• Withdrawal from friends and activities, school avoidance, decline of grades, or depression.
• Indications that your child is being bullied at school.

Action Steps and Options
•Make sure your child knows not to retaliate, to save the evidence, and to ask for help if he/she is having difficulties.
• Identify the person cyberbullying. Ask your Internet service provider for help.
• There are different ways your child or you can respond to cyberbullying:
•   Ignore the cyberbullying by leaving the online environment, blocking communications, or both.
•   File a complaint with the Internet or cell phone company.
•   Contact the parents of the child cyberbullying and share evidence of the cyberbullying. Demand that the actions stop and harmful material be removed.
•   Seek assistance from administrators at school.
•   Contact an attorney to send a letter to or file a lawsuit against the parents of the child cyberbullying.
•   Contact the police if the cyberbullying involves threats of violence, coercion, intimidation based on hate or bias, or any form of sexual exploitation.

Reprinted with permission from Nancy Willard © 2007. Willard is the author of Cyber-Safe Kids, Cyber-Savvy Teens *(2007, Jossey-Bass),* Cyberbullying and Cyberthreats *(2007, Research Press), and* Cyber Savvy: Embracing Digital Safety and Civility *(2011, Corwin Press). She also is the founder of Embracing Digital Youth (program of the Center for Safe and Responsible Internet Use), which promotes positive approaches that will best ensure that all young people become cyber savvy. For more information: http:// embracecivility.org or info@embracecivility.org*

   ALL RIGHTS RESERVED. © 2014 FAMILY EMPOWERMENT NETWORK™

Related Resources for Further Exploration

30 Activities for Getting Better at Getting Along by SuEllen Fried and Lynne Lang. Kansas City, KS: BullySafe USA, 2011.

Best Friends, Worst Enemies: Understanding the Social Lives of Children (2001) and *Mom, They're Teasing Me: Helping Your Child Solve Social Problems* (2002) by Michael Thompson, PhD, Lawrence J. Cohen, PhD, and Catherine O'Neill Grace. NY: Ballantine Books.

Cliques: 8 Steps to Help Your Child Survive the Social Jungle by Charlene Giannetti and Margaret Sagarese. NY: Broadway Books, 2001.

Easing the Teasing: Helping Your Child Cope with Name-Calling, Ridicule, and Verbal Bullying by Judy S. Freedman. NY: Contemporary Books, 2002.

The Friendship Factor: Helping Our Children Navigate Their Social World–and Why It Matters for Their Success and Happiness by Kenneth H. Rubin. NY: Skylight Press, 2002.

The Kids' Guide to Working Out Conflicts: How to Keep Cool, Stay Safe, and Get Along by Naomi Drew, MA. Minneapolis: Free Spirit Publishing, 2004.

Masterminds & Wingmen: Helping Our Boys Cope with Schoolyard Power, Locker-Room Tests, Girlfriends, and the New Rules of Boy World by Rosalind Wiseman. NY: Random House, 2013.

No More Mis-behavin': 38 Difficult Behaviors and How to Stop Them (2003) and *Nobody Likes Me, Everybody Hates Me: The Top 25 Friendship Problems and How to Solve Them* (2005) by Michele Borba, EdD. San Francisco, CA: Jossey-Bass.

Odd Girl Out: The Hidden Culture of Aggression in Girls (2002) and *Odd Girl Speaks Out* (2004) by Rachel Simmons. NY: Harcourt.

Queen Bees & Wannabes: Helping Your Daughter Survive Cliques, Gossip, Boyfriends and Other Realities of Adolescence (2002) and *Queen Bee Moms & King Pin Dads: Dealing with the Parents, Teachers, Coaches and Counselors Who Can Make–or Break–Your Child's Future* (2006) by Rosalind Wiseman. NY: Crown Publishers.

The Unwritten Rules of Friendship: Simple Strategies to Help Your Child Make Friends by Natalie Madorsky Elman, PhD, and Eileen Kennedy-Moore, PhD. Boston: Little Brown and Company, 2003.

Organizations/programs:

   Be a Friend–Lend a Hand. A program of Embrace Civility in the Digital Age that encourages young people to be helpful allies if they witness hurtful behavior. www.embracecivility.org

   Sources of Strength. A wellness program that uses peer leaders to change norms around codes of silence and help seeking. www.sourcesofstrength.org

   Stand for Courage. An organization that works with youth to provide celebrity recognition for individuals who stand up for one another and themselves. www.standforcourage.org

© 2014 Family Empowerment Network™ All Rights Reserved.

Peer Mistreatment

Artist Unknown

chapter five
Peer Mistreatment:
Protecting, Supporting, and Empowering Our Kids

"It is not enough to be compassionate; you must act."
- Tenzin Gyasto (14th Dalai Lama)

Previous chapters have delved into the complicated world of relationships, starting with that critical first relationship with parents or primary caregivers. As children grow older, they explore the nuances of peer relationships. If we value having friends, most of us learn how to balance what we want with what others want. We experiment with behaviors that make us likeable–and those that do not–and figure out how to relate so that people will play with us. We share stories, tease each other, form groups, and navigate the muddy waters of accidentally hurting and excluding others. The support we receive in our families about how to get along with others often can carry us through the negative social influences of media, screens, stress, and competition.

This chapter explores peer mistreatment (bullying). Even if your child has not personally had these experiences, nearly all have witnessed others who have been mistreated and who may be traumatized by that experience. A child who understands and recognizes peer mistreatment can become a leader, support mistreated peers, and be much more resilient if mistreatment should happen to him.

Peer mistreatment goes on every day in our schools, in our neighborhoods, in our homes (e.g., sibling rivalry, texting meanness, Facebook rumors, etc.), and even in our corporate meetings. Here are a few examples of real-life peer mistreatment which manifested as gossip and exclusion:

- *As a quarterback in football, Chris, a seventh-grade boy, has friends and social standing. Another boy, Tom, who covets Chris' position, starts spreading rumors that Chris is gay. Friends start avoiding Chris. He tells no one, asks no one for help. His grades begin to suffer and he loses focus on the team. The coach replaces Chris with Tom.*

- *When Amanda was in ninth grade, her boyfriend broke up with her. At first she was heartbroken, but, when he started dating a classmate, she became enraged. She sought revenge by spreading ugly sexual rumors about them, which her peers believed.*

Peer mistreatment has been around for a long time. We probably all have a story or two about bullying that we witnessed or experienced first hand. The digital world, however, is creating new opportunities for exacerbating peer mistreatment. From "sexting" (the sharing of sexual photos online) to creating a website to bash someone to Tweeting threats–digital technology provides youth with a multitude of novel ways to hurt and defame each other in addition to "old-fashioned" face-to-face meanness.

This chapter offers basic tools to understand peer mistreatment (aka bullying) and offers research-backed approaches to support all children. For organizational purposes, we have divided the chapter into three sections:

Part I: Peer Mistreatment 101
Part II: Protecting and Supporting Our Kids
Part III: Changing Social Norms

If you believe that your child is suffering from serious peer mistreatment, you will need to delve deeper than this chapter to fully protect your child. For these situations, we have included a list of references that will be invaluable in helping you to share information and to collaborate with the school or institution where the mistreatment is occurring.

© 2014 FAMILY EMPOWERMENT NETWORK™ ALL RIGHTS RESERVED.

Months later, she realized what she had done, apologized to the couple, and told her classmates she had lied. But it was too late. Her rumors had become "true" to her classmates.

- *The "in group" rules the social life of a sixth-grade classroom. Four of the 12 girls decide each day who will be allowed in the group. The rules change daily, but the best way to get in is to criticize another girl. The girls on the "out" haven't figured out how to create their own friendship groups. They just wait to see if maybe today they'll get lucky and be allowed in.*

Twenty years ago we did not have the research to recognize how harmful ostracism, verbal taunting, and rumors can be. Now we do. As the adults of this society, we are responsible for the social norm–i.e. which behaviors are allowed or not allowed. We can address mistreatment, but doing so takes patience and commitment, and it takes all of us! We can change the social norm by changing how we treat one another–starting in our homes, then in our neighborhoods and schools, then in our community at large. We can strive to build a world in which all people are respected and treated with consideration, even those with whom we disagree.

One person who has taken up the mantle of social responsibility for peer mistreatment is Stan Davis (www. stopbullyingnow.com). Davis is a family and child therapist, school counselor, author, and researcher on peer mistreatment who has had a profound influence on our understanding of bullying and peer mistreatment and how to support kids in this arena. His trainings and books, *Schools Where Everyone Belongs* and *Empowering Bystanders in Bullying Prevention*, have helped schools across America to implement comprehensive programs to help youth feel safer and thrive. Ever exploring new information and strategies, Davis, along with Dr. Charisse Nixon, is about to publish a new book based on ground-breaking research on what actually helps mistreated kids. Passionate in his youth advocacy, he also has been a tireless mentor to other human rights activists and his ideas can be found on nearly every page of this chapter.

Inspired by the work of Stan Davis, we begin this chapter with an exploration of peer mistreatment. Then, in Part II, we examine how to best support children experiencing peer mistreatment by addressing both short-term and long-term goals:

- Short-term goals: Protecting everyone involved, preventing harm, and enacting clear consequences that foster empathy and learning
- Long-term goals: Building resiliency, cultivating peer connections, and reducing the incidents of peer mistreatment

---

PART I: PEER MISTREATMENT 101

"You should be nicer to him,' a schoolmate had once said to me of some awfully ill-favored boy. 'He has no friends.' This, I realized with a pang of pity that I can still remember, was only true as long as everybody agreed to it." – Christopher Hitchens, *Hitch-22: A Memoir*

Based on the weapon used to hurt another, peer mistreatment takes various forms:

- **Physical:** Using physical force such as hitting, tripping, taking a backpack, touching another inappropriately, etc.
- **Verbal:** Using words to tease, taunt, slander, or call names
- **Non-verbal:** Using gestures, dirty looks, eye-rolling, turning one's back, etc., whereby hurting another's feelings
- **Relational/Emotional:** Using the target's social relationships with others to manipulate or attempt to damage his/her social relationships
  - *Gossip:* Spreading rumors
  - *Exclusion:* Telling others not to play or associate with another
  - *Silent treatment:* Purposefully ignoring someone

ALL RIGHTS RESERVED. © 2014 FAMILY EMPOWERMENT NETWORK™

TOPICS COVERED IN PART I
OF THIS CHAPTER

- Types of Aggression
- The Significance of Relational Aggression
- Insights into Cyberbullying
- Sexual Mistreatment
- The Problem of Labeling Kids as "Bully" or "Victim"
- Focus on the Behaviors Rather Than the Label
- Does the Action Cross the Line? Does It Have Potential for Harm?
- Reasons Some Children Mistreat Others
- How Mistreated Kids Can Become Kids Who Mistreat Others
- Short- and Long-term Effects of Serious and Repetitive Mistreatment

- **Cyberbullying:** Using technology to attempt to harm others such as texting threats and posting unflattering photos or rumors; this form of peer mistreatment can occur 24/7 inside and outside of school except for schools that are successful at silencing phones and deterring social networking during school hours.
- **Sexual:** Touching someone inappropriately, calling people names of body parts, using sexual terms to denigrate another, etc.

Each of these forms of peer mistreatment has varying degrees of potential harm. Thankfully, our culture, media aside, has taken a stand on physical violence. Today in schools, for example, overt physical fights are usually handled by school support staff, and the consequences are guided by school policy. But, have we taken an equally strong stand on the other forms of mistreatment? Are there policies in place against leaving someone out, spreading rumors, and calling someone names?

The Significance of Relational Aggression

Early on, "anti-bullying" programs focused primarily on direct (verbal and physical) mistreatment, and many felt that boys did most of the hurting. Then, in 1994, Nicki Crick coined the phrase "relational aggression" to identify what she found in her research–that gossip, exclusion, and silent treatment (i.e., relationship-based mistreatment) are types of mistreatment that are covert, secretive, and difficult to detect. Adults struggle to catch kids engaging in this indirect form of peer mistreatment, let alone deal with it.

Research shows that kids view relational aggression as the:

- Most acceptable way to mistreat others, even in preschool
- Most hurtful type of mistreatment to experience (second is physical; third is verbal)
- Easiest, most effective way to retaliate when "wronged by someone"

(Werner, N.E. and Hill, L.G. [Nov., 2003] "An Exploration of the social-cognitive basis of relational aggression." Invited presentation at the Aggression Workshop, Berlin, Germany.)

A question to ponder is: If kids disclose that relational aggression is the most harmful type of mistreatment, why do kids believe that relational aggression is the most acceptable mistreatment to use? A possible answer might lie in considering responses to the following situation: If a group of children excludes your preschooler from playing with them, what would your reaction be if your kid:

1. Hits them with a rubber chicken?
2. Calls them "poopy heads"?
3. Says, "You can't come to my birthday party"?

If you are like the majority of parents in a study that used this as a research question, the consequences for hitting or name-calling would be somewhat severe, such as a "time-out," whereas the consequence for the birthday party comment might be saying, "That is not nice." So, in small, subtle ways, we teach our kids that we prefer them to use relational aggression, and, thus, we establish

© 2014 FAMILY EMPOWERMENT NETWORK™ ALL RIGHTS RESERVED.

as the social norm: "It is better to leave someone out rather than to hit or call him names." We often model this, too. We wouldn't hit or name-call, but many of us routinely gossip and exclude people who have offended us.

In addition to a frank consideration of what we are modeling in our homes, we can check out the school policy in our area to see if it addresses *all* forms of peer mistreatment (including emotional/relational aggression). Does it have the clarity of this policy example?

"Relational aggression is defined by Riverdale as any behavior that harms others through damage or threat of damage to relationships or feelings of acceptance, friendship, or group inclusion. Examples of such behavior include unwelcome teasing, name-calling, exclud-

---

A SUMMARY OF THE LATEST RESEARCH ON PEER MISTREATMENT REVEALS THAT:

• 1 in 4 students have reported exclusion or emotional mistreatment at least twice a month (National Data Set [Spring 2010] Youth Voice Project of Stan Davis and Charisse Nixon. www.stopbullyingnow.com/yvp.htm)

• 1 in 10 have been physically mistreated regularly (National Data Set [Spring 2010] Youth Voice Project of Stan Davis and Charisse Nixon. www.stopbullyingnow.com/yvp.htm)

• 48% of bystanders observed emotional mistreatment of others; 54% of bystanders observed others being verbally mistreated; and 30% of bystanders observed others being physically mistreated (National Data Set [Spring 2010] Youth Voice Project of Stan Davis and Charisse Nixon. www.stopbullyingnow.com/yvp.htm)

• Just witnessing mistreatment can lead to anxiety and a dislike of school (Nishina and Juvonen [2005] "Daily reports of witnessing and experiencing peer harassment in middle school." Child Development, 76: 435-450)

---

ing, humiliating, spreading rumors, playing harmful practical jokes, threatening to isolate or to harm, disrespecting another's property, coercing, or manipulating power in a relationship." – Riverdale School District Policy, Portland, OR

When we treat all forms of mistreatment—including exclusion, gossip, and taunting—with equal consequences and clear boundaries, then we send the message: It is not acceptable to harm another in any way. We also can model and teach consideration, respect, and confidential venting to replace gossip and taunting.

Insights into Cyberbullying

It is up for debate as to whether or not kids today are meaner than they were in previous generations, although research suggests they may be dramatically less empathetic (Spretnek, *Relational Reality*, p. 41). What is not debatable, however, is that digital devices give kids the ability to magnify a hurtful action a thousand-fold; digital messages reach more people, and they reach them faster. What many fail to realize is that postings are like "digital tattoos" that can never be totally removed.

Cyberbullying has taken mistreatment to levels never seen before. In the "old days," before the Digital Age, a nasty note may have been passed in class about us. We would have been hurt, but only a few saw the note, we ripped it up, the episode faded, and we were usually able to move on. In today's world, the same note may get posted on Facebook or texted. It might go "viral," as with this tragic example:

Melanie, an eighth-grade girl, was drunk and allowed herself to be talked into undressing and sending a sexually explicit video to an online "friend." The "friend," who turned out to be an adult, posted his video recording of this on a porn site. During the school week, a former student visited the middle school and showed the video to everyone who would watch after school. Melanie became distraught and depressed, and she missed many days of school. Eventually, she and her family moved to another state.

ALL RIGHTS RESERVED. © 2014 FAMILY EMPOWERMENT NETWORK™

ACCORDING TO CYBERBULLYING STATISTICS FROM THE i-SAFE FOUNDATION

- Over 50% of adolescents and teens have been mistreated online, and about the same number have engaged in some degree of meanness online.
- More than 1 in 3 young people have experienced cyber threats online.
- Over 25% of adolescents and teens have been bullied repeatedly through their cell phones or the Internet.
- Well over half of young people do not tell their parents when cyberbullying occurs.

www.bullyingstatistics.org/content/cyber-bullying-statistics.html
accessed 9/1/13

The targeted child can get additional degrading posts from others, adding to the horror of the situation. She may feel extremely anxious and compelled to constantly monitor these messages so she can defend herself. Even though others may defend her, the damage could be amplified to such a degree that her coping mechanisms are completely overwhelmed. "The incident creates a cavernous trauma deep within her," said Elizabeth Englander, the director of the Massachusetts Aggression Reduction Center (http://elizabethenglander.com), who spoke at the 2011 and 2012 International Bullying Prevention Conferences. Stress could peak to damaging levels, reactions from everyone involved might be amplified, and a molehill just turned into a "mountain range" of damage.

Parents clearly have a critical role to play when it comes to setting and monitoring agreements around proper Internet use. You can help your child and yourself be cyber savvy by checking out the numerous resources available online, which are updated on a regular basis, given that technology changes so fast. We highly recommend the following:

- **Anti-Defamation League's A World of Difference® Institute** develops and provides anti-bullying and anti-cyberbullying training, curriculum, and resources for youth, educators, and families including a downloadable PDF entitled, "Internet Safety Strategies for Youth." http://www.adl.org/education-outreach/bullying-cyberbullying/

- **Common Sense Media** has a comprehensive webpage that features a short video, links to age-appropriate Cyberbullying Toolkits for educators and parents, and more. http://www.commonsensemedia.org/cyberbullying

- **Embrace Civility in the Digital Age**, run by Nancy Willard, author of *Cyberbully and Cyber Threats*, provides students as well as adults with a wealth of information and handouts. Go to www.embracecivility.org and check out "Be a Friend–Lend a Hand" as well as Nancy's articles in this book: **"Screen Savvy Parents"** in Chapter 3, and **"CyberbullyingNOT"** in Chapter 4.

- **Massachusetts Aggression Reduction Center** (MARC) is an academic center run by Dr. Elizabeth Englander at Bridgewater University in Massachusetts. The center conducts bullying and cyberbullying research and offers great programs and resources, many that are free or low-cost. http://webhost.bridgew.edu/marc/

Sexual Mistreatment

As founder of BullySafeUSA.com, SuEllen Fried has interviewed over 50,000 students about peer mistreatment. According to her work, although verbal mistreatment is the most common, it is sexual mistreatment (aka sexual harassment) which students, elementary through high school, generally fear the most.

Even the chase-and-try-to-kiss games of early childhood friends can be experienced as sexual mistreatment if there is unwanted, physical contact, especially if it

© 2014 FAMILY EMPOWERMENT NETWORK™ ALL RIGHTS RESERVED.

happens repeatedly. When Fried interviewed children as young as fourth grade, they reported many forms of sexual mistreatment such as: "touching someone in a place they shouldn't be touched," "calling people names of body parts," "humiliating students if they have developed too slowly or too quickly," "pressuring kids to do something they are uncomfortable about," and " showing them vulgar pictures."

As noted earlier, today's media world with its confused sexual messages, coupled with the introduction of digital devices into children's lives, opens many new doors for mistreatment. Students report that it is the combination of cyber/sexual mistreatment that is most likely to cause relentless pain. Sexting–sending or requesting sexually explicit images or messages, usually between mobile phones–has become rampant in adolescence.

Boys are not immune from the toll of sexual mistreatment; consider the sexually humiliating hazing of young men on sports teams that has been in the news far too often in the last few years. The introduction of alcohol into teens' social lives can potentially open many possibilities for everything from sexual harassment to drug-induced date rape. The pervasive use of sexual language like "gay, queer, homo, lesbo, slut" and worse has led to tragedy. Whether spoken or splattered across the Internet, homosexual accusations have caused horrifying results.

It is challenging to address sexual mistreatment, but when students are willing to raise these issues, we are compelled to match their courage with our own.

The Problem of Labeling Kids as "Bully" or "Victim"

Think of a time you nagged, yelled, or screamed at your child. Maybe you even spanked him. How would you feel if someone observed you in that instant of time and labeled you "an out-of-control, incompetent, uncaring parent"? And what if that label led to shunning you every time you went out of the house? Would this treatment

WALK THE TALK

What you say can influence what you think. What you think can influence what you do. Start by changing what you say and you will start changing what you think. When your thinking changes, your attitudes and perceptions can change, and your habitual response can change. When our habitual responses and actions are consistent with our values, we may find ourselves at peace, ease, and calm.

bring out your best self? What alternative reactions might be helpful instead? Labels don't help anyone, anytime.

When peer mistreatment occurs, we traditionally talk about the three roles of "bully," "victim," and "bystander." These labels, however, can contribute to a cascade of negative reactions. For example, labeling someone a "bully" triggers stereotyping. Words that come to mind are: mean, inconsiderate, dangerous, manipulative, Queen Bee, King Pin, disrespectful, nasty, self-centered, power-hungry, bad, and feared.

Some people demonize or ostracize the "bully" to protect their own children. Others may try to kick the "bully" out of the school, which marginalizes the child who aggressed. Then that child may feel justified to retaliate by continuing to mistreat others. It rarely works to "remove the bully," as there is always another child ready to step into the role.

Imagine if your own child were accused of being a "bully." Your knee-jerk reaction may be to defend and deny: "My child would/could never bully!" Unfortunately, that reaction takes attention away from what actually happened and the harm the behavior may have caused. When, instead, we hear a specific description of the harmful behavior and its impact on the other child, we are more apt to be open to hear about our own child's missteps. Any child can say or do hurtful things; all of us have done things that have hurt others at times. When we avoid

ALL RIGHTS RESERVED. © 2014 FAMILY EMPOWERMENT NETWORK™

Focus on the Behaviors Rather Than the Label

When we take the focus off the labels of "bully" and "victim," we can reduce peer mistreatment more effectively. The bigger, more important questions then become:

- Was the behavior acceptable or unacceptable?
- What is the best course of action to help reduce further incidents of mistreatment?

This allows us to put our energy into creative problem solving, understanding what is going on for all kids involved, and choosing the unique course of action for the situation. When we use an approach based on behavior, our advice and consequences are more likely to be effective and fair. When a consequence is fair, the tendency for revenge goes down, and the chances of empathy go up.

Take a few minutes to review the vocabulary guide on the next page. It can help you to change your words, which will change your thoughts, which will ultimately change your actions with regard to peer mistreatment. A change of language can lead to a focus on changing actions.

Children who are clear about what behavior is expected, what is acceptable or unacceptable–in the home, in the classroom, in hallways, on playgrounds, and on the school bus–find it easier to get along. On the contrary, not having clear boundaries or rules can foster peer mistreatment. (Think of the work office 30 years ago where sexual harassment was rampant with no laws to protect employees.) Having small, predictable consequences and making amends also are important elements in deterring peer mistreatment. Furthermore, we would like to empower bystanders to shift from being passive to being active by spending time with, talking to, giving advice to, or encouraging the child being mistreated. Other useful strategies for bystanders include helping the target to get away from the situation or to tell an adult. In the new paradigm, there are clear boundaries and rules.

labeling children and focus on behavior instead, we help them to see that they, and others, can change.

Labeling someone a "victim" also triggers stereotyping. Words that come to mind are: inept, weak, helpless, insecure, hopeless, and "a loser." Adults may treat "victims" as incapable or pathetic and micro-manage them. Peers may disengage with the "victim" to protect themselves from being aligned with someone "weak."

These labels are so powerfully negative that, when our own child is labeled, we may get emotionally triggered, defensive, and over-react to the situation. Nothing triggers "Father Bear" or "Mother Bear" more than seeing his/her child hurt or accused! We are biologically wired to protect our offspring, so it is easy to over-react and jump to the conclusion that the incident was "bullying"!

Finally, regarding the "bystander," some researchers prefer using "witness" instead. SuEllen Fried, author of *Banishing Bullying Behavior,* coined the term "witness" in her first book in 1993 in relation to bystanders and bullying. She explains that kids watch a lot of TV law programs that educate kids that "witnesses" are people who see something happen and have to tell the truth. She and others feel this word is more empowering than "bystander," especially given the bystander/witness's key role in the prevention of peer mistreatment.

© 2014 FAMILY EMPOWERMENT NETWORK™ ALL RIGHTS RESERVED.

Replace Old Way of Talking	With New Way of Thinking and Communicating
Bullying	Peer mistreatment
Bully	Child who mistreated another: This puts focus on the actions of peer mistreatment. Did the child cross the line into unacceptable behavior?
Victim	Child who was mistreated or targeted–and deserves protection from future peer mistreatment
Bystander	Witness–someone who sees something happen and has to tell the truth
Rather than focusing on, "Is it bullying?" or "Is he a bully?"	Focus on the questions: "Did peer mistreatment occur?" and "Is there potential for harm?"
Tattling	Reporting or asking for help: When we call kids "tattletales," we shame them into silence and eventually they stop telling us anything. It is imperative that adults encourage kids to tell us when they are experiencing actions by their peers or interactions with their peers that they (or others) can't handle on their own.
Zero Tolerance (can lead to a vicious cycle of punishment and revenge)	Replace "punishment" with "discipline," consequences that teach a lesson: The goal is for the kids who mistreat to see and own the hurtfulness and impact of their behavior on another. This can foster empathy, understanding, and cooperation. Some call this "restorative justice" or "making it right."

Does the Action Cross the Line? Does It Have Potential for Harm?

Parents, school staff, and anyone who engages with children all struggle with these questions: How will I know when conflict has crossed the line into peer mistreatment? If the action did cross the line, how serious is it? And, what is the best way to support the children involved?

The first challenge is to get an accurate story. (We will talk about this more in the second half of the chapter.) When we hear of an incident from one person, the story can be distorted. Think of the many stories told in a courtroom to determine whether someone is guilty or not guilty. Kids who perceive they have crossed the line and worry they will get into trouble have a strong inclination to lie in order to stay out of trouble! And friends often lie to protect friends.

Once you think you have an accurate story, you still may struggle to identify whether or not peer mistreatment occurred. In "bullying" literature, these three criteria are often used as the guideposts:

1. Imbalance of power (physical or emotional)
2. Intent to harm
3. Pattern of repetition

Nonetheless, if you solely rely on these three criteria, you still might not have a clear answer. First, more often than not, deciding who has more "power" can be challenging. Secondly, the only person who really knows if there was "intent to harm" is the one who did the mistreatment–and confession is unlikely. Also, repetition can happen with everyday conflict; it is not always peer mistreatment. Because getting clarity on these criteria can be so confusing, time-consuming, exhausting, and nearly impossible, we may still get nowhere with our investigation. In addition, some peer mistreatment does not meet these criteria but still has potential for harm.

ALL RIGHTS RESERVED. © 2014 FAMILY EMPOWERMENT NETWORK™

Here is an example to highlight the challenges we may face at home:

In the Franks' home, there was one clear rule: No physical mistreatment ever. Whenever someone hit someone else for any reason, Mom gave the hitter an automatic time-out. One day, the two older brothers did not let the youngest join their soccer game. He was so young and small; they were worried about him getting hurt. Plus, they wanted a competitive game. The youngest reacted by disrupting the game and stealing the ball again and again. Eventually, in frustration, the older brother pushed his little brother away from the ball. The youngest wailed to Mom loudly about being pushed. The older brother was punished for pushing with "no soccer for a week." The youngest had no consequence.

Who was the child who mistreated another? Did the youngest cross the line? What were the consequences? How could this have been a learning experience that might have reduced the chance of the situation happening again? There are only three kids involved here, and look how difficult this is! Imagine the complexity with schools of many hundreds of kids:

A group of first-grade girls was standing in line at the drinking fountain. A group of first-grade boys kept lifting up the girls' skirts, laughing, and running away. The girls asked them to stop. The boys kept lifting the skirts and laughing.

Were these first-grade boys "bullying?" Was there intent to harm, imbalance of power, or repetition? When this question was asked at the 2011 International Bullying Prevention Conference, the session participants responded by splitting equally three ways: 1) Yes, peer mistreat-ment; 2) Not sure; 3) Innocent. How can we intervene effectively when there are so many different perceptions?

What happens when we replace, "Is it bullying?" with, "Was there potential for harm?" (physical or emotional). It is easier to agree that excluding someone who wants to be included, pushing, and lifting skirts are all behaviors that could cause harm. Whether a behavior crosses the line into peer mistreatment can be determined by *focusing on the actions.* Peer mistreatment happens if one or both parties cross the line into *unacceptable behavior.* Once we know that behavior crossed the line, we can begin to focus on consequences and discussions about reducing future mistreatment.

Reasons Some Children Mistreat Others

Children mistreat others for various reasons. They might mistreat each other for revenge, to look good in front of their friends, or to get a rise out of the other child as a challenge or to have "fun." They might initiate aggression (proactively forming a club to leave someone out) or react in self-defense (reactively hitting another who pushed him or called him "stupid"). Or, they might feel overwhelmed and stressed, angry about flunking a test, or frustrated for being yelled at or hit by Mom or Dad.

Our chart on the next page illustrates the fact that, according to Stan Davis, "most children who mistreat others do so for peer approval, thinking the actions are fun, trying to get away from someone, and/or finding a way to cope with emotion. For others, the behaviors have to do with a skill deficit–self control or impulsivity or anger management or social skills. For the very

© 2014 FAMILY EMPOWERMENT NETWORK™ ALL RIGHTS RESERVED.

few (perhaps one child in 10,000) callous, unemotional youth (described by Paul Frick's research), there is a real desire to hurt others. This is very rare." If you're trying to figure out why a child mistreated another, decide which of these two categories fits and recognize that ostracism of the child who mistreated is not a helpful nor effective long-term solution to the mistreatment.

THE MOST COMMON REASONS KIDS MISTREAT OTHERS		
Reasons	**Settings That Foster Mistreatment**	**Approaches that Help**
Peer approval/ acceptance (70%)	Acceptance, power, to be "cool" and fit in, boy or girl code, honor code	Education can help here. Empathy programs would help members of this group to see the impact of their behavior on others.
Life skills deficits (30%)	**Internal Factors** e.g., Poor social skills, anger management issues, and lack of impulse control	Specific intervention is needed here: Instruction and role playing to improve anger management, social skills, perspective taking and empathy would help this group. For some children, something outside of themselves, such as an unhappy home, is exacerbating their problems. These children would benefit from mentoring.
	External Factors e.g., Abuse, school failure, loss of loved one, etc.	

How Mistreated Kids Can Become Kids Who Mistreat Others

Because many people subscribe to the idea that the best defense to avoid being targeted is a good offense, a child who mistreated someone today may have been a target yesterday or last month. Research shows that about 20-30% of third through eighth graders are both giving and receiving relational or emotional mistreatment (Northwest Regional Lab). So, the child mistreating your child today may have been the recipient of your child's mistreatment last week!

Amy cried as she recounted being tormented in middle school by her classmates. For some reason, she was targeted as a "dog." Day after day, Amy had to walk the halls with kids barking at her. There was silence in the room as we imagined the horror of that kind of rejection. Finally, we asked her, "Then what happened? How did it stop?" She replied softly, "I stopped it." We breathed a sigh of relief. Great! Thank goodness. "How?" we asked. Her voice was so quiet that we had to strain to hear her. "I picked out another girl, someone worse off than me, and started to call her a dog. Then the others forgot about me. We barked at her instead."

It is not always easy to figure out where the mistreatment started. Most children do not identify their behavior as aggressive. One thing that is clear is that "removing the bully" rarely solves anything. Someone usually steps in to take her place, and the "removed" child can continue her destructive patterns in the new environment.

Short- and Long-term Effects of Serious and Repetitive Mistreatment

The consequences of peer mistreatment can be serious. Surprisingly, the outcomes look equally bleak for the child receiving *and* for the child giving the mistreatment. In short, givers and receivers of mistreatment are *both* at risk for:

- Depression
- Drug and alcohol abuse and early use
- Eating disorders, poor body image, self-harm
- Violence toward self or others
- School failure, suspension, dropping out, absenteeism, avoidance, delinquency, being disruptive in class
- Peer rejection, loneliness, isolation, low self-worth

 ALL RIGHTS RESERVED. © 2014 FAMILY EMPOWERMENT NETWORK™

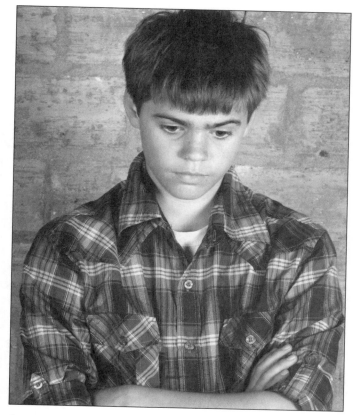

In addition to the risk factors listed above, *recipients* of mistreatment may suffer other negative effects. Short-term ramifications may include humiliation, sadness, distressed affect, confusion, anxiousness, psychosomatic symptoms, and poor concentration. The long-term outcomes for targets also include:

- Insecurity about their place in the social hierarchy, which manifests as social avoidance and anxiety
- Lower levels of leadership
- Fear, which may lead to absenteeism, truancy, or dropping out
- Poor self-concept

With regard to the children who choose to mistreat others, according to research, boys who get identified as a "bully" by age eight have a six-fold increase of getting in trouble with the law by 25 years of age (Saufler and Gaugne. [June 2000] "Maine Project Against Bullying: Final Report").

Also, boys who "bully" by age 14-15 have a 60% chance of criminal conviction by age 24 (Banks, R. [Spring 2000] Sec. 1 of "School Safety: A Collaborative Effort." *ERIC Review* 7[1], 12-14. Retrieved Sept. 1, 2013, from http://files.eric.ed.gov/fulltext/ED440640.pdf). In addition, at the 2012 International Bullying Conference, Diana Schroeder reported about the 2012 Highmark Foundation study that showed that the estimated cost to society per year per student who bullied others is nearly a million dollars ($951,327)!

A long-term consequence for children who seriously and repeatedly mistreat others can be "escalation." That is, people who bully as children not only have an increased chance of incarceration, but they also have increased chances of:

- Having kids who mistreat others
- Domestic abuse
- Having difficulty getting along with neighbors and colleagues
- Eventually abusing their elders as well (Beane, *Protect Your Child from Bullying*)

Research also shows that self-esteem for a child who mistreats others may be high or low. Those with *low* self esteem may get jealous and frustrated easily, need a lot of attention from other people, need to feel accepted, need to be noticed, and need to gain power and control. Those with unrealistically *high* self esteem feel good about their ability to manipulate others and do not take responsibility for what they have done.

One of the things that fuels relational aggression in friendship is sharing friends. Learning to share friends is a developmental step, but, if a child doesn't learn how to do this by adolescence, the issue can turn into jealousy and possessiveness. Often, children who mistreat others may have difficulty recognizing their hurtful behavior. Relational aggression may work at getting the child's needs met in the short term, but much is lost in the long term.

© 2014 FAMILY EMPOWERMENT NETWORK™ ALL RIGHTS RESERVED.

In this part of Chapter 5, we focus on two major steps parents and educators can use to support and protect kids: "Get the Whole Story" and "Help All Kids Involved." Here is a quick outline of the upcoming section:

GET THE WHOLE STORY
- Connection and Empathy Matter Most
- Evaluate What Happened, So Your Support and Advice is Helpful
- Teach to Report and Remove "Tattling" from Your Vocabulary
- Avoid Advice that Doesn't Work

HELP ALL KIDS INVOLVED
- Support the Child Who Was Mistreated
- Support the Child who Mistreated Another
- Strategies That Help: Accountability, "Making It Right," and "Win-Win"
- What about the Bystander?

PART II: PROTECTING AND SUPPORTING OUR KIDS

"Once thought to be simply an unpleasant rite of passage, bullying can actually result in long-term social, academic, psychological, and physical consequences." – "The Challenge" Vol. 11 (3), a Publication of the U.S. Department of Education's Office of Safe and Drug-Free Schools

One of the most difficult challenges we face as parents today is to figure out when conflict crosses the line into peer mistreatment. What can we do to keep our children safe? How can we protect our children from mistreatment and help them heal? How can we help our children stop mistreating other kids? How can we empower bystanders in ways that actually help the targeted children and reduce overall peer mistreatment? Most people–adults and children alike–have been on both the receiving and giving end of hurting others. We all play the bystander role and have witnessed mistreatment.

To truly make a difference, it is important to keep the big picture in mind. We want our interventions to be effective in reducing the harm of the current incident as well as in reducing the chance of further incidents, but every situation that involves possible peer mistreatment is unique. Human interactions are complex! What might look simple on the surface might have many more nuances as you delve deeper. (Consider sibling rivalry.) What this means is that each and every situation of peer mistreatment deserves special consideration and attention. In this chapter, we offer general guidance on how to deal with peer mistreatment, emphasizing important concepts to keep in mind.

By far the most effective way to reduce peer mistreatment is an integrated approach involving all parties (parents, school, students, etc.) working together to change social norms. We advocate for:

- **Clear guidelines for behavior/expectations that apply to everyone, and consistent effective follow-through with small, escalating consequences paired with opportunities to learn through reflection**

- **Support for mistreated youth:** Listen with empathy, offer supportive advice, and follow up to see if things get better; avoid telling mistreated youth that they would not be mistreated if they acted differently or that they should have reported the incident to an adult earlier.

- **Support for the child who mistreats:** Help the child to change his/her behavior, repair the harm ("make it right") while continuing to be a valued part of the community, and find positive ways to meet his/her needs.

- **Empowerment of the silent majority:** Empower bystanders to notice, care, support targets, and tell adults.

- **Modeling all of this in the adult world**

ALL RIGHTS RESERVED. © 2014 FAMILY EMPOWERMENT NETWORK™

What is frustrating as a parent involved in an incident is that system change takes a long time–and you want action now! Reducing the harm of the peer mistreatment is the first priority in supporting your child. We still encourage you, however, to invest in both short- and long-term solutions. We will give you some ideas on how you, as an individual parent, can be helpful regardless of the actions of your child. For a quick overview of the ideas, see **"Approach to an Incident: What Parents Can Do."**

If the peer mistreatment is serious or pervasive, we encourage you to look into resources beyond this book and potentially to get outside help. Our resource section has many books and websites that offer detailed information to maximize your effectiveness.

GET THE WHOLE STORY

Connection and Empathy Matter Most

No matter how your child is involved in mistreatment–as the giver, receiver, or bystander–what matters most is your child's close, trusting, connected relationship with you. Otherwise, you may never even hear about peer mistreatment incidents. The shroud of silence around peer mistreatment is pervasive and powerful, especially as kids get older. We cannot help our kids if we do not know what is going on. Once we do know what's going on, connection will be powerful in helping your child through it.

Thousands and thousands of kids suffer from peer mistreatment every single day, and many don't tell an adult!

> ### KEY STRATEGIES FOR REDUCING THE HARM OF PEER MISTREATMENT
>
> ---
>
> • Build connections among youth and adults
>
> • Encourage supportive behavior by peers/ bystanders and by adults
>
> • In each setting (home, school, sports, etc.), establish consistent expectations and interventions for unacceptable behavior
>
> From Stan Davis at www.stopbullyingnow.com

And the kids who watch often don't report either. As parents, we can be incredibly valuable by changing one thing: Listening well! Listening brings peer mistreatment out in the open so we will know when, where, and how it happens. Then, we as individuals and as a community can figure out what to do about it.

Parents who prioritize connection find that issues (grades, friends, chores, responsibility, risky behavior, safety, romantic relationships and sexuality, peer mistreatment, conflict, etc.) are all best handled by being closely connected with their child. Connection is facilitated by a certain frame of mind, which Daniel Siegel, M.D., calls "COAL": curiosity, openness, acceptance, and loving kindness (Siegel, *The Mindful Brain*, p. 15). Only when we are truly connected to our kids will they feel safe enough to tell us what is really going on in their lives. Then, with curious questions and neutral dialogue, we can maximally influence their decision making, their problem-solving skills, and even help our kids to tap into their own core values.

CONNECTION

- Connection matters if your child is mistreating others.
- Connection matters if your child is being targeted.
- Connection matters if your child is a bystander.
- Connection matters for every kid and adult involved in a peer mistreatment incident.

© 2014 FAMILY EMPOWERMENT NETWORK™ ALL RIGHTS RESERVED.

Research studies confirm that connection matters. Fifty years of research at the Search Institute (www.searchinstitute.org) has explored one big question: What best supports kids to be safe and to thrive? In a nutshell, the answer can be summarized in three words: Connect with Kids. Return to the articles of Chapter 3 and review the **"40 Developmental Assets"** and **"Family Assets"** for more specifics on the Search Institute research.

Similarly, in a study published in the American Medical Association journal, 12,000 youths were surveyed to find out what protects kids from the risky behaviors of substance abuse, violence, depression, suicide, and promiscuity. The researchers found that the most protective factor was close connection with parents, defined as "children perceiving they are loved, wanted, and cared for by the way their parents treat them." The second factor was being "connected" at school, feeling that teachers treat them fairly and that they are a part of the school and its activities ("Protecting Adolescents from Harm," *Journal of American Medical Association*, 278 [10]: 823-32, 9/10/97).

> *"Listening with attention and intention can be the best thing you'll ever do for others and yourself. . . . When you listen with an open heart, you are providing dignity and a sense of worth to others. You may hear their deepest and most important stories put into voice and connect yourself to your own truth."*
>
> – Amy Beltaine, Minister at First Unitarian Church, Portland, OR

Both studies reinforce for professionals–counselors, teachers, educational administrators, and health professionals–what parents know intuitively: that it is fruitful to focus more attention on relationships. Plus, they reinforce for parents that the absolute core of parenting is to connect. Even in a media world where the message "separate from your parents to be cool" is reinforced every day and teens put up a front of defiance and shunning, parents who have the courage to take the emotional risk will be able to connect deeply and often with kids–their kids and all kids.

Evaluate What Happened, So Your Support and Advice is Helpful

Once you hear about the peer mistreatment, the next step is to stay as calm and neutral as possible so you learn the whole story. Check out the steps outlined in the article **"Approach to an Incident."** If you find yourself getting triggered and upset, take a five-minute break to calm down or postpone the discussion until a better time. At this moment, more than ever, your child needs you to be grounded, whether he was the target, the bystander, or the child who chose to mistreat another. As you hear the story and ask questions for clarity and details, here are some key distinctions you want to make to evaluate the seriousness and determine the next steps:

- Do you need to get others involved to get the whole story?
- If mistreatment did occur, was the mistreatment done only by one side or by both sides?
- How serious was the mistreatment?
- How troubled was your child by the incident?
- Do you need to get others involved to help you decide what to do next? (It is okay to get support. You don't need to handle the dilemma alone.)

 # TAKE THE TIME

Molly loved to talk and really valued connecting with her kids. However, what she often experienced is that her three boys did not easily share stories about what happened at school or on the soccer field. They also seemed to struggle with sharing their feelings. She explored various ways to connect with her kids and found unique connecting strategies for each son: With Joe, she chatted while they shot hoops; with Shane, she talked in the car; and with Ben, she connected while massaging his feet at bedtime. Knowing that these activities maximized connection helped Molly to prioritize and take the time for these experiences even on busy days.

ALL RIGHTS RESERVED. © 2014 FAMILY EMPOWERMENT NETWORK™

- Answer these two questions to help you decide if this is a reportable incident:

  1. How unacceptable was the behavior? If serious, such as a racial slur or sexual harassment, report even if it didn't bother your child at all.
  2. Was the impact of the mistreatment on your child serious? Reporting is important not only to enlist others to help stop the mistreatment, but also to help build protective connections with peers and caring adults.

Knowing the extent to which the mistreatment has impacted your child emotionally is critical information in helping you decide how to proceed. Assess your child's emotional state as you would a physical ailment. You already have this skill; you use it every time your child has a stomach ache, the flu, etc. Watch your child and ask questions. For an idea of how to proceed, use the analogy of a physical ailment as presented in our chart.

What is great about this approach is that you focus your attention on how your child is doing rather than focusing on changing the behavior of the child who mistreated your child. Also, know that not all kids are affected the same way when a peer mistreatment inci-

dent occurs. To help frame this, let's explore the impact of frequent mistreatment on the 13,000 5th-12th graders in the Youth Voice Project study. Twenty-two percent reported experiencing either physical or emotional peer mistreatment at least twice a month in the past month. So, how many of these kids were traumatized emotionally? Surprisingly, of these kids who received peer mistreatment regularly, half said they experienced only mild trauma, even when the mistreatment was serious (Youth Voice Project, Charisse Nixon and Stan Davis. www. stopbullyingnow.com/yvp.htm). This reminds us to stay calm and neutral when the child is seemingly okay; then we avoid projecting the pain we expect on to them and creating or accentuating pain.

As parents, however, we need to remember that some categories of peer mistreatment are automatically serious no matter how our children have reacted. These unequivocally unacceptable behaviors include sexual harassment, racial and sexual orientation slurs, expensive or extensive physical damage, and safety issues. Nevertheless, it is important to keep in mind that children (and some adults) often don't understand the subtleties or have the ability to see the mistreatment from the perspective of the target. For example, sexual harassment has to do with the target feeling uncomfortable, even if the child approaching the target does not think what they

Assessment	Physical Ailment	Emotional Ailment
Low suffering/ risk:	Try self care, such as rest or change in diet	Listen well. Brainstorm solutions or give advice, if asked. Check back to be sure your child is okay.
Moderate suffering/ risk:	Should we go to the doctor? Try different approaches. Monitor closely!	Shall we go to the school/the coach? Is there something else to try? Someone else who could help? Check back to see if your child is okay.
Severe suffering/ risk:	Go to the doctor right away!	Go to school/coach. . . as soon as you are calm and know you can be respectful. Check back to see if your child is okay.

© 2014 FAMILY EMPOWERMENT NETWORK™ ALL RIGHTS RESERVED.

are doing or saying is a violation. (For example, asking a girl out again and again, after she has said "no" three times, is considered unwanted sexual harassment; this is called the "Three-No Rule.") The inappropriate actions of tweens/teens can be seen as perfect opportunities for educating our youth rather than opportunities for harsh punishment. Check out this example of how we as adults might do better to educate our children regarding completely unacceptable behavior (especially given how prevalent the unacceptable behavior is in the media today):

> *Inspired by the movie* Jackass, *two middle-school boys in a small town in Oregon were arrested for slapping girls' bottoms and touching their breasts in the school hallways. The boys thought their behavior was funny. Three months later—after national media coverage, the threat of possible prison time, and the prospect of being placed on a sex offender registry for life—the judge dismissed the case following public outcry and at the request of the girls.*

These boys did cross the line and needed an appropriate consequence and thorough education about sexual harassment, as did their peers. But prison time? Being on a sex offender registry for life? No. Instead, we would advocate for smaller consequences and support to understand why the behavior was unacceptable.

Many children (and adults) who are competent social beings learn to "filter" minor conflicts and mistreatment in order to solve problems and enjoy life. They may be surprised, however, to find that ignoring or filtering doesn't work for sexual and other more serious forms of harassment. In fact, ignoring unacceptable behavior gives the message that the aggressor can continue with the harassment.

Mob mentality deserves special mention here as well, especially if you find your child doing behavior way out of character. As we all know, people can act differently in groups and may be more likely to mistreat others than they would if they were alone face-to-face with someone.

You can see, from the details in the story below, the steps a caring adult might need to take to get clarity in a complex incident. It sometimes requires a lot of patience, thinking, and problem-solving to figure out what is going on. Tenacity and determination are key ingredients:

> *Margie Abbott was a vice principal in a school committed to reducing peer mistreatment. An incident occurred in which a group of popular seventh-grade boys were suspected of serious peer mistreatment. The target and a few bystanders gave a story of mistreatment that was consistent and that Ms. Abbott suspected was true. However, the implicated group of popular boys and their bystander allies consistently stuck to a different version of the story. The school year ended before Ms. Abbott could get the clarity she needed to take action. The next fall, because she had taken detailed notes, she was able to take up right where she left off. It still took two months for the key instigators to fess up to their mistreatment.*

Ms. Abbott's tenacity had a profound impact on the school climate. The popular group of boys, who had been regularly mistreating others, got to experience consequences for their actions in a way that felt fair. They stopped their mistreatment habit. Even better was that every child in that school knew this vice principal spent four months getting to the bottom of what happened. They learned that adults cared, were watching to keep kids safe, and that their behavior mattered. Here are some tips from the vice principal, Margie Abbott, who is currently an adjunct professor at Marylhurst College:

- Students want people to listen to them, they want to be heard, and they want to be treated respectfully.
- People may act aggressively in a group in ways they would never act alone; we all need to learn about mob mentality, so we can identify it when it happens.
- Students want adults in their lives to be responsible and follow through on what they say they will do.
- Time can be a wonderful tactic—even if it seems you need to respond right away.

ALL RIGHTS RESERVED. © 2014 FAMILY EMPOWERMENT NETWORK™

- Keep detailed notes, so you can track discrepancies in the story. Kids who lie will contradict themselves later.

Elsbeth Martindale, PsyD, has developed this wonderful tool for counselors, parents, and other caring adults. The cards provide an engaging, accessible, and even playful way to learn when peer conflict crosses the line into mistreatment. The solution cards go beyond identifying a problem to give clear and specific steps for resolution.

www.couragetobloom.com

Teach to Report and Remove "Tattling" from Your Vocabulary

Even if you have great connection with your kids, they still might not share their stories of peer mistreatment. What else can be getting in the way? Why the shroud of silence and secrecy around peer mistreatment? Why don't our kids tell us what is going on when they are being mistreated, especially the more painful exclusion and gossip? Why do bystanders who see the peer mistreatment not tell anyone, especially as they get older?

Four major obstacles get in the way of reporting—and they all have to do with the reaction of adults:

- Being shamed as a "tattler"
- Fearing an over-reaction from an adult
- Experiencing adult inaction when kids do report peer mistreatment
- Fearing that telling someone might make the peer mistreatment worse

We have an unacknowledged cultural problem with teaching the concept of "tattling" in our country, and major consequences ensue. For example, it can lead to the "code of silence" that promotes tolerating violence of many kinds (e.g., military sexual harassment). The problem starts when adults say, "Don't be a tattletale" to young children who are telling us about something bothering them, something we have decided is unimportant or insignificant. The labeling that "tattling is bad" is reinforced by a plethora of books and TV programs about not being a snitch or a tattletale. So, when kids are older and experience or witness peer mistreatment, they go out of their way not to tell an adult to avoid being called a "snitch," which often makes suffering even worse.

Young children are not capable of distinguishing minor from major infractions. Developmentally, they have limited skills to assess or deal with conflict and limited ability to see the big picture of important and unimportant. They, hopefully, learn this ability over time with our gentle guidance. Thus, when adults discourage young people from reporting minor infractions, kids pick up the simple message that adults don't want to hear their concerns and are not interested in helping them out.

If we want our kids to report incidents, we have to hear it all—big and small—and say, "Thanks for letting me know that Tommy took your pencil." Then we can move on quickly so as not to reinforce the reporting of insignificant incidences. Over time and with patience, we can

© 2014 FAMILY EMPOWERMENT NETWORK™ ALL RIGHTS RESERVED.

teach children what is serious mistreatment and what is a mild infraction. We do this by encouraging them to try two to three solutions on their own before they go to an adult. We ask them what they tried on their own before brainstorming new solutions. We talk to them about when mistreatment is too big for them to handle on their own and when to get an adult involved. (See **"Kelso's Wheels"** in the previous chapter on page 4:27.)

In addition to stopping the culture of silence by encouraging our kids to tell us all their concerns, we also need to avoid over-reacting to incidents of peer mistreatment. An over-reacting parent might aggravate the situation. For example, when we are so triggered by the story that our Mother/Father Bear kicks in, we may storm the school and, in anger, mistreat others–doing the very thing we are angry about happening to our child. This can cause more damage ("making a mountain out of a molehill"), and we lose sight of the long-term goals of teaching how to treat others with fairness and respect.

> *Kurt was a 12-year-old boy, full of gregariousness and testosterone. During a Scout meeting, he incessantly whispered to his friend beside him. Doug, sitting nearby, was irritated and kept turning around and saying, "Shhh!" Kurt totally ignored Doug, but, after the tenth "Shhh!" he impulsively took his pencil and stuck it into the air pocket of Doug's expensive basketball shoes. Minutes later, the boys were out in the parking lot with their parents. Before the boys could talk, Doug's mother started yelling at Kurt. Kurt's father kept saying, "I think the boys could work this out," but he was drowned out by Doug's mother. When Kurt got home, he told his mother that he had done something "really stupid." She listened and replied, "Wow. What are you going to do?" Kurt said he was going to write a letter to Doug right away, saying he would replace the shoes. For Kurt, that meant he was going to have to cut a whole lot of lawns to earn the money. He asked his mom to help him find the exact shoes at one of the outlet store. Kurt avoided the angry mom by delivering the shoes when Doug was at his dad's house.*

In this story, Doug's "mother-bear" mom went into overdrive and reacted with blame, shame, and anger to

deal with the situation. Kurt's parents chose a restorative approach, which allowed Kurt to use his creative and work skills to solve the problem and "make it right." How did Kurt feel when he had finished making amends? He felt happy with himself, supported by his parents, fine about Doug, and he knew he never wanted to do anything that impulsive again. What about Doug? On the contrary, his mother's embarrassing parking lot rant interfered with Doug speaking up for himself and left him being upset with his mother as well as feeling less confident in general.

On the other hand, parents and other adults who under-react may also inadvertently aggravate the situation. When we under-react and do nothing, not only could the mistreatment continue or get worse, but the targeted child also may think he is unimportant, uncared for, unsupported, and alone. Eventually, the child who is repeatedly mistreated may not bother to report and start to believe she deserves the mistreatment.

Empowering the bystander to report peer mistreatment just might be one of the most influential changes we could make toward changing the social norm. We will talk more about witnesses/bystanders later in this chapter, but one factor deserves mention here: If a bystander reports an incident and the adults do nothing, the reporting will soon stop, as evidenced in this example:

> *One school that was having trouble with peer mistreatment in the second grade started a mentor program that encouraged the second graders to report peer mistreatment incidents to fifth-grade peer mentors. This worked great. Most incidences were being reported. After four months, however, reporting went down to the initial rates again. It turns out that the adults who were welcoming the stories about the peer mistreatment took no action to stop it. Nothing changed. The kids saw no value in continuing to report.*

Avoid Advice That Doesn't Work

Once you have heard the whole story, determined there was peer mistreatment, and framed its severity, it is

ALL RIGHTS RESERVED. © 2014 FAMILY EMPOWERMENT NETWORK™

important to take some time for reflection in order to avoid doing and saying things that are likely to make the situation worse. Here is a story that illustrates the damage even caring advice can do:

Peter moved to a new middle school district in sixth grade. For 1½ years, a group of boys in his new school harassed him, stopping him in the hall, making insinuating comments that he was a homosexual, stroking his cheek, making fun of the way he walked. At first, Peter was too embarrassed to tell his parents. When he did tell them, they told him to tell the principal. When he finally told the principal, the principal replied that she could not help him, because he hadn't reported the behavior right away. Peter, feeling scared and vulnerable, vowed never to talk to the principal again. Next, Peter's parents suggested he talk to the counselor, who told him to tell the mistreating boys the behavior bothered him. Then the boys teased him for being a baby, who could not take a joke. Peter returned to the counselor, who set up a meeting with all the boys. Then they teased him for running to an adult for help. Peter talked to his PE teacher, who suggested that Peter pretend that the mistreatment did not bother him. This didn't work either. First, Peter did not have the level of acting training necessary to convince the boys that he didn't mind what they were doing. Second, the boys reacted to his efforts by trying harder to get a reaction out of Peter. At this point, it was clear that each adult intervention left Peter worse off—more isolated, with fewer people to appeal to, and experiencing more harassment. - From Stan Davis, author of Schools Where Everyone Belongs)

In 2010, Stan Davis and Charisse Nixon conducted an extensive survey of approximately 13,000 students in grades 5-12. This Youth Voice Research Project uncovered the fact that some commonly recommended responses to peer mistreatment do more harm than good. See their **"Tip Sheet to Support Children Who Are Mistreated by Peers,"** which clearly outlines the most helpful, neutral, and least helpful actions of adults, the targeted children themselves, and bystanders. For serious peer mistreatment situations, for example, the following advice does not work:

- **Get a backbone:** Counseling a target to stand up to the kids mistreating her, fight back, or tell them how she feels is like telling an abused wife to tell her husband she doesn't like it when he beats her.
- **Change Your Behavior:** Telling a target to change his behavior to stop peer mistreatment often leaves the targeted kid thinking and feeling the mistreatment was somehow his fault.
- **Pretend peer mistreatment doesn't bother you (the target):** This requires acting skills beyond the capacity of most students. In the Youth Voice Project report, this was espe cially true for elementary students who said pre tending makes it worse. High school students say this can sometimes help. (Youth Voice Project of Stan Davis and Charisse Nixon, www.stopbullyingnow.com/yvp.htm)
- **Use mediation:** In a peer mistreatment sit- uation, mediation often results in re-injury to the targeted child, as the kids who mistreated her may sneer, give "lip service," and say what the adult wants to hear.
- **Rely solely on prevention programs/ assemblies:** These programs often do not change the behavior of kids who are mistreating others. Individual attention to the problem and clear consequences do work.

The best way to have a positive impact is to focus on the behaviors of mistreatment rather than looking for reasons why a child was targeted (i.e., too fat, too shy, too passive, cries easily, too sensitive, too clueless, too awkward, autistic, physically disabled, etc). There is no justification for mistreatment under any circumstances.

When kids internalize this fact through discussions, empathy, and consistent consequences, treating each other fairly and respectfully will prevail. We have made giant strides in sexual harassment in the last few decades by saying, "No more!" and by having laws that back this up. We can do the same for the mistreatment that goes on in our kids' lives.

© 2014 FAMILY EMPOWERMENT NETWORK™ ALL RIGHTS RESERVED.

HELP ALL KIDS INVOLVED

Support the Child Who Was Mistreated

Supporting a child who has been mistreated is one of a parent's most important roles. When kids find a safe haven at home, much of their hurt can be healed with unconditional love and nurturing support. How do we know this is true? Beyond our intuition and inner knowing, the Youth Voice Project supports the important role of parental empathy. When Davis and Nixon asked thousands of mistreated youth what adult actions in response to peer mistreatment most often made things better, the youth said:

- Listened to me
- Gave me advice
- Checked in with me afterwards to see if the behavior stopped
- Kept up increased adult supervision for some time

This advice is surprisingly simple. Elaborated, these words mean, "I want to be heard. I want to say out loud what happened to me. This will help me feel better. Then, from your more experienced voice, give me some tips for dealing with the situation. And also check back with me later, because I might be too embarrassed to come back to you. Ask how I am doing and keep an eye on me. Perhaps I need more support or a 'Plan B.'"

Two big-picture ways to support a targeted child that are both powerful and helpful include: 1) reducing the harm, and 2) increasing a sense of belonging and security. See the chart below for key points related to both.

Parents need to contemplate what they can and cannot control and remind themselves to put their energy into long-term as well as short-term solutions. For an overview of how to support a targeted child, check out the article **"Empowering Kids Who are Targeted."**

	Reducing the Harm	Increasing a Sense of Belonging and Security
Short Term	• Listen. • Give advice. • Check back later to be sure the child is okay. • Supervise more closely for a while. • Teach tools to "filter" and not let mean behavior "soak in." • Foster appropriate interventions that lead to learning, empathy, and changed behavior in the child who mistreated another.	• Brainstorm immediate ways to help the child to connect with peers and adults, in and out of the environment where the mistreatment occurred. • Seek "safe havens" where your child will be welcomed, accepted, and safe.
Long Term	• Cultivate children's resiliency and autonomy. • Get involved in schools and community organizations to change social norms. • Develop policies, clear boundaries, and clear consequences. • Empower peers and adults to reduce the severity and volume of mistreatment.	• Empower bystanders to include and give emotional support and help. • Change the social norm to: "We all belong; we all matter." • Provide safe havens in the home and in the community, so everyone belongs somewhere.

ALL RIGHTS RESERVED. © 2014 FAMILY EMPOWERMENT NETWORK™

Determining the severity of a peer mistreatment incident is an important first step. For mild mistreatment with low impact, we encourage you to review articles in the last chapter on conflict skills and anger management. If you decide the incident of peer mistreatment is serious, you most likely will need to get others involved from the institution where the incident occurred. In some circumstances, serious incidents can even lead to restraining orders or changing schools. Please get support for yourself as well, to help you figure out all you can do to protect your child physically and emotionally for long-term health and the well-being for all involved. Our **"Resource Guide,"** at the end of this book, also can steer you toward resources, experts, and organizations that may be helpful.

Connection protects kids from being seriously emotionally impacted by mistreatment. Connection, therefore, has to be our short-term and long-term goal with our children.

As previously discussed, assessing the emotional impact of mistreatment on your child is critical. In the Youth Voice Project of Stan Davis and Charisse Nixon, half the kids who received regular peer mistreatment reported experiencing moderate to very severe trauma, and half reported experiencing only mild trauma. Of those who were impacted, one might guess it was mostly due to the severity of the mistreatment. In fact, it was the *degree* of isolation, ostracism, and exclusion experienced that mattered most. Truly, kids who are alienated suffer the most. This is especially true for kids with mental, physical, or emotional disabilities.

The next logical question to consider is: "What led half of the kids to be protected from 'soaking in' the mistreatment?" One factor stood out in the research above all else: the quantity and quality of connections in the child's life. Connections with peers, with adults, with passions, with meaningful work, and even with self—all buffered kids from isolation. It makes sense. If ostracism and exclusion are the most damaging, connections are the antidote.

Here are some strategies Stan Davis proposes that may also help to reduce the harm of peer mistreatment:

- Help your child **find "escape valves"** for when peer issues (and the digital world) are just too much to handle. Sometimes, your kid simply needs to talk out loud to someone. Sometimes, she needs the endorphins of running or playing music or singing or walking in the woods.

- Help your child **reframe his story**. Suggest: "Rewrite the story to make this clear that the other child chose to do this to you because of needs or problems he or she has, and that this has nothing to do with who you are or what you are like or what you did." Talk to your child about the story.

- Help your child to **develop an internal filter**, so low-level or occasional hurtful comments slide off rather than soak in. (Imagine a rain coat with the rain rolling off and you are dry on the inside.)

Ian was over at our house playing. Zoe called him a "baby." He was upset and told his mom. I was listening and asked him, "If Zoe had said, 'Ian, you have blue hair?' would that bother you?" "No," Ian said. "I don't have blue hair, silly." Then I asked, "Well, are you a baby?" "No," he answered. Then he got it. He chose not to let it in. He ran off smiling.
– One of many tips from *Easing the Teasing* by Judy Freedman

A mom of a 14-year-old who wanted to come out as a lesbian reminded the girl that people will say mean things and helped her to develop a filter, which she could use to question criticism and opinions rationally. The filter was a little voice in her head that asked, "Does this judgment fit or have merit for me or does it not?" "Soaking it in" is a personal choice.

© 2014 FAMILY EMPOWERMENT NETWORK™ ALL RIGHTS RESERVED.

- **See the difficulty of peer mistreatment as ostracism and exclusion** (rather than the mistreatment by itself). Focusing only on the mistreatment can have a negative message for your child. For your child it may mean, "I am stuck. If they continue to be mean, I can't feel better." If the worst part of bullying is ostracism, several things can help: Adults can help by listening, and peers can help by being inclusive.

- Address loneliness and ostracism of peer mistreatment by **building a better peer network**. Belonging and acceptance can be fostered when a child joins clubs such as Scouts or a religious congregation youth group, participates in creative group activities such as dancing or band, or engages in interest-related organizations such as Chess or Math Club.

- **Encourage hobbies and service** to others where kids experience mastery, which is independent of peer approval, and where positive mentoring by adults occurs. Volunteering and making a difference for others can make your child feel strong and assist her in building connections.

- Help your child **find his natural peer group**. It might not be obvious. Explore the qualities of the children to which your child naturally gravitates. Sometimes, really bright kids do better with older kids or adults. Or really shy kids do better with younger kids with whom they often take natural leaderships roles.

- **Focus on what is working and the strengths in your child's life** rather than "fixing" what is not working. Encourage your child to journal about the many good times he has had with his friend(s). You may need to help your child brainstorm: "Think of the best time you have had with a friend. What activities were you doing? Where do you feel you can relax and be yourself?"

What is good about this process is that kids figure out solutions to their problems rather than doing what parents think they should do. (Think marriage counseling. Rather than focusing on the fights, focus on the last time you had fun together and analyze that. What made it positive? Do more of that.)

- **Forgiveness** is always a good choice. Marshall Rosenberg, author of *Nonviolent Communication*, gives us a different perspective on forgiveness: "Forgiveness is not about letting the other person 'off the hook.' It is about letting *you* off the hook."

> *We spent yesterday afternoon in the emergency room with my son, Michael. He was playing football, and things got out of hand. Another seventh grader punched Michael, causing a badly swollen eye and a laceration that needed a few stitches. Michael said that John is a nice guy and someone he considers a friend. Michael doesn't know what got into John. John came to the ER with his mother. He was upset and scared about what he had done. When we came home, Michael asked if he could invite John over for dinner. John came with his mom, and the boys seemed to work it out. I was proud of Michael for inviting John over for dinner and to bring "closure" to this event.* – Linda Johnson, from *Wings*, Winter 2000. Used with permission from Full Esteem Ahead.

Support the Child Who Mistreated Another

When we think about how to support kids who mistreat others, it is important to consider the perspective of Ken Rigby, research professor at the University of South Australia. He says children who mistreat others are weak in three areas (which you may recognize as the developmental stages discussed in Chapter 2):

- Empathy (feeling)
- Perspective taking - seeing issues from different angles (thinking)
- Impulse control (will)

ALL RIGHTS RESERVED. © 2014 FAMILY EMPOWERMENT NETWORK™

As you learned earlier in this book, we learn empathy in our homes, our neighborhoods, our schools, our communities. It begins at birth. Babies are wired for empathy, crying in response to another newborn's cries (Perry and Szalavitz, *Born for Love*, p. 23). A person needs constant reinforcement to stay in touch with this natural drive. For people to give empathy, they must receive it. And what so often happens is that when a kid hurts others she typically receives very little empathy from the adults involved in that situation.

To assist you in the case of your child mistreating a peer, we have included the article **"Changing the Pattern of Peer Mistreatment: What to Do If Your Child Mistreats a Peer."** You might also keep the following ideas in mind as you explore ways to support your child during this challenging time:

- **Connect!** Connection is a priority. A child who feels loved and cared for in all situations is a child who will feel included and part of the community. Be sure she knows this first. Children who are unconditionally loved will be more likely to open up with honesty and accountability. We take you down a very personal journey into how one mom supported her son when he chose to treat another boy meanly in **"Empathy: Healing the Bully Within."**

WALK THE TALK

Why do kids mistreat others when they know it is against the rules? When you think about it, kid mistreatment is similar to adults speeding. Do you speed even though you know the speed limit? Most of us would say, "Yes." But, what if there were a device on our car that automatically charged a dollar on our credit card for each mile over the speed limit? How long would it take to change our driving behavior? One month? Bottom line? Frequent little consequences for unacceptable peer mistreatment behavior will lead to more rapid change than big consequences used infrequently.

- **Stay calm and neutral.** Adults who are calm can offer the patience and neutrality that will best support the child. Remind yourself that the mistreatment is not about you or done to "make you mad." If you are triggered, you need to find strategies to calm down or find confidential places to vent. If you want your kids to be respectful, friendly, and fair in all settings, you must model it—especially in stressful mistreatment-related situations.

- **Focus on the behavior** rather than the label. Your child may have mistreated another, but he is not a "bully." Once you get clarity on what happened, explore the underlying needs beneath the behavior and brainstorm other ways your child can meet those needs. Modeling empathy in this difficult situation will help your child to develop their empathy over time.

- **Have consistent expectations and consequences** at home and at school related to the severity of the peer mistreatment rather than your mood. Small, consistent consequences are easier to implement and more effective. Because your child's processing and understanding of the situation is critical to his learning, a consequence can be as simple as a conversation with you or a counselor. The consequence does not have to be big; it just has to be something. When we do nothing, we inadvertently teach kids that what they are doing, however bad, is okay.

- **Making amends** is also a critical part of consequences. Brainstorm ways to "make it right." See more below on restitution and restorative justice.

At one elementary school, one of the small consequences for small infractions was for the child to call his/her parent(s) about the misbehavior. The goal of this process was that kids would own up and parents would know what was going on early, would help out with insights, and would give clear consequences and empathy at home. What actually happened

© 2014 FAMILY EMPOWERMENT NETWORK™ ALL RIGHTS RESERVED.

when the counselor or teacher called was that many of the parents went into denial and anger—even with little issues. The result was that teachers stopped calling until the problem was much bigger. Then parents were even more irate and complained, "Why didn't you call me earlier?" It felt like a lose-lose for everyone. What might work better?

Strategies That Help: Accountability, "Making It Right," and "Win-Win"

We live in a country that has 5% of the world's population but 25% of the world's prisoners (Perry and Szalavitz, *Born for Love*, p. 296). Are Americans more evil than others? Is America safer than other countries because all these people are "locked up?" We are not so sure, but we are certainly a culture that uses a lot of blame and punishment.

Unfortunately, punishment marginalizes the child who mistreats. Children who mistreat others end up seeing themselves as "victims" of the punishment rather than the cause of another's harm or pain. They feel justified in retaliating any way they can, because the adult or school or organization is "against them." They may become heroes to their peers, because defying adults is revered. In environments with harsh discipline policies, connectedness is undermined. Animosity and distrust can be created between youth and adults.

> *"[Justice] means bringing the parties together, looking at the deep implications, and agreeing to restoration instead of shame. This is social inclusion."*
>
> – Kim John Payne

What can happen when we use the "blame and punish" approach or have "zero tolerance?" One thing is that the mistreatment often continues or may even get worse, as in this case:

In tenth grade, Emily was a great student, a great athlete, and had lots of friends in many different groups. She was thriving until popular Will got angry when she did not want to go out with him. He started threatening her in emails.

Emily told her mom and, eventually, the school counselors about the disturbing emails. Will was suspended for two weeks, but what then happened was worse. Knowing how to "play the system," Will got their entire class, except for one friend, to turn against Emily. The kids would taunt her daily with "loser" signs and sneers in the hallways. The counselors kept trying to convince Emily to meet with Will, but Emily did not feel safe, because everything adults had done so far had made things worse. The ostracism and meanness lasted for months. Eventually, Emily changed to a new school, where she was able to thrive again. What did Will learn? That he can get away with anything!

A mistake is an opportunity for learning. What if Will were able to really see the impact of his threats or of aligning their friends against Emily? Or what if he had gotten the counseling he needed to not end up continuing to use threats to get what he wanted and get away with it?

Even when horrendous events occur, we can have discussions that lead us to understanding—and use what we learn to help us stay tapped into our own values. Consider this story Kim John Payne tells of his experience with a group of school children on September 11, 2001.

"I was in a school in New York on 9/11 when the news came through about the attacks. In working with a class to bring this news in the best way we could, one nine-year-old boy said earnestly, "But why do they hate us so much?" Another child answered, "Because we won't talk to them. Because everybody thinks they are just bad." The children, without prompting, went on to talk about how that very same thing happens on their playground. As the children got ready to go out to recess, a child who was known to tease and bully others . . . said, "I hit kids because they won't listen to me." A small group gathered and agreed that this was happening. Right there, they made a plan to try to listen when the boy wanted to speak. While . . . adults struggled to understand the

ALL RIGHTS RESERVED. © 2014 FAMILY EMPOWERMENT NETWORK™

unimaginable, [these kids] made the clear link between being marginalized on their own playground to the dynamics of terrorism." – Kim John Payne in "From the Bathrooms to the Balkans, Teasing to Terrorism" (http://simplicityparenting.com/downloads/FromTheBathroomsToTheBalkansTeasingAndTerrorism.pdf)

Here is a group of nine-year-olds who excel in self reflection and empathy! They take a horrific situation, examine the underlying needs, and look at how they can change their own behavior for a better world. This does not condone the behavior, which was dreadful. This is not saying there should be no consequences for serious crimes. It is, however, an example of looking at what might be behind the behavior so we can understand where it came from and explore what we can do in the future to make it less likely to happen again.

This is where empathy starts–with everyday actions of consideration, respect, and fairness in our own classrooms, living rooms, and backyards! Payne says, "It is about looking at our behavior everyday and being honest about how our joking can lead to teasing to putdowns to peer mistreatment to dehumanizing others."

Restorative justice is a "social inclusion method" that communities can use to solve problems. The system focuses on the needs of the targets and the offenders, as well as the involved community. This story from Kim John Payne demonstrates how a community came together to work through mistreatment:

Two boys took a car for a joy ride and totaled it. The owner was a pregnant teen mom, who had worked at minimum wage for two years to buy the car. She needed it to drop her two kids off at a relative's house, so she could attend nursing school. Without the car, she could not go. This community was close and called a town meeting, during which the boys heard this story first-hand. The two boys were treated respectfully during the entire process yet were held accountable. A grocery store owner offered jobs to the boys so they could earn

---

SORRY!

Check out **Trudy Ludwig's book** *Sorry!* for an insightful story addressing peer mistreatment and restitution. All of Ludwig's children's books (*My Secret Bully, Just Kidding, Trouble Talk, Too Perfect, Better Than You, The Invisible Boy,* and *Confessions of a Former Bully*) can be used as invaluable tools to supplement life skills, character education, and anti-bullying curricula.

www.trudyludwig.com

---

the money needed to buy a new car. Other neighbors took turns loaning their car to the teen mom for the day until the money was earned. The boys became good workers and upstanding citizens. The teen mom continued her career path and got a car from the boys.

This story illustrates "making it right" and restoring justice in a way that involves the entire community. "Making it right" is a multifaceted process, one that greatly differs from many traditional punishment formats. Barbara Coloroso, in her book *The Bully, The Bullied, and The Bystander,* outlines an alternative discipline process that also works well in incidences of peer mistreatment. Her recommended approach, which requires adult oversight, features three Rs: restitution, resolution, and reconciliation:

- **Restitution:** The child who mistreated another fixes what she did (e.g., figures out how to make money to pay for the chair that was broken when she pushed another child, shows she is sorry by having lunch with the child she belittled in front of others, or writes a sincere apology letter to the friend she threatened). Physical or material damage is much easier to fix than personal or emotional damage, but the effort to fix the latter needs to be made. Note that a repentant apology cannot be forced. We do not want to teach our children to

© 2014 FAMILY EMPOWERMENT NETWORK™ ALL RIGHTS RESERVED.

spout an in-sincere "I'm sorry"; instead, we need to ensure that our children show they are sorry.

- **Resolution:** The child who mistreated another admits he mistreated another, acknowledges that the behavior is wrong, stops the mistreatment, and learns alternatives for getting his needs met. This may require some counseling or therapeutic assistance from caring adults.

- **Reconciliation:** The child who mistreated another "makes up" with the person she harmed. This involves a commitment by the child who mistreated to make a plan of restitution and for her to keep her word about the resolutions. This process allows the harmed child to experience the goodness within the child who mistreated her; it also allows the child who mistreated the opportunity to practice being respectful and fair. Truly, a child who has been mistreating others can be taught ways to shift his energy into leadership and actually become an asset to his community. (Barbara Coloroso, *The Bully, The Bullied and The Bystander*, p. 108).

What About the Bystander?

One of the reasons kids engage in peer mistreatment is to win peer approval. In fact, Wendy Craig, in *Making a Difference in Bullying*, describes bystanders as the "audience" for the "theater" of peer mistreatment. She observes that peers are drawn into mistreatment interactions by arousal and the excitement of mistreatment, and that peers can assume many roles in the mistreatment "act." We lump those "watching the show"—whether they get involved or not—under the title "bystanders."

Research shows that bystanders can play a critical role in reducing the harm of peer mistreatment, but, most often, they do nothing. They often don't help the target or report the peer mistreatment incident for two basic reasons: 1) fear of being targeted next, and 2) they don't know how to help. Unfortunately, when witnesses are silent, the aggressors may have the incorrect assumption that the majority of their peers don't mind their behavior. In reality, most kids don't want other kids to be mean. One way to combat this is to collect real data from a school and feed this data back to the kids.

What else can we do to encourage bystanders to support the targets? First of all, we cannot expect children to do something we, as adults, would or could not do. For example, why don't we speak up to the mom slapping her child in the grocery store or to the dad screaming at the referee at a soccer game? Because no one wants to be the next target! Our article, **"The Pivotal Role of the Bystander,"** provides an overview of bystander roles, information about why bystanders don't intervene more often, and ideas for empowering this often-silent majority.

According to the Youth Voice Project, instead of teaching our children to *only* focus on stopping the peer mistreatment, we can encourage them to:

- Spend time with, support, and encourage the target. This can be done in the moment or later with a phone call or text message (using technology for good!)
- Distract the child who mistreats and help the target get away
- Help the target to tell an adult about the mistreatment

One friend can buffer the effects of peer mistreatment. One child can make a difference with any of these actions.

Part III: Changing Social Norms

We will reduce peer mistreatment when we decide to make it a priority.

We can do something about the meanness in the world—starting at home at the dinner table and on our play-

ALL RIGHTS RESERVED. © 2014 FAMILY EMPOWERMENT NETWORK™

PEER SUPPORT PROGRAMS

Given what the research now shows about the incredible power of peer support, a number of programs have cropped up as tools for empowering bystanders/witnesses. Check out this sampling:

- **Be a Friend–Lend a Hand:** A program of Embrace Civility in the Digital Age that encourages young people to be helpful allies if they witness hurtful behavior. (www.embracecivility.org)
- **Sources of Strength:** A wellness program that uses peer leaders to change norms around codes of silence and seeking help. The program has a preventative aim in building multiple sources of support around individuals. (www.sourcesofstrength.org)
- **Stand for Courage:** With the support of celebrities and culture makers, Stand for Courage provides various forms of recognition to bring attention to youth engaged in pro-community, positive behavior. They also offer peer mistreatment education for youth and educators. See Nicole Jon Carroll's article, **"A Movement to Stand for Courage."** (www.standforcourage.org)
- **Steps to Respect:** A program of the Center for Children that works on a school-wide level to get everyone to recognize and learn to deal with peer mistreatment issues. Children learn through well-researched lesson plans how to "recognize, refuse, and report bullying." (www.cfchildren.org/steps-to-respect.aspx)
- **Support Groups:** See Wendy Craig's article at the end of this chapter on establishing goals, strategies, and methods for setting up **"Empowerment Groups to Reduce Peer Mistreatment Among Girls"** and the short article, **"Boys' Support Groups"** that accompanies Ms. Craig's article. On the same page, you will also find a list of support groups for both girls and boys.

grounds. We must be mindful to "walk our talk," because joking and disrespectful behavior at home can lead to teasing and putdowns that dehumanize others.

The basic concept of "social norms" is very important, because, more than anything else, established social norms are what drive peer mistreatment. Social norms are the "expected rules for behavior," and they are based upon beliefs that people have about the acceptability of a behavior. As described in Chapter 3, these beliefs are often "taught" to our children by the "outside influences" that make up the culture in which they dwell, especially the media.

Adults establish the "social norms" of acceptable behavior over time. How would you react, for instance, to your own child hitting someone versus hearing him say, "You can't come to my birthday party"? Even though kids say exclusion is the worst form of peer mistreatment (they would rather be hit or called names), we adults tend to react strongly to hitting but erratically to exclusion. We then have established a "norm" that it is more okay to exclude someone than it is to hit that person.

Likewise, when teachers do not intervene in incidents of peer mistreatment, they create a "social norm" that says it is okay to: mistreat other kids when you get away with it, put someone down for a laugh, exclude others, or spread rumors. Teachers who "don't have time to deal with it" will end up spending more time with the results of not dealing with it. They will be disciplining kids who mistreat others, counseling targeted children, and dealing with angry parents–leaving destruction in the wake.

Many social norms within the adult world perpetuate mistreatment among adults and between adults and children. How many times do we hear gossip about someone or give the "silent treatment" to someone with whom we are angry? We might talk about a teacher disparagingly at the dinner table or tell our kids not to play with certain kids. We put up with coaches yelling at children

© 2014 FAMILY EMPOWERMENT NETWORK™ ALL RIGHTS RESERVED.

who might not have played particularly well in a game. Because these messages are repeated over and over, children learn them well–and the cycle of mistreatment continues.

Our lives do not have to involve gossip, exclusion, and meanness. We can protect our kids from perpetuating the mistreatment–by modeling the behavior we want to see! It starts with treating everyone, no matter what they have done, with respect and fairness. Children from an early age can be taught to be "friendly and fair" to all their classmates.

Other ways to change the social norm of accepting peer mistreatment is to stop gossiping and allowing exclusion

ourselves and to be vigilant about watching out for "accidental" harm. As you read in the previous chapter, mistreatment is not black or white. We all share stories, tease for fun, and form groups with our friends to connect and be close. Sometimes, we "cross the line" and hurt someone, maybe accidentally, maybe sub-consciously. We can invite honesty, so people let us know when they are hurt and we can "make it right."

We have covered a lot of material in this chapter–hopefully empowering you to take a stand and do what you can to change the social norms surrounding peer mistreatment. As inspiration for the journey ahead, we leave you with an innovative **"Rights and Responsibilities"** contract developed by an elementary school in Canada.

I have a RIGHT to learn and grow.	It is my RESPONSIBILITY to listen to instructions, work quietly, raise my hand if I have a question or concern, and to complete assignments. I will cooperate, participate and do the best that I can do.
I have a RIGHT to hear and be heard.	It is my RESPONSIBILITY not to talk, shout or make loud noises when others are speaking.
I have a RIGHT to be respected as an individual.	It is my RESPONSIBILITY not to tease or bother other people, or to hurt their feelings, but to show respect and consideration for others and their ideas.
I have a RIGHT to be safe.	It is my RESPONSIBILITY not to threaten, kick, punch or physically harm anyone else, and to adhere to the rules of this school.
I have a RIGHT to privacy and to my own personal space.	I have a RESPONSIBILITY to respect the personal property of others, and to accept their right to privacy.
I have a RIGHT to enjoy school.	I have a RESPONSIBILITY to have a good attitude and to participate in a way which helps make our school a place where others can enjoy school too.

Used with permission from Thorndale Elementary, Quebec, Canada. http://thorndale.lbpsb.qc.ca/rights.htm

ALL RIGHTS RESERVED. © 2014 FAMILY EMPOWERMENT NETWORK™

What do you worry about most regarding peer mistreatment?

POSSIBLE DISCUSSION QUESTIONS

1) Share a story about how you supported a child who a) was mistreated, b) chose to mistreat others, or c) was a witness in a peer mistreatment incident.

2) Share your ideas about focusing on behavior and substituting "peer mistreatment" for "bullying." Will it make a difference?

3) What sorts of peer mistreatment occur at your child's school or on her sports' teams? Talk about some typical situations where children feel excluded and brainstorm together possible solutions. Describe the challenges of identifying emotional or relational mistreatment (gossip, teasing, exclusion, etc.).

4) In what ways are you mindfully cultivating empathy in your child(ren)?

5) When your child shares a hurtful incident, how do you support him in a way that both protects him and empowers him with skills to resolve the conflict?

6) What are some things your child's school is doing to create a safe social climate and reduce peer mistreatment? How could you or your discussion group help?

7) Share strategies that help your child to "filter" a peer mistreatment incident and not let it "soak into her soul."

8) What are some ideas for how kids can find places and groups where they can be accepted for who they are? How might parents help?

9) Discuss challenges you have faced intervening as a bystander (in a store, at a sports game, etc.).

10) Share ways to reduce mistreatment among adults. Take a stab at being a "gossip-stopper," notice when teasing crosses the line, etc.

PUTTING IT INTO PRACTICE

- When your child is involved in peer mistreatment, find ways to stay calm and neutral, listen, brainstorm solutions, and check back later to see if the situation is better.

- Get your child's opinion on the ideas from the Youth Voice Project. Ask him to share what would work for him in a peer mistreatment incident if he were the target.

- Get involved with your child's school to reduce peer mistreatment and promote a healthy social climate of acceptance and inclusion.

PUTTING IT TOGETHER—YOUR VERSION

Write down a few ideas you have been inspired to implement in your own life after reading/discussing this chapter.

_____

_____

_____

© 2014 FAMILY EMPOWERMENT NETWORK™ ALL RIGHTS RESERVED.

Approach to an Incident:
What Parents Can Do

Listen Without Judgment and Stay Neutral
- Do take the problems seriously.
- Don't over-react or under-react.

Seriousness?
Most children experience peer mistreatment.
- 70-80% are minor or transitory and improve with minor intervention/support.
- 10-15% are concerning and enduring and require support and intervention to get the kids back on track.
- 5-10% are serious and require prolonged and comprehensive intervention.

Get the Whole Story
- Be an active listener.
- Ask open-ended questions.
- Talk to others if the situation is serious.
  - School staff
  - Parents of other kids involved
- Don't assume you are hearing the whole story from your child.
- Don't just do something… stand there! i.e., Get calm and think before you talk or act.

Remember
- Empathy and compassion are key.
- Kids can change "roles."
- Don't "demonize" a child who has mistreated another.

MILD INCIDENT
- Role-play/brainstorm a response.
- Discuss social milieu of school.
  - What are the groups/cliques? Think of the table groups in the cafeteria.
  - What, When, Who, Why, Does peer mistreatment happen?
- Possible Solutions:
  - Network with parents and school staff.
  - Keep in touch when problems are little.
  - Safe Spaces: fun, let kids be themselves.
- Check back wtih your child!

CONCERNING INCIDENT
- Brainstorm possible solutions.
- Decide if teacher, counselor, principal, or coach should be involved.
- If yes, decide who will report to the other adult(s): child or child with parent.
  - If incident is concerning enough, child may need parental support in the meeting with school/sport/club staff.
- Check back with your child!

SERIOUS INCIDENT
- Parent meets with team of teacher, school counselor, principal, etc.
- Work together to develop strategies.
- Communicate regularly to assess effectiveness of the interventions implemented.
- If chronic…
  - Monitor progress. Keep log of events, meetings, etc.
  - Watch for chronic signs.
  - Support domains of competence for both kid who did the mistreatment and kid who was mistreated.
- Check back with your child regularly!

If you are concerned about peer mistreatment at your child's school, get involved!

Mild Incident Resources
Grade School: Thompson *et al*'s *Best Friends, Worst Enemies*
Middle School: Giannetti & Sagarese's *Cliques: 8 Ways to Survive the Social Jungle*
Kid Books:Trudy Ludwig's books: *My Secret Bully, Just Kidding, Sorry!, Confessions of a Former Bully*, etc.
Concerning Incident Resources
Wiseman's *Queen Bees & WannaBes* or *Masterminds & Wingmen*
Simmons' *Odd Girl Speaks Out*
Freedman's *Easing the Teasing*
Fried's *Banishing Bullying Behavior* and *Bullies, Targets & Witnesses*
Serious Incident Resources
Coloroso's *The Bully, the Bullied, and the Bystander*

ALL RIGHTS RESERVED. © 2014 FAMILY EMPOWERMENT NETWORK™

Tip Sheet to Support Children Who Are Mistreated by Peers
What actually helps in mistreatment situations?

- Based on data from the Youth Voice Research Project, 2010, Stan Davis & Charisse Nixon, PhD
- Survey of approximately 13,000 students in grades 5-12, from 31 schools in 12 states
- Focus: what helped and what didn't help in coping with mistreatment situations
- **Conclusion: Some commonly recommended strategies do not, in fact, appear to be helpful in resolving or coping with peer mistreatment situations. However, other strategies do appear to be helpful.**

The following are overall results of data from youth who were repeatedly mistreated. Some actions were more or less helpful depending on grade level and gender. See the detailed study at http://www.youthvoiceproject.com

	Most Helpful Actions *These made things better more often than they made things worse.*	**Neutral Actions** *These worked sometimes but sometimes made things worse.*	**Least Helpful Actions** *These made things worse more often than they made things better.*
What Adults (Parents/ Educators) Can Do	• Listened to me • Gave me advice • Checked in with me afterward to see if the behavior stopped • Kept up increased adult supervision for some time	• Talked about the behavior in class more than once • Said they would talk with the other student(s) • Sat down with me and the other student(s) together • Used punishment for the other student(s) • Talked with the whole class or school about the behavior • Brought in a speaker to talk with the whole class or school about the behavior	• Ignored what was going on • Told me that if I acted differently this wouldn't happen to me • Told me to solve the problem myself • Told me to stop tattling
What Children Who Are Targeted Can Do	• Made a joke about it. *NOTE: It is not clear that using humor stopped the mistreatment. Many youth told us that humor stopped them from feeling bad even though the mistreatment continued.* • Told a friend(s) • Told an adult at home • Reminded myself that what they are doing is not my fault and that they are the ones who are doing something wrong • Told an adult at school	• Walked away • Pretended it didn't bother me • Hit them or fought them • Did nothing • Made plans to get back at them or fight them • Told the person or people how I felt about what they were doing • Told the person or people to stop • Told the person to stop in a mean or angry way	
What Bystanders Can Do	• Spent time with me, sat with me, or hung out with me • Talked to me at school to encourage me • Helped me get away from situations where the behavior was going on • Listened to me • Gave me advice about what I should do • Called me at home to encourage me • Helped me tell an adult • Distracted the people who were treating me badly • Told an adult • Asked the person to stop being mean to me in a friendly way		• Ignored what was going on • Made fun of me for asking for help or for being treated badly • Blamed me for what was happening

Empowering Kids Who are Targeted

OFFER SUPPORT

Reassure your child. It is your child's right to feel safe at school and in the community. Let her know this and that you view peer mistreatment as serious and hurtful. Your child wants to know she is not alone.

Talk to school personnel. If the incident is serious and/or traumatizing to your child, you will need to intervene and involve your child's school teacher, counselor, and/or principal. Consult with your child about taking this step to empower her and so she doesn't feel that you are going behind her back. If your child is afraid of retaliation, be sure that she is protected. Convince her of the importance of getting adults involved.

Check your anger. Be aware of any feelings you may have of revenge or anger so you can model calmness in the face of crisis and to prevent falling into the trap of saying things you will regret later.

Identify an ally. There is safety in numbers. Until you are sure the mistreatment has stopped, encourage your child to hang out with a trusted friend or two so he is never alone, especially going to and from school, during lunch, and during recess.

Document the mistreatment. By keeping a detailed account of the incidents–listing names, times, and places–your child can build a record that can be helpful in an intervention plan. Also, for some kids, keeping a record of the abuse helps them to make more informed choices when choosing friends.

Persevere until the mistreatment stops. For severe cases, schedule regular meetings with school staff until the mistreatment stops. Keep a journal of what is said, promised, and followed through on. Some mistreatment is serious enough to remove your child from the school and/or get legal help.

Preserve your child's self worth. If the aggression is/was repetitive, your child might begin to believe he "deserves" to be treated poorly. This can eventually lead to low self worth and self-destructive behaviors. If you suspect such a shift, browse the literature, talk to the school counselor, or get help from a professional therapist to help you decide what to do. Also look at your own self worth. One of the best gifts you can give your kids is to have and model self worth in yourself and eliminate self-deprecating remarks.

FOSTER COMMUNICATION AND REFLECTION

Continue to talk to your child to be sure she is safe, still being open with you, and not retaliating with aggression. Keeping the lines of communication open will allow you to know the "script" your child is telling herself about the mistreatment.

ALL RIGHTS RESERVED. © 2014 FAMILY EMPOWERMENT NETWORK™

What does he get out of it)? What needs are not being met in that child (e.g., kindness, empathy, inclusion…). Check out www.cnvc.org for more about this powerful approach to a mistreatment incident.

Talk about letting go of a "friend" who continually uses aggression. Many children think that being popular is going to make them happy, so they accept mistreatment from popular friends in the belief that this will help solidify their social position as part of the popular crowd.

Find safe havens for your child. As adults we hang out with people who like us for who we are, and most of us have the skills to let go of unhealthy relationships. Many kids mature into these skills around tenth grade. Until then, we need to help them find safe havens where they are accepted. Sometimes this means going outside of school academics and sports.

Resources

Coloroso, B. *The Bully, the Bullied, and the Bystander: From Preschool to High School—How Parents and Teachers Can Help Break the Cycle of Violence* (2003)

Fried, P., & Fried, S. *Bullies, Targets and Witnesses: Helping Children Break the Pain Chain* (2003)

Giannetti, C., and Sagarese, M. *Cliques: 8 Steps to Help Your Child Survive the Social Jungle* (2001)

Simmons, Rachel. *Odd Girl Out: The Hidden Culture of Aggression in Girls* (2002) and *Odd Girl Speaks Out* (2004).

Wiseman, Rosalind. *Queen Bees and Wannabes: Helping Your Daughter Survive Cliques, Gossip, Boyfriends and Other Realities of Adolescence* (2002); *Queen Bee Moms and King Pin Dads: Dealing with the Parents, Teachers, Coaches and Counselors Who Can Make—or Break—Your Child's Future* (2006); and *Masterminds and Wingmen: Helping Our Boys Cope with Schoolyard Power, Locker-Room Tests, Girlfriends, and the New Rules of Boy World* (2013)

Youth Voice Research Project (2010) by Stan Davis and Charisse Nixon, Ph.D. (www.youthvoiceproject.com)

Encourage him to "let it out." Whether by writing in a journal or diary, creating art, making music, exercising, or playing sports, having outlets for all his emotions will help him to understand and work out his feelings. If your child seems to have completely lost his "friendship" confidence because of the peer mistreatment, you might seek out cooperative play groups and expressive education/therapy programs where he can act, write, draw, and talk about his experiences.

Help her to "rewrite the stories." Having an alternative viewpoint can be beneficial and healing. Check out the fascinating work of Byron Katie (www.thework.com), author of *Loving What Is*. As a way of identifying and questioning the thoughts that cause the anger, fear, depression, and mistreatment in the world, she encourages asking: "Is that true? Is that really true? What is the factual evidence? What are the assumptions? What is another explanation for what happened?"

Use Compassionate Communication to discover what values or needs are not being met for your child when he is the target of aggression. What values or needs are being met for the child who mistreated him (i.e.,

© 2014 FAMILY EMPOWERMENT NETWORK™ ALL RIGHTS RESERVED.

Changing the Pattern of Peer Mistreatment:
What to Do If Your Child Mistreats a Peer

One of the most difficult challenges parents face is recognizing and accepting when their child has crossed the line into peer mistreatment. Once children develop the habit of getting what they want by exerting power over others, the pattern often continues–and can carry into adulthood. So it is imperative to stop the peer mistreatment as soon as it occurs, not only to protect the person being targeted, but also for the well being of the aggressive child.

WHERE TO START

Deny Your Denial
Keep an open mind about the possibility that your child mistreated another. What is difficult for any adult is that kids who are skilled at peer mistreatment often have great social skills and easily "pull the wool over our eyes." These kids might be wonderful, sweet tempered, and cooperative with adults and only show their aggressive side with peers, when it serves them. Also, peer aggression is rarely black and white. Targets today can become aggressors tomorrow. Many kids do both.

Get the Facts
If you observe your child being mean or your child tells you about mistreating a peer, then you know it happened and you can start a conversation with your child. If you weren't present or if you suspect the mistreatment but are unsure, talk to your child's teacher or counselor or perhaps even the parents of your son's or daughter's friends.

In talking to your child and the others, be sure to get all the facts and don't jump to assumptions. Also, be prepared for your child to completely deny the mistreatment, say that "everyone does it," or "it's no big deal." Peer mistreatment is so ingrained and accepted in our culture as the social norm that kids often really don't see it, especially when they are doing it.

In discussing the incident with your child, keep in mind that most kids won't come right out and admit to being mean to others, so you need to ask questions in an empathetic way. For example, "I heard about an incident today on the school bus that involved you and some other kids.

Because you were there, can you fill me in so I don't have to rely on one story?"

Think Short and Long Term for Intervention
Once you have enough information to know your child was engaged in aggressive behavior, you need to think short and long term. The main goals for immediate intervention are to have your child stop the behavior and support your child in "making it right." The goals of long-term intervention are to stop the aggressive pattern of behavior and help your child to develop empathy for others.

IMMEDIATE ACTION

Focus on the behavior, not the label. No matter what the underlying cause of your child's aggression, you must first provide two clear messages:
- I love and care about you.
- Peer mistreatment is not acceptable.

Listen and talk to your child. Find out the details of the mistreatment, why it occurred, etc. Keep your judgment at bay. After all, our kids didn't get a roadmap on how to be a good friend any more that we got one on how to parent. They need to be taught social skills. Part of getting the facts is to stay calm yourself; if your frustration and embarrassment lead to an angry outburst, your child may clamp up defensively or became enraged herself.

An enormous step is to help your child see that his behavior crossed the line into peer mistreatment. If you can help your child to reflect on her behavior, she may be able to gain insight into the impact of her behavior on the other child. Brainstorming positive choices and role playing with your child being in the position of target can be helpful in reminding your child of how his behavior was unacceptable or inappropriate.

Assess the seriousness. As one of the initial steps, you'll want to assess the severity, frequency, complexity and pervasiveness of the problem. Your short- and long-term strategies for dealing with your child will depend on knowing how widespread or ingrained the behavior is.

Have clear consequences. Clear consequences are important. Make sure the consequences are age appropriate and proportional to the severity of the aggression. For example, if the aggression is mild, you might talk through the incident with your child and brainstorm being pro-social next time. Or, you might withdraw some privileges and assign an awareness activity such as observing people using their power to create good.

Support your child to "make it right." Your child will need to figure out how to make amends. Depending on the seriousness of the incident, this may involve working with a teacher, counselor, principal, the parents of the target, etc. Note: Apologizing or writing a note may be one approach, but a forced apology will feel like further abuse to the target. Kids see honesty better than adults do! The apology must be genuine to be effective. A powerful question to teach kids to use when they know they have crossed the line is, "What can I do to help?" This is a simple yet powerful way for your child to gain a new perspective and develop empathy.

Supervise your child's activities and whereabouts more closely. To support your child to avoid repeating transgressions, pay extra special attention to him for a while. You might have his friends come to your house to play and hang out or you might be the chaperone for some of your child's activities with his friends. You also might monitor more closely the TV and video games your child is playing, to reduce exposure to violent content that may be influencing his behavior.

Verify follow through. Set up a way to verify that your child has followed through with making amends. You may need to contact the school to help ensure that the undesirable activities don't sneak back. If the target's parents are involved, fill them in on what your child is doing to "make it right" and to prevent the incident from happening again. Ask them to contact you if there are any further troubles. Another proactive strategy is to network with other parents so you all can monitor the behavior of a particular friendship group and perhaps provide a consistent front on acceptable and unacceptable treatment of others.

Channel "leadership" for good. Being the ringleader in peer mistreatment can be an unhealthy form of leadership. Help your child to channel his or her leadership skills into healthy areas by supporting areas of competence.

- Support your child to take on leadership positions at school. "Insider" teachers can help with this.
- Build connections within the community for leadership opportunities such as teen advisory boards.
- Model leadership by starting a program at school that supports kids to treat one another respectfully. A great model is the Sources of Strength program at www.sourcesofstrength.org.

Acknowledge and encourage your child's efforts to overcome aggressive behavior.

LONG-TERM STRATEGIES

Identify and understand why your child is engaging in peer mistreatment. Your child may be acting out as "a cry for help." Try to be very honest about anything at home that may be contributing to why your child treated another meanly. It is important to note that, in dealing with the underlying causes of your child's poor behavior, sometimes you might need the help of a professional counselor or psychologist. (These ideas come from Charlene Giannetti and Margaret Sagarese's book *Cliques: Eight Steps to Help Your Child Survive the Social Jungle*.)

- If someone at home is **abusing** your daughter, she may carry that hurt, fear, frustration, and anger to school and take it out on others. Consider verbal belittling as well as physical and sexual abuse. Confront this problem strongly and seek outside therapy to help change long held patterns of abuse.
- If your son is **powerless** at home, he may be trying to gather power at school by mistreating others. Does he have a vote in family outings and decisions? Does he get acknowledged for chores done well or good effort on school work?
- If your daughter is **lonely**, because she has just moved or comes home to an empty house, she may be "forcing" friendships with coercion and power.
- If your son is **ignored** because of a new stepdad, overly busy working parents, or a needy other child, he may be trying to get extra attention at school. Get involved in your child's life and talk about his interests and concerns.

© 2014 FAMILY EMPOWERMENT NETWORK™ ALL RIGHTS RESERVED.

Spending one-on-one time with him or going out on "dates" together can give him the alone time with you he craves.

- If your daughter **does not have enough supervision**, she may be stretching her lack of boundaries at home into the school. Children benefit from clear boundaries on their behaviors.
- If your son is **struggling academically**, that can be extremely frustrating. A failure in school can easily be masked by being a successful leader of a clique, even if he rules by "dominance."
- If your daughter **has trouble with anger**—easily angered, hangs on to it too long, overreacts—she will benefit from learning venting and self-management skills.
- If your daughter is worried **about her physical appearance**, she may deflect being mistreated by mistreating others. Talk to her about her concerns about her appearance, if you suspect there is a body image issue.

Teach and model empathy. No parent ever intends to raise a child who could be capable of hurting another, but it happens. What goes wrong? What can be done? Because chronic peer mistreatment can have such dire consequences for all kids involved, teaching and modeling life skills that help your child relate to others with empathy and understanding is critical.

A tragic story comes from *Born for Love* (Ch. 6, pp. 120-127) by Bruce Perry and Maia Szalavitz:

Ryan, at his graduation party before going off to an Ivy League college, raped a mentally disabled teenage neighbor. His comment was: "She is lucky she had me first." No remorse. It turns out that Ryan had been abusive to his peers during his entire childhood. His extremely wealthy parents used their influence to buffer him from consequences of his transgressions. So he continued aggressing until he ended up in jail. Who knows what he will be like when he gets out? Restored, empathetic, and conscious, or even more angry and abusive? What makes this story even more tragic is looking into Ryan's early childhood to when he could have learned empathy. His mother became jealous of any caregivers she hired. Every time Ryan got close to one of his nannies, his mom fired the caregiver. He had had 18 nannies by the time he was three! And, with his parents being very busy, Ryan experienced little real connection in his daily life. Sadly, his ability for empathy never developed.

Helping your child to become aware of her impact on others (empathy) and teaching skills to interact respectfully are as equally important as having consequences and making amends for a peer mistreatment incident. Consider creating opportunities for your child to learn about empathy by doing good through volunteering or traveling, so he sees new perspectives. Other ideas for teaching empathy include:

- Find and discuss books or films such as *Finding Kind* (www.findingkind.indieflix.com) that deal with positive handling of peer aggression.
- Identify and discuss pro-social behavior from community and world leaders that illustrates the link between power and positive leadership.
- Share stories from your own life about making difficult choices.
- Discuss how words and actions seem from another person's view.
- Practice "acts of kindness," like baking bread or raking leaves for an elderly neighbor.

Here's an example of how one man taught empathy to youth:

I know a mentor who was trying to help a group of young people whom he considered selfish and unaware of how well-off they were. Their only contact with suffering people was on TV. In discussions with them, he recognized they weren't seeing the pain which many people in their community were experiencing, so he arranged a "sleep-over." At about 11:00 pm, the kids and the event chaperones got into cars and headed for the charity hospital. They sat in the emergency room waiting area, watching victims of heart attacks, drug overdoses, knifings, shootings, and auto accidents being rolled in on a busy, icy Friday night. The next day, after a little sleep, the youth talked about the difficult experience. They had encountered real suffering, and their reflection was no longer theoretical. Several years later, I met one of the young men who told me it was a life-changing event for him.
– Stan Crow, founder of Rite of Passage Journeys (www.riteofpassagejourneys.org)

Model and teach pro-social skills:
- Give family time top priority, even when your child appears to not need or want the family.
- Find an adult mentor for your child.
- Be a good role model. Practice social & friendship skills at home—assertive, respectful, and peaceful ways to relate to others. Don't talk negatively about others. Let your child see you "make it right" when you're wrong.

ALL RIGHTS RESERVED. © 2014 FAMILY EMPOWERMENT NETWORK™

Empathy:
Healing the Bully Within
By Jody Bellant Scheer MD

I remember the day clearly. I received a phone call that stopped my heart and chilled my senses. My son's school had just called to tell me that my son had been disciplined for bullying a fellow classmate. My son and I were expected to meet the next day with counselors and the principal before he could return to his daily classes. As the panic subsided, I wondered how to best deal with this problem in a way that would most benefit everyone involved. Unfortunately, nobody had ever taught me how to handle this kind of mess when I signed up for parenthood! And, as my son was due home off the bus in exactly 35 minutes, I didn't have enough time to consult parenting experts, online advice, or even my trusted group of mothering friends before I had to deal with him on the issue. I realized that I was on my own in this crisis, so I spent the next 35 minutes trying to calm myself by collecting my thoughts on paper. These were the points that most helped me:

The Message of Love Comes First
First of all, I wrote down how much I loved my son. Exuberant, feisty, testy, and smart, he was often a handful for me, his family, and teachers. But, he was a good person. His friendships were solid, and his values were strong. He did tend to hide his tenderness with a strong dose of bravado, and he was well known to show off a bit to earn the approval of his peers, but he was not a cruel or sadistic person. How was it, I wondered, that he could have bullied another?

All Behavior Has a Positive Intention
I next remembered that *all* behavior has a positive, underlying intention. This is often difficult for parents to remember, especially when their child is involved in hurtful behaviors. However, all behaviors simply reflect a child's strategies to meet his/her own basic needs. As such, almost all behaviors have a positive, underlying intent. Meeting one's needs is certainly a good thing, but many times the behavioral strategies we choose to meet them do not get us what we are seeking and may even have negative effects on ourselves and others. Part of becoming accountable for our actions requires that we

have the self-awareness to judge whether our behaviors are getting us what we want and, secondly, to understand how our actions affect other people's feelings and needs.

Therefore, to really understand the situation at hand, I needed to hear my son's story so I could understand the reasoning behind his behavior from his point of view. To help this occur, I made a note to avoid blaming or punishing him in our upcoming encounter. My goal was to understand what my son did, why he did it, and to help him understand the consequences of his behavior for himself and for the feelings and needs of others. This last goal only can be accomplished if a person can see him- or herself as whole and valuable.

It was important for me to remind my son that, while mistakes are inevitable and serve as our most valuable opportunities to learn, they do not mean that we are terrible people when we make them. Finally, my job as a parent was to help him to move beyond self blame and self hatred to a place of compassion for himself and others. This would be the only method likely to lead my son to enough self acceptance to be willing and able to think creatively, so that the next time these same needs arose, he could think of different ways to meet them that would be more fun and less costly.

Focus on Feelings and Needs
Thirdly, I remembered that most conflicts can more easily be resolved if we simply focus on each other's feelings and needs. It is our human nature to want to be a positive force in our world, and seeing a conflict in the context of universal human feelings and needs helps us to move beyond judgment, anger, competition, and negative thinking toward resolution. It allows us to resolve conflicts in ways that respect the dignity of all parties involved, despite the details of our disputes.

Encouraging Accountable, Respectful Behavior
Lastly, I wanted to support my son in taking responsibility for his behavior, for being respectful of fellow students and school authorities, and for maintaining his own self

© 2014 FAMILY EMPOWERMENT NETWORK™ ALL RIGHTS RESERVED.

respect. The best way to teach these complicated goals to my son was to model them as best I could in our upcoming conversation. I would remember that this was *his* problem, not mine. And, if I wanted him to be honest with me, I would have to maintain my composure and refrain from preaching, blaming, or punishing. Only by accepting my son completely would he be able to do the same, and so come to terms with his problem.

My hopes were to encourage my son to be able to see the effects of his behavior on himself, the other child, and his school. I would talk with him about ways of making amends. I would brainstorm with him how to manage himself the next time a similar situation might arise. In short, without blame, ridicule, or demands, I would try to help my son resolve his problem in a way that would respect his dignity, create a safe environment at school for all children, and encourage him to be respectful and accountable. On a final note, I would ensure him that I would let him take the lead in the meeting at school the next day, and intervene only if and when he asked. I would also reiterate to him that I felt confident that he could handle the situation, and that I would be there to fully support him in doing so.

How It All Worked Out
While I can't remember the exact details of our encounter so many years ago, I will try to recreate it here to the best of my memory. My son did successfully resolve his predicament, and it wasn't nearly as painful for him or me as I had imagined. We both learned a great deal from the experience, which went something like this:

1. Message of Love: When my son came home, I told him how much I loved him, and that I had heard from the school that he had had a bad day. I then asked him if he would like to tell me about it.

2. All Behavior Has a Positive Intention: My son first denied that anything at all had happened at school. He then ducked into his room, stating that he had lots of homework. Instead of getting angry with him, I simply noted that I would prefer to talk with him about our upcoming meeting at school the next morning so that I could understand the situation from his point of view, before hearing the story from the school. I asked him if he would be willing to talk with me before dinner, as I thought it would be easier for him than waiting until his father got home, when he would be outnumbered 2:1. I was careful to stay calm and neutral, and he did agree to

talk with me in a half hour. I waited patiently for him to make the first move.

When we did talk, the story actually came out piece by piece, only because I continued to ask neutral, open-ended questions without rancor or blame, while eating a bowl of popcorn (boys often find it easier to talk when doing something else at the same time.) My son's story was that there was a pickup basketball game during lunchtime at the outdoor basketball court. He recounted that a classmate with a history of impulsive and provocative behavior had inserted himself into the game and then refused to share the ball after several of the boys (including my son) had teased and taunted him. My son finally lost his temper, pushed the fellow down, called him a few colorful names, and wrestled the ball away. "He deserved it, Mom. He's an annoying little brat who had no business bothering us in our game. He shouldn't play ball if he can't take a little ribbing now and then. He's lucky I didn't pound him into dust. It's not my fault he's such a pest."

At this point, my son had gotten quite worked up. He was very defensive and angry. It was unlikely that at this point he would have any ability to be rational about his situation. However, I was able to see that the positive, underlying intentions of my son's behavior were to connect and hang out with his friends, to have fun, to play a good game of basketball, and to gain the approval of his buddies by taking care of an irritating situation in a macho, risky, and aggressive way. Underlying all of this was a strong need to belong, to prove his manhood, and to protect and enhance his closest relationships. The problem was, however, that my son's behavior was also aggressive, potentially dangerous, and intentionally cruel.

How could I get my son to move from his self-righteous, entrenched position to a more compassionate one? The secret was empathy: By offering empathy to someone who is steeped in negative energy, you can meet their needs for connection and understanding, and create the safety they need to become vulnerable and compassionate enough to see another person's point of view. The simplest way to empathize is to connect with another's feelings and needs. By guessing my son's underlying feelings and needs, I was able to break through his wall of defensiveness towards a shred of compassion.

3. Focus on Feelings and Needs: Giving empathy starts with guessing your child's underlying feelings and needs and expressing them. Giving empathy does *not*

ALL RIGHTS RESERVED. © 2014 FAMILY EMPOWERMENT NETWORK™

mean that you are condoning your child's behaviors. It is simply an attempt to connect with what is alive in your child: his strong feelings and unmet needs. Making an empathic connection in this way with your son will empower him to feel trusted and supported enough to do the hard work of hearing another person's point of view.

So, I asked my son, "Are you feeling angry because you value fair play in your games? "Were you feeling annoyed because you needed connection with your friends, and you wanted to play your game uninterrupted?" "Were you irritated and wanting to be accepted and looked up to by your friends?" After a few such guesses at his feelings and his unmet needs (some were right, others off base… this doesn't seem to matter when you are truly interested in creating an empathic connection), my son calmed down and became quiet. I knew that this change likely indicated that he had finally felt "heard" and might be willing to crack open a bit. So, next I asked, "Were you feeling a bit frustrated because you would have liked everyone's needs to be met and you just didn't know how to both get on with your ball game and to deal with the negative behaviors created by and directed back at Billy?"

This seemed to hit paydirt. My son was finally able to acknowledge his frustration at a number of issues, including the fact that the teasing and taunting he and his friends had directed toward Billy had not deterred him from bothering them. Instead, it had provoked Billy to disrupt their game and to get <u>all</u> of their undivided attention. Carefully, I suggested we consider how Billy might have felt at the time, and what he might have been needing that afternoon. It took my son a while to empathize with Billy's feelings and needs; it helped him a lot when I role played with him by taking on Billy's role. Grudgingly, he conceded that Billy was probably feeling sad, angry, irritated, and hurt during and after their encounter, and was needing attention, respect, empathy, reassurance, and a safe school environment. It became obvious that my son's needs and Billy's were really quite similar. As well, my son's and Billy's behaviors shared another common trait: Neither one of them was getting anything close to what he really wanted.

At the level of feelings and needs, my son was able to make an empathic, human connection with a boy whose social skills and behavioral strategies were weak. However, this in no way implied that Billy "deserved" to be mistreated, and my son was finally able to come to that understanding. While my son's temper outburst had solved his problem momentarily, it had left him feeling bad about himself, remorseful about the harm it could have caused Billy, and defensive about being held accountable for his actions. He discovered that there were better ways to deal with the "Billys" in his life.

From this position of self-awareness, it did not take too long for my son to think of some ways to make amends to Billy. It took a bit longer to brainstorm more effective ways to deal with Billy's behavior in the future that would preserve everybody's self respect and ability to play ball.

I wish I could say that similar interactions did not recur, but it seems that the universe repeats those lessons that we haven't yet mastered until we finally "get it." My hope is that my son's ability to step back and look compassionately at himself and the effects of his behavior will be enhanced by the prolonged time we spent together that afternoon. Watching him struggle over the next few years to develop compassion and empathy within a social structure that encourages competition and callousness was sometimes painful and sometimes gratifying. The fact that he did not incorporate this type of bullying into his permanent behavioral repertoire is especially comforting to me as his mother.

4. Encouraging Accountable, Respectful Behavior

The meeting with the school officials the next day went well. My son led the conversation, with my silent support, as he discussed with them what we had discussed the afternoon before. By showing he was open to feedback, my son earned the trust of the school officials and was able to negotiate a resolution to the problem that worked for everybody.

As a parent, I was grateful to have helped my son resolve his own conflict in a way that held him accountable, encouraged him to be respectful to others, respected the school requirement for a safe emotional and physical environment, and increased his own self respect and self awareness. While I will never quite understand the male predilection toward put-downs, one-up-manship, teasing, and rough-and-tumble play, I was happy to see that my son could resolve with dignity his own role and responsibility in such behavior. The side benefit was that he (and I) learned an important lesson about the power of empathy to make amends, to strengthen ties with family and friends, and to heal the bully within.

© 2014 FAMILY EMPOWERMENT NETWORK™ ALL RIGHTS RESERVED.

The Pivotal Role of the Bystander

*"All that is necessary for the triumph of evil
is that good men do nothing."*
– Edmund Burke

When people think of a peer mistreatment incident, it's usually the aggressor and target who come to mind. However, there is a third participant: the bystander or witness. A bystander is more than just an onlooker. Without the audience a bystander provides, the aggressor is usually unlikely to act. Studies have shown that, in as many as 88% of bullying incidents, bystanders were involved in some way (Hawkins, Pepler & Craig). Although most people might think the aggressor holds the power in mistreatment incidents, in reality, the bystanders are the most powerful players because there are usually more bystanders than aggressors or targets involved, mistreatment rarely happens without their presence, and they can affect or alter the course of events.

Bystander Roles

Bystanders may assume different roles during an episode of peer mistreatment:
- Try to help the target
- Join in the mistreatment
- Cheer on and active support the mistreatment
- Passively watch (inadvertently supports the mistreatment)

This last role is particularly interesting. In essence, kids who passively watch and don't do anything allow the children doing the mistreatment to think they approve, even if they don't. And the target interprets the bystander's silence as approval of the mistreatment.

Why Bystanders Don't Intervene More Often

According to research, only 11% to 19% of students who witnessed mistreatment tried to stop it (Hawkins, Pepler, & Craig). The reasons most often given by bystanders as to why they don't try to help the target are the following:
- Fear of getting hurt.
- Fear of becoming the new target of the mistreatment. Even if the bystander intervenes, he or she may be singled out at a later date for retribution.
- Apparent lack of negative consequences should the retaliation occur.
- Being swayed by strong and conflicting emotions.
- Fear of worsening the situation for the target.
- Feeling helpless. Do not know how to respond and/or do not have the skills to do so.
- Think the situation should be an adult's responsibility.
- Group dynamics. The social norm is to NOT intervene.
- Status "management." Has a strong desire to be associated with the "cool" crowd, not the "uncool" target.

Empowering the Bystander

Most children have not directly been involved in mistreating others but have seen it unfold in front of them. How can we involve this group of kids in a positive way? Here are some suggestions for what to teach them:

- **Notice the mistreatment.** Seeing that mistreatment is even happening can be challenging in a school where mistreatment happens so frequently and regularly that it is easy to accept it as the norm.
- **Don't encourage the aggressor** by laughing, clapping or joining in on the mistreatment.
- **Care about the target**. Switch from "There's nothing I can do" to "What can I do?"
- **Comfort the target.** This can be done in the

ALL RIGHTS RESERVED. © 2014 FAMILY EMPOWERMENT NETWORK™

moment or afterward in private if it is awkward or the bystander is afraid of being the next target. Children who have been targeted report that having peers support them through kind words or actions is extremely helpful.

- **Get help from someone you trust.** Tell an adult.

Examples of Effective Bystander/Witness Actions from the Youth Voice Research Project:

- Spent time with me, sat with me, or hung out with me
- Talked to me at school to encourage me
- Helped me get away from situations where the behavior was going on
- Listened to me
- Gave me advice about what I should do
- Called me at home to encourage me
- Helped me tell an adult
- Distracted the people who were treating me badly
- Told an adult
- Asked the person to stop being mean to me in a friendly way

Teaching Pro-Social Skills

Additional tips for intervention, prevention, and befriending (for kids as well as adults) include:

- Be the one to stop gossip. Walk away when you hear someone start talking meanly about someone you know, ask him to stop being mean, or stand up for a friend about whom others are gossiping.
- Always be open to getting to know new people.
- Give positive strokes to another when they are deserved, even if you don't know that person well.
- Compliment or acknowledge others.
- Try to talk out conflicts with your friends. Try not to hold grudges.
- Live the Golden Rule. (Do onto others, as you would have them do unto you.)
- Ask your child what she would like someone to do for her if she were in a target's shoes and hold that expectation as a family value.

Parents as Role Models

The most effective long-term strategy for peer mistreatment intervention is for parents to take their job as role models and forces for positive change seriously. This means we adults must:

- Set a new standard: always comfort the target or intervene to stop mistreatment when it can be done safely.
- Work to instill feelings of empathy and compassion in our children.
- Stand up to injustice.
- Create awareness among children and adults about the power of being a supportive bystander.
- Model all the things that we expect our children to do in similar situations.

Resources

Fried, S., & Fried, P. *Bullies, Targets and Witnesses: Helping Children Break the Pain Chain.* NY: M. Evans & Company, Inc., 2003.

Fried, S., and Sosland, B. *Banishing Bullying Behavior.* 2nd Ed. Lanham, MD: R & L Education, 2011.

Hawkins, D.L., Pepler, D.J., & Craig, W.M. (2001). "Naturalistic Observations of Peer Interventions in Bullying." *Social Development* 10 (4), 512-527.

Youth Voice Research Project (2010) by Stan Davis and Charisse Nixon, Ph.D. (www.youthvoiceproject.com)

© 2014 FAMILY EMPOWERMENT NETWORK™ ALL RIGHTS RESERVED.

A Movement to Stand for Courage

By Nicole Jon Carroll, MSW, LCSW

Imagine this scenario: Ramon notices a wheelchair-bound student being harassed. Bothered by what he sees, Ramon arranges to have five wheelchairs brought into his school and challenges peers to spend a full school day in a chair. He then puts up posters with the statements peers made about the challenges of navigating school in a wheelchair. Witness the character of a hero. Ramon uses his personal power to influence others to be empathetic and aware of peer mistreatment—behavior worthy of recognition and reinforcement.

Wanting to recognize and celebrate our youth heroes, Stand for Courage was born. We are a foundation that encourages students to "get caught doing the right thing." We do this through recognizing youth who stand up for one another and

Stand for Courage Youth Advisors joined Roger Waters of Pink Floyd on stage at a sold-out performance of "The Wall" tour.

themselves. For example, a peer might go online and nominate Ramon for a Stand for Courage award. If he wins, he might be honored through Stand for Courage in a number of ways. Ramon might be singled out at a school assembly for his leadership or innovative thinking. He might get red-carpet treatment at a Stand for Courage award ceremony, be recognized at a sporting event during half time or at a concert intermission, or receive a personal congratulatory call or video chat from a favorite musician, athlete, or politician. There might even be donations to his school, a scholarship, or tickets to concerts or sporting events.

Stand for Courage recognizes and rewards positive behavior by using the power of cultural currency—from local to international celebrities and other social status symbols—to publicly shift power to the youth who engage in pro-community, positive behavior. Doing so creates a domino effect among youth, encouraging others to "do

the right thing."

Students play a major role in the success of Stand for Courage's programs. Youth nominate one another to be recognized for their positive choices and actions. Plus, our Youth Advisory Board, consisting of 20 students ages 14-18, meet regularly to come up with ideas for program development and for promoting Stand for Courage to their peers. They also help to establish Stand for Courage clubs at schools and community centers and present talks to audiences of peers about personal power and healthy relationships. In addition, students assist in implementing Stand for Courage's online platform and mentor younger students to actively "do the right thing."

Backed by the evidence-based methodology of positive reinforcement and a strengths perspective, Stand for Courage is a nationally recognized organization. By promoting a healthy and positive environment conducive to personal growth and learning, the foundation offers a cultural movement based on hope, possibility, and encouragement for the future of our youth.

To nominate someone or find out how your school can become a Stand for Courage school, check out www.standforcourage.org. You'll also find on the website articles, media clips, and information about *Your Mind: Own It. A Manual for Every Teen*, a forthcoming book for teens about dealing with peer mistreatment.

Nicole Jon Carroll, MSW, LCSW, is the founder and director of Stand for Courage (www.standforcourage.org), author of Your Mind: Own It, *an executive coach, an IMAGO therapist, as well as the mother of three sons and two bonus sons.*

 ALL RIGHTS RESERVED. © 2014 FAMILY EMPOWERMENT NETWORK™

Empowerment Groups to Reduce Peer Mistreatment Among Girls

For 5th-12th Graders

By Wendy Craig, PhD

TWO TENETS OF EMPOWERMENT GROUPS

1. It is easier to awaken empathy and reduce tolerance of peer mistreatment among the silent majority than it is to change the behavior of individual aggressive girls.

2. Girls who use peer mistreatment are more likely to respond to peer censure than to adult censure. Therefore, by working with a group of girls to help them understand the dynamics of power, the abuse of power, the experience of being targeted, and the strategies for positive power, significant change can occur within girls' peer groups.

GOALS FOR EMPOWERMENT GROUPS

- Gain greater understanding of power in relationships and how violation of power causes harm to individuals and to the group
- Awaken empathy for targets of peer mistreatment
- Empower the silent majority to support those being mistreated
- Reduce stigma associated with being mistreated
- Decrease the support, prestige, and power that mistreatment behavior might achieve for the aggressor or the leader of the mistreatment
- Transform the group atmosphere to become more cohesive, caring, and trusting
- Girls who use peer mistreatment choose to stop
- Targeted girl no longer feels isolated and humiliated, has strategies for responding, and a support network

EMPOWERMENT GROUP STRATEGIES

Leader:
- Communicates a respectful, collegial attitude, rather than a punitive or blaming one
- Creates a working alliance with the group to engage everyone productively
- Communicates an accepting and nonjudgmental attitude about the personal worth of all the girls
- Doesn't condone mistreatment of others but also doesn't label the child who mistreated another

Group Process promotes:
- Moving beyond limitations of stereotyping
- Recognizing that individual behaviors may reflect the internalization of harmful social, ethno-cultural, and political factors
- Recognizing traits that are culturally defined as "masculine" or "feminine" stereotypes.

SAMPLE AGENDA TOPICS
- Power: Its use and abuse
- Popularity: What does it mean?
- Self-worth: Consideration of self worth beyond boys; positive female role models, etc.
- Emotions that happen when girls get together:
  - Anger, envy, jealousy
  - Embarrassment, shame, intimidation, shyness
  - Joy, excitement, silliness
- Relationships: Their importance and what it takes to maintain healthy relationships
- Thin line between mistreatment and flirting with boys
- How to speak up for people in need

© 2014 FAMILY EMPOWERMENT NETWORK™ ALL RIGHTS RESERVED.

EMPOWERMENT GROUP METHOD

- Can be done with all the girls in a class or with a specific group of girls, depending on situation
- Meet in a special place; establish a schedule
- Openly tell students why you are there
- Engage girls in establishing rules for group meetings (e.g., no specific names and incidents, respect, listen without interruption, etc.)
- Have an agenda for discussions, but be flexible
- Use subgroup/large group format (to encourage everyone to talk, go around in a circle, etc.

GIRLS' EMPOWERMENT GROUP EXAMPLES

Girl Scouts helps girls develop their potential; relate to others; develop values to guide positive actions; and contribute to society. www.girlscouts.org

Girls Circle aims to counteract social and interpersonal forces that impede girls' growth and development by promoting an emotionally safe setting and structure within which girls can develop caring relationships and use authentic voices. www.onecirclefoundation.org/GC.aspx

Girls Inc.® inspires all girls to be strong, smart, and bold™ through programs and experiences that help them navigate gender, economic, and social barriers. www.girlsinc.org

Girls Leadership Institute (GLI) offers camps and workshops designed to teach girls the core practices of emotional intelligence, healthy relationships, and assertive self expression. www.girlsleadershipinstitute.org

New Moon Girls is a safe, fully moderated online community where girls connect and support each other while creating poetry, artwork, stories, and videos. www.newmoon.com

---

Adapted from Lewis, J.A. (1992). Gender sensitivity and family empowerment. Topics in Family Psychology and Counseling 1, 1. Used with permission from Wendy Craig from Making a Difference in Bullying *(with "peer mistreatment" substituted for "bullying" and "target" substituted for "victim").*

Support Groups for Boys

Educators and professionals working with boys often find that the challenges boys face in our schools and communities arise out of limited relational abilities. One avenue for supporting them is to engage them in strengths-based groups where they can practice relational skills in a safe environment and connect with positive role models.

Two particular examples of boys support groups are **BAM! Boys Advocacy and Mentoring** and **The Council for Boys and Young Men** of One Circle Foundation. **BAM!** uses methods that reflect an understanding and respect of boys' communication styles and activities that honor boys' need for movement. Each BAM! group meeting begins with a facilitator telling a childhood story. Sharing stories allows the leaders to connect with the boys, because stories showcase openness and vulnerability. After the facilitator story, the boys engage in group physical challenges. These offer outlets for boys' energy as well as create group cohesion, make abstract ideas more concrete, and build a playful learning atmosphere. Finally, the boys practice the skills they need to become more relationally competent.

The Council for Boys and Young Men promotes boys' and young men's safe and healthy passage through adolescent years by focusing on their developmental need for strong, positive relationships. During Council meetings, boys engage in organized activities, dialogue, and self-expression to question stereotypical concepts and to increase their emotional, social, and cultural literacy. In a safe and action-oriented context, the boys build valuable relationships with peers and adults.

For more information on the above programs, check out their respective websites: www.bamgroups.com *and* www.onecirclefoundation.org/TC.aspx.

ALL RIGHTS RESERVED. © 2014 FAMILY EMPOWERMENT NETWORK™

Related Resources for Further Exploration

Banishing Bullying Behavior: Transforming the Culture of Peer Abuse by SuEllen Fried and Blanche Sosland, PhD. Lanham, MD: Rowman & Littlefield, 2011. 2nd Ed.

Bullied: What Every Parent, Teacher and Kid Needs to Know About Ending the Cycle of Fear by Carrie Goldman. NY: HarperCollins, 2012.

Bullies, Targets & Witnesses: Helping Children Break the Pain Chain by SuEllen Fried and Paula Fried, PhD. Lanham, MD: Rowman & Littlefield, 2003.

The Bully, the Bullied, and the Bystander by Barbara Coloroso. NY: Harper Resource, 2003.

Bullying Beyond the Schoolyard: Preventing and Responding to Cyberbullying by Sameer Hinduja and Justin Patchin. Thousand Oaks, CA: Corwin Press, 2009.

Cliques: 8 Steps to Help Your Child Survive the Social Jungle by Charlene Giannetti and Margaret Sagarese. NY: Broadway Books, 2001.

Cyberbullying and Cyberthreats: Responding to the Challenge of Online Social Aggression, Threats, and Distress by Nancy Willard, MS, JD. Minneapolis, MN: Research Press, 2007 2nd Ed.

Easing the Teasing: Helping Your Child Cope with Name-Calling, Ridicule, and Verbal Bullying by Judy S Freedman. NY: McGraw-HillContemporary Books, 2002.

Mom, They're Teasing Me: Helping Your Child Solve Social Problems by Michael Thompson, Lawrence J. Cohen, and Catherine O'Neill Grace. NY: Ballantine Books, 2002.

Nobody Likes Me, Everybody Hates Me: The Top 25 Friendship Problems and How to Solve Them by Michele Borba, EdD. San Francisco, CA: Jossey-Bass, 2005.

Odd Girl Out: The Hidden Culture of Aggression in Girls (2002) and *Odd Girl Speaks Out* (2004) by Rachel Simmons. NY: Harcourt, 2002.

Protect Your Child from Bullying: Expert Advice to Help You Recognize, Prevent, and Stop Bullying Before Your Child Gets Hurt by Allen L. Beane. San Francisco, CA: Jossey-Bass, 2008.

Queen Bee Moms & King Pin Dads: Dealing with the Parents, Teachers, Coaches and Counselors Who Can Make—or Break—Your Child's Future by Rosalind Wiseman. NY: Crown Publishers, 2006.

Queen Bees & Wannabes: Helping Your Daughter Survive Cliques, Gossip, Boyfriends and Other Realities of Adolescence by Rosalind Wiseman. NY: Crown Publishers, 2002.

Masterminds & Wingmen: Helping Our Boys Cope with Schoolyard Power, Locker-Room Tests, Girlfriends, and the New Rules of Boy World by Rosalind Wiseman. NY: Random House, 2013.

© 2014 FAMILY EMPOWERMENT NETWORK™ ALL RIGHTS RESERVED.

Sticks and Stones: 7 Ways Your Child Can Deal with Teasing, Conflict, and Other Hard Times by Scott Cooper. NY: Random House, 2000.

Sticks and Stones: Defeating the Culture of Bullying and Rediscovering the Power of Character and Empathy by Emily Bazelon. NY: Random House, 2013.

Organization and program: *Stand for Courage.* An organization that works with youth to provide celebrity recognition for individuals who stand up for one another and themselves. www.standforcourage.org

Organization and programs: *Massachusetts Aggression Reduction Center* http://webhost.bridgew.edu/marc/

SPECIFICALLY FOR SCHOOLS

Bully Free Classroom: Over 100 Tips and Strategies for Teachers K-8 by Allan Beane. Minneapolis, MN: Free Spirit Publishing, 1999.

Bullying and Cyberbullying: What Every Educator Needs to Know by Elizabeth Englander, PhD. Cambridge, MA: Harvard Education Press, 2013.

Bullying Prevention Handbook: A Guide for Principals, Teachers, and Counselors by John H. Hoover and Ronald Oliver. Bloomington, IN: National Educational Service, 1996.

Bullying at School: What We Know and What We Can Do by Dan Olweus. Malden, MA: Blackwell Publishing, 1993. www.olweus.org

Empowering the Bystander in Bullying Prevention K-8 by Stan Davis with Julia Davis. Minneapolis, MN: Research Press, 2007. www.stopbullyingnow.org

No Kidding About Bullying: 125 Ready-to-Use Activities to Help Kids Manage Anger, Resolve Conflicts, Build Empathy, and Get Along by Naomi Drew. Minneapolis, MN: Free Spirit Publishing, 2010. (Book with CD-ROM)

Nobody Left to Hate: Teaching Compassion After Columbine by Elliot Aronson. NY: Owl Books, 2000.

Owning Up® Curriculum: Empowering Adolescents to Confront Social Cruelty, Bullying, and Injustice by Rosalind Wiseman. Minneapolis, MN: Research Press, 2009. (Book with CD-ROM)

Schools Where Everyone Belongs: Practical Strategies for Reducing Bullying by Stan Davis with Julia Davis. Minneapolis, MN: Research Press, 2007. www.stopbullyingnow.org

ABC-TV "20/20" News Special: "The In Crowd and Social Cruelty." 02/15/2002 John Stossel, focusing on what it takes to be popular, interviews kids and uncovers why they dish out social cruelty, why they take it, and what schools can do to make it better. (Enter Product Code S020215 01. Cost $29.95.)

BOOKS FOR ELEMENTARY SCHOOL KIDS

My Secret Bully (also in Spanish), ***Just Kidding*** (also in Spanish), ***Trouble Talk***, ***Sorry!***, ***Too Perfect***, ***Confessions of a Former Bully***, ***The Invisible Boy,*** and ***Better Than You*** by Trudy Ludwig. All must-haves for every elementary school. Fantastic, to-the-point learning through picture-book stories. Check out www.trudyludwig. com, who also gives assembly presentations to kids.

ALL RIGHTS RESERVED. © 2014 FAMILY EMPOWERMENT NETWORK™

Fostering Resilience 6

Stefani Graap, 8th Grade, Rosemont Ridge Middle School

chapter six
Fostering Resilience

"Every adversity, every failure, every heartache carries with it the seed to an equal or greater benefit." – Napoleon Hill, *Think and Grow Rich*

It is difficult to see our kids suffer—whether from peer mistreatment, normal friendship troubles, failing a test, falling down, or just plain being sad along the rocky road of life. As parents, we'd all like our children to be happy and full of joy. Trying to ensure a child's continual happiness, however, is an impossible task. Disappointment is an inevitable part of the fabric of human life. Whether the "downs" of your child's life are caused by internal struggles (such as learning to wait for something or grasping the week's Calculus concept) or by external struggles (such as being teased by friends or not getting into the college of choice), there is one key asset that will allow your child to push through the hard times and thrive: resilience. Resilience is the ability to withstand disappointment and failure, manage the unexpected, find creative solutions to problems, and bounce back in the face of adversity and emotional hurts. Resilience allows people to move through their trials and tribulations with flexibility and courage.

In general, experts agree that resilient people tend to have these three traits in common:

1. **Emotional Hardiness:** They have tools and skills to handle feelings of sadness, disappointment, discomfort, and upset, and they trust in their ability to deal with their emotions effectively.
2. **Competence and Confidence:** They have had practice overcoming challenges; are capable and competent; and believe in themselves as capable, competent human beings.
3. **Support:** They have someone who believes in them and has faith in their abilities.

All life-serving, these are traits we hope to see in our children by the time they are grown, so they can bravely face challenging outside influences and the inevitable hard knocks of life.

In service of exemplifying the power of resilience, one of our authors shares her story of how she developed resilience and how she and her husband cul-

Resilience is a powerful antidote to the challenges we and our children face every day. This invaluable skill can enable us to make and keep friends, deal with the ups and downs of our world, and find peace and fulfillment in our lives.

With so much to gain, how do we foster resilience in our children? By being lovingly present, teaching them skills, and letting them have their own experiences from which to grow strong. Unfortunately, some parents may inadvertently compromise a child's resilience.

- Part I of this chapter discusses some of the ways this may happen, and
- Part II delves into ways we can help our children build and exercise their resilience.

The bottom line is that our children will, hopefully, be on their own some day. We want them to have the skills to face their challenges and problems head on and with gusto. As loving adults in their lives, we can only foster this by teaching, modeling, and then letting go!

© 2014 FAMILY EMPOWERMENT NETWORK™ ALL RIGHTS RESERVED.

tivated resilience in their children:

Resilience was the gift I received from a less than perfect childhood. My dad died after a prolonged coma, and my mother gave me up for adoption. She later reclaimed me from the orphanage when her situation stabilized, and I learned to survive with homemade clothes and 150 ways to cook hamburger. I fought my family, cultural expectations, and poverty to enter college and put myself through medical school. By comparison, I knew that my own children were being raised in a great big tub of butter! They had two physician parents in a stable, loving relationship, a large extended family, no experiences of deprivation, and never a period of worry in their lives about the basic necessities of survival.

How would these children of mine ever become resilient, given their privileged beginnings? This was a subject my husband and I often pondered. We decided that we would have to imbue resilience in our children by creating experiences where they would have to struggle to meet their own needs. Some examples included:

- *We created financial struggles by putting our kids on a budget, starting in the fourth and sixth grades. They negotiated their yearly budget with us after researching the cost of their basic needs. We increased the number of items in their budget and went from a monthly disbursement to a yearly one as they grew. As parents, we learned to live with the consequences of their decisions, needing to resist rescuing them when they made (frequent) poorly thought out choices. As a result, I sewed all my daughter's prom dresses, at her request. My son's wardrobe was a bit shabby, but he had a terrific music collection. During college, we provided a basic living allowance that would cover a very frugal budget. This encouraged the kids to find supplemental jobs to complement their lifestyles and studies.*

- *We looked for challenging physical experiences that would help our children gain confidence and a sense of well-being. We kayaked every summer off the coast of Vancouver Island. Our kids rode bicycles, went on rafting trips, climbed mountains, went backpacking, and enjoyed summer science excursions. They knew how to survive torrential downpours in a tent, how to stay calm in a pod of barking sea lions, and how to paddle through a storm. I like to think that these hardships built resilience, as well as life-long memories.*

- *We made a conscious choice to encourage creativity, physical activity, and reading by investing in craft supplies, living on a houseboat, playing outside, and collecting a large library of children's books and games. During our prolonged post-graduate years of study and work, my husband and I never had time for TV, and we elected not to buy one while our kids were growing up. This forced all of us to develop hobbies and activities that enriched our lives to a degree that more than made up for the time usually lost to TV shows and commercials.*

- *We mindfully included a diversity of people in our kids' lives. Our neighborhood included a lot of diversity in income and livelihood, the kids' school drew students of all races and socioeconomic levels from all over the city, and our spiritual community was culturally diverse. We reached out to those in need through charitable work and shared our home with a number of kids and individuals in need of respite and shelter.*

- *We traveled as a family to Third World countries. Privileges that our children took for granted were so obviously missing from the peoples we met and lived with abroad, yet happiness and joy in life were not.*

Our efforts seem to have born fruit! All three of our kids are now marvelous, independent young adults who are pursuing their dreams in a way that is consistent with their own sets of values. Each of them can live on a dime when they need to, and they are pursuing careers that will reward them more with passion than with monetary rewards. I am proud of their choices and gratified to see them so resilient, happy, and self-supporting as adults.

ALL RIGHTS RESERVED. © 2014 FAMILY EMPOWERMENT NETWORK™

What are the lessons learned from this reflection? That resilience is built one struggle at a time starting at an early age, and, as parents, we can consciously encourage and/or facilitate those productive struggles. Read: Let them fall down so they have to learn how to get up on their own. Sometimes we might ponder, "My child is doing fine, so why put him/her through trials and frustration?" The answer is that childhood is the time to tackle little mistakes and failures so that children will be prepared for the bigger challenges that surely will come their way when they are older. Without those early struggles and gradual strengthening of the resiliency muscle, bigger challenges may seem insurmountable.

Before we get to our suggestions and tips for building resilience skills and competencies, we are going to explore what gets in the way of this important work.

PART I: WHAT COMPROMISES OUR CHILDREN'S RESILIENCE?

". . . Childhood is full of frustrating moments. Nature has designed life for children in such a way as to guarantee that they'll have their wishes denied many times a day.... When parents intervene because their children are frustrated—believing they're doing so out of love and care—they prevent [their children] from learning the lesson of adaptation. . . . There's value in helping [children] chalk up another adaptation, knowing that each time they do, they're adding to the internal reservoir of confidence and resourcefulness that will help them navigate life's ups and downs." – Susan Stiffelman, *Parenting Without Power Struggles*

One of the most difficult tasks parents face in raising their children to be resilient may be to stand by them while they experience the pain, discomfort, and hardship of their own struggles. This is challenging work! Because it is so important, however, we want to explore some of the ways we may undermine our children's resilience. If you see yourself in any of these behaviors, don't be too hard on yourself; at times we do what's easiest in the moment instead of keeping the long-term goals in mind. Hopefully, some of our ideas of what compromises our children's resilience will help you in these particular moments.

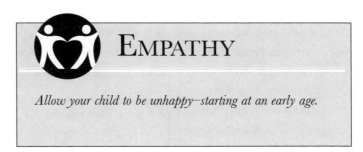

EMPATHY

Allow your child to be unhappy—starting at an early age.

Not Allowing Children to Have Their Natural Emotions

In order to develop resilience, children must fully experience challenging emotions and, starting at an early age, learn to get through to the other side of them. Over time and with practice, children can learn strategies to cope with confusing feelings and difficult situations. Gradually, they can become confident in their own abilities to handle anger and sadness, disappointment and frustration—and trust that these, like any other emotions, are impermanent.

Unfortunately, it's difficult for us to see our children unhappy, and we may do all we can to avoid triggering tantrums and tears. The irony is, however, that when we parent to avoid our children's unhappiness we ultimately instigate unhappiness within our children. Here's how this works: Children who perceive their parents' discomfort at their displays of unhappiness learn quickly that being unhappy gets them what they want. Displays of unhappiness "work". . . to avoid having to do something or get the toy, the food, the experience, the car, the iPhone that they believe will make them feel good in the moment. So kids have much to gain from being unhappy! They learn that, when they show they are unhappy, especially really loudly, their parents will jump in to fix (quiet) the situation by providing the object of desire of the moment. A pattern is, thus, established—which creates exactly what

© 2014 FAMILY EMPOWERMENT NETWORK™ ALL RIGHTS RESERVED.

the parents have been working hard to avoid: their child's displays of discontent.

At some point, parents may begin to feel as though they are held captive by their children's difficult emotions. At first the goal was to avoid their children feeling bad. Eventually, parents realize that they are "giving in" or going back on their word in order to avoid their own embarrassment and challenging emotions in the face of their children's exuberant public displays of dismay. It is a pattern that begins with good intentions and yet ends up being a trap, detrimental to both children and their parents.

If you find yourself in this scenario, you are not alone. In the heat of the moment, we often forget that, when we parent to avoid challenging emotions in our kids, we unwittingly end up robbing them of the opportunity to build their own capacity for resilience, as they practice encountering and overcoming discomforts in their daily lives.

Rescuing

University professors are calling the young adults they are seeing these days "tea cups": They are very fragile, are used to being served, and crack at the slightest stress. Obviously, parents don't set out to purposefully handicap their kids. They don't purposely parent in a way to nurture fragility

and incompetence. If we asked parents who delivered these kids to their first semester of college why they parented them the way they did, the parents would say, "Because we love them so much!"

In truth, loving them really is the easy part! What we need to do is love them in a way that encourages them to develop the tools, skills, and character traits that will allow them to be prepared to live an independent, fulfilling life. To do so, we need to stop interfering with our children's struggles and–little by little, skinned knee by skinned knee, squabble by squabble–let them experience adversity first hand. It's good for them! When we "helicopter" over our children of any age and swoop down and rescue them whenever needed (even if not needed), we convey the message, "You are fragile and clearly can't do this on your own."

One particular area of our parenting that ultimately causes over-parenting or helicoptering is when we take on too much responsibility for our children's future success. For example, we might believe our children will only be successful if they get into the right pre-school, play on the most elite sports team, get perfect grades, and get into an Ivy League college. Any vestige of these attitudes can push us into feeling we have to fix everything for our children and do everything for them so

---

THE DOWNSIDE OF "FIXING" BAD FEELINGS

When we make it our goal to "fix" bad feelings and work overtime to ensure our children's continued uninterrupted happiness, our good intentions send negative messages that we often don't recognize we are passing on. For example, when we go back on our word, change our plans, and ignore our own family rules so that our children can avoid being upset, the messages they receive are detrimental to healthy self development:

- "Feelings are powerful and sometimes frightening."
- "Feeling bad is so horrible that rules, patterns, and standards must shift so I don't have to feel like this."
- "My parents don't want me to have to deal with this; it must be too difficult for me to handle."
- "My parents feel I am not strong enough or capable enough–and so I must be taken care of and served."

Kids who grow up with these messages rarely feel competent, self reliant, or resilient. They also often equate being served and pampered with being loved and then don't recognize or value the many wonderful ways that people show they care.

ALL RIGHTS RESERVED. © 2014 FAMILY EMPOWERMENT NETWORK™

WALK THE TALK

Consider the growth that occurred in this scenario for a young college freshman:

> *Lisa was in her first year of college. Upon departing a campus bus, she realized, too late, that she had left her wallet on the seat. She called the school security office, but the wallet was nowhere to be found. Lost were her debit card, credit card, driver's license, and student ID, in addition to $20. So she called home, which was 3000+ miles away and a three-hour time difference, and asked her mom what to do. Her mom didn't get upset and reprimand or shame her. Nor did she start looking up information and making phone calls for Lisa. Instead, Mom told Lisa she would have to look up the financial information online and visit her local bank in person. A few hours later, Mom got this text: "Thanks for making me call and take care of it. I'm glad I know how and it was sort of empowering."*

Lisa learned some valuable lessons and became more competent and confident in the process. Next time she loses her wallet—or faces another challenge—she may call home just for connection and support rather than expecting a rescue.

they attain these goals. In truth, what helps kids be resilient and successful is to practice overcoming challenges with the support of someone who believes in them yet doesn't constantly prop up or rescue them. The article **"How to Ground Your Helicopter Parenting"** shares tips on what we can do to reduce our helicoptering and empower our kids to develop healthy competency and decision-making skills.

With too many rescues under their belt, our children also may develop a sense of entitlement. Children who begin to feel entitled—who think they deserve all the best things without any effort on their part—have more difficulty developing a sense of inner strength and self esteem. (Note: Entitlement is the direct outcome of a parenting style that gives too much and asks too little.) As the adults in their lives let children experience working hard, overcoming difficulties, and helping others, the children will begin to shed the "beast" of entitlement (as Charles Fay and his father, Jim Fay, call it). Children need to know that their level of success is dependent on their level of personal responsibility and perseverance.

Fear

If we empower our children to be resilient, connected, and empathetic, they will find their own good place in their world—just as we can. But fear compromises resilience. To foster resilience in children, we must recognize we cannot parent wisely, nor really prepare our children for the future, if we parent out of fear. For example, when we get unreasonably scared about our kids' safety or success, we usually react reflexively and lose our long-term perspective. So, one of the steps for raising resilient children is being resilient ourselves. We can do this by holding on to both sides of modern life: On one hand, we need to be realistic about potential negatives and dangers, and, on the other, to affirm the goodness of the world we live in—the kindness of people; the beauty of the Earth; the forces for positive change; the deep satisfaction of family, friends, and fulfilling work; the wonders of the modern world; and the ability of our kids to grow.

A lot of our fear about our kids' safety comes from the distorted perception of the world we glean from the media. George Gerbner, the University of Pennsylvania professor who coined the phrase "mean world syndrome," conducted three decades of research on violence on television and how it shapes perceptions of society. He showed that the more television people watch, the more likely they are to believe that the world is an unforgiving and frightening place. As early as 1981, before a Congressional subcommittee on communications, he warned us: "Fearful people are more dependent, more easily manipulated and controlled, more susceptible to deceptively simple, strong, tough measures and hard-line postures. They may accept and even welcome repression

© 2014 FAMILY EMPOWERMENT NETWORK™ ALL RIGHTS RESERVED.

if it promises to relieve their insecurities." Is this what we want for our children? Fear causes us to be over-protective (intrusive) and over reactive (alarmist) and limit our children's autonomy in counterproductive ways. In looking for ways to curb fear, we might start with being proactive about the content and amount of what we and our kids watch on movies, TV programs, and the nightly news.

RESOURCE FOR PARENTS WITH FEARFUL AND ANXIOUS CHILDREN

If your child seems especially fearful and anxious, a great place to start your education is with Donna Pincus' book, ***Growing Up Brave: Expert Strategies for Helping Your Child Overcome Fear, Stress, and Anxiety*** (2012). Dr. Pincus is the Director of the Child and Adolescent Fear and Anxiety Treatment Program at Boston University. Her work guides parents in identifying and understanding anxiety in their children, outlines effective parenting techniques for reducing anxiety, and shows parents how to promote bravery for long-term confidence.

Scarcity

"I can see exactly how and why more people are wrestling with how to believe they are enough. I see the cultural messaging everywhere that says that an ordinary life is a meaningless life. And I see how kids that grow up on a steady diet of reality TV, celebrity culture, and unsupervised social media can absorb this messaging and develop a completely skewed sense of the world. 'I am only as good as the number of likes I get on Facebook or Instagram.'"
– Brené Brown, *Daring Greatly*, p. 23

Just as the media in our culture promotes fear, that fear begets a sense of scarcity–the attitude that you are never good enough and never have enough–which is great for the twin evils of consumerism and lookism promoted by the media! In a scarcity culture, we measure ourselves with these questions: What is your work? How powerful and influential are you? How busy are you? How much money do you have? How much stuff do you own? How

thin and beautiful are you? Then there are the kids: How perfect are they? How many friends do they have? How obedient are they? How many "As" do they get? What college do they go to? How "superstar" are they in sports? And, finally, how does scarcity show up in parenting? Do you attend all your child's soccer games? Do you buy your kids the latest fashions so they fit in? How many hours do you volunteer at your child's school? Do you sit with her every night so she gets "As" on her homework? Wow! What pressure! Here's the real deal: In a culture of scarcity, no matter what, there is never enough and you can never do enough! This attitude surely does not promote resilience; it kills it.

In a scarcity culture, we feel inept and desperately look around, trying to find comfort in whom and what we are. Unfortunately, often the only strategy we can come up with is to compare and put down those around us. Then we "feel" better in some shallow, self-defeating way–self-defeating because we end up alienating others. To top it off, because we are sure we will never measure up and because we are so afraid of being ordinary, we also quickly learn to never show our true colors.

What's the antidote to the scarcity dilemma? Brené Brown, a shame and vulnerability researcher and author of *Daring Greatly*, has the answer: whole-hearted living. Her research shows that to live a whole-hearted life, we need to truly believe, to the core of our being, "I am enough, I have enough, and I am grateful." We need to shift from "human doing" to "human being." We need to be satisfied that just being human is magnificent enough. This belief will, ultimately, translate into confidence and flower into resilience and strength to face uncertainty.

Shame

Another way we short circuit cultivating resilience in our children is with shame. Shame makes a person feel hopeless. If a child is told "You are bad," he eventually soaks in the words and begins to believe, "I am bad, and nothing can be done about it." On the contrary, if

ALL RIGHTS RESERVED. © 2014 FAMILY EMPOWERMENT NETWORK™

the child is separated from the negative action ("One of my actions was bad"), he can have hope, try something different, and do better next time. Proactive, positive experiences with setbacks over the course of childhood plant the seeds for a flourish of resilience.

In truth, we use various strategies to guide our kids. Some are positive–cheerleader, supporter, advisor, hugger, carpooler–and some are not so positive: bribery, humiliation, punishment, guilt, demands, and, worst of all, shame. Shame is using ridicule and belittling to get your child to do what you want, and it has been a strategy used to keep people in line for generations. But shame has a devastating negative impact on our kids. Nothing good comes from it!

In her book, *Daring Greatly*, Brené Brown dissects the appalling and scary power shame has and shows that it directly correlates with addiction, depression, aggression, violence, eating disorders, and suicide–all the things we fear the most for our kids through the teen years and beyond. Parents have a lot of influence on our children's internalization of shame, which means we need to be vigilant about separating our children from their behaviors. Brown offers a good example: "If a child *tells a lie*, she can change that behavior. If she *is a liar*–where is the potential for change in that?" (*Daring Greatly*, p. 224)

Perfectionism

"Our kids are going to spend a lot more time being imperfect than being perfect. It is up to us to teach them to learn and grow from times of imperfection." – Glenda Montgomery

Demanding perfection is another roadblock to raising a resilient child. Believing that perfection is the road to emotional acceptance actually makes us weak, anxious, and unable to love ourselves and our children as we are, with all our foibles. Perfectionism doesn't leave enough room for the normal struggles and mistakes of life, which are often the very events that muster grit and build psychological muscle.

Be real. Are you perfect? Perfectionism makes us fear failure more than we desire success, and, by avoiding failure at all costs, we minimize the ability to learn resilience from our potential mistakes. This is as likely to be a problem for adults as well as children.

If you have a child who is veering toward perfectionism, give her the extra support she needs to begin to accept herself and open up to the complexity of life. Celebrate your own mistakes aloud and be gentle with your child's mistakes.

Trudy Ludwig's book *Too Perfect* is an excellent resource for pre-adolescents and their parents, and *The Curse of the Good Girl: Raising Authentic Girls with Courage and Confidence* by Rachel Simmons should be a go-to book for any woman or girl struggling with perfectionism.

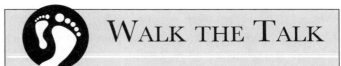 WALK THE TALK

In the Smith family home, "Nobody is perfect" were watchwords from the get-go. Whenever Kira would complain about the immature boys at school, her mother would remind her, "Nobody is perfect; they haven't learned yet how to follow the rules." One day, when Kira came home from first grade, she was excited to share her news of the day. Apparently, one of the boys in her class had gotten into trouble and her teacher had kept him in from recess. Kira's take-away from the altercation was: "Mom, I don't think that Ms. Taylor has learned yet that 'nobody is perfect.'"

Over-scheduling, Overdoing ... Too Much Stress

For people of all ages, over-scheduling and overdoing can lead to stress, which not only compromises our health but also our resilience. Unfortunately, stress–that "state of arousal that involves both the mind and the body in response to demands" (Webster's dictionary)–is a salient factor for many families today as we rush from

© 2014 FAMILY EMPOWERMENT NETWORK™ ALL RIGHTS RESERVED.

one activity to the other and feel pressure to keep up with the Joneses. The anxiety that a too-much, too-fast life produces can be paralyzing. Even for adults, stress can lead to yelling, dissatisfaction, complaining, and unhappiness–and interfere with the very relationships that mean the most to us.

For our kids, stress can happen, too. It's a rare kid taking academics or sports seriously who doesn't succumb to feeling overly stressed from the ridiculous pressure put on them to go to Harvard and get into the NBA! But other kids feel stress just in response to our stress. This is "second-hand stress," where one person's anxious flurry and freak-out spreads to the other people in the house.

Granted, it is important to note that stress is not always a bad thing. A little stress or tension is required to stretch and grow and learn or to get hyped for a big project or an athletic event. It can help us maximize our potential. Where we get in trouble is when there is too much stress. Unchecked, stress impacts behavior, attention, emotional learning, academic learning, and anxiety. To be resilient, we need to be able to have good emotional regulation, but, when we're stressed, we tend to "flip our lids"–disconnect from our Upstairs Brain–as Dan Siegel would say. Families can make a commitment to apologize when this happens.

According to John Medina, author of *Brain Rules* and *Brain Rules for Babies,* excelling in school is impossible when our brains are bathed in constant adrenaline, our stress hormone. Medina says: "Stressed people don't do math well. They don't process language very efficiently. They have poorer memories, both short and long forms. Stressed individuals do not generalize or adapt old pieces of information to new scenarios as well as non-stressed individuals. They can't concentrate. In almost every way it can be tested, chronic stress interferes with our ability to learn. One study showed that adults with high stress levels performed 50 percent worse on certain cognitive tests than adults with low stress. Specifically, stress hurts declarative memory (things that you can declare) and executive function (the type of thinking that involves problem solving). Those, of course, are the skills needed to excel in school and business" *(Brain Rules,* p. 178).

Medina goes on to say that parents' fighting is deeply disturbing and stressful for kids. Children as young as six months old react to parent fighting. Part of why it is so upsetting to the children is that they have no control over the situation. Medina's #1 rule of 12 for a healthy baby brain is not to fight and yell (i.e., stress) in front of your baby. If it does happen, one way to mitigate the negative effect is for the parents to make up in front of the children!

Area of Optimal Stress/Challenge

Performance Happiness, Health

Low Stress Boredom Depression

High Stress Anxiety

Stress/Challenge Level

PART II: TIPS FOR FOSTERING RESILIENCE IN OUR CHILDREN

Knowing what compromises our children's resilience provides us with a springboard from which to consider what fosters their ability to deal with life's ups and downs. Let's begin by asking ourselves how we can support our kids to: 1) be emotionally hardy enough to handle feelings of disappointment and upset, 2) be competent and believe in their ability, and 3) know they have someone who supports them and has faith in their ability to handle their lives.

ALL RIGHTS RESERVED. © 2014 FAMILY EMPOWERMENT NETWORK™

Start with the Touchstones in Mind

The touchstones can be used as tools to guide us on the path to creating strong, competent, caring, resilient children. Connection and Empathy help to nurture a child to feel loved for who he is, who learns readily to be a good friend to others, and who is not overly influenced by the need for another's approval. Play and Creativity cultivate both the social skills and the imagination/inner world of the child, which will help her to know her own mind, communicate it to others, be intrinsically motivated to learn, and, ultimately, have a rich, satisfying life. Safe Haven and Take the Time teach your child to have self care, inner structure, and the ability to handle stress and be resilient in the face of setbacks. And, of course, when we Walk the Talk, we model the kind of people we would like our children to grow up to be.

Allow Your Child to Experience Disappointment, Frustration, and Even Failure

"Success is the ability to go from one failure to another with no loss of enthusiasm." – Winston Churchill

Children who don't experience disappointment and who aren't given opportunities to experience the sadness, tears, and grief that go with not having things turn out the way they want (aka "life") will not learn how to cope and move on to something else. They will most likely grow into adults who don't know how to cope when things don't conform to their liking. Wouldn't it be better to find the value in the tears and the tantrums, to let children work through all their feelings in order for them to accept the facts as they are? Wouldn't it be wonderful to let our children discover early on in their lives that life may not always unfold to their liking, but that they can adapt and find their way back to joy?

Walking your child through all the stages of grief over life's disappointments and encouraging him/her to hit the Wall of Futility (accepting that there is no use in fighting it anymore) is how to help him/her move from being stuck in anger and aggression to making new, healthy choices. As Glenda Montgomery discusses in her article, **"Learning to Be OK with Plan B: Helping Your Child to Develop Resiliency,"** the only way for a young child to "develop his disappointment muscle is to be disappointed, and learn that he can get through it." Brené Brown also explores this need for having a Plan B–which she identifies as "hope" in the "Wholehearted Parenting" chapter of her book, *Daring Greatly* (pp. 239-240). She writes that hope happens when:

- We can set realistic goals.
- We can figure out how to achieve those goals.
- We have faith in ourselves.

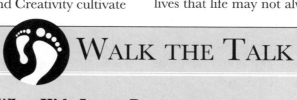

WALK THE TALK

What Kids Learn By Doing Things Themselves

When children have to rely on themselves and have to struggle with challenges through the point of frustration on to success, they develop a belief in themselves. As patience testing and time consuming it is to let kids do as much as possible for themselves, the benefits hugely outweigh the trouble. Letting kids do for themselves allows them to learn that they are:

- Capable
- Self reliant
- Stronger than they think
- Clever and good problem solvers
- Responsible (and can clean up their own messes)
- An integral part of the universe, not the center of the universe

They also internalize the messages: "My parents trust me," "My parents believe in me and my efforts," and "My parents think I can do it...and so do I."

© 2014 Family Empowerment Network™ All Rights Reserved.

When our teens and young adults experience their inevitable heartbreaks and disappointments, they may turn to screens–social networking, games, the Internet–for solace. Although this can be natural for digital natives and we all deserve some privacy in working through our struggles, online activities are enticing enough that they can potentially interfere with healing or lead kids down unproductive paths. Parents, family members, and friends can all play an important role in drawing struggling kids back into real life where the power of unconditional love and acceptance can empower them to find their way. After all, it is a combination of a proactive engagement of Plan B with empathy, reflection, physical activity, engaged learning or work, and helping others that promotes healing–rather than staying glued to a screen.

Teach the Life Skills of Self Control and Cognitive Flexibility

Social emotional learning (SEL) is key to happiness in life and getting along with others. One skill critical to the development of resilience–and life, in general–is self control. Ellen Galinsky, in her landmark book *Mind in the Making: The Seven Essential Life Skills Every Child Needs*, notes that "Focus and self control . . . [may be] as important as IQ" (p. 13). Galinsky's book and website (www.mindinthemaking.org) are filled with specific examples of how to help your child develop self control, focus, and inhibitory control (the ability to resist a strong inclination to do one thing and instead do what is appropriate).

Everyday life presents many opportunities to exercise these skills–unless we sabotage the process by giving children things immediately, doing things for them they can do themselves, or using an electronic babysitter. Consider, for example, a common scene in public places today: A family goes out to eat and the kids are handed iPads. Suddenly the children are mesmerized and quiet, and this is very reinforcing to the adults. Yet how can children learn to anticipate and participate in family events if they entertain themselves at the table with a screen? Think of all the skill building they miss: how to sit still and wait, observe others, order from a menu, talk to the family, use manners, etc. Instead, technology in this setting reinforces the idea that they are entitled to be entertained at all moments, they are not really part of the family but off on their own experience, they couldn't possibly learn to sit still or entertain themselves, and they are not responsible for waiting for good things. When everyone gives in to immediate gratification, children miss out on connection, time to practice valuable life skills, the enjoyment of others' company, and a sense of competence that they can handle themselves in a public space.

Closely tied to self control is the ability to exercise cognitive flexibility, another life skill critical to resilience. According to Adele Diamond of the University of British Columbia, cognitive flexibility is the ability to think and respond flexibly, switch perspectives and the focus of attention, adjust to changes in demands or priorities, try another solution when things don't work, and take on new ideas (in *Mind in the Making*, pp. 8-9). It often involves inhibiting our own thoughts to consider someone else's perspective, in order to see a situation in different ways, in other words "flexibly" (Ellen Galinsky, *Mind in the Making*, p. 6).

LEARNING TO WAIT

Children don't usually like to wait and often get angry, so waiting can be a great opportunity for exercising your child's self control muscle. A good rule of thumb is to have him wait one minute per age. That is, have your three-year-old wait three minutes to be given something she wants, your four-year-old, four minutes, etc. The training and patience early on pays off; the more self control a child has, the more proud of himself he is and the happier he will be.

ALL RIGHTS RESERVED. © 2014 FAMILY EMPOWERMENT NETWORK™

We actually can see the beginnings of this important skill in children's social play when they listen to the cues from their friend(s) and quickly move from one game to another. Whispering to your child, "Listen to your friend" can remind them to interact flexibly. Like other skills, however, cognitive flexibility develops slowly, and young children have difficulty seeing the perspective of another person (while holding their own in mind), especially when they are stressed or upset.

Cognitive flexibility is clearly an essential skill for adults as well as children. Given our fast-paced world that changes in a blink, our children will only be able to thrive in their future jobs and families if they are creative, flexible, and adaptable thinkers. Cognitive flexibility is an important tool for parents, because our "knee jerk" reactions are rarely as nurturing as our better thought-out ones. Our ability to listen and take in a variety of perspectives before moving ahead will certainly help us to stay connected to our children as they grow. In this way, we model cognitive flexibility for our children. Clearly being able to control one's self as anxiety and anger rise is critical for maintaining an open mind at any age. These are skills that can be practiced through more attention to pausing, breathing, and positive self-talk.

Daniel Siegel in *The Whole Brain Child* calls this integrating the Upstairs/Thinking Brain with the Downstairs/Feeling brain. We can engage the Upstairs Brain by staying calm ourselves, asking questions, requesting alternatives, and letting kids be involved in decision making. If kids have lost touch with their Upstairs Brain, physical activity can help them to get balanced again.

Help Kids Ascend the Steps to Resilience

Self esteem or self worth also plays a role in developing resilience. If a child has healthy sense of self worth, he feels competent, which gives him the confidence to forge ahead. But we can't give self esteem to our kids on a silver platter. It is the culmination of a process of their needs being met over time combined with the quality of their experiences as they grow. Joanne Nordling in *Taking Charge: Caring Discipline That Works at Home and at School* pictures it this way:

STEPS TO RESILIENCE: CLIMBING THE STAIRCASE OF NEEDS

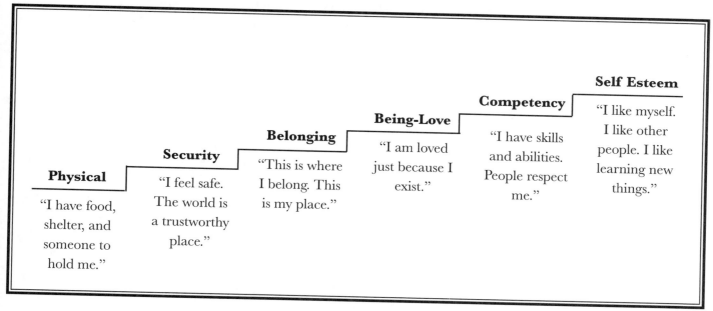

Physical
"I have food, shelter, and someone to hold me."

Security
"I feel safe. The world is a trustworthy place."

Belonging
"This is where I belong. This is my place."

Being-Love
"I am loved just because I exist."

Competency
"I have skills and abilities. People respect me."

Self Esteem
"I like myself. I like other people. I like learning new things."

© 2014 FAMILY EMPOWERMENT NETWORK™ ALL RIGHTS RESERVED.

As you can see from the Staircase, the steps to self esteem include feeling safe and belonging, feeling loved for who one is (Being-Love), and continually learning new life skills, which create a sense of competency. This sense of competency sounds like this: "I am capable. I can influence what happens to me. I contribute in meaningful ways, and I am genuinely needed" (Stephen Glenn in *Positive Discipline* by Jane Nelsen, p. 6). (This is elaborated on in **"Developing Capable People Guidelines"** by Stephen Glenn and Jane Nelsen at the end of this chapter.) On the other hand, children who do not feel they are loved for who they are and do not get to practice real-life skills feel much more vulnerable to outside influences, have an exaggerated need for approval, and their inner strength is compromised (all the more so if they indulge in a great amount of media).

Although we cannot give our children their self-esteem on a silver platter, we can boost them along on the Staircase by ensuring their physical safety and their sense of security and by cultivating their sense of belonging and being loved. Perhaps the most important step of all is Being-Love–unconditional love–being loved for who they are in all their quirkiness and with all their blunders. This deep confidence in being loved allows the child to internalize the message: "I am loved for who I am and I am enough." With this inner message, the child does not equate his self-worth with how well he does things in life.

In essence, we need to teach our child at an early age the distinction between personhood and behavior. We need to let him know that we will correct his behavior at times but we always love him no matter what happens. This loving connection and the sense of significance it gives the child sets the stage for the development of resilience. This child has someone who believes in her!

We all occasionally experience a back slide on the Staircase when things are not going well or when we are too stressed. But not to fear: This regression also is an opportunity to develop resilience, to learn to regulate negative emotion in healthy ways, so we can deal with adversity and move ahead into a strong and capable stance. As we mentioned earlier in the chapter, children (including teens) who are protected from experiencing setbacks, failure, and mistakes do not learn to take responsibility, and they are less likely to develop the knowledge and strength to deal with adversity and frustration in general. Kids need to have frustrating experiences, such as losing at games and contests, and they need to not get their way all the time. In fact, the more we protect and rescue our children, the more we send the message that they are too weak to handle their challenges. For a good summary about developing resilience in children, see Kelly Bartlett's article, **"Understanding Resiliency in Kids."**

When we recommend letting our children fail, we are not advocating for disengagement. Hopefully, we are always our children's consultants–a listening ear–when things go wrong at any age. When we listen and express empathy for their problem, they learn to face reality, take responsibility, and come up with a plan for recovery. When kids are actively involved and complete this process, they often experience a boost in self esteem, because they were able to work things through even though it was challenging. On the other hand, when parents take on their kids'

ALL RIGHTS RESERVED. © 2014 FAMILY EMPOWERMENT NETWORK™

problem or act very upset about a situation (i.e., own the problem for the child), the child will usually experience a diminishment in self esteem. For one mother's take on the value of supporting our children rather than rescuing them, read **"Super Mom: Ditching the Cape."**

Empower Your Child to Take on Challenges: Fixed versus Growth Mindset

University of Pennsylvania's Angela Duckworth and her colleagues in *How Children Succeed* by Paul Tough (p.76) called "grit" one of the main character traits that predict life satisfaction and high achievement. According to their research, people with grit evaluate themselves this way: "Setbacks don't discourage me," "I am a hard worker," "I finish whatever I begin."

In general, all challenges can be stressful, even when they are positive. What helps kids to develop the skill of tackling challenges is having safe, dependable people to turn to and not having too much stress that lasts too long. Kids who fear failure or are being shamed while learning can develop a bad habit of not trying. In his famous "visual cliff" experiment (www.youtube.com/watch?v=p-6cqNhHrMJA), UC Berkeley's Joseph Campos demonstrates the role of non-verbal parental communication in giving children, from the beginning of their lives, the courage and impetus to take on challenges.

Other researchers such as Stanford's Carol Dweck have examined children's ability to take on challenges and the effect praise has on determination. Check out Dweck's work on fixed versus growth mindset at www.youtube. com/watch?v=TTXrV0_3UjY or see her book, *Mindset: The New Psychology of Success.* Her bottom line? Cultivate a growth mindset in your child–as well as yourself! Her research has shown that people who believe ability is not fixed but that it grows with effort experience a healthy approach to tackling challenges. According to Dweck,

"Never do for a child what he can do for himself."

– Rudolf Dreikers, eminent Adlerian psychologist

one of the ways we can cultivate a growth mindset in our children is to acknowledge their effort and strategies, not their personality or intelligence. Dweck's research also shows that having a growth mindset and teaching about the malleable nature of people's thoughts, feelings, and behavior can lead to reduced aggression and other behavior problems.

Help Children Connect to Their Own Inner Compass

When children have enough practice falling down and getting back up or enough practice shifting to Plan B when Plan A doesn't work out, they tend to start hearing an encouraging inner voice. This inner voice essentially is a child thinking for himself despite pressure from others or the culture. Over time, that inner voice becomes the child's "true North." He develops the ability to access and connect with his personal "inner compass" that sheds light on a path to positive behavior in the face of negative influences and roadblocks.

If a child does not have a strong connection with her inner compass, she is more apt to engage in risk taking. For example, without the inner compass which is developed through the exercise of resilience, a child might abuse or overuse technology. Here is a true story about how a teen's inner compass helped her to avoid getting into trouble:

Six 13-year-old girls were an extroverted social group. During the summer, they texted each other to arrange get-togethers in the park. This was harmless enough until the group decided to tell their parents they were going to the park and, instead, slipped off to try marijuana. Remarkably, one of the six girls simply said, "I can't do this. My dad would be so disappointed in me." And she didn't hang out with the rest of the group for the remainder of the summer. One of the other girls' mothers eventually noticed her daughter's sneakiness while texting, read her messages, and discovered what was going

© 2014 FAMILY EMPOWERMENT NETWORK™ ALL RIGHTS RESERVED.

on. She contacted the other parents, who were all very shocked. They talked to the girls about trust and took their girls' phones for a month. The girls also met as a group with a counselor to process their experience; they all remained close friends with the girl who had said "No."

Just think about the strength of the one girl and her ability to think for herself despite her need to belong. Consider the role digital devices played in getting the girls into trouble. Notice how closely the one strong girl's inner compass is tied to her strong connection with a parent, in this case her father. You can introduce your children to the idea of the inner compass that helps us to find our true North, even when we feel lost at sea.

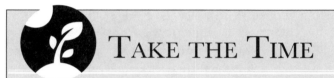

TAKE THE TIME

"Each time you are tempted to do something for your children that you know they can do themselves, use that love, patience, and selflessness to give time and encouragement as they fumble through doing it on their own instead of using your love to do it for them. This is an effective way to show your love. Allowing your kids to develop a belief in their own capability and competence is a far better gift."
– Glenda Montgomery

Teach Emotional Self-Care

What are other ways we can we encourage our kids to develop comfort with their own discomfort and to bounce back when they face seemingly insurmountable challenges? What else can we do as parents to help them become resilient and able to manage their own emotions and difficult situations with competence?

Our children need to learn emotional self care: Allow your children the space to feel their own feelings and to develop strategies to self soothe. Then guide them to practice these strategies.

To inspire the growth of resilience and inner strength in our children, it is important to show our kids we have faith in their abilities to work through strong emotions and tackle tough tasks in their everyday journeys in the process from disappointment to acceptance. Of course, this also means we must have the strength ourselves to witness their discomfort and to comfort them and express empathy while they feel badly–without acting to fix or change the situation. Clearly, there are exceptions to this. If our children are in danger in any way, we need to act– and act swiftly–to ensure their safety. However, day-to-day sadness and disappointment, anger and frustration about the ups and downs of an average day are times when we don't need to intervene. We need to be there as witness and support, while allowing the waves of feelings to pass over and reminding them that "things change."

When parents can accept a child's emotions without being triggered themselves, the child sees that you trust that this emotion is not something to be frightened about or pro-voked by but rather something to discuss and explore. We can ask questions about the feeling and acknowledge it before moving on: (e.g., "Oh, I see. You are really angry that you have to start your homework.") Once parents have allowed some space and time to be there with their child and attempt to understand the emotion and wish, they can offer a choice: "I know you are mad, and I know it is really tough being mad. Sometimes I feel mad when I have to do something I don't want to do. So I understand what that feels like."

We also can be curious about how our kids can make themselves feel better: "You are feeling mad about start-ing your homework. What can you do to make yourself feel better? Do you think you'd like to grab a snack first before you begin your homework? What would make you feel better, do you think?"

Asking children to be in charge of making themselves feel better is a radical thought. Yet, it is now, while young, that they need to begin to learn healthy self soothing. Our culture has not promoted the development of healthy

ALL RIGHTS RESERVED. © 2014 FAMILY EMPOWERMENT NETWORK™

emotional self care, and so we have adults who do not soothe themselves and instead suffer from high blood pressure, high stress, heart attacks, and hypertension. Unfortunately, some of us have learned to self soothe in unhealthy ways such as with smoking, drinking, drugs, and overeating.

How might we as parents begin to consciously cultivate self-connection while immersed in our busy lives with family and community? We can start by slowing down and giving ourselves empathy when we are triggered, lash out in anger, or are upset by something going on with our child. Ask yourself, "What are my feelings?" "What values do I long for right now that are triggering me to be so upset?" This can be not only calming, but also energizing. Follow with the next question: "How will I respond to this conflict in a way that respectfully conveys my concerns and honors my highest values?"

Read on for how one mother put this lesson into practice:

My teenage daughter had to study for a big final exam one evening, and it was her night to clean up the kitchen after dinner, when she got a call from one of her best friends. They talked for nearly an hour, and then she practically ran me over running up the stairs to her room. "Kendra really needs me. She just broke up with her boyfriend. I have to go over to her house right away," she murmured effusively. Usually, this would be where I would launch into a tirade and lecture Cassandra about her schoolwork and chores, about responsibility and all that. This time, I bit my lip and refrained from saying what I might eventually regret. I could feel my anger, but I also tapped into my desire for mutual connection, respect, and consideration, even in the midst of conflict. I took three big breaths and closed my eyes for a moment. Could I do this differently? I said to my daughter simply, "Wow, that must really be hard!" Cassandra looked at me like I was from the planet Mars and continued to her room. An hour later, I went to the kitchen for coffee, and it was spotless! What had happened? I wandered up to my daughter's room and found her studying. She told me that, after she thought about it, she decided just to call Kendra on the phone, then she did the dishes and got back to her schoolwork. Wow! What a

difference taking a few breaths and prioritizing connection and self reflection can make! – Carole, Mother of three children

There are various ways we can teach our kids emotional self care. We can teach it through modeling–by taking care of ourselves through engaging in activities such as yoga, exercise, and conscious breathing. We can teach it by conversing with our kids about strategies that might work for them. (e.g., "Does bouncing help you to calm yourself and feel better? Does it help to listen to music? What about curling up in a blanket in the dark?") We can teach it by encouraging our kids to experiment with different ways to manage their own difficult emotions. Be curious and commend them when they find something that has worked for them. (e.g., "Wow, you got over that anger quickly! What did you do to get through it so fast? That really worked well for you!") If we, as parents, assume it is always our responsibility to soothe our kids, make them feel better, and work out their problems for them, they cannot learn these extremely important skills for themselves.

Master and Model Stress Reduction

"Good habits formed at youth make all the difference." - Aristotle

To thrive, children do best with balance. We all do! Getting enough sleep, eating right, exercising, having face-to-face social time with family and peers, playing, being creative, having non-screen downtime, and getting outside–these are all critical ingredients to healthy development and the building of resilience. When life is not balanced, kids feel stressed, which leads to anxiety and reduced ability to deal with challenges. The mixed messages of our culture and the "if-it-bleeds-it-leads" news also fuel stress, just as does being over busy and over scheduled, as noted earlier in the "What Compromises Our Children's Resilience" section.

Kim John Payne beautifully addresses the influence of stress on kids today in his book, *Simplicity Parenting.* He lovingly shares accounts of children who are not thriving

© 2014 FAMILY EMPOWERMENT NETWORK™ ALL RIGHTS RESERVED.

despite the best intentions of their parents. He notes that, "when a child accumulates enough little pieces of stress, with enough frequency," the child is more apt to be hyper-vigilant, nervous, and anxious and have a lack of resilience, impulse control, empathy, and perspective taking. All tolled, this can lead to high levels of anxiety sometimes similar to the symptoms of post-traumatic stress disorder (Payne, *Simplicity Parenting*, p. 9).

The type of consistent stress Payne speaks of is different from the stress of a special activity such as being in a school play or of an individual, intense event such as the loss of a pet. These types of stress, which happen and then are over and resolved, actually can produce resilience. In contrast, children who live their lives with daily stress that never lets up are at risk. Unfortunately, some kids are experiencing stress from the over-stimulation of today's digital world. Payne says that we need to watch out for "soul fever" when our children are emotionally stressed. He suggests we care for those with soul fever as though they have a high temperature. We need to hunker down with them, give them extra care, possibly more

---

MINIMIZING STRESS TO MAXIMIZE DEVELOPMENT

One author and expert who offers pointers on minimizing stress to maximize social and emotional development is Ellen Galinsky. In her book, *Mind in the Making* (pp. 284-288), Galinsky offers these pointers:

- First, manage your own stress, turn to others who can help you manage your stress, and take time for yourself.
- Don't shield your child from everyday stresses.
- Know that a warm, caring, and trusting relationship with your child makes you a stress buster.
- Work on keeping your own alarm button on low.

---

home time, and let the fever runs its course. This "Rx" works for teens and little children—as well as for us!

What else can parents do about childhood stress? Foremost, it is not helpful to get stressed over kids being stressed! Difficult as it may be at times, we need to walk the talk and strive for balance—keeping our lives calm and our attention focused. How we do this for ourselves will carry over into how we teach our children to do the same.

One of the easiest ways to find balance and peace is by regularly spending time outdoors. Read Richard Louv's article **"Nature's Neurons"** for an eloquent recap of what we've said in this book about the importance of the natural world in shaping the lives of our children.

Another stress-busting strategy we suggest is to teach your children how their brains work. A book for learning how to do this is Daniel Siegel's and Tina Payne Bryson's *The Whole Brain Child: 12 Revolutionary Strategies to Nurture Your Child's Developing Mind, Survive Everyday Parenting Struggles, and Help Your Family Thrive*. This book provides parents with a vocabulary about how the brain works and explains how chronic stress undermines human development and resilience. Siegel and Bryson also suggest activities that enhance brain development and help children to be adaptive and flexible under trying circumstances.

Yet another resource to explore is Goldie Hawn and Wendy Holden's book, 1*0 Mindful Minutes: Giving Our Children—and Ourselves—the Social and Emotional Skills to Reduce Stress and Anxiety for Healthier, Happy Lives*. One of the many research studies Hawn and Holden reference shows that "ongoing stress shrinks the executive function areas of our brain and stimulates the habit-forming parts that keep us repeating actions in a negative pattern" (Hawn and Holden, *10 Mindful Minutes*, p. 32).

To diffuse the impact of stress on children's lives, Hawn also has designed, with education professionals and researchers, a school curriculum that shows significant results. In her MindUP™ program (www.thehawnfoun-

ALL RIGHTS RESERVED. © 2014 FAMILY EMPOWERMENT NETWORK™

dation.org/mindup), children learn about the biology of their own brains in simple terms. They learn how the emotional part of the brain can hijack the more clear-thinking areas that keep them calm and focused. Then, once they grasp the brain basics, they talk about how their thoughts and feelings affect their behavior, discover how breathing affects the brain, practice focused awareness regularly, and learn how to appreciate the sensory aspects of their lives. Results are showing that children participating in MindUP™ programs throughout the country can handle their stress better than their peers not in the program and that, subsequently, they have greater working memory, better reading scores, better attention, and more (Hawn and Holden, *10 Mindful Minutes*).

Unfortunately, because of intense financial pressures, too many schools are being forced to cut the activities that give kids the energy and incentive to be ready to learn.

LESSONS FROM THE MAT

Yoga is a fun way for kids and adults to connect and share special time together. Attending yoga classes especially designed for kids and families, or doing yoga together at home, offers opportunities to enjoy physical activity, play, mindfulness, rest, and health as a family. **Yoga Calm®** is a social-emotional learning curriculum developed by Jim and Lynea Gillen of Portland, Oregon. An award-winning program, Yoga Calm offers opportunities for kids and adults of all ages to learn yoga in a safe and nurturing environment, while also learning about strength, flexibility and balance—lessons which can be easily applied to life. With a focus on physical, emotional, and social well-being, Yoga Calm offers many learning games, mindfulness activities, opportunities to learn effective ways of communicating, ways to integrate the importance of being outdoors in nature, and invitations to take on leadership roles in class and the community at large.

www.yogacalm.org

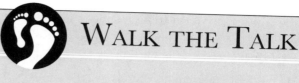

WALK THE TALK

Do your children have time to read for pleasure, go for bike rides, play outside for fun, or just be? If not, help them Make the Time! Do *you* have time to read for pleasure, go for bike rides, play outside for fun, or just be? If not, Walk the Talk and Make the Time!

Some elementary schools are cutting PE, music, recess, and art. High schools have fewer shop classes, choirs, and drama programs. In the place of these activities, which could help a child to balance out his day, the emphasis is all too often solely on academic achievement. Consider also the vast amount of homework many children get—and their sacrifice of precious sleep hours to complete it. Ponder the pressure parents put on their children to get good grades and to do well on standardized tests. In our fast-paced, high-achieving world, children barely have time to breathe—even when it comes to school.

Promote a Balanced Life

In the end, the children who are the most resilient and the most connected and empathetic are those who were given a multitude of opportunities to live a balanced life—experiencing loss, success, happiness, struggle, and how it feels to be understood by caring adults and peers. Our ability to live a balanced life also involves good self care, and the health and the vitality that come with good self care can be learned in our childhood homes. At the heart of balance is having enough non-screen time in the day to read, be alone and reflect, connect with friends, eat and play with family, sleep until rested, exercise, and be outdoors. This template sets the stage for learning how to handle our own personal brand of anxiety and stress in healthy ways. See the article **"Helping Kids Manage Anxiety–Ages and Stages."** As we discussed in Chapter 2, our homes can be safe havens where we feel loved for who we are and where we can release stress through fun, conversation, art, and reading.

© 2014 FAMILY EMPOWERMENT NETWORK™ ALL RIGHTS RESERVED.

One critical activity for leading balanced lives is getting enough physical activity. Physical activity is also one of the most effective ways of reducing stress—anything from playing outdoors to going for family swims. Families that exercise together enhance family bonding while also lessening everyone's stress.

Especially for tweens and teens, playing on sports teams can be a "stress buster" and offers many other wonderful benefits for building resilience. Boundaries are big in sports and provide many opportunities for learning self control. Kids also get lots of practice with failure in sports, as they often find themselves on the losing end of games. They also have many opportunities during practices and games to observe how others respond to stressful situations. In addition, the car rides to and from sports events can be perfect times for discussing and reflecting upon the experiences with peers and parents.

In short, playing on teams can be instrumental in promoting responsible social behaviors, confidence in one's physical abilities, strong bonds with individuals and institutions, and, most significantly, the skills and discipline needed for establishing a lifelong commitment to personal health and fitness. See our article **"Put the Play Back Into Sports"** at the end of this overview for some ideas about how to keep organized sports from becoming unhealthy. Also, check out the list of other resources about healthy sports in our resources section at the end of this chapter.

PLAY/CREATE

". . . [P]laying prepares us for real-life situations, allowing us to practice making decisions under pressure, lead a group, and think abstractly. Group play teaches us to socialize and to cooperate. Play also gives us a chance to better know ourselves through self evaluation and self reflection. . . . Play also encourages creativity."

– Kevin Carroll, creativity guru and author of *What's Your Red Rubber Ball?*

kevincarrollkatalyst.com

Introduce Technology in a Way That Does Not Interfere with the Development of Resilience

Our consumer culture encourages us to have more, faster, sooner, but if you want to have a strong, resilient, caring child and a contented home, you may want to prioritize "less, slower, later."

Clearly, in today's times, we need resilient, independent (yet connected and caring) kids who can be themselves despite the powerful influences of our consumer/media-driven culture. Another way we can help kids to accomplish this is by introducing technology in a way that doesn't interfere with the development of resilience. We can do this by teaching and modeling living a balanced, active life as a prerequisite to the use of technology.

How will we know when our children are ready for more technology in their lives? These questions can be a starting point for consideration:

- Are they courteous people and empathetic, trustworthy friends?
- Do they have the self-control to be respectful and to get their work done at school and at home?
- Have they internalized the basic values of the family, and do they follow those values when they are out in the community? Do they obey the law?
- Are they contributing and involved in the family, the community, and the school?
- Do they know how to converse with adults with appropriate eye contact and engagement?

Will our children always meet these expectations? No, of course not, but we can respectfully and persistently teach these standards. Wouldn't it make sense for our daughters to develop life skills before they spend hours of their time immersed in the world of social networking? Wouldn't our sons be much less likely to get lost in their games if they had basic life experiences and competencies first? Let's contemplate some specific examples of how the unconscious use of technology can interfere with our children's healthy development and honing of resilience:

ALL RIGHTS RESERVED. © 2014 FAMILY EMPOWERMENT NETWORK™

The World's Longest Umbilical Cord, the Phone: Phones can be helpful for safety and communication, yet think about how dependent they have made our children. When it comes to parent-child relationships, phones may be the world's longest umbilical cord! Recall that we all used to be out and about without cell phones (or GPSs), and somehow we found our way, stayed safe, developed a sense of direction, and asked kind strangers for help. Without phones, we generally had much more independence than kids do today. When we were out in the greater world, we had a feeling of competency that contributed to our self-esteem and resilience. Here's a story where not using the phone for rescue empowered children:

When I was at work, my sixth- and eight-graders missed the school bus. They knew to call my receptionist only for emergencies. Not considering the situation an emergency, they decided to walk to school–approximately three miles. After that, they rarely missed the bus. If they did, they took the city bus, rode their bikes, or got a ride from friends. Not using the phone empowered them.

"Reading" Other People: Most of us use emailing and texting to communicate with our friends. Of course, it's convenient to use our cell phones to make arrangements about when and where to meet. Not so long ago, we exclusively interacted with people face-to-face or voice-to-voice. Remember when we told each other we would meet at such and such a time and place–and it was an agreement we remembered and kept? Our honor depended on our showing up; we couldn't text and say at the last minute we couldn't come (i.e., something better came up). We couldn't possibly get away with communicating via a screen and, thereby, protecting ourselves from the other person's feelings. We had a lot of practice reading people's faces, and it really helped us to do well in our lives. Digital natives, however, often have trouble perceiving non-verbal communication cues, because they just aren't practicing enough. Furthermore, it's just too easy to "unfriend" someone or erase them from a game. But how do we learn to handle disagreements with friends unless we practice regularly?

IN CONCLUSION

Envision what you really want for your child. Does your vision include that your child:

- Is emotionally hardy, competent, and confident?
- Has self control and is able to wait for what is important to her?
- Knows it is his effort that makes the difference?
- Learns to be resilient in the face of disappointment and adversity?
- Sees mistakes as an opportunity for learning?
- Knows her own mind and is able to communicate her needs, thoughts, and feelings?
- Is able to understand others, take the perspective of others, and empathize?
- Develops the skills to be a trustworthy friend who can make repairs when disagreements occur?
- Develops habits of self care that encourage a healthy, balanced life in spite of anxiety or stress?
- Becomes a lifelong learner who takes on challenges with gusto?
- Practices being a respectful, responsible person in the real world, and develops all the skills he needs to live independently?

Clearly, this vision is a process that takes years. When you offer your children your faith in their abilities to get through difficult feelings and situations, your guidance in teaching them how, and your willingness to let them practice, you give your children gifts that will positively influence them for the rest of their lives. You give them the opportunities to become emotionally strong and resilient, full of faith in their own abilities to withstand setbacks and challenges–and to keep *themselves* happy.

The bottom line? Our kids will face difficulties and struggles when they leave home. We want them to face their problems as challenges to be mastered rather than threats to be avoided. With your nurturance, guidance–and your letting go–they will become hardy, thriving citizens of the world.

© 2014 FAMILY EMPOWERMENT NETWORK™ ALL RIGHTS RESERVED.

THE WHOLEHEARTED PARENTING MANIFESTO
by Brené Brown, PhD, LMSW

Above all else, I want you to know that you are loved and lovable.

You will learn this from my words and actions—
the lessons on love are in how I treat you and how I treat myself.

I want you to engage with the world from a place of worthiness.

You will learn that you are worthy of love, belonging, and joy
every time you see me practice self-compassion
and embrace my own imperfections.

We will practice courage in our family by showing up,
letting ourselves be seen, and honoring vulnerability.
We will share our stories of struggle and strength.
There will always be room in our home for both.

We will teach compassion by practicing compassion with ourselves first;
then with each other. We will set and respect boundaries;
we will honor hard work, hope, and perseverance.
Rest and play will be family values, as well as family practices.

You will learn accountability and respect
by watching me make mistakes and make amends,
and by watching how I ask for what I need and talk about how I feel.

I want you to know joy, so together we will practice gratitude.

I want you to feel joy, so together we will learn how to be vulnerable.

When uncertainty and scarcity visit,
you will be able to draw from the spirit that is a part of our everyday life.

Together we will cry and face fear and grief.
I will want to take away your pain,
but instead I will sit with you and teach you how to feel it.

We will laugh and sing and dance and create.
We will always have permission to be ourselves with each other.
No matter what, you will always belong here.

As you begin your Wholehearted journey, the greatest gift that I can give to you is
to live and love with my whole heart and to dare greatly.

I will not teach or love or show you anything perfectly,
but I will let you see me,
and I will always hold sacred the gift of seeing you.
Truly, deeply, seeing you.

From *Daring Greatly* (pp. 244-245) by Brené Brown, copyright © 2012 by Brené Brown. Used by permission of Gotham Books, an imprint of Penguin Group (USA) LLC. Copies of this manifesto can be downloaded from www.brenebrown.com. A beautifully illustrated rendering of the manifesto is also available on her website.

What are the strengths of each of your children?
How do you use these strengths to help your children to learn to manage their own lives?

POSSIBLE DISCUSSION QUESTIONS

1) Who loved you unconditionally when you were a child? When did love sometimes feel contingent upon performing well? How would your children answer these questions?
2) What are some ways your child gets to practice self control? Under what circumstances are you able to let your children deal with age-appropriate adversity and experience the consequences of their mistakes?
3) Can you think of a time when someone in your family was able to turn lemons into lemonade?
4) How is modern technology interfering with your child's sense of social competency and resilience? What can be done about this?
5) What are your biggest challenges when it comes to handling your child's or your stress? How do you support your child in managing his/her own stress and anxiety?
6) Discuss the differences between "fixed" and "growth" mindset. What are some ways to foster "growth" mindset?
7) How does your family attempt to live a balanced life? What are your main challenges?
8) How important are organized sports to your child? How have sports affected your child and your family?
9) What are some of the ways your family helps kids to integrate their upstairs and downstairs brains, in other words, handle strong emotions without flipping one's lid?
10) What compromises your child's strength and resilience? How do you think you might work on this in the future?

PUTTING IT INTO PRACTICE

- Set a goal for having a more balanced life for your family.
- To promote growth mindset, focus on the qualities and the effort of your children rather than praising their actions.
- Find one way that your child's strength and resilience might be compromised and support your child to make a plan that will empower him/her.
- Identify an arena where you struggle with letting your child experience the consequences (i.e., failure) of his/her decisions or actions. Create a new habit/strategy.

PUTTING IT TOGETHER—YOUR VERSION

Write down a few ideas you have been inspired to implement in your own life after reading/discussing this chapter.

© 2014 FAMILY EMPOWERMENT NETWORK™ ALL RIGHTS RESERVED.

How to Ground Your "Helicopter" Parenting

By Kathy Masarie, MD

"Helicopter parent" is eloquently described by Wikipedia:

....a parent who pays extremely close attention to his or her child's experiences and problems. These parents rush to prevent any harm or failure from befalling their children and won't let them learn from their own mistakes, sometimes even contrary to the children's wishes. They are so named because, like helicopters, they hover closely overhead, rarely out of reach, whether their children need them or not. An extension of the term, "Black Hawk parents," has been coined for those who cross the line from a mere excess of zeal to unethical behavior, such as writing their children's college admission essays.

Helicoptering starts out with bringing forgotten homework and lunch to school, goes on to berating the teacher for an "unfair" grade or assignment, or overly helping on school projects. It evolves to calling your kid at college to be sure he/she got up for class or flying to Harvard to protest your child's biology grade or demanding the college provide more desirable plumbing for your child studying abroad in China. Colleges and now even companies are actually hiring extra staff to ward off helicopter parents.

One outcome is that helicoptering parents feel stressed to the max. A study by the Society for Research in Child Development determined that helicopter parents reported "more sadness, crying, and negative beliefs about themselves, and less joy, contentment and life satisfaction," whether the children were succeeding or failing. Helicoptering's message to the child is that "you are too ineffective to succeed on your own"; however, we all need to learn how to cope with adversity to be effective in life. How can a 22-year-old who can't address setbacks, disappointments, goals, and progress at the university level adjust to a complex job situation and an independent adult life?

Caring for our children's welfare and helping them along the way is a fundamental part of a parent's role. But some parents have made this nurturing an extreme sport. Some reasons for this parenting phenomenon are:

• Technological advances that allow 24/7 connection. This makes it easy to cross the line from involved to over-involved.

• Concern for our children's safety–after Columbine, Sandy Hook shootings, 9/11, etc.

• Rejection of the less engaged, "latch-key" parenting style with which many of today's parents were raised.

You are helicoptering when you:

• Equate "love" with "success"

• Feel ashamed when your child fails

• Fight your child's battles for him/her, such as protesting an unfair grade

• Take over your child's school projects

• Start sentences about your child with "we," as in, "We are applying for scholarships."

• Are preoccupied with the details of a child's activities, practices, schedules and performances

• Lurk on Facebook to see if your child is hanging out with any "bad seeds"

– Erin Wade, *Dallas Morning News*, Aug. 15, 2005

So what are some antidotes?

1. Consider what is the best support to enable your child to succeed toward independence, to learn to make his or her own decisions and become self-sufficient. That answer will vary from child to child.

ALL RIGHTS RESERVED. © 2014 FAMILY EMPOWERMENT NETWORK™

5. Offer support rather than rescue. Communicate that you are not going to step in every time a child needs help. We can ask our kids, "What are you going to do to solve this problem?"

6. Allow every opportunity for your child to practice making his/her own decisions. Think of yourself as a life coach who provides structure and gives suggestions. However, children need to "step up to the plate." Start small when they are young and gradually give them more responsibility as they grow.

7. For every intervention, **ask yourself, "Is this action going to lead my child toward independence, competence and confidence or take away from it?** In this way we give our children what they need: roots to grow and wings to fly.

Resource:
Mom Needs an "A": Hovering, Hyper-involved Parents the Topic of a Landmark Study by Kay Randall at www.utexas.edu/features/2007/helicopter/

2. Connect and communicate with your child. When your kid complains about an unfair math grade, get curious about what your child sees as the problem behind it rather than storm the school. It may be s/he just wants to vent or that your child doesn't realize the value of completing an unpleasant task in realizing a long-term goal.

3. Model healthy listening and conflict skills. If an angry parent yells and coerces a teacher or administrator into doing what he wants, the message the kids learn is: "Might makes right." The teacher's perspective on the issue can be very insightful.

4. Be involved in your child's education. The Harvard Family Research Project found that teens whose parents play an active role do better in school and are more likely to enroll in college. Communicate regularly with the teacher and volunteer on school projects in ways that don't stress you.

© 2014 FAMILY EMPOWERMENT NETWORK™ ALL RIGHTS RESERVED.

Learning to Be OK with Plan B:
Helping Your Young Child
Develop Resiliency
By Glenda Montgomery

Based on the work of Jane Nelsen and Lynne Lott of the *Positive Discipline* books

---

". . . [T]he only way a child can develop his disappointment muscle is to be disappointed and to learn that he can get through it. Instead of taking away your children's 'opportunities' to feel disappointed, be there with them as they experience their emotions (without telling them 'you are OK' when they clearly are not feeling OK), show empathy and faith in their ability to weather the emotional storm, and then help them come up with a Plan B. Instead of showing love by rescuing your children, show it by teaching them the tools they can use to competently rescue themselves and carry on with strength and confidence."
– Jane Nelsen

Our children will encounter upset, disappointment, discomfort, and frustration in their lives, even if we work really hard to make sure this doesn't happen. What may be counter intuitive is that, in the effort to rescue our kids from these situations, we make sure that they are *less* prepared to meet problems effectively when they inevitably arise. In our quest to keep them happy and calm by doing things for them and owning their emotions ourselves, we have not taught our kids the skills they need to build resilience.

There are many ways to help to develop resiliency. Our reaction to our children's distress is a place to start. Use these four steps:

1. Allow kids to have their emotions.
When children are upset, it makes sense they experience difficult emotions. Let them have those, even if it means a temper tantrum. Refrain from taking on your children's upset; these are their emotions, not yours. Squat down to their level and let them know you understand they are really disappointed/mad/frustrated/embarrassed/unhappy. You don't have to agree that their emotion is justified in this moment; you just need to recognize they are feeling badly–and listen. Offer a hug and sincere empathy, acknowledging they are feeling something

challenging to feel. Refrain from fixing it for them. Just *be* with them.

Remember that you need to respect the situation as well as yourself and your child. If your child is having a temper tantrum somewhere such as the mall or the park or your own house, then hanging out and patiently waiting at a child's eye level until she "finishes" is fine. If you are somewhere where your child's temper tantrum is creating disruption for others, firmly but kindly pick him up and bring him to a place where he can finish in privacy.

2. Show faith that he/she will get through this.
When we rescue our kids from feeling upset, our kids get this message: "Wow, strong emotions must be really, really horrible. My mom clearly thinks this feeling is too difficult for me. I am not capable of handling this." They also may figure out a strategy. "Dad feels really uncomfortable when I am upset, so all I need to do to get what I want is to get upset." These messages are received at the subconscious level, but neither one helps to develop a resilient child. Instead, show your child that you have complete faith he can handle the situation and get through it: Your words might sound like this: "You are feeling awful now, I know, but you will get through this. You are strong."

3. Talk about Plan B.
When your child is *not* upset, introduce the idea of Plan B. Tell her that a Plan A is what you really *want* to happen and that Plan B is what you might do when Plan A does not work. Bring up times when you were disappointed and didn't get what you wanted or things did not go your way. Tell your kids what you did instead, when your Plan A didn't work. Then, bring up a time your child was disappointed in the recent past. Ask what a Plan B might have been. We *all* have to learn at one time or another to be OK with giving up on Plan A and finding a Plan

ALL RIGHTS RESERVED. © 2014 FAMILY EMPOWERMENT NETWORK™

B. There are examples in picture books and movies and real life. Point them out to your kids. Once kids get the idea, they will have fun finding them and pointing them out to you.

4. After letting them have their emotions and showing empathy and faith, invite them to help choose a Plan B.

Sometimes, you can begin helping your child figure out what he can do when what he wants to do is not an option. Children who are upset, however, often cannot jump into problem solving. Wait until they are calm and then invite them to help choose a Plan B. You can offer two or three (no more) ideas and ask what they think. Sometimes, you'll just have to choose an option yourself, and go with it, but as your kids get used to this process and feel more comfortable with their own resilience, they will begin to engage more (and more calmly) in thinking of and choosing a Plan B.

> ### Tips for Parents to Help Children Find Their Tears
>
> • Remain calm and clear about your position: "It really is bed time right now."
>
> • Don't engage in any bargaining or heated negotiations: "This isn't up for discussion." "No, sweetie, not this time."
>
> • Explain your position once but no more than that: "I've already told you why."
>
> • Don't lecture, advise, or teach when your child is frustrated. It will get you nowhere. Silence is very powerful. Silence with listening ears and a smile is even better.

When you use these four steps, not only will you help your children to develop resiliency, but you also will help them to develop emotional intelligence, empathy, patience, faith in themselves, trust in the world, creative thinking, problem solving, cooperation, response flexibility, and confidence.

Many times your child's frustration and anger may be in response to you kindly and firmly enforcing the rules and boundaries set in your home. When you use these steps, and keep your boundaries and rules intact, you are also allowing your child to develop trust in you, as well as a sense of security and faith in the predictability of his world. These things provide deep comfort, despite what the temper tantrum may seem to say to you in the moment.

SPECIAL TIP for When Kids Dig In Their Heels

Sometimes when the screaming starts and you can tell that your child's heels have dug in, parents can get sucked into confusion and despair–and give in to the children's demands. It's helpful to understand that often a tantrum follows a pattern: the stages of grief. When you know the pattern–and that it has a beginning, middle, and end–the more emotionally detached you can be and the less you will be triggered yourself. The more readily you can accept the run of the pattern without jumping in to intervene, the more your child can focus on the process of grieving himself and trust that he *can* get through it. Practice with the run of the stages tends to equal comfort with the whole process. Miraculously, your child will eventually begin to take less time to move from denial to acceptance.

To illustrate, consider this adaptation of a handout on the **Stages of Grief** and what they sound like by Positive Discipline instructor Colleen Murphy from the work of Susan Stiffleman:

#1. Denial: "No!" "It's NOT bed time!" "You're NOT the boss of me!" "I AM going to keep watching TV!"

#2. Anger: "Go away!" "Get out of my room!" "I don't like you!" "You're mean!" "Stupid head!" "I'm gonna scream until you let me watch more! AAAAAAHHHH!"

#3. Bargaining: "PLEASE!" "I promise just this once!" "One more minute!" "But WHY?"

With your help, this is the point where the child hits what's called "The Wall of Futility." If you manage to refrain from reacting to the anger, giving in at the display of emotion, or getting involved in the process of bargaining, children can get past the first three stages. When they do, they shift from trying to change things to beginning to accept things. This is when the tears often come.

#4. Depression: "But I really wanted to watch that show."

#5. Acceptance: "Okay . . . but after my bath, I get to pick out the book to read for bedtime, okay?"

You have great love for your kids, and the temptation to rescue them is strong. Instead, show your love by helping them to become the competent, capable, resilient adults you want them to become.

Glenda Montgomery is a Positive Discipline lead trainer as well as the mother of a daughter and son.

© 2014 FAMILY EMPOWERMENT NETWORK™ ALL RIGHTS RESERVED.

Developing Capable People Guidelines

By H. Stephen Glenn and Jane Nelsen, EdD

From the book *Raising Self-Reliant Children in a Self-Indulgent World*

SEVEN STRATEGIES FOR DEVELOPING CAPABLE PEOPLE

#1. Recognize that the rate and intensity with which knowledge, technology, and lifestyle are changing have created conditions in which resiliency and personal resources are critical to effective living and learning.

#2. Encourage the development of seven resources of highly resilient and capable people:

1) **Strong perceptions of personal capabilities.** "I am capable of facing problems and challenges and gaining strength and wisdom through experience."

2) **Strong perceptions of significance.** "My life has meaning and purpose, and I contribute in unique and meaningful ways."

3) **Strong perceptions of personal influence over life.** "I can influence what I do in life and am accountable for my actions and choices."

4) **Strong intrapersonal skills.** The ability to manage personal emotions through self-assessment, self-control, and self-discipline.

5) **Strong interpersonal skills.** The ability to communicate, cooperate, negotiate, share, empathize, listen, and work effectively with people.

6) **Strong systemic skills.** The ability to respond to the limits and consequences of everyday life with responsibility, adaptability, flexibility, and integrity.

7) **Strong judgmental skills.** The ability to make decisions based on moral and ethical principles, wisdom, and understanding.

#3. Provide opportunities in homes and classrooms for children to develop the significant seven. Strategies such as family/class meetings, mentoring, and firmness with dignity and respect can provide opportunities for children to develop all of these resources.

#4. Create and use rituals, traditions, and service projects as opportunities for growth and empowerment for children.

#5. Increase the use of dialogue (a meaningful exchange of ideas and perceptions) as the essential process for encouraging closeness, trust, and learning: "What are your thoughts about that?" *Avoid* "Did you? Can you? Will you? Won't you? Is everything okay?" etc. Instead *use* "What? How? When? In what way . . . ?" etc.

#6. Build closeness and trust, and convey respect by avoiding the **Five Barriers** and using the **Five Builders** instead:

Barrier 1: **Assuming:** Acting on limiting assumptions about what a person can or can't do, say, think, etc. "I didn't tell you because you always get upset." "You always think ...." "You're too young to try that!" etc.

Builder 1: **Checking:** Giving people a clean slate: "How do you want to deal with this?" "What are your thoughts about ....?" "What will you need to have ready for ....?" etc.

Barrier 2: **Rescuing/Explaining:** Problem solving for a person: "........ is what is happening." " .... is why it is happening." " .... is how to deal with it." "Do it this way." etc.

Builder 2: **Exploring:** Problem solving with a person by letting him/her try something and then asking: "What did you experience in that situation?" "Why is that significant?" "How might you apply what you have learned in the future?" etc.

Barrier 3: **Directing:** Telling people what to do: "Pick up your shoes." "Put that away." "Don't forget your lunch." "Be sure and ...." etc.

Builder 3: **Inviting:** Asking for participation/assistance: "I would appreciate any help you could give me in straightening up this room." "How do you plan to ....?" "What will you need in order to ....?" etc.

Barrier 4: **Expecting (too much too soon):** Using potential as a standard and discounting people for not being there already: "I was expecting this room to be spotless." "You should know that already." "I appreciate .... but you forgot ...." etc.

Builder 4: **Celebrating:** Focusing on effort, progress, and/or what was gained by trying. "I appreciate the effort you have made to clean up this room." "What did you learn from trying to do that?" "What progress do you see yourself making?" etc.

Barrier 5: **Adultism:** Using stereotypes when dealing with people: "Teenagers are like that." "You know better than that! Surely you realize!" "You are too young to appreciate that." "Grow up!" "Why are you so childish." etc.

Builder 5: **Respect:** Allowing for people's uniqueness and individuality: "What is your perception of ....?" or "Let me check out what you think." "How do you see this issue?" etc.

#7. Improve your relationships 100% by avoiding the **Five Barriers.** Where can you get that kind of return for doing less? Replace the Barriers with the **Builders** and double the positive impact of your contributions!

Reprinted with permission from Jane Nelsen, author of the Positive Discipline *books (www.positivediscipline.com and www.empoweringpeople.com).*

Understanding Resiliency in Kids
By Kelly Bartlett

Resilience =
- The ability to handle things going wrong
- The ability to cope with adversity
- The ability to find creative solutions to problems
- The ability to bounce back from emotional hurts

Some of the most common challenges that children encounter bring up unavoidable feelings of frustration, anger, sadness, or fear. These are futile situations; children are powerless to change them. It is in these situations that we, parents, tend to want to protect our kids. We are inclined to offer rationalization, justification, and protection from life's futilities. Common futilities in a child's life are ones such as:

- Trying to make something work that doesn't
- Not feeling smart enough
- Not being perfect
- Failing
- Wanting to hold on to a good experience
- Not being able to have mom or dad all to oneself
- Wishing to go back in time (wanting to change something they've done)
- Trying to defy the laws of nature (make magic work)
- Losing at games or contests
- Wanting to "send back" a sibling
- Not being able to know what will happen in the future
- Not being big enough/ tall enough/ strong enough for their own satisfaction

How Resilience Develops in Children

1. Allow kids to get to the point of futility. They must experience adversity, frustration, and mistakes.

2. Kids will express their feelings through tears. Tears are a healthy and necessary step to move toward resiliency.

3. Parents must acknowledge and accept those feelings. Provide a safe environment for kids to express their feelings by allowing tears, empathizing, and supporting them through their difficult emotions.

4. Parents offer encouragement. Help kids through their hardships; help them find success after failure.

- Being excluded (among peers or siblings)
- Not being able to control another's decisions/ choices/ outcomes
- Not being able to have their own way all the time

The more we try to protect children in these kinds of situations, the more we send the message that we're afraid they won't be able to handle them. But they can. And they will, if they're given both opportunity and support.

Here are some things you can do at home to create a safe, supportive environment and encourage a child's development of resiliency:

- **Have one-on-one time each day** (with a young child), or each week (with an older one). Allow the child to decide the activity, and to take the lead in the topics of conversation. Your focus is on listening and getting to know your child just a little bit better.

- **Substitute punishment and consequences with problem solving.** The unpleasantness of a punishment may work in the short-term, but it is

© 2014 FAMILY EMPOWERMENT NETWORK™ ALL RIGHTS RESERVED.

much more effective to teach kids how to own their mistakes and fix them. Instead of approaching mis-behavior with the thought of, "What can I do to you so that you'll learn a lesson?" approach it with the perspective of, "How can we solve this problem?"

• **Tell kids, "It's OK to cry."** Don't rescue them from their feelings, but acknowledge all feelings as real and acceptable. The more they are allowed to feel their feelings when they are young, the more capable they will be of understanding and managing them when they are grown.

• **Switch from time-outs to time-ins.** A time-out is sending a child away to an isolated area to deal with his feelings alone. A time-in is a connective moment spent with a child to help him calm down and learn how to regulate his emotions. Help a child feel better so he can do better.

• **Provide opportunities for autonomy and responsibility.** Give kids control over as many areas of their lives as possible. From choosing their own clothes to fixing their own food to deciding how to spend their allowance…let them make their own choices–and their own mistakes. Recovering from mistakes is where resilience comes from, but they need to have those opportunities in the first place.

• **Offer encouragement** through failures and mistakes…
> "I trust you."
> "You have my support."
> "These are some really big feelings."
> "You are capable of finding a solution."
> "I have faith that you'll figure this out."
> "What can I do to help you right now?"
> "What are your ideas?"
> "Is there a solution that will meet everyone's needs?"
> "Trust yourself."
> "I'm confident we can find a workable solution."
> "You have the freedom to choose."
> "I love you."

Kelly Bartlett is a writer, parent educator, and author of Encouraging Words for Kids.

ALL RIGHTS RESERVED. © 2014 FAMILY EMPOWERMENT NETWORK™

Super Mom: Ditching the Cape

By Eryn Rodger, MA

I meditate quite often on the myth of the "Super Mom," the one who's always off saving the day, getting everything done for everyone with an unflappably upbeat attitude and a smile interrupted only occasionally by the trademark sigh of resignation: "Those kids," I imagine she says, with a grin and a little shake of her head, cape flapping in the wind.

Transforming my own inner Super Mom has been a bigger challenge than I expected it to be. I have had to keep her in check: She's always wanting to rescue and protect and make sure everyone gets his needs met without stress or tears or–God forbid–anyone getting angry with her. She lives in denial of her own needs.

Over the years, with lots of hard work and plenty of mistakes, I've managed to change my parenting style and philosophy, but first I had to acknowledge the ways in which I was still buying into the myth and get clear on the harm I was causing my entire family by donning the cape. I learned that I was enabling my children when I was constantly "doing for" them in the name of care-taking, instead of "doing with" them with the intention of fostering a sense of capability and independence.

Seldom do we think about doing things for our children that they could do themselves as *depriving* or *robbing* our children of the experiences they need in order to learn, grow, and thrive. That by doing it all we are not merely "coddling" or "spoiling" a little, but we are potentially causing our children harm by setting up (co-)dependency, self-esteem problems, or "slacker" mentality.

What are you doing that your child could do, or learn to do? Are you taking time for training, or are you stuck in the notion that "It's easier if I just do it myself"? Do you succumb to whining, crying, and demands, or do you hold your line with dignity, love, and respect, letting natural consequences do the teaching? Are you expressing faith in your child's abilities, both with words and actions? Our children deserve this from us, to be given the chance to develop life skills that will allow them to become confident, capable adults. It's not always easy–I like to feel needed!–but parenting with long-range vision requires me to ditch the cape.

What about protecting or rescuing our children from emotional experiences? Super Mom doesn't like her cubs to feel any of the "bad" feelings: sadness, anger, hurt, frustration. But what are the long-range effects of depriving our children from experiencing these emotions? Many parents come to me wanting tools that will spare their children any "negative" feelings; they don't think a tool is working if their children lose their tempers, become frustrated, or cry. They don't want to "hurt their feelings," even if they are acting with love and respect.

If we really want our children to decide the world is a safe place, and feel comfortable taking appropriate risks, we must let our children experience a full range of emotions without judgment or fear. We let go, without abandoning. We can create sacred, safe space to hold our children and their intense feelings, and teach them to heal and grow from them. We can teach and model optimism even while we are facing sadness or loss. If we think back on times in our own lives when we felt sad, angry or hurt, we can see the good that came from living through these ordeals, especially if we were supported and loved.

I continue to dispel my personal "Super Mom" myth, letting my children develop competency with everything from packing their own lunches and doing their own laundry to allowing them to feel frustration and rage as well as joy and accomplishment–keeping in mind that they will need to learn these things if they are to experience a happy, productive adulthood. I provide the training, the encouragement, the shoulder to cry on, the belief in their abilities when they don't have it.

And what do I do when I'm not flying around, taking care of everyone else? I get to take care of my own needs. It turns out I've got quite a few!

Eryn Rodger, MA, is a Certified Positive Discipline Educator and the mother of four.

© 2014 FAMILY EMPOWERMENT NETWORK™ ALL RIGHTS RESERVED.

Nature's Neurons:

Do Early Experiences in the Natural World Help Shape Children's Brain Architecture?

By Richard Louv

What role do early childhood experiences in nearby nature play in the formation of brain architecture? It's time for science to ask that question.

In January, 2012, *New York Times* columnist Nicholas Kristof reported on the American Academy of Pediatrics' "landmark warning that toxic stress can harm children for life." This was, he wrote, a 'policy statement' from the premier association of pediatricians, based on two decades of scientific research," and he added that the statement "has revolutionary implications for medicine and for how we can more effectively chip away at poverty and crime."

Understanding the "plasticity" of the brain is a key to this relatively new approach. While genetics are responsible for the brain's basic foundation, its architecture–structure and connections–can literally be shaped by factors outside the body.

From conception through early childhood, brain architecture is particularly malleable and influenced by environment and relationships with primary caregivers, including toxic stress caused by abuse or chronic neglect. By interfering with healthy brain development, such stress can undermine the cognitive skills and health of a child, leading to learning difficulty and behavior problems, as well as psychological and behavior problems,

heart disease, obesity, diabetes and other physical ailments later in life.

"We're beginning to get a pretty compelling biological model of why kids who have experienced adversity have trouble learning," according to Jack Shonkoff, a pediatrician and director of the Center on the Developing Child at Harvard. "You can modify behavior later, but you can't rewire disrupted brain circuits," he told Kristof. Does this mean that brain development stops at age three? No. Original circuits may be disrupted, but the brain does have a remarkable ability to create neural detours throughout a lifetime, especially during periodic windows of brain-development opportunity. So don't write off teenagers or the rest of us. Still, neuroscientists believe that it's vastly better to get brain circuitry right the first time, during the first years of life.

To reduce toxic stress in early childhood, Shonkoff and others call for early intervention, including home visitation by childcare experts to vulnerable women pregnant for the first time. Kristof reports on one such program: "The nurse warns against smoking and alcohol and drug abuse, and later encourages breast-feeding and good nutrition, while coaxing mothers to cuddle their children and read to them. This program continues until the child is 2." In addition, better urban design and public health and economic policies could relieve toxic stresses caused by excessive noise,

ALL RIGHTS RESERVED. © 2014 FAMILY EMPOWERMENT NETWORK™

Several years ago, I worked with the Center on the Developing Child, then associated with Brandeis University, to help with communications. When I would ask the neuroscientists how the natural world itself affects brain development, they, in turn, would ask, rhetorically, "How do you define nature?" Ironically, these same scientists were simulating more "natural" conditions for control groups of animal subjects in their labs. Defining nature may be a scientific stumbling block, but it shouldn't be an insurmountable problem.

For all of human history and prehistory, experience in the natural world has helped shape our species, including our brains. That huge and ongoing influence cannot be ignored.

So here are a few questions to challenge neuroscientists and other researchers to explore these questions: What is nature's role in reducing toxic stress early in life and improving parent-child attachment? Does disconnection from nature help cause toxic stress? What is already being done by people in vulnerable neighborhoods to create more naturally nurturing environments? Are proliferating community gardens, especially in urban neighborhoods, already having a positive impact on early childhood development, including brain development? And could one form of early intervention be to assure early, positive childhood experiences in the natural world?

It's time for science to ask these questions, and more, about the shaping of young brains. Defining nature will be the easy part.

pollution, traffic, the threat of crime, and unemployment. Unfortunately, researchers have not focused on the impact a child's attachment to the natural world may have on brain development. On related fronts, here's what we do know.

A growing body of primarily correlative evidence suggests that, even in the densest urban neighborhoods, negative stress, obesity and other health problems are reduced and psychological and physical health improved when children and adults experience more nature in their everyday lives. These studies suggest that nearby nature can also stimulate learning abilities and reduce the symptoms of attention deficit hyperactivity disorder, and we know that therapies using gardening or animal companions do improve psychological health. We also know that parks with the richest biodiversity appear to have a positive impact on psychological well-being and social bonding among humans. While we can't say with certainty that these influences play a direct role in early brain development, it's fair to suggest that the presence of nature can soften the blow of toxic stress in early childhood and throughout our lives. It's understandable that researchers have yet to explore the natural world's impact on brain development because the topic itself is rather new. Also, scientists have a hard time coming up with an agreed-upon definition of nature—or of life itself.

Richard Louv is the author of eight books about nature and development including Last Child in the Woods: Saving Our Children from Nature-Deficit Disorder *and* The Nature Principle: Human Restoration and the End of Nature-Deficit Disorder. *For more information on the movement to connect children with nature, see www.richardlouv.com or www.childrenandnature.org.*

© 2014 FAMILY EMPOWERMENT NETWORK™ ALL RIGHTS RESERVED.

Helping Kids Manage Anxiety:

Ages and Stages

By Sue Campbell

From time to time, most of us wish for the carefree days of childhood, but children have plenty of stresses of their own. They absorb stress from their parents and face pressures related to friendships and schoolwork. Sometimes just the pace of daily life can be overwhelming for children, causing anxiety that can manifest in stomachaches, crying, sleeplessness, and other troubling symptoms.

The goods news is that awareness of childhood anxiety–and what parents and kids can do to curb it–is increasing, and, like so many aspects of parenting, helping your child manage anxiety begins with modeling the behavior you hope to teach them. From dealing with postpartum anxiety to developing and practicing healthy coping strategies to maintaining reasonable schedules for everyone in the family, parents can set the tone for a balanced, low-stress lifestyle.

The Early Years (Ages 2 and under): The Mama-Baby Connection . . . How Maternal Anxiety Affects Babies and Toddlers

We don't need to tell you how becoming a parent, or adding another child to your family, can throw you for a loop. It's perfectly normal to worry about your child's well being. Questions such as "Is that cough normal?" or "Is that rash serious?" come up all the time, but for five to 20 percent of new mothers, postpartum anxiety is a serious issue–and what's a serious issue for mom is a serious issue for baby.

"Most new moms have a level of anxiety, but they don't spend a disproportionate amount of time thinking about all the bad things that could happen," says Deb Mertlich, a licensed clinical social worker who specializes in anxiety disorders. When worry becomes so prevalent it impacts a mother's ability to function, it starts to impact the baby, too.

"When children are infants and toddlers, they are completely dependent on their mothers and often pick up on any emotion the mother is feeling," Mertlich notes.

While statistics specifically related to the effects of maternal anxiety on babies are hard to come by, anxiety often accompanies postpartum depression, and studies have shown that babies and toddlers of mothers suffering from postpartum depression can have a difficult time learning to self soothe and have a higher risk of behavioral problems. If left untreated, there's also a risk that mom and baby won't form a strong attachment.

"If a new mom finds herself asking a lot of 'what if' questions that lead her to feel something terrible is going to happen to her child," says Mertlich, "it might be time to talk to a friend, family member, or possibly a professional."

Indeed, experts agree that new moms are not to blame for their anxiety. Hormonal changes, sleep deprivation, genetic predisposition, or even an underlying medical issue such as hypothyroidism can set the stage for postpartum anxiety. Difficulty breastfeeding or hormonal changes associated with weaning also can be factors.

ALL RIGHTS RESERVED. © 2014 FAMILY EMPOWERMENT NETWORK™

Some of the most effective strategies for combating anxiety–getting adequate sleep, maintaining a healthful diet, exercising regularly, and talking about your feelings–are only possible if you've got a good support network of friends and family to assist you. If you need help getting a support network in place, Mertlich recommends connecting with a medical social worker. "Social workers can be a wonderful resource to help new moms get connected to outside organizations," she says. Talk to your health care provider or your child's pediatrician to learn more.

The Preschool Period (Ages 3 to 5): Please Don't Go! . . . Managing Separation Anxiety

It's a familiar scene for parents everywhere: You've found the perfect preschool for your child. The teacher is wonderful. Your child is excited. But when it comes time for you to leave him, there are tears and yelling and little hands wrapped tightly around your neck. What's a parent to do?

First of all, says Susan Andrews, a preschool teacher at Cedarwood Waldorf School in Portland, Oregon, who's been an early childhood educator for 24 years, don't panic. "Separation anxiety in a child is very normal and

quite important for the adults to honor and respect in a child," she says. Most children overcome their anxiety quickly after a parent leaves, and, it's important to remember, this stage of development eventually will pass.

In the meantime, a few simple strategies can help. Andrews encourages parents "not to talk too much about their leaving beforehand, as this builds the anticipation within the child."

> *For some children, severe separation anxiety can be a sign they're not ready for the program in which they're enrolled. If your child's anxiety is severe, prolonged, and not manageable with the help of your child's teacher and simple techniques such as those detailed in this article, it may be time to discuss the possibility of separation anxiety disorder (SAD) with your family's pediatrician.*

Parents also need to manage their own emotions about the separation. "If the parent is internally stressed about leaving his or her child," Andrews explains, "the child picks up on that energy, even if the parent is outwardly acting like everything will be fine." She suggests parents "visualize a positive transition" to foster confidence for both the parent and the child.

If possible, try to help your child get engaged in a fun activity before you leave, but don't be tempted to sneak away while she's not looking. It also can be helpful to create some sort of ritual for the drop-off period–reading a short story together or sharing a special goodbye hug or handshake, for example.

The key is keeping it brief. Not only can a long, drawn-out goodbye increase your child's anxiety, but it also can have a cascading effect on the rest of the classroom. In fact, if your child could put it into words, she'd probably tell you to go quickly.

It's also important to clearly let your child know what to expect, and to follow through on your promises. If you say you'll be back after lunch, for example, make sure you're there on time, and don't tell him you're going to pick him up and then send somebody else.

The symptoms of separation anxiety will decrease as your child becomes more familiar with new environments and routines, but be prepared for some regression after long absences from school, such as winter and spring break.

© 2014 FAMILY EMPOWERMENT NETWORK™ ALL RIGHTS RESERVED.

Dealing with separation anxiety can be as stressful for the parent (if not more so!), as it is for the child, but all you can do is try to ease the transitions with consistency and care, and keep reminding yourself that it's a normal part of your child's development.

Elementary Concerns (Ages 6 to 10): Child's Pose . . . Yoga for Kids

If you've ever taken a yoga class, you know nothing matches the feeling of relaxation and calm you feel after a session of intentional breath and body work. All your cares seem to melt away. The positive effects of yoga are well documented by scientific studies and--you guessed it–it's never too early to start reaping the benefits.

Just imagine the effect an hour of Lion's Breath and Downward Dog can have on an amped-up, stressed-out grade schooler. And then imagine the emotional leg up your child can gain by developing positive tools for coping with anxiety at an early age.

"There are so very many benefits to learning yoga as a child," says Rosey Wyland, a licensed clinical social worker, yoga teacher, and mother. Wyland teaches yoga to children, families, and adults. "It's fun and a great way [for kids] to connect with their bodies and practice quieting their minds. It can help reduce stress and help with sleep."

Kids often don't know what to do with feelings of anxiety, strong emotions brought on by trauma, or even daily stresses such as homework and life on the playground. "Yoga teaches children to manage emotions and cope with stress and anxiety through poses, breathing techniques, visualization, mindfulness practices, and relaxation," Wyland says.

Her students use yoga to manage stress "before tests or a sports game and to help during times of transition," she says. "They use it before bed and when they wake up in the middle of the night. They use it to help manage difficult emotions and get along with their friends and families."

Recent studies have shown that a yoga practice that incorporates breathing and mindfulness techniques has a measurable effect on a child's ability to cope with stress. Kids are even able to generalize the concepts they learn during yoga practice in their everyday lives.

Wyland says the kids in her classes say yoga helps them feel calm and peaceful. One eight-year-old student says, "Yoga gets the stress out of my mind."

"One child would roll out her yoga mat in the middle of the living room, put on her eye pillow, and practice her relaxation," says Wyland.

Some schools are beginning to catch on to the benefits of incorporating yoga into the curriculum. Allyson Copacino Move Yoga (www.moveyogastudio.com) teaches yoga to kids in several elementary schools. She says kids this age "aren't quite sure how to identify stress, but they understand hyper energy that they feel."

Copacino finds the best poses for helping kids manage anxiety are those that promote relaxation and a sense of focus, such as deep breathing exercises and balancing poses. She also recommends a simple pose for relaxation where children lay on their backs on the floor with their legs up against a wall. Her students tell her they could lie like that for hours.

"Kids at this age are really interested in sharing what they've learned." Copacino says. "I get a lot of parents telling me their kids have been teaching them yoga classes."

Wyland says her students do the same, sharing what they've learned with their siblings and parents. Not only is that great for stress management; it's a wonderful way for families to spend quality time together.

ALL RIGHTS RESERVED. © 2014 FAMILY EMPOWERMENT NETWORK™

The "Middle Ages" (Ages 11 to 14 and beyond): Overbooked and Overwhelmed . . . Time Management for Tweens and Teens

Tenth grader Emilie is a typical modern teenager. She has a busy social life, does her best to stay on top of her schoolwork, and loves to dance. As a member of a local dance company as well as the dance company at her school, Emilie devotes between eight and 13 hours per week to practicing. Whenever she's not at school or dancing, she's studying. Anxiety tends to spike for her one to two weeks before a big dance performance. "Before shows, I usually get really stressed out and really nervous, and I'm always afraid that my grades are going to fall," Emilie says.

Her mom knows that when Emilie gets grumpy, it's the stress talking, "Usually the temper gets a little short," says her mom, "or she gets a little snippy when she responds to simple questions or things I'm asking her to do around the house."

Deb Mertlich, the social worker mentioned earlier, says irritability is a common symptom of anxiety in overscheduled teens. "Kids don't know how to regulate themselves," Mertlich says. "They are relying on their parents to know when they should take a break." To help keep things under control, Mertlich recommends parents check in with their kids regularly and help them create a schedule that includes adequate down time.

There's no exact formula for figuring out how much is too much for your child. Focus on whether his activity level seems to be causing the symptoms of anxiety—irritability, sleeplessness, weepiness, constant worrying, and even headaches and stomachaches—rather than simply counting the number of commitments.

When Emilie's mom sees the warning signs of stress and anxiety in Emilie, she steps in, giving her daughter a temporary reprieve from chores and helping her limit social activities so she can focus on schoolwork and dance practice. When things get really bad, she encourages Emilie to speak with her teachers and ask for deadline extensions to relieve some pressure. She also reminds her to eat and get enough sleep. "Sometimes I can't get to sleep and I start to freak out and I just need to talk to my mom or my friends," Emilie says.

Sleep troubles often accompany anxiety in teens, says Mertlich. This compounds the problem, as a lack of sleep depletes the child's ability to cope with anxiety.

Cutting back on activities isn't the only solution. It's important to help your child find an outlet for his stress—something that helps him feel calmer and happier. That's why giving up dance isn't an option for Emilie. "Dance helps me with my stress," she says. When she feels overwhelmed, she adds, "I actually just stop everything and dance."

Many educators and researchers believe the effect of stress on tweens and teens is so detrimental to their health that a change in society's attitude toward achievement is in order. Stanford University began a program called Challenge Success (challengesuccess.org), which offers a data-driven curriculum and resources to help educators, parents, and students set a new standard of success that values mental and physical health, not just academic performance.

"Help kids understand that they don't need to do everything," Mertlich urges. The best way to do that? Show them what a balanced life looks like.

As Mertlich says, "Parents need to look at their own schedules and see if they are modeling good limits before trying to set limits with their kids."

Sue Campbell is a freelance writer and mom who lives in Portland, Oregon. Her article, "Helping Kids Manage Anxiety: Ages and Stages" first appeared in the August 2012 issue of Metro Parent.

© 2014 FAMILY EMPOWERMENT NETWORK™ ALL RIGHTS RESERVED.

Put the Play Back into Organized Sports

By Kathy Masarie, MD, and Ruth Matinko-Wald, MA

"Sports are a double-edged sword. They can do our children a lot of good or a lot of harm. They can give them a sense of belonging, character, self-esteem, and good health. Or they can cripple them in body, warp them in mind, teach them bad values, and lead to a crushing sense of failure."
– Steve Biddulph, *Raising Boys*

How can we help our kids to develop a life-long love of moving their bodies and of being on teams where they can practice decision-making, conflict resolution, and teamwork skills? Organized sports can enhance children's lives, but they also can increase our children's and family's stress levels and turn kids off from continuing to be physically active. So, picking developmentally appropriate sports and considering balance for the whole family can maximize benefit.

By age 13, 70% of the 20 million American kids playing organized league sports quit–and never play that sport again. Kids cite multiple reasons for quitting: too much pressure, coaches who yell and shame/punish for mistakes, no time for other interests, and over-involved parents who obsess and lecture on the way home. Ironically, kids often quit or burn out on organized sports before they get to their high school years, when being on a sports team can be a supportive safe haven. High school sports, in fact, are generally more palatable and much more family friendly than club or classics teams, because of their seasonal, weekday format.

> ### Tips for Putting the Play Back Into Organized Sports
>
> Make fun the top priority.
>
> Talk to your kids about their sports in empowering and connecting ways. Regularly explore what they think about the team, coach, games, their role, etc.
>
> Encourage kids to play seasonal sports. By changing sports per season, kids can avoid burn-out and overuse injuries.
>
> Although difficult, consider delaying year-round sports until your child nears adolescence to maximize free play and family time.
>
> Model exercise. If you can't find time to exercise, stop watching and start moving. You could walk around the park/track while your child is practicing.
>
> Start a sports club (complete with pick-up games, pinnies, caps, and a fun season-end party) as an alternative to the demands of a competitive team.
>
> Introduce your children to alternative sports that have a better chance of becoming life-long habits such as hiking, yoga, playing tennis, and bike riding.
>
> Most importantly, when a child says, "I'm bored," say four magical words: "Go outside and play." Even better, go join him and remember to have fun!
>
> *These ideas could reduce unhealthy sports attitudes and practices (too much competition too early, win-at-all cost mentality, and parents who get caught in the "intensity web") and replace them with character-building practices that bring fun and skill-building with respect back into the game.*

In truth, we need our kids to be physically active at *every* age, to engage in *any* exercise such as swimming, yoga, fencing, running, walking, hiking, kayaking, or rock climbing–because regular, lifelong exercise is critical to healthy living. People were made to move! With one in three children overweight or obese and with astronomic increases in diabetes, heart disease, and stress among children, this may be the first generation to have a shorter life expectancy than their parents.

Done well, healthy youth sports are best used as a tool for learning life lessons and firmly establishing the relationship between physical activity and positive physical and mental health. Youth involved in sports can learn the social and moral skills (ethical understanding of fair play, sportsmanship, integrity, and compassion) needed to function well in adult life. Sports also can provide many unique situations for discussing appropriate and inappropriate behaviors and can foster enhanced self esteem and self confidence when kids are taught to feel good about the improvements they make in their skills and performance.

Finally, youth athletes also can be helped to understand that effort is the most important aspect of any competition, and that the outcome is less important than how one reacts in response to a win or a loss. The Positive Coaching Alliance (www.positivecoach.org) is a good resource for more information on healthy sports. Also, see more resources at the end of the chapter.

ALL RIGHTS RESERVED. © 2014 FAMILY EMPOWERMENT NETWORK™

Related Resources for Further Exploration

The Blessing of a Skinned Knee: Using Jewish Teaching to Raise Self-Reliant Children (2008) and *The Blessing of a B Minus: Using Jewish Teachings to Raise Resilient Teenagers* (2011) by Wendy Mogel, PhD. NY: Scribner.

Building Moral Intelligence: The Seven Essential Virtues that Teach Kids to Do the Right Thing by Michele Borba, EdD. San Francisco, CA: Jossey-Bass, 2002.

Building Resilience in Children and Teens: Giving Kids Roots and Wings by Kenneth Ginsburg, MD. Washington, DC: American Academy of Pediatrics, 2011.

The Curse of the Good Girl: Raising Authentic Girls with Courage and Confidence by Rachel Simmons. NY: Penguin Books, 2010.

Daring Greatly: How the Courage to Be Vulnerable Transforms the Way We Live, Love, Parent, and Lead by Brené Brown, PhD, LMSW. NY: Gotham Books, 2012.

Growing Up Brave: Expert Strategies for Helping Your Child Overcome Fear, Stress, and Anxiety by Donna Pincus, PhD. NY: Little Brown & Co., 2012.

How Children Succeed: Grit, Curiosity & the Hidden Power of Character by Paul Tough. NY: Houghton Mifflin Harcourt, 2012.

Mind in the Making: The Seven Essential Life Skills Every Child Needs by Ellen Galinsky. NY: William Morrow, 2010.

Mindset: The New Psychology of Success by Carol Dweck. NY: Ballantine, 2007.

No: Why Kids–of All Ages–Need to Hear It and Ways Parents Can Say It by David Walsh, PhD. NY: Atria Books, 2007.

Parenting without Power Struggles: Raising Joyful, Resilient Kids While Staying Cool, Calm & Connected by Susan Stiffelman, MFT. NY: Atria Books, 2012.

The Price of Privilege: How Parental Pressure and Material Advantage Are Creating a Generation of Disconnected and Unhappy Kids by Madeline Levine, PhD. NY: HarperCollins, 2006.

Raising Resilient Children (Drs. Robert Brooks & Sam Goldstein, McGraw Hill: 2001); *Nurturing Resilience in Our Children: Answers to the Most Important Parenting Questions* (Drs. Brooks & Goldstein, McGraw Hill: 2002); *Angry Children, Worried Parents: Seven Steps to Help Families Manage Anger* (Drs. Brooks, Goldstein, & Sharon Weiss, Specialty Press: 2004); *Seven Steps to Help Your Child's Social Skills: A Family Guide* (Drs. Brooks, Goldstein & Kristy Hagar, Speciality Press: 2006); *Raising a Self-Disciplined Child: Help Your Child Become More Responsible, Confident, and Resilient*, (Drs. Brooks & Goldstein, McGraw Hill: 2007); *Resilience in Children* (Drs. Brooks & David Richman, Springer Press: 2012).

© 2014 FAMILY EMPOWERMENT NETWORK™ ALL RIGHTS RESERVED.

Raising Self-Reliant Children in a Self-Indulgent World: Seven Building Blocks for Developing Capable Young People by H. Stephen Glenn and Jane Nelsen, EdD. 2nd ed. NY: Harmony Books, 2000.

Student Success Skills: Helping Students Develop the Academic, Social, and Self-Management Skills They Need to Succeed by Greg Brigman, PhD, and Linda Webb, PhD. www.studentsuccessskills.com

Taking Charge: Caring Discipline That Works at Home and at School by Joanne Nordling, MS, MEd. Portland, OR: Parent Support Center, 2007.

Too Much of A Good Thing: Raising Children of Character in an Indulgent Age by Dan Kindlon, PhD. Bel Aire, CA: Miramax Books, 2003.

ON STRESS REDUCTION

10 Mindful Minutes: Giving Our Children–and Ourselves–the Social and Emotional Skills to Reduce Stress and Anxiety for Healthier, Happier Lives by Goldie Hawn and Wendy Holden. NY: Penguin Group, 2011.

The Homework Myth: Why Our Kids Get Too Much of a Bad Thing by Alfie Kohn. Cambridge, MA: De Capo Press, 2007.

The Opposite of Worry: The Playful Parenting Approach to Childhood Anxieties and Fears by Lawrence Cohen, PhD. NY: Ballantine, 2013.

Simplicity Parenting: Using the Extraordinary Power of Less to Raise Calmer, Happier, and More Secure Kids by Kim John Payne. NY: Ballantine Books, 2009.

The Whole-Brain Child: 12 Revolutionary Strategies to Nurture Your Child's Developing Mind by Daniel Siegel, MD, and Tina Payne Bryson, PhD. NY: Bantam, 2012.

Organization and film: *Race to Nowhere* www.racetonowhere.com

ON HEALTHY SPORTS

Beyond Winning: Smart Parenting in a Toxic Sports Environment by Kim John Payne, Luis Fernando Llosa, and Scott Lancaster. Guilford, CT: Lyons Press, 2013.

The Double Goal Coach: Positive Coaching Tools for Honoring the Game and Developing Winners in Sports and Life by Jim Thompson of the Positive Coaching Alliance at www.positivecoach.org (2003)

Dr. Rob's Guide to Raising Fit Kids: A Family-Centered Approach to Achieving Optimal Health by Robert Gotlin, DO. NY: DiaMedica Publishing, 2008.

Raising Our Athletic Daughters: How Sports Can Build Self-Esteem and Save Girls' Lives by Jean Zimmerman and Gil Reavill . NY: Main Street Book, 1998.

Whose Game Is It Anyway? A Guide to Helping Your Child Get the Most from Sports, Organized by Age and Stage by Amy Baltzell, Richard D. Ginsburg, and Stephen Durant. NY: Mariner Books, 2006.

 ALL RIGHTS RESERVED. © 2014 FAMILY EMPOWERMENT NETWORK™

Courage to Act 7

Andrea Millen, 14 yrs. Private School

chapter seven

Courage to Act

"We must not, in trying to think about how we can make a big difference,
ignore the small daily differences we can make which, over time,
add up to big differences that we often cannot foresee."
– Marian Wright Edelman, president and founder of the Children's Defense Fund

As parents, we play a major role in our children becoming who they will be. Parenting's core demands have basically stayed the same over time, but our job now needs to evolve to deal with the new dilemma of the Digital Age: how to enjoy the gifts of modern technology while simultaneously protecting our children from its untoward effects. This takes courage and effort. Given the all-powerful influence of media and technology, it takes daring to transcend fear and the negative messages that bombard us on a daily basis. It takes guts to chart our own course, to stick to our values, and to walk our talk. It takes real courage to change social norms to more fully nurture and protect our nation's youngest and most vulnerable citizens.

We know courage when we see it, especially on the big screen, in great literature, or in the realm of history. Think about Martin Luther King, Jr., and the tremendous impact of his words and work. Consider how First Lady Michelle Obama's signature "Let's Move" campaign–which encourages healthy eating and exercise–has helped to decrease childhood obesity rates in the United States. The truth is, social norms *can* be changed. Over the last decades, there are many compelling examples: decreasing tobacco use, car seat safety protocols, recycling, and everyday improvements for Americans with disabilities.

What do we really want for our children and our families? Don't we all want to raise resilient, empathetic, and capable kids? Don't we want to raise children who will experience the happiness of rich relationships? To develop such competencies and relationships, children need strong social and life skills that come through real experience and face-to-face interaction. They must actively engage in the complexity of the real world if they are to learn the art of being present, reaching out, navigating difficulties, staying connected, setting boundaries, and letting go.

But what does courage look like in our ordinary lives? What does it look like for you? How can you take what you've learned through *Face to Face* and have the courage to act to make your world, your child's world, a little bit better?

This final chapter of *Face to Face* challenges you to take the first small steps toward creating health, resilience, and connection for children in your own home, your child's school, and your community. We offer our touchstones and share the stories of others to help inspire you to forge your own path of action. Then we encourage you to take the leap and venture boldly with your advocacy and passion into the wider world.

© 2014 FAMILY EMPOWERMENT NETWORK™ ALL RIGHTS RESERVED.

STAY CONNECTED

"The most precious gift we can offer others is our presence. When mindfulness embraces those we love, they will bloom like flowers."
– Thich Nhat Hanh

As humankind is biologically wired for rich, active, face-to-face interaction, holding connection as one of our highest values is an important first step to take. Yet, we are all at risk of feeling more isolated as we are seduced by communicating via quick texts, immediate Facebook posts, and the 140 characters of Twitter! So we must mindfully consider, "How can I increase connection with my child, my community, and myself?"

Creating Connection with Your Child

Never forget that the most important connection for your child is with you. The development of children's autonomy can grow hand-in-hand with connection. In other words, it is healthy for you to be connected to your child as he/she grows toward independence. Hang on to this, even if your child pushes you away.

As a young child, Jon was easy going, open, and fun loving, yet in high school we got disconnected to the point of not being able to stand to be in the same room together. Starting in middle school, Jon focused his energy on friends, popularity, and social success over academics and sports. This led to taking easy classes, doing minimal homework, if any, and being with friends 24/7. Then he crossed the line by skipping many classes in high school. The more my husband and I insisted he go to school, the more he resisted. The defiance spread.

By the time he was 16, we were in major conflict over pretty much everything–chores, school, where he was going, what he did. Jon even ran away for a few days to a friend's house. This was a wake-up call for me. I realized that we had grown so far apart that: 1) He might not be safe. I did not know if he was doing risky drinking, driving, or drugs,

because we never talked; and 2) He might walk out the door at 18 (or before) and never come back.

I was sad when I realized what we had lost–that close connection, sharing, and involvement in each other's lives. I valued his going to school and learning very much, but I valued Jon's safety and my being a part of his life more.

I went back to something I knew, something that got lost in trying to make him go to school. What I had forgotten is that, by far, the most important ingredient in raising a resilient, competent, caring kid is having a strong, healthy connection with him. I asked myself, "How do I begin again?"

The first thing I did was ask if he would agree that neither of us talk to each other in anger. If one of us escalated to anger, we agreed to take a pause. Second, I fired myself from school-pushing. I decided to let it be his problem if he did not get a high school degree. I let him know I was leaving the responsibility to him to choose work, a GED, or a different school. He chose to continue to go to his high school.

But how to connect? I noticed a possible space in the late evening, after Jon's friends went home. I would just "hang," sitting in a big blue chair in his room. At first Jon was suspicious about what I wanted from him. When I slipped and brought up even the slightest agenda, the visit was cut short. So I learned, the less judgment and agenda I brought with me, the more the connection.

Over time we began to feel a peaceful, comfortable acceptance of each other. He slowly started sharing more about what was going on in his life and where he was going–so I felt better about his safety. He even started helping out around the house and agreed to hitting golf balls and going out to dinner together. As far as school went, it remained Jon's business to figure out. My husband and I continued to share our values about learning and education and kept zipped lips when he skipped classes. This process began the healthy, respectful relationship we have today. And, by the way, he went on to get re-engaged with learning and graduated from college in 3½ years, with great grades and a degree and career about which he is passionate.

ALL RIGHTS RESERVED. © 2014 FAMILY EMPOWERMENT NETWORK™

Creating Connection with Your Community: Form Villages

Build a supportive network for yourself. Parenting is too complex to do alone. Find other adults with whom you can connect openly and honestly.

Drawn by a new job, my husband and I moved to the West Coast early in our marriage, leaving behind our East Coast families. We started our own family and established roots. Raising our two girls without grandparents or aunts and uncles nearby was challenging; we seemed to be on our own. Then, when our youngest daughter was in third grade, we heard Dr. Kathy Masarie speak at school and decided to give her Raising Our Daughters *book a try. Being a Room Parent, I posted a flyer about starting a parent discussion group, and our "Friendzies" group was born.*

We originally started with seven couples participating, reading a chapter and meeting once a month. Our kids played games or pool or watched a movie together in our downstairs family room, while we parents shared our deepest dreams and fears for our girls.

Although we finished reading and discussing the book, five of the seven couples continued to meet irregularly over the next 10 years. We also conferred and commiserated with each about braces, club soccer, middle school garbage, and high school challenges for our girls. We celebrated rites of passages with the girls, and we supported each other through all the ups of downs of raising them.

Needless to say, our families have grown close over all those years. When the girls graduated, we had a special "Friendzies" dinner party for them and presented each of the girls with a photo collage and a necklace, a reminder of their caring "village" back home.

We parents still get together and send care packages to all our daughters who are now off in college forging their own paths. We know they are stronger and bolder because of the love and support of their "Friendzies" throughout all those formative years.

Creating Connection with Yourself

Parenting is always enhanced when you take time for yourself, but self reflection and self care can be particularly challenging in today's times. Nonetheless, we encourage you to prioritize connection with yourself. What this looks like will be different for everyone. Perhaps what works for you is finding a few moments of alone time in your day, or carving out a space for shared reflection through journaling, or engaging in a daily practice of a stress reduction activity such as yoga. Taking the time to contemplate and live your deepest values will serve you well–and provide a healthy model for your children that will benefit them throughout their lives.

When I practice Quiet Time (QT), everyone in my family notices. I am more present as a parent, more intuitive and aware of my children's feelings and needs, and a lot more patient. I feel calm, balanced, flexible, and able to deal with stress so much better. The little things (and big ones!) don't bother me as much. I solve problems more easily and feel more energetic, optimistic, and creative, too. My magic formula? The simple and easy practice of Quiet Time recommended by Trevor Blake. (See Natalie's website/blog, www.movedbyinspiration.com, for step-by-step instructions on this technique.)

You don't need special equipment or a budget for the practice.. Just 20 minutes of time alone each day to notice your breath. The beauty of this practice is that you can adapt it to your own personal situation. Blake recommends taking QT in the morning, or the first half of the day, before our brains get overloaded with too much information. For that reason, I usually don't watch TV or use my computer before my QT. Instead, I usually begin my daily practice around 11:00 am. (I am not able to take the time first thing in the morning, because one of my daughters gets up at the same time as I do!) When I am ready, my husband "takes over" and spends time with our daughters. He engages them in activities such as watering the plants, doing stretching exercises, reading, drawing, or painting. After practicing QT daily for almost a year, I can truly say this simple practice has been life-transforming for me–and has been a blessing to my family. – Natalie, Mother of two young daughters

© 2014 FAMILY EMPOWERMENT NETWORK™ ALL RIGHTS RESERVED.

Taking the time to nurture your own health, hobbies, and interests can refresh your heart and soul and allow your gifts of service to be given to others with joy rather than resentment. Connecting with your own feelings and needs can help your relationships to grow and flourish through harmony as well as through conflict. Truly, self reflection and self care are at the core of a life well lived.

> **What calls you to connection? What small step might you take to connect in a deeper way with your own children, your community, yourself?**

CULTIVATE EMPATHY

"I believe empathy is the most essential quality of civilization." – Roger Ebert

The practice of simply being present and accepting the experiences, feelings, and needs of ourselves and others is at the heart of cultivating empathy. The great news about cultivating empathy in our children is that it is most successfully accomplished through parents modeling mindfulness, respect, and gratitude in our daily connections and conflicts with other humans and living things. Most significantly, our children learn the art of empathy when others, especially their parents, are empathetic toward them. For example:

- How do you interact with your two-year-old when he spills the entire container of milk on the floor?
- What do you say when your 16-year-old new driver slinks home with the car 1½ hours after her curfew?
- How do you treat yourself when you have done or said something unfortunate that you now regret?
- What words do you use to talk about politicians, authorities, or family members with whom you have widely divergent views of our world?
- Alternatively, how do you celebrate the multitudes of life-serving interactions and events in your life for which you are grateful?

Your children will learn that loving relationships can actually grow and be improved through conflict as well as joy. They also learn that paying attention to and honoring another's values and needs is the critical ingredient for living in community with respect and cooperation—and where everyone's needs matter.

Truly, it is difficult to knowingly harm another with whom one feels connected and accepted. An even more onerous task is to stay connected, open, and accepting when you disagree with someone. Your child, in fact, will likely be the person who crosses you at times. What can be invaluable is to prepare for these stressful times by learning a respectful and mindful way of being present with your child no matter what he or she does. What values do you want to be expressed by your words and actions, and how do you want to treat yourself and your child in times of conflict? This is at the heart of developing a practice of empathy and why we spent so much time in the first chapter of this book clarifying your highest personal values.

I know I need "me" time. It doesn't have to be a luxurious trip somewhere alone. Usually all I need is my morning yoga and my evening walk in the park with my dog. Then the rest of the day works out just fine.

A few weeks ago, my middle schooler, Ellie, spent Friday night at a friend's house. When she came home on Saturday morning, she was in "one of her moods." Despite knowing she was responsible for watching her little brother so I could go to my yoga class, she entered the house, went straight to her room, and slammed the door. I wasn't sure what to do. In the past when this happened (and it had!), I got really upset, we got into a fight, I ended up not going to yoga, and, needless to say, I wasn't a happy camper for the rest of that

ALL RIGHTS RESERVED. © 2014 FAMILY EMPOWERMENT NETWORK™

day. This time, having just had the benefit of participating in a Compassionate Communication class, I paused, stopped myself from overreacting, and thought through the values that were triggering me to be so upset. I also remembered from the class to ask myself, "How will I respond to this conflict in a way that respectfully conveys my concerns and honors my values?"

So, I did something I never did before. I wrote a note to Ellie and slipped it under her door. The note read, "I know you're tired, but I really was counting on you to watch Henry. It's important to me to go to yoga. Will you please come and watch him for an hour or so while I'm gone, and then you can take a nap when I get home?" A few minutes later I knocked lightly on the door and waited for a reply. Sheepishly, Ellie opened the door and smiled at me. "I'm sorry, Mom," she said. "I am exhausted, but I know how important your yoga class is to you and I can take a nap when you get back." Crisis averted. Respect retained. Connection confirmed.
– Leticia, Mother of five

You can foster empathy in your home by practicing standing in another person's shoes–literally with role playing if you like–and by using mindful and respectful communication practices in your everyday relationships. Imagine being someone's age or gender, with their personality. Then imagine what you would be feeling or doing in a particular situation. Practicing empathy and acceptance of other viewpoints is really a life-long process for all of us.

> **When we summon greater empathy for ourselves, we become better parents, better friends, and better citizens. This shift alone can make the world a better place.**

WALK THE TALK

"Mindlessness is sinking your feet into the deep, deep tracks society has worn and following those wherever they lead. Mindfulness is about making informed, ethical decisions, choosing your own path."
– Robert Slatford

Having a clear understanding of our values makes life and parenting more satisfying. But it takes courage to live our lives in service of our values, especially when the messages from society are not in support of our parenting. This is when our courage to walk our talk can make a huge difference.

Just as I supported my children in their first cautious steps before walking, and finally running, I am asking that they master the basics of relationships before they embrace social media. The idea of handing out cell phones and personal email addresses to my children who can just barely manage their own emotions feels frightening. In the same way, I will require they prove their maturity before giving them a driver's license. I want to see well-developed compassion, empathy, and personal accountability before giving them media tools that have the power to destroy a reputation or demolish someone emotionally with the tap of a finger. They can't decipher body language in text. They won't see tears or hear laughter in an email, and I'll be the first to admit how easy it is to say something mean or even cruel with the shelter of electronic anonymity. It is only when looking into another face during sibling squabbles and transgressions with friends that the practice for their future relationships can take place. By insisting on a strong sense of positive communication, I am also empowering my children to be more savvy and sophisticated in reading cues and, thereby, arming them against cyber bullying and ether predators.

I understand it'll be awkward for them at times, but they know the limit is not an outright "No," but instead a "When." I hope on some level they appreciate my conviction to facilitate

© 2014 FAMILY EMPOWERMENT NETWORK™ ALL RIGHTS RESERVED.

their future success as friends, co-workers, lovers, and parents. I'm providing the opportunities for plenty of practice, so they can soon own the windfall of their increasingly positive human interactions. They took hundreds of falls in order to be agile athletes, so, too, I know they need thousands of face-to-face interactions to become healthy communicators. I think they're well on their way. – Berdine, Mother of two sons

> **This story reminds us of the power of starting small and walking your talk. Small steps lead to bigger changes and ultimately can shift social norms.**

CREATE SAFE HAVENS

"What goes right in childhood is more important than what goes wrong. The positive effects of even one loving relative, mentor, friend can overwhelm the negative effects of the bad things that happen." – George Vaillant in *Triumphs of Experience*

Safe havens provide children with places where they can be themselves, feel secure, and develop a sense of significance and belonging. They are the "safety nets" that give our children a sense of trust in the world while they are finding themselves. When we pioneer or reinvigorate safe havens, at home and beyond, we build and amplify this trust for our children.

Safe Havens for Safety

The following is a story about providing a safety net for a community of kids who were experimenting with alcohol. Notice all the various "village" members who were engaged, all the support structures put in place, and how the social norm in this community changed.

When Alex was 16, I learned he was experimenting with drinking. I was a big drinker in high school–a "good" girl by day with grades, sports, and cooperation, and a "bad" girl by night, crawling out the window to drink and do drugs. My parents' very clear rule of "No drinking" just shoved my behavior underground and out of sight.

With a strong "alcohol gene" in our family, I did not want Alex doing a lot of uncontrolled drinking and drugs. I pursued every avenue I could think of. First and foremost, even through his high school years, I prioritized connection, so he would feel safe letting me know about serious things going on in his life. We hung out, went out to dinner, shot hoops, and played card games.

My short-term solutions to address the drinking included discussions about: always having a designated driver, the signs of alcohol poisoning, and the relationship between alcohol and sexual behavior. In addition, I stored all of our alcohol in our neighbors' garage (for two years), knowing that 70% of kids raid their parents' liquor cabinets. I also collaborated with his friends' parents to watch for drinking and conferred with close neighbors so they knew to watch for parties if we weren't at home. My husband and I did not go out of town together for two years after Alex hosted an 80-person party that was highlighted by a visit from the police, a broken table, and vomit on the couch.

We also did our best to think of long-term solutions. We wanted Alex's friends to hang out here–so we knew what was going on. To that end, we stocked our refrigerator with good snacks (i.e., junk food), moved Alex's room to a bigger location with a sofa, bought Alex a comfortable bed so he would want to sleep at home, and, yes, bought video games (caved in, but held the line at "no violence"). I also started a program at Alex's high school that organized parent-teen assemblies with trauma nurses, a state liquor commissioner, lawyers (you can be sued if you serve liquor to kids), and police. I paid (bribed) Alex to go. He took his friends. I even developed guidelines on how to host a teen party in your home, after I botched supervising ours. Any parent who signed an agreement to these guidelines got designated in the school directory as a "safe teen home."

ALL RIGHTS RESERVED. © 2014 FAMILY EMPOWERMENT NETWORK™

Throughout all of this, Alex and I had on-going discussions about how he was doing with his drinking. Now, at 26 years old, Alex claims these discussions were pretty honest. Today, he is a "now and then" drinker, has developed healthy habits of self-care, and, best of all, we remain close, connected, and open with each other.

Safe Havens at School

Schools (and their before- and after-school activities) are potentially important safe havens for children. They provide regular opportunities for kids to engage with peers and adults and to practice face-to-face communication skills. Ideally, schools can act as safe havens by ensuring that every single student gets proactive attention from at least one adult.

Benold Middle School principal Randy Adair wanted to be sure that no child fell through the cracks at his Georgetown, TX, school. At a staff planning meeting, he gave each teacher stickers and asked them to put a sticker next to the students with whom they had the closest relationships. It turned out that the outgoing students got lots of stickers, but many of the kids who really needed attention were the ones who didn't get any stickers at all. The staff then brainstormed ways to reach out to those children, with teachers putting a star next to the names of the kids with whom they would initiate a relationship in the near future. – Summarized from "Assets… Every Student a Star." *Assets: The Magazine of Ideas for Healthy Communities and Healthy Youth.* Copyright © Spring 2000 Search Institute® www.search-institute.org

Safe Havens for Acceptance

All of our children deserve to have safe havens in their lives, but not all kids "fit" in school. That's why adults need to be proactive about volunteering for community organizations and mentoring youth.

When I was in ninth grade, I felt like such a misfit in my high school. I had a great life being a tomboy growing up and just could not figure out how to be a "girl" as I went through puberty. To top it off, we moved. I had a few girlfriends but no guy friends, which I really missed. I was too tall, quiet, insecure, and not confident in my classes or any social settings. I was in search mode. Somehow I happened upon a place for myself: the youth group at my church. It was very small. Five of us: me, a nerdy guy, a quiet girl, a punk girl, and a "hood" who was kind and cute, even though he played the tough guy. For some reason, these were my "peeps," a place where I could really be myself and just have fun. Belonging to this youth group helped me to gain the confidence that I actually was OK.

Safe Havens for At-Risk Youth

Some youth need extra special attention to protect and support them. The following shows the power of one man, one idea, one website, leading to a safety net for LGBT youth.

Responding to repeated news reports of students committing suicide after being bullied at school, Dan Savage, an author and syndicated columnist, decided to send a message of hope and inspiration to LGBT (lesbian, gay, bisexual, or transsexual) youth facing harassment. Savage and his partner, Terry Miller, created a YouTube video entitled "It Gets Better." Since that video was released in September, 2010, a non-profit organization and a book of the same name have been created. The "It Gets Better Project" (www.itgetsbetter.org) is now a worldwide movement that has inspired more than 50,000 user-created videos that have logged more than 50 million views. Video submissions of hope have been received from celebrities, politicians, media personalities, the President, and scores of regular folks. What started as one man's idea bloomed into a concrete action and is now a wellspring of support, inspiration, and help to a large segment of our at-risk youth.

> **These are what nurturing villages look like. One proactive parent, teacher, principal, witness, or friend can build a stronger social safety net for one—and for all.**

TAKE THE TIME

"Kids spell love T-I-M-E."
– John Crudele

While our daily lives are often busy with work, activities, and family obligations, we all can benefit from period-ically stopping and taking the time to reflect on our core values. Pursuing what matters takes time, but in the long run, doing what we value and love expands our energy because of the "juice" it gives us—and we are the better for it.

Take the Time to Care of Yourself

Put your oxygen mask on first. Meeting other people's needs graciously is difficult if your own basic needs for sleep, fun, good nutrition, downtime, and companion-ship haven't been met.

Amy, like many of her friends, was a bit overwhelmed with her parenting responsibilities and her family life. She often felt anxious trying to keep all the balls in the air of morning rou-tine, carpooling to lessons and sports, homework help, volun-teering at school, meals, household stuff, then bedtime routine . . . before starting it all over again. When she saw the neatly folded laundry get thrown back in the dirty clothes basket as her son was straightening up his room, she hit the tipping point. To calm herself, she went for a long walk. She thought about her daily "to do" list and of all the fun things she wasn't doing because of all the household chores. She decided to do things differently. She started with the laundry, teaching her nine- and 11-year-olds to do their own. (Eventually, they bragged about it to friends.) She also realized her kids could take care of getting themselves ready in the morning, so she started to jog at that time. She even made a monthly date with girlfriends for hiking and coffee and joined a book club. Most importantly, Amy began having more fun with her family. She found more time for one-on-one dates with her kids as well as for playing board games and reading together.

Take the Time for One-on-One Connection

Although family time is precious, each of our children craves one-on-one connection with each of his or her parents. Carve out space in your week for each child and nurture the special connection that will blossom.

When our son was born, I made the very conscious decision to be an active and integral participant in his upbringing. As a fresh new parent, I wasn't exactly sure what that would look like. Looking back over the last eight years though, I have a long list of of parental accomplishments I never anticipated. I got to be the solo "dad" at Music Together and Storytime at the library, I've run hundreds of miles with Raffi blaring from inside the jogger in my grip, and I taught Math and History for a year when we decided to homeschool for first grade. But the most recent, unexpected, and personally fulfill-ing of my "integrated parent" accomplishments was receiving my Black Belt in Tae Kwon Do with my son.

We enrolled our son into the Tiny Tigers program at our local Dojang when he was four years old. There were no pre-conceived notions that he'd be the next Chuck Norris, but we had heard good things and it seemed like a solid activity for a rambunctious boy: a healthy dose of structure, emphasis on respect, and lots of calories burned. Win, win, win. When he finished the Tiny Tigers program a year later, it was an easy choice to enroll him in the color belt classes and keep him rolling. Up until that time, my involvement in TKD was primarily as uniform finder and taxi driver. I'd play with our daughter in the waiting room during class, give our son a high five at the end, and that was that. Now he was taking classes with "big kids" and, to my surprise, many adults. At first it seemed a little strange to see my five-year-old in class with 30-, 40-, 50-year-olds, but then the light bulb turned on. If I was going to be here for 45 minutes twice a week, why not join the fray and share the experience with my son?

The Black Belt was hanging so far up the wall that I didn't really even set it as a goal. I figured we'd ride it out for a year and see what happened. What happened was that three years flew by, and we were soon in the midst of a hard-core 10-week training period for Black Belt testing. Along the

ALL RIGHTS RESERVED. © 2014 FAMILY EMPOWERMENT NETWORK™

way, I had had the pleasure of participating alongside my son (and now my daughter, too) in an activity that meets all of us where we are—something we can do side by side and all be challenged at the same time. Instead of just talking to my kids about "respect" or "hard work," I get to show them in class how I interpret those challenges.

We prepared for belt testings together. In the beginning, it was me who did all of the coaching at home, remembering the order of movements in the forms and adjusting technique here and there. Now we are peers, and my son is able to learn new forms faster than I can. He teaches me the movements and reminds me of my technical short-comings. I expect that very soon the tides will shift permanently and he will be performing feats that I can no longer hope to master. When that day comes though, we will still be able to do this activity together. Regardless of where our future leads us, we will always be able look back on the common path we shared to earn our Black Belts together. – Jeff, Father of two

Take the Time for Family Rituals

When we think back on what we remember and cherish most in our childhood, rituals, holiday celebrations, vacations, everyday meals, and bedtime routines often top the list.

Our family has the tradition of holding hands for a few moments before dinner. We were waiting for our almost two-year-old grandson to join us, but his independent toddler nature prevented him from holding hands (even the hands of his sweet little girlfriends). One evening, all three generations were having a family meal. About five minutes into the meal, Ray suddenly stopped eating, looked around, and held out his hands. We all stopped eating and talking and joined hands (again), while he beamed at us and we beamed back. He had finally joined the circle! We all went back to dinner, but five minutes later he held out his hands again and we all stopped, held hands, and beamed at each other again. Ah, the joys of being a grandparent!

As a special treat and for inspiration, read Lizanne Ryan's beautiful reflection on the time she spends with

her grandchildren, **"Visite Chez Grand-maman,"** at the end of our book.

Take the Time for Rites of Passage

"If we do not initiate the young, they will burn down the village to feel the heat." – African proverb

Our culture (with a few exceptions such as the Jewish community's Bar and Bat Mitzvah) has largely forgotten how to welcome our adolescents into adulthood. Nevertheless, engaging in rites of passage rituals is an important cultural task which can buffer the tendency our kids have to create their own rites (i.e., smoking, drinking, and other risky behavior). Families can create their own rites of passage ceremonies to commemorate the growing maturity of their teens as well as to honor their teens' needs for new responsibilities and new connections to community. There are countless ways to do this such as:

- Having a gathering of adults important to your child's life
- Planning and going on a wilderness trip alone or with others
- Drawing on the natural world for inspiration for the rite of passage
- Creating a commemorative book, quilt, bracelet, etc., and presenting the symbolic gift during a special ceremony

A group of 14 women from our family and circle of friends gathered to celebrate my daughter's passage into womanhood. We began the evening by sharing stories of our own first menses and, then, why we were glad we were women. Four hours went by in a flash. We heard stories of finding our first blood and thinking we were going to die; one grandmother was terrified she would get pregnant because she liked the boy who sat across the room from her in her eighth-grade class; and one aunt read several hilarious selections from the journal she kept as a 13-year-old about the foibles of growing up with younger sisters, a nosey mother, and fickle girlfriends. Tears were shed and laughter abounded. The joys and sorrows of

© 2014 FAMILY EMPOWERMENT NETWORK™ ALL RIGHTS RESERVED.

motherhood, careers, adventures, and pranks were shared. It was like group therapy! Many of us had never had the honor of sitting in a circle of women sharing the joys, the fears, the struggles, and triumphs of womanhood. At 10:00 pm, we finally paused to eat our well-overcooked dinner. What a memorable night for my daughter, and, really, for all of us women. My daughter couldn't have experienced more love and support than in that group of powerful women, for her new journey into adulthood. – Maya's Mother

Take the Time for Mentoring

"Relationships are the oxygen of human development. All young people need and deserve many adults who connect–and connect deeply–with them." – Dr. Peter Benson of the Search Institute

The 40 Developmental Assets that we highlighted in Chapter 3 remind us that all children need several interested, caring adults in their lives during their transition into adulthood. One of the great ways to be a part of children's lives is through sharing your passions. For example, if you're a ham radio enthusiast, avid bird watcher, or poetry buff, find a way to connect with kids who have similar interests and support them in developing their interests. Good mentors help kids to see the strengths and gifts they have. They help children reflect upon and learn from their wins and losses. Good mentors accept children as they are and avoid trying to "fix" them.

Healthy communities help kids to use their time constructively and connect them with adults who serve as their mentors, youth group leaders, and sports team coaches. According to Dr. Peter Benson, founder of the Search Institute and the 40 Developmental Assets, the importance of adults in the lives of teens cannot be overly emphasized. Benson's groundbreaking research led him to this magic formula:

SPARK + 3 ADULTS WHO SEE THAT SPARK + OPPORTUNITY = THRIVING YOUTH

In other words, when a child's spark is ignited and encouraged by adults who care, the child thrives. One father shares how his daughter's interest in science was cultivated throughout her childhood and fostered her motivation to become a doctor:

At first it was rats and koalas, and then it was dolphins and whales. Abby's fascination with animal science led her to begging to bring home the class rabbit and rat when her preschool teacher (Adult #1) was ready to "move them along." Of course, we wanted to encourage her interest and caring. . . . In elementary school, projects on dolphins and whales sparked her fancy (aka obsession)–and, facilitated by the children's librarian (Adult #2), she read every book on the subjects in our local library.

Then the nagging started, which led to family whale-watching vacations and to training through the dedicated volunteers of Whale Watching Spoken Here. In 9th grade, Abby's Physics teacher (Adult #3) recognized her "spark" and nominated her to attend a National Youth Leadership Forum on Medicine, and her fascination with science shifted to the human species. Abby has taken the pre-med track in college, and through opportunities offered through other adults who see her spark, is well on her way to medical school and a career of putting her love of science to a rewarding use. – Barry, Father of two girls

Take the Time to Teach Kids the Magic of Helping Others

Gradually, and especially as kids approach adolescence, they can find safe havens with extended family, with friends and their families, and in community programs. Examples of community safe havens include sports teams, youth groups, music activities, and science clubs. A particularly important safe haven for teens can be service activities such as working at the food bank or the soup kitchen. When youth serve in the community, it's a win-win situation, because adults see youth as a valuable resource and the kids feel empowered. Many who volunteer, in fact, feel they receive more than they give.

ALL RIGHTS RESERVED. © 2014 FAMILY EMPOWERMENT NETWORK™

The Petrie family decided to commemorate Earth Day by planting trees through the organization Friends of Trees in their community. The Petrie kids were not thrilled about getting up early on a Saturday morning, but they were proud of themselves at the end of the morning as they looked over the field of young trees they had helped to plant. They learned to appreciate the work it takes to keep our world green, and the kids convinced their parents that they should volunteer at least once a month with different organizations in their hometown.

When kids volunteer, they:

- Have the opportunity to be valuable resources
- Experience the good feeling service to others offers
- Learn that their community values them
- Develop relationships with adults and role models
- Have positive peer influence (friends who set good examples)
- Develop a sense of purpose, caring, empathy, and sensitivity

Take the Time to Advocate for a Child-Friendly Society

Advocating for our children's well-being is one important area to which you can contribute your time. In our culture, we say we value children, but we often don't put our money where our mouths are. How did we let this happen?

Where are the laws protecting our children from guns? Where is stable school funding? Where are our government regulations on video game violence? What protects our children from predatory advertising?

A school counselor focused her April activities on teaching children and reminding parents (through newsletter articles and online blogging) to be screen smart: understanding advertisements, having a balanced life, and the importance of limiting screen time and content. The month culminated in a

school-wide Screen Turn Off week. Written feedback from families and provocative classroom discussions confirmed the positive impact the experience had on their lives. Kids even wrote thank-you notes to the counselor, making her day.

> **Simply choose one thing you can do in the community. When you get that done, choose one more. . . .**

DON'T FORGET TO PLAY AND CREATE!

"Love life, engage in it, give it all you've got. Love it with a passion, because life truly does give back, many times over, what you put into it."
– Maya Angelou

Ours is a precious place to be alive–and it is our responsibility as parents and caring adults to pass along this message, this legacy, to our children. Introduce them to the wonders of our world through gardening in your backyard, playing in the neighborhood park, or walking through the woods, through sharing books and poetry, making music and art together, or volunteering with the very young or the very old. Encourage children to pursue hobbies such as hiking, drawing, bird watching, nature photography, gardening, or caring for animals. The options are endless when it comes to exploring and engaging in the world.

Our children need to know that this is a world worth loving, that we live in a good world. As adults we must hold both the pain and the wonder of the world. When we start to feel out of balance toward the fearful side rather than the open and happy side–or sense that our children do–it may be time to get outside and play. So underrated, play and creativity are right in front of us, easier than therapy, and cheaper than a vacation. They

© 2014 FAMILY EMPOWERMENT NETWORK™ ALL RIGHTS RESERVED.

are the perfect remedy for smoothing out life's imbalances triggered by the demands of school, work, and the intrusion of media.

So, go out and do something for the sheer joy of it! Every parent has built in mentors—our kids! Play and creativity can help us to re-balance our thoughts and emotions so we have the energy to nurture ourselves, our families, our communities, and the world at large.

A FINAL NOTE

"The world changes when we change." – Marianne Williamson

In small steps, parenting calls us to acts of love and courage. Through mindfulness and conscious decision making, and with a light heart, we can ensure that our children have enough time in the real world and an abundance of caring, face-to-face relationships to develop the skills they need—the skills that are the building blocks of happiness, the building blocks of reaching human potential.

We do not need a big fix, or paradigm shift, to take us to a place where we trust our instincts again and enjoy the journey. Nor do we need data to provide us with an anatomy of caring—what it feels like and why it matters so much. Our hearts know the way.

"Where, after all, do universal human rights begin? In small places, close to home—so close and so small that they cannot be seen on any maps of the world. Yet they are the world of the individual person; the neighborhood he lives in; the school or college she attends; the factory, farm, or office where he works. Such are the places where every man, woman, and child seeks equal justice, equal opportunity, equal dignity without discrimination. Unless these rights have meaning there, they have little meaning anywhere. Without concerted citizen action to uphold them close to home, we shall look in vain for progress in the larger world."

– Eleanor Roosevelt

ALL RIGHTS RESERVED. © 2014 FAMILY EMPOWERMENT NETWORK™

What social norms would you like to change and how can you get started?

POSSIBLE DISCUSSION QUESTIONS

1) Who makes up your village–the people who love and care about you and your family? Who are the mentors in each child's life? How might you expand your village?

2) Share your strategies for open, connected relationships with each of your children. What times of day or activities keep you regularly connected?

3) What are the safe havens in the lives of each of your family members, and what type of safe haven could you provide for other children in your community?

4) Share memories of rites of passage and celebrations from your childhood. What rites of passage or celebrations will you facilitate for your children?

5) What sparks or passions are you recognizing in your child(ren)? What specifically do you notice or hear? Brainstorm how you might help them find their passion. What other adults might your child enlist for support? How might you fan the sparks of another child?

6) What support structure(s) do you need to put in place to have the time in your busy world of parenting to ensure you live your family values?

PUTTING IT INTO PRACTICE

- Have a family meeting to talk specifically about making your home a safe haven for everyone. What rituals, habits, rhythms, one-on-one dates, family outings, comfort/self-soothe areas does everyone want?

- Create a safe haven for children about whom you care (e.g., a support group for kids, a Girls' or Boys' "Night Out," an after-school club, etc.).

- Provide opportunities for children to give to others (e.g., volunteering, helping around the house, pet sitting, reading to an elderly neighbor, etc.).

- Explore ways to bring the 40 Assets into your child's school, your neighborhood, or your congregation.

- In prominent places throughout your home, post reminders of the six touchstones: Stay Connected, Cultivate Empathy, Take the Time, Create Safe Havens, Walk the Talk, and Play/Create.

PUTTING IT TOGETHER—YOUR VERSION

Write down a few ideas you have been inspired to implement in your own life after reading/discussing this book.

_____

_____

_____

_____

Visite Chez Grand-maman

By Lizanne Ryan

I love to have the grand-children at the chalet. (cottage)
It allows a very special time together,
A time that is very different
From when I am visiting and fold myself into their lives
Their parents', their home life, their world.

First, I must situate you.
My chalet is in the country
On a very quiet road,
And it faces a small mountain,
Surrounded by a huge forest.
Between the mountain and the chalet,
There is no civilization.

It is a terrain for wild animals —
Deer, moose, birds of all kinds, squirrels, rabbits, wild turkeys,
And the underworld of forest and swamp.
On my property, there is a nice expanse of land,
Framed by an apple orchard and large trees.
There is grass to run and play games on, trees to climb,
Nooks and crannies to discover nature's secrets.

And the house sits on this piece of land
As if it were an integral piece of it.
A little house tailored to children
Like something out of a fairy tale.

Inside, it is very cozy and intimate
with a small wood stove at the center of the living area,
And the furniture is well used, chabby chic, children friendly.

Into this world, I love to receive my grand-children
Who leave behind their iPhones, iPads, video games, TV.
They are plunged into a world of intimacy
With nature, with themselves, with me.

And around this world I create rituals.
Rituals that they come to seek, even as they grow older.
Games we play: cache cache, treasure hunts, frog hunting;
Fishing with the locals on the dock, marshmallows and camp fires,
Beaching and jumping off rocks and docks,
Creating slides, skiing and snow shoeing.

The animals are an integral part of this world
And I love to witness the grand-children's discoveries
Of the wild.

Watching my granddaughter sit on a snow bank
Hands outstretched, holding sunflower seeds,
Listening to the flutter of chickadees in the bush,
Waiting patiently for them to land on her hand;

My grandson awakened from sleep and wrapped in a warm blanket,
peering into the dark of night to glimpse the shadows of the deer
and listen to them as they crunch apples in the orchard;
Or taken out on the patio to gaze at the sky full of stars,
and hear the rustling sounds of the night in the forest;

The excitement of my step-granddaughters as they see the wild turkeys
dragging their big stomachs across the snow to the bird feeder,
leaving traces of a round balls with little feet marks in the snow;

The continual chase of chipmunks snapping at blue jays
and running into their tunnels,
The play of raccoons and their big round eyes shining in the night,
The chickadees chatting to me as I come with the food,
The excitement of discovering a moose or fox tracks.

These are but a few of the rich experiences
that the grand-children live in the wild of the country.

Their creativity is greatly stimulated here, as they are occasionally,
and deliberately, left to their own devices.
As I busy myself in the house, I watch to see where it will take them,
And I marvel at their resourcefulness:

The creation of a piece of art from a slice of wood off a log,
The imagination running wild as one climbs a tree and creates stories,
The games they play with plastic pots and sticks from nature,
Beautiful sculptures made with stones piled in Eskimo fashion,
The making of a house out of a large cardboard box,
The simple play in tents and houses made from bits of wood,
Sitting on their thinking chair and taking a moment of quiet,
The stories, songs and dances they create around the campfires.

There is no end to their creativity, play and joy in this very simple place,
where all is there for them to discover.

In the house, the wood stove is the center of our life in cold seasons.
Children of all ages are attracted to fire —
To sit by it, to watch it, to poke it,
to carry the wood in and prepare it, to light it.
It is a continuous fascination to them.
And many beautiful evenings are spent
With children in my lap on the big rocker,
Reading stories and telling tales.

My most memorable moment with the fire is
when one of my grand-children carefully set himself up by the fire,
Bringing the mattress from the sofa, adding cushions at head and feet
and finding a soft blanket to stretch himself out onto the floor
with his feet warmed by the fire.
Enveloped in his warm cocoon, we talked and I read to him
And he said to me, Grand-maman, this is heaven!

The flowing days and nights of our lives there,
Pulled away from their home routines,
Bring them into a special place of simplicity,
Rooted in Mother Earth.

It is our privileged time
To have that intimate contact together.
They come into my world,
And the absence of the other world
Opens them up totally to it
And to what I can give them —
My love, my laughter, my song, my creativity, my bond with nature.
These times are my most precious offerings.
And my most precious memories.

My grand-children and I have been blessed to
To have such a special place
And I know it is anchored deep down in their being for life.
To quote my grand-son, it is heaven!

Related Resources for Further Exploration

POLITICAL ACTION GROUPS FOCUSED ON FAMILY-RELATED ISSUES

Family Forward Oregon engages parents, employers, and policymakers to create innovative, forward-thinking approaches to work and family. www.familyforwardoregon.org (or similar in your area)

MomsRising is a transformative online and on-the-ground multicultural organization of more than a million members and over a hundred aligned organizations working to increase family economic security, to end discrimination against women and mothers, and to build a nation where both businesses and families can thrive. www.momsrising.org

The Mother PAC endorses and supports pro-family candidates for public office and builds a political voice for families. www.motherpac.org

Stand for Children educates and empowers communities to demand excellent public schools; advocates for effective education policies and investments; ensures the policies and funding reach classrooms and help students; and endorses leaders who will stand up for educational priorities. www.stand.org

RITES OF PASSAGE

Documentary: Frederick Marx' documentary on rites of passage at www.warriorfilms.org/rites-of-passage

Organization: ***The National Rites of Passage Institute*** facilitates child, youth, and community development through an African-centered Rites of Passage program that promotes identity, resiliency, and village building. http://ritesofpassage.org/

Organization: ***Rite of Passage Journeys***, established in 1968, fosters self-discovery, community, and connection with the natural world. Their mission is to mentor youth, adults, and elders through life transitions through intentional rites of passage experiences and rite of passage education. http://riteofpassagejourneys.org

Chapter 9 of *Raising Our Daughters* or *Raising Our Sons* by Kathy Masarie, MD, Kathy Keller Jones, MA, and Jody Bellant Scheer, MD, at www.family-empower.com

SPARKS

For more information on "igniting sparks," check out Peter Benson's book, *Sparks: How Parents Can Ignite the Hidden Strengths of Teenagers*, or go to the Search Institute's website at www.search-institute.org and click on the "Sparks" link. This will lead you to an evidence-based curriculum that will help children discover and explore their unique interests and passions. The site also offers suggestions on how you can be that adult who ignites a spark.

RACE TO NOWHERE FILM

This a thought-provoking documentary that "challenges current assumptions on how to best prepare the youth of America to become healthy, bright, and contributing citizens." Go to www.racetonowhere.com to learn how to arrange for a screening and follow-up panel discussion at your school or within your community. The website also features resources on "healthy" homework and the perils of high-stakes testing.

© 2014 FAMILY EMPOWERMENT NETWORK™ ALL RIGHTS RESERVED.

1

2

3

4

5

6

7

8

Supplemental Information 8

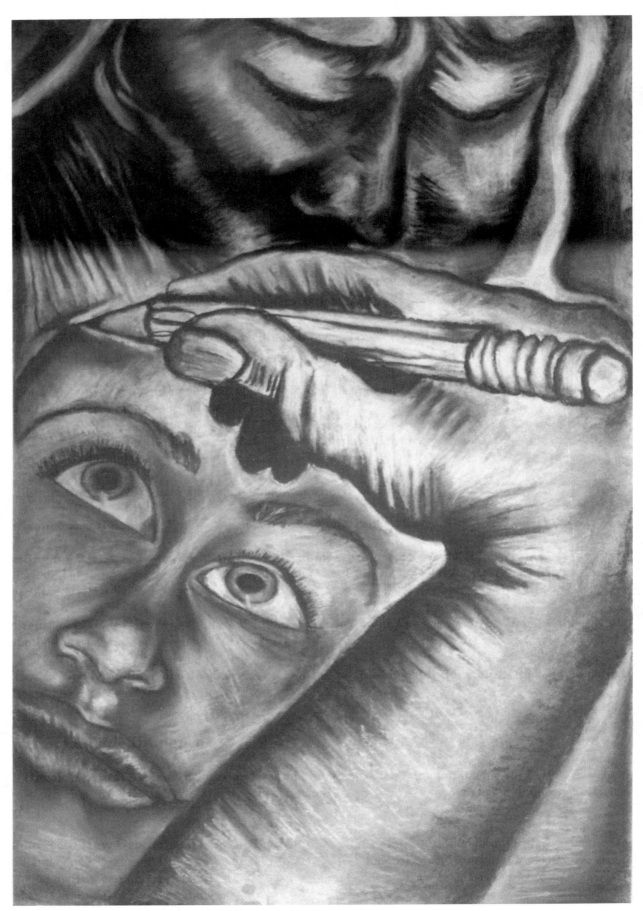

Sally Nelson, Class Instructor & Children's Art Institue Teacher

GUIDELINES FOR DISCUSSION GROUPS

Face to Face supports you to explore ways to help children navigate their social world. Some people prefer to use the book as an informational resource. Others use it as a guide for discussion groups. Parent groups discuss one chapter weekly or monthly, sharing concerns, brainstorming solutions, and supporting each other. Many groups find that, when the facilitator role/leadership rotates, every participant is empowered and the group's shared wisdom can be maximized. For a 12-minute video on "How to Run a Successful Parenting Group," check out: www.family-empower.com/running-a-successful-parenting-group. Family Empowerment Network also offers free monthly webinars on starting groups. Check out our website calendar for details at www.family-empower.com/all-events.

HOW TO START YOUR OWN PARENT DISCUSSION GROUP
- Talk to your friends, parents of your child's friends, scout or soccer team parents … Find a co-leader.
- Share these guidelines with your school counselor and ask if s/he would like to get involved.
- Talk to the principal about putting an ad in your school newsletter to announce an "info meeting."
- Host a parent seminar with a local speaker. Distribute a sign-up sheet to tap interest in a class.
- An ideal group size is 8-12 participants.

FACILITATOR GUIDELINES
- The role of **facilitator** can rotate each session among participants. Facilitators generally take time to read the entire chapter. They are not expected to be experts on the topic.
- Start on time with an opening inspirational quote or story. (See "Opener Guidelines" below.) End on time with exploring action steps. Groups generally meet for one-and-a-half hours.
- After the inspirational opening, the discussion can be kicked off with the **Circle Question.** Each participant can take a turn answering the question, so everyone's voice is heard (allow approximately 20 minutes). The group then can choose the most relevant **Discussion Questions,** and the facilitator can guide the discussion for about 30 minutes. The final 30 minutes can be devoted to brainstorming action steps.
- The facilitator's principal role is to keep the focus on the topic and to foster a comfortable environment for everyone to share ideas respectfully. The articles and the discussion questions are only a guide to the topic. Add your own ideas. If the discussion branches off in a relevant, fruitful direction, follow it. Conversation that drifts off topic too far, however, can be gently brought in with a comment such as, "I noticed we are talking about … rather than …"
- One difficult aspect of facilitating groups is when a participant dominates the discussion. You may want to agree ahead of time how to handle individuals monopolizing the discussion. For example, you might thank that person for his/her opinions, and then ask someone else for an opinion. If overtalking continues, share your concern with the individual privately later.
- Listen carefully and talk less to help guide the discussion effectively. Keep in mind:
  › Consensus is not the goal of the group. Disagreements should be expected and welcomed.
  › Interrupt any discussions during which respect is jeopardized.
  › Consider having a visible clock or using a sand timer or a talking stick to foster fair sharing.
  › Keep the discussions moving along, so there is time to discuss the Putting It Together action steps.
- This discussion group is for personal exploration and to discover how the participants can make a difference in their own lives in connection with their families, communities, and schools. Always be sure to save time to write down the personal ideas you want to implement in Putting it Together—Your Version.

OPENER GUIDELINES
- The role of **opener** can rotate each session among participants.
- The purpose of the opening is to transition from the outside distractions of daily life to the discussion. The opening can be an opportunity to express appreciation of parenting or child(ren). This could take the form of sharing a personal story or family ritual, reading a poem or a passage from a favorite book, doing a short activity with the group, singing a song, doing a dance, leading a meditation, etc.
- Start on time. Late members can join in as they arrive. Groups committed to starting on time may add 15 minutes to the beginning of the meeting for socializing and snacks.

CLASS SCHEDULE AND SIGN-UP

All participants fill out this sheet at the first session. Two volunteers are needed for each session: someone to provide an **Opening** and someone to serve as **Facilitator**. Snacks might be provided by the hosting member.

Group Coordinator: .... Email: ....

Co-Coordinator: .... Email: ....

	CHAPTERS	DATE	OPENER	FACILITATOR	LOCATION
1	Exploring Values and the Lay of the Land				
2	Parenting Touchstones: Friendship Begins at Home				
3	Outside Influences				
4	Navigating Friendship and Social Groups				
5	Peer Mistreatment				
6	Fostering Resilience				
7	Courage to Act				
	Gathering to Celebrate				

TIPS FOR A MEANINGFUL, CONNECTED, SUPPORTIVE DISCUSSION GROUP

- Bring an open mind and acceptance to each meeting. Share honestly.
- Attend every meeting and show up on time for the opening.
- Prepare for each session by doing as much reading as you can. At least, try to read the chapter, if not all the articles.
- List one or more goals for what you want to create in your life during this discussion group time.
- Take your turn with the co-leader roles: **opener** and **facilitator**.
- Ideally everyone monitors his/her own talking and makes sure it is a "fair amount of time." This is critical. Putting structures in place to support equal sharing can be helpful.
- Allow time for discussion of solutions and action steps in each session.
- Take ownership of actions. Focus your energy on what you can change personally or contribute as a group. Avoid "should" as in: "my child, partner, the media, school, counselor … should …"
- **Set ground rules for the group** at the first meeting and share how you are best supported by others:
  - › Observe confidentiality of personal stories.
  - › Seek clarity, not consensus. Maintain respect for everyone's opinions.
  - › Avoid finger pointing, blaming others or ganging up on someone with a differing opinion.
- Handle conflict directly and early, such as one or two people dominating the discussions.
  - › Avoid third party talk.
  - › If you have a problem with a fellow participant, talk with him/her directly and when the problem is small and easier to resolve. Everyone matters, and the group success depends on honest interactions.
  - › If a problem continues, or a group problem arises, bring it up at the next meeting to discuss together.
- Participants with serious problems with their child or with themselves will find more effective support from outside, for example, from professional counseling.

          ALL RIGHTS RESERVED. © 2014 FAMILY EMPOWERMENT NETWORK™

Resources

American Psychological Assn. Task Force on the Sexualization of Girls. "Report of the APA Task Force on the Sexualization of Girls." Washington, DC: American Psychological Assn., 2007. www.apa.org/pi/wpo/sexualization.html.

Aronson, Elliot. *Nobody Left to Hate: Teaching Compassion After Columbine.* NY: Owl Books, 2000.

Baltzell, Amy, Richard D. Ginsburg, and Stephen Durant. *Whose Game Is It Anyway? A Guide to Helping Your Child Get the Most from Sports, Organized by Age and Stage.* NY: Mariner Books, 2006.

Bazelon, Emily. *Sticks and Stones: Defeating the Culture of Bullying and Rediscovering the Power of Character and Empathy.* NY: Random House, 2013.

Beane, Allan L., PhD. *Bully Free Classroom: Over 100 Tips and Strategies for Teachers K-8.* Minneapolis, MN: Free Spirit Publishing, 1999.

---. *Protect Your Child from Bullying: Expert Advice to Help You Recognize, Prevent, and Stop Bullying Before Your Child Gets Hurt.* San Francisco, CA: Jossey-Bass, 2008.

Beck, Carol, MS. *Nourishing Your Daughter: Help Your Child Develop a Healthy Relationship with Food and Her Body.* NY: Perigee Trade, 2001.

Benson, Peter, PhD. *Parent, Teacher, Mentor, Friend: How Every Adult Can Change Kids' Lives.* Minneapolis, MN: Search Institute, 2010.

Biddulph, Steve. *Raising Boys: Why Boys are Different—and How to Help Them Become Happy and Well-Balanced Men.* NY: Celestial Arts, rev. 2008.

Borba, Michele, EdD. *Building Moral Intelligence: The Seven Essential Virtues that Teach Kids to Do the Right Thing.* San Francisco, CA: Jossey-Bass, 2002.

---. *Nobody Likes Me, Everybody Hates Me: The Top 25 Friendship Problems and How to Solve Them.* San Francisco, CA: Jossey-Bass, 2005.

---. *No More Mis-behavin': 38 Difficult Behaviors and How to Stop Them.* San Francisco: Jossey-Bass, 2003.

Brigman, Greg, PhD, and Linda Webb, PhD. *Student Success Skills: Helping Students Develop the Academic, Social, and Self-Management Skills They Need to Succeed.* www.studentsuccessskills.com.

Bronson, Po, and Ashley Merryman. "Why White Parents Don't Talk About Race." *NurtureShock: New Thinking About Children.* NY: Twelve, 2009.

Brooks, Robert, PhD, and Sam Goldstein, PhD. *Nurturing Resilience in Our Children: Answers to the Most Important Parenting Questions.* NY: McGraw-Hill, 2002.

---. *Raising Resilient Children: Fostering Strength, Hope, and Optimism in Your Child.* NY: McGraw-Hill, 2001.

---. *Raising a Self-Disciplined Child: Help Your Child Become More Responsible, Confident, and Resilient.* NY: McGraw-Hill, 2009.

Brooks, Robert, PhD, Sam Goldstein, PhD, and Sharon Weiss, MEd. *Angry Children, Worried Parents: Seven Steps to Help Families Manage Anger.* Plantation, FL: Specialty Press/A.D.D. Warehouse, 2004.

Brooks, Robert, PhD, Sam Goldstein, PhD, and Kristy Hagar, PhD. *Seven Steps to Help Your Child's Social Skills: A Family Guide*. Plantation, FL: Specialty Press/A.D.D. Warehouse, 2006.

Brown, Brené, PhD, LMSW. *Daring Greatly: How the Courage to Be Vulnerable Transforms the Way We Live, Love, Parent, and Lead*. NY: Gotham Books, 2012.

Brown, Stuart, and Christopher Vaughan. *Play: How It Shapes the Brain, Opens the Imagination, and Invigorates the Soul*. NY: Avery Trade, 2010.

Brizendine, Louann, MD. *The Female Brain*. NY: Broadway Books, 2006.

---. *The Male Brain: A Breakthrough Understanding of How Men and Boys Think*. NY: Three Rivers Press, 2010.

Carr, Nicholas. T*he Shallows: What the Internet is Doing to Our Brains*. NY: W.W. Norton & Co., 2010.

Carroll, Kevin. *Rules of the Red Rubber Ball: Find and Sustain Your Life's Work*. NY: ESPN, 2005.

---. *What's Your Red Rubber Ball?! Discover Your Inspiration and Chase It for a Lifetime*. NY: ESPN, 2008.

Cash, Hilarie, PhD, and Kim McDaniel, MA. *Video Games & Your Kids*. Enumclaw, WA: Idyll Arbor Press, 2008.

Cohen, Cathi. *Raise Your Child's Social IQ: Stepping Stones to People Skills for Kids*. Silver Springs, MD: Advantage Books, 2000.

Cohen, Lawrence, PhD. *Playful Parenting*. NY: Ballantine Press, 2002.

---. *The Opposite of Worry: The Playful Parenting Approach to Childhood Anxieties and Fears*. NY: Ballantine, 2013.

Coloroso, Barbara. *The Bully, the Bullied, and the Bystander*. NY: Harper Resource, 2003.

Cooper, Scott. *Sticks and Stones: 7 Ways Your Child Can Deal with Teasing, Conflict, and Other Hard Times*. NY: Random House, 2000.

Csikszentmihalyi, Mihaly. *Flow: The Psychology of Optimal Experience*. NY: Harper, 2008.

Davis, Devra, PhD, MPH. *Disconnect: The Truth about Cell Phone Radiation, What the Industry Has Done to Hide It, and How to Protect Your Family*. NY: Dutton, 2010.

Davis, Stan, and Julia Davis. *Empowering the Bystander in Bullying Prevention K-8*. Minneapolis, MN: Research Press, 2007. www.stopbullyingnow.org.

---. *Schools Where Everyone Belongs: Practical Strategies for Reducing Bullying*. Minneapolis, MN: Research Press, 2007.

DeBenedet, Anthony, MD, and Lawrence Cohen, PhD. *The Art of Roughhousing: Good Old-Fashioned Horseplay and Why Every Child Needs It*. Philadelphia, PA: Quirk Books, 2011.

Doherty, William J., PhD. *The Intentional Family: Simple Rituals to Strengthen Family Ties*. NY: William Morrow, 1999.

---. *Take Back Your Kids: Confident Parenting in Turbulent Times*. Notre Dame, IN: 2000.

Doidge, Norman, MD. *The Brain that Changes Itself: Stories of Personal Triumph from the Frontiers of Brain Science*. NY: Penguin Books, 2007.

Dodson, Shireen. *The Mother-Daughter Book Club*. Harper Perennial, 2007.

---. *100 Books for Girls to Grow On*. William Morrow, 1998.

 ALL RIGHTS RESERVED. © 2014 FAMILY EMPOWERMENT NETWORK™

Drew, Naomi, MA. *The Kids' Guide to Working Out Conflicts: How to Keep Cool, Stay Safe, and Get Along.* Minneapolis, MN: Free Spirit Publishing, 2004.

---. *No Kidding About Bullying: 125 Ready-to-Use Activities to Help Kids Manage Anger, Resolve Conflicts, Build Empathy, and Get Along.* Minneapolis, MN: Free Spirit Publishing, 2010. Book with CD-ROM.

Duke, Marshall, PhD, Stephen Nowicki, Jr., PhD, and Elizabeth Martin, MEd. *Teaching Your Child the Language of Social Success.* Atlanta, GA: Peachtree Publishers, 1996.

Dutwin, David. *Unplug Your Kids: A Parent's Guide to Raising Happy, Active, and Well-Adjusted Children in the Digital Age.* Avon, MA: Adams Media, 2009.

Echevarria, Pegine. *For All Our Daughters: How Mentoring Helps Young Women and Girls Master the Art of Growing Up.* Worcester, MA: Chandler House Press, 1998.

Elkind, David. *The Power of Play: Learning What Comes Naturally.* Cambridge, MA: Da Capo Press, 2007.

Englander, Elizabeth, PhD. *Bullying and Cyberbullying: What Every Educator Needs to Know.* Cambridge, MA: Harvard Education Press, 2013.

Freedman, Judy S. *Easing the Teasing: Helping Your Child Cope with Name-Calling, Ridicule, and Verbal Bullying.* NY: Contemporary Books, 2002.

Fried, SuEllen, and Blanche Sosland, PhD. *Banishing Bullying Behavior, Transforming the Culture of Peer Abuse.* NY: Rowman & Littlefield, 2011 rev.

Fried, SuEllen, and Lynne Lang. *30 Activities for Getting Better at Getting Along.* Kansas City, KS: BullySafeUSA, 2011.

Fried, SuEllen, and Paula Fried, PhD. *Bullies, Targets and Witnesses: Helping Children Break the Pain Chain.* NY: Rowman & Littlefield, 2003.

---. *Bullies, Targets & Witnesses, Helping Children Through the Schoolyard Battlefield.* NY: Rowman & Littlefield, 1996.

Galinsky, Ellen. *Mind in the Making: The Seven Essential Life Skills Every Child Needs.* NY: William Morrow, 2010.

Giannetti, Charlene, and Margaret Sagarese. *Cliques: 8 Steps to Help Your Child Survive the Social Jungle.* NY: Broadway Books, 2001.

Ginsburg, Kenneth, MD. *Building Resilience in Children and Teens: Giving Kids Roots and Wings.* Washington, DC: American Academy of Pediatrics, 2011.

Glenn, H. Stephen, and Jane Nelsen, EdD. *Raising Self-Reliant Children in a Self-Indulgent World: Seven Building Blocks for Developing Capable Young People.* 2nd ed. NY: Harmony Books, 2000.

Goldman, Carrie. *Bullied: What Every Parent, Teacher and Kid Needs to Know About Ending the Cycle of Fear.* NY: HarperCollins, 2012.

Goleman, Daniel. *Emotional Intelligence: Why It Can Matter More Than IQ.* NY: Bantam, rev. 2007.

---. *Social Intelligence: The New Science of Human Relationships.* NY: Bantam, rev. 2005.

Gordon, Mary. *Roots of Empathy: Changing the World Child by Child.* Ontario, Canada: Thomas Allen Publishers, 2005.

Gotlin, Robert, DO. *Dr. Rob's Guide to Raising Fit Kids: A Family-Centered Approach to Achieving Optimal Health.* NY: DiaMedica Publishing, 2008.

© 2014 FAMILY EMPOWERMENT NETWORK™ ALL RIGHTS RESERVED.

Hamkins, SuEllen, MD, and Renee Schultz, MA. *The Mother-Daughter Project: How Mothers and Daughters Can Band Together, Beat the Odds and Thrive Through Adolescence.* NY: Hudson Street Press, 2007. www.themother-daughter-project.com.

Hawn, Goldie, and Wendy Holden. *10 Mindful Minutes: Giving Our Children–and Ourselves–the Social and Emotional Skills to Reduce Stress and Anxiety for Healthier, Happier Lives.* NY: Penguin Group, 2011.

Hinduja, Sameer, and Justin Patchin. *Bullying Beyond the Schoolyard: Preventing and Responding to Cyberbullying.* Thousand Oaks, CA: Corwin Press, 2009.

Hiton, Howard, MS, Stephen Grant, LCSW, and Peter Mortolla, PhD. *BAM! Boys Advocacy and Mentoring: A Leader's Guide to Facilitating Strengths-Based Groups for Boys.* NY: Routledge: 2007. www.bamgroups.com

Home, Arthur M. *Bully Busters: A Teacher's Manual for Helping Bullies, Victims, and Bystanders.* Minneapolis, MN: Research Press, 2000.

Hoover, John H., and Ronald Oliver. *Bullying Prevention Handbook: A Guide for Principals, Teachers, and Counselors.* Bloomington, IN: National Educational Service, 1996.

Kelly, Joe. *Dads and Daughters: How to Inspire, Understand, and Support Your Daughter.* NY: Three Rivers Press, 2003.

Kimmel, Michael. *Guyland: The Perilous World Where Boys Become Men (Understanding the Critical Years Between 16 and 26).* NY: Harper, 2008.

Kindlon, Dan, PhD. *Too Much of A Good Thing: Raising Children of Character in an Indulgent Age.* Bel Aire, CA: Miramax Books, 2003.

Kindlon, Dan, PhD, and Michael Thompson, PhD. *Raising Cain: Protecting the Emotional Life of Boys.* NY: Ballantine Books, 2000.

Kohn, Alfie. *The Homework Myth: Why Our Kids Get Too Much of a Bad Thing.* Cambridge, MA: De Capo Press, 2007.

Levine, Madeline, PhD. *The Price of Privilege: How Parental Pressure and Material Advantage Are Creating a Generation of Disconnected and Unhappy Kids.* NY: HarperCollins Publishers, 2006.

Linn, Susan. *Consuming Kids: Protecting Our Children from the Onslaught of Marketing & Advertising.* NY: Anchor Books, 2004.

Louv, Richard. *Last Child in the Woods: Saving Our Children from Nature-Deficit Disorder.* NY: Algonquin Books, 2008.

Ludwig, Trudy. *Better Than You.* NY: Borzoi Books, 2011. www.trudyludwig.com.
---. *Confessions of a Former Bully.* NY: Dragonfly Books, 2012.
---. *The Invisible Boy.* NY: Knopf Books for Young Readers, 2013.
---. *Just Kidding.* Berkeley, CA: Tricycle Press, 2006. Also available in Spanish.
---. *My Secret Bully.* Berkeley, CA: Tricycle Press, 2004. Also available in Spanish.
---. *Sorry!* Berkeley, CA: Tricycle Press, 2006.
---. *Too Perfect.* Berkeley, CA: Tricycle Press, 2009.
---. *Trouble Talk.* Berkeley, CA: Tricycle Press, 2008.

Mackoff, Barbara. *Growing a Girl: Seven Strategies for Raising a Strong, Spirited Daughter.* NY: Dell, 1996.

Marche, Stephen. "Is Facebook Making Us Lonely?" *Atlantic Monthly,* May 2012. Available online at http://www.the-atlantic.com/magazine/archive/2012/05/is-facebook-making-us-lonely/8930/

Masarie, Kathy, MD, Jody Bellant Scheer, MD, and Kathy Keller Jones, MA. *Raising Our Daughters: The Ultimate Parenting Guide for Healthy Girls and Thriving Families.* Portland, OR: Family Empowerment Network, 2009. www.family-empower.com

  ALL RIGHTS RESERVED. © 2014 FAMILY EMPOWERMENT NETWORK™

---. *Raising Our Sons: The Ultimate Parenting Guide for Healthy Boys and Strong Families.* Portland, OR: Family Empowerment Network, 2009. www.family-empower.com

McCoy, Elin. *What To Do…When Kids Are Mean To Your Child.* NY: Reader's Digest Adult, 1997.

McNamara, Barry, and Francine McNamara. *Keys to Dealing with Bullies.* NY: Barron's, 1997.

Medina, John, PhD. *Brain Rules: 12 Principles for Surviving and Thriving at Work, Home, and School.* Seattle: Pear Press, 2009.

---. *Brain Rules for Baby: How to Raise a Smart and Happy Child from 0 to 5.* Seattle: Pear Press, 2011.

Mogel, Wendy, PhD. *The Blessing of a B Minus: Using Jewish Teachings to Raise Resilient Teenagers.* NY: Scribner, 2011.

---. *The Blessing of a Skinned Knee: Using Jewish Teaching to Raise Self-Reliant Children.* NY: Scribner, 2008.

Nelsen, Jane, EdD. *Positive Discipline.* NY: Ballantine Books, 2005, revised.

Nordling, Joanne, MS, MEd. *Taking Charge: Caring Discipline That Works at Home and at School.* Portland, OR: Parent Support Center, 2007.

Olweus, Dan. *Bullying at School: What We Know and What We Can Do.* Malden, MA: Blackwell Publishing, 1993. www.olweus.org

Orenstein, Peggy. *Cinderella Ate My Daughter: Dispatches from the Front Lines of the New Girlie-Girl Culture.* NY: Harper Collins, 2011.

Payne, Kim John. *Simplicity Parenting: Using the Extraordinary Power of Less to Raise Calmer, Happier, and More Secure Kids.* NY: Ballantine Books, 2009.

Payne, Kim John, Luis Fernando Llosa and Scott Lancaster. *Beyond Winning: Smart Parenting in a Toxic Sports Environment.* Guilford, CT: Lyons Press, 2013.

Pica, Rae. *Your Active Child: How to Boost Physical, Emotional, and Cognitive Development Through Age-Appropriate Activity.* NY: McGraw-Hill, 2003.

Pincus, Donna, PhD. *Growing Up Brave: Expert Strategies for Helping Your Child Overcome Fear, Stress, and Anxiety.* NY: Little Brown & Co., 2012.

Pipher, Mary, PhD. *Reviving Ophelia: Saving the Selves of Adolescent Girls.* NY: Riverhead Trade, rev. 2005.

---. *The Shelter of Each Other: Rebuilding Our Families.* NY: G.P. Putnam's Sons, 1996.

Pollack, William, Ph.D. *Rescuing Our Sons from the Myths of Boyhood.* NY: Owl Books, 1998.

---. *Real Boys' Voices.* NY: Penguin Books, 2001.

---. *Real Boys' Workbook: The Definitive Guide to Understanding Boys.* NY: Villard Books, 2001.

Pope, Harrison, MD, Katharine Phillips, MD, and Roberto Olivardia. *The Adonis Complex: How to Identify, Treat, Prevent Body Obsession in Men and Boys.* NY: Free Press, 2002.

Rao, Anthony, PhD, and Michelle Seaton. *The Way of Boys: Raising Healthy Boys in a Challenging and Complex World.* NY: William Morrow, 2009.

Rowan, Cris. *Virtual Child: The Terrifying Truth About What Technology is Doing to Children.* 2010.

© 2014 FAMILY EMPOWERMENT NETWORK™ ALL RIGHTS RESERVED.

Rubin, Kenneth H. *The Friendship Factor: Helping Our Children Navigate Their Social World—and Why It Matters for Their Success and Happiness.* NY: Skylight Press, 2002.

Sax, Leonard, MD, PhD. *Boys Adrift: The Five Factors Driving the Growing Epidemic of Unmotivated Boys and Underachieving Young Men.* NY: Basic Books, 2007.

Schor, Juliet. *Born to Buy: The Commercialized Child and the New Consumer Culture.* NY: Scribner, 2004.

Siegel, Daniel, MD. *Brainstorm: The Power and Purpose of the Teenage Brain.* NY: Tarcher, 2014.

Siegel, Daniel, MD. *The Mindful Brain: Reflection and Attunement in the Cultivation of Well-Being.* NY: Norton & Co., 2007.

---. *The Neurobiology of "We": How Relationships, the Mind, and the Brain Interact to Shape Who We Are.* (CD – 2008). www.drdansiegel.com.

Siegel, Daniel, MD, and Tina Payne Bryson, PhD. *The Whole-Brain Child: 12 Revolutionary Strategies to Nurture Your Child's Developing Mind.* NY: Bantam, 2012.

Siegel, Daniel, MD. and Mary Hartzell, MEd. *Parenting from the Inside Out: How a Deeper Understanding Can Help You Raise Children Who Thrive.* NY: Tarcher Publishing, rev. 2004.

Simmons, Rachel. *The Curse of the Good Girl: Raising Authentic Girls with Courage and Confidence.* NY: Penguin Books, 2010.

---. *Odd Girl Out: The Hidden Culture of Aggression In Girls.* NY: Harcourt, 2002.

---. *Odd Girl Speaks Out.* NY: Harcourt, 2004.

Spretnak, Charlene. MA. *Relational Reality: New Discoveries of Interrelatedness That Are Transforming the Modern World.* Topsham, ME: Green Horizon Books, 2011.

Sterling, Diana. *The Parent as Coach Approach.* White Oak Publishing, 2008.

Steyer, James P. *Talking Back to Facebook: The Common Sense Guide to Raising Kids in the Digital Age.* NY: Scribner, 2012.

Szalavitz, Maia, and Perry, Bruce, MD, PhD. *Born for Love: Why Empathy is Essential—and Endangered.* NY: William Morrow, 2010.

Thomas, Susan Gregory. *Buy, Buy Baby: How Consumer Culture Manipulates Parents and Harms Young Minds.* Boston: Houghton Mifflin, 2007.

Thompson, Jim. *The Double-Goal Coach: Positive Coaching Tools for Honoring the Game and Developing Winners in Sports and Life.* NY: HarperCollins, 2003. www.positivecoach.org.

Thompson, Michael, PhD, and Teresa Barker. *It's a Boy: Your Son's Development from Birth to Age 18.* NY: Ballantine Books, 2009.

Thompson, Michael, PhD, Lawrence J. Cohen, PhD, and Catherine O'Neill Grace. *Best Friends, Worst Enemies: Understanding the Social Lives of Children.* NY: Ballantine Books, 2001.

---. *Mom, They're Teasing Me: Helping Your Child Solve Social Problems.* NY: Ballantine Books, 2002.

Turkle, Sherry, PhD. *Alone Together: Why We Expect More from Technology and Less from Each Other.* NY: Basic Books, 2011.

Walsh, David, PhD. *No: Why Kids—of All Ages—Need to Hear It and Ways Parents Can Say It.* NY: Atria Books, 2007.

Wenner, Melinda. "The Serious Need for Play," *Scientific American Mind,* February/March 2009, pp. 21-29.

 ALL RIGHTS RESERVED. © 2014 FAMILY EMPOWERMENT NETWORK™

Wilson, Susan. *Sports Her Way: Motivating Girls to Start and Stay with Sports.* NY: Fireside Books, 2000.

Wiseman, Rosalind. *Masterminds & Wingmen: Helping Our Boys Cope with Schoolyard Power, Locker-Room Tests, Girlfriends, and the New Rules of Boy World.* NY: Random House, 2013.

---. *Owning Up® Curriculum: Empowering Adolescents to Confront Social Cruelty, Bullying, and Injustice.* Minneapolis, MN: Research Press, 2009. Book with CD-ROM.

---. *Queen Bee Moms & King Pin Dads: Dealing with the Parents, Teachers, Coaches and Counselors Who Can Make–or Break–Your Child's Future.* NY: Crown Publishers, 2006.

---. *Queen Bees & Wannabes: Helping Your Daughter Survive Cliques, Gossip, Boyfriends and Other Realities of Adolescence.* NY: Crown Publishers, 2002.

Zimbardo, Philip, PhD, and Nikita Duncan. *The Demise of Guys: Why Boys are Struggling and What We Can Do About It.* TED Conferences: 2012.

Zimmerman, Jean, and Gil Reavill. *Raising Our Athletic Daughters: How Sports Can Build Self-Esteem and Save Girls' Lives.* NY: Main Street Books, 1998.

FILMS OR DVDS

Empower Our Girls: Seven Strategies That Work (with Dr. Kathy Masarie). 2010. DVD. www.family-empower.com
Finding Kind. Dir. Lauren Parsekian. Indieflix, 2011. Film. www.findingkind.indieflix.com/movie
A Girl's Life with Rachel Simmons. PBS "Frontline" Special. 2009. DVD. www.shoppbs.org
The In Crowd and Social Cruelty (with John Stossel). ABC "20/20" Special. Interview with Michael Thompson, others. ABC. 15 Feb., 2002. DVD.
It's Elementary: Talking About Gay Issues in School (1999) and *It's Still Elementary* (2009). Dir. Debra Chasnoff. GroundSpark Productions. Films. www.groundspark.org
Merchants of Cool: A Report on the Creators & Marketers of Popular Culture for Teenagers. PBS "Frontline" Special. 2001. DVD. www.shoppbs.org
Miss Representation. Dir. Jennifer Siebel Newsom, 2011. Film. www.missrepresentation.org.
No Time to Think. Dir. Brian Huston and Brian Grubb. Road Trip Productions. 2013. Film. www.notimetothink.net
Play Again. Dir. Tonje Hessen Schei. Ground Productions, 2010. Film. http://playagainfilm.com.
Race to Nowhere. Dir. Vicki Abeles. Reel Link Films, 2010. Film. www.racetonowhere.com
Straightlaced: How Gender's Got Us All Tied Up. Dir. Debra Chasnoff. GroundSpark Productions, 2011. Film. www.groundspark.org
Tough Guise: Violence, Media and the Crisis in Masculinity. Dir. Sut Jhally. Media Educational Foundation, 1999. DVD.
What About Boys? Connecting with Our Sons (with Dr. Kathy Masarie). 2010. DVD. www.family-empower.com

ORGANIZATIONS

Campaign for a Commercial Free Childhood (www.commercialfreechildhood.org)
Common Sense Media (www.commonsensemedia.org)
The Council for Boys and Young Men (www.onecirclefoundation.org)
The Dad Man and Dads & Daughters (www.thedadman.com)
Embrace Civility in the Digital Age (www.embracecivility.org)
The Girls' Circle: (www.onecirclefoundation.org)
Girls Inc. (www.girlsinc.org)
GroundSpark (www.groundspark.org)
Hardy Girls Hardy Women (www.hghw.org)
Massachusetts Aggression Reduction Center (http://webhost.bridgew.edu/marc/)
New Moon Girls (www.newmoon.com)
Positive Coaching Alliance (www.positivecoach.org)
Sources of Strength (www.sourcesofstrength.org)
Stand for Courage (www.standforcourage.org)

© 2014 FAMILY EMPOWERMENT NETWORK™ ALL RIGHTS RESERVED.

Permissions

All material in this list is copyright protected. Please contact authors directly for reprint requests. For permission of material not listed here, please contact info@family-empower.com.

Chapter 2: Parenting Touchstones: Friendship Begins at Home

Excerpt on 2:3 from *Daring Greatly* (p. 216-217) by Brené Brown, copyright © 2012 by Brené Brown. Used by permission of Gotham Books, an imprint of Penguin Group (USA) LLC.

Excerpt on 2:11 from *Daring Greatly* (p. 68) by Brené Brown, copyright © 2012 by Brené Brown. Used by permission of Gotham Books, an imprint of Penguin Group (USA) LLC.

Excerpt on 2:11 from poem by Lizanne Ryan entitled **"Visite chez grand-maman."** Poem in its entirety found on 7:14. Printed with permission of the author.

Story on 2:17, **"Embracing the Low-Tech Life,"** by Berdine Jordan, writer and visual artist, Portland, OR. Printed with permission of the author.

Brain illustration on 2:23 created for Family Empowerment Network by Jonathan West.

"Significance and Belonging." Printed with permission from Glenda Montgomery.

"Parenting for Peace." Reprinted with permission from Inbal Kashtan. Copyright © Inbal Kashtan. A version of this article appeared in *Parenting From Your Heart*, by Inbal Kashtan, and also published in *Paths of Learning* (Spring 2003) and *California Home Schooler* (Oct. 2002).

"The Steps of NVC." Copyright © Inbal Kashtan. Excerpted from *Parenting From Your Heart* by Inbal Kashtan and also published in *Mothering*, Jan./Feb. 2002.

"The Key to Surviving the Negative Impact of Digital Technology? Moderation." Printed with permission from Doreen Dodgen-Magee, PsyD.

Chapter 3: Outside Influences

The 40 Developmental Assets® are used with permission from Search Institute®. Copyright © 1997 Search Institute®. 615 First Ave. NE, Ste. 125, Minneapolis, MN 55413; 800-888-7828; www.search-institute.org. All rights reserved.

"Straightlaced: How Gender's Got Us All Tied Up." Reprinted with permission from Debra Chasnoff, President and Senior Producer of GroundSpark, 901 Mission Street Suite 205, San Francisco, CA 94103. Excerpt from "Background for Teachers and Facilitators" from the Curriculum Guide to *Straightlaced: How Gender's Got Us All Tied Up.* Copyright © GroundSpark. www.groundspark.org

 All Rights Reserved. © 2014 Family Empowerment Network™

lay Again: **Reconnecting Children to Nature."** Printed with permission from Meg Merrill, MSW, producer of the film
 Again. More about the film at PlayAgainFilm.com or www.facebook/PlayAgainFilm.

voiding the Addictive Potential of Internet Use." Printed with permission from Hilarie Cash, PhD.

creen Savvy Parents: Embracing Civility in a Digital Age." Reprinted with permission from Nancy Willard, MS, JD,
 ector of Embrace Civility in the Digital Age. www.embracecivility.org

mily Assets® are used with permission from Search Institute®. Copyright © 2012 Search Institute®. 615 First Ave. NE, Ste.
 , Minneapolis, MN 55413; 800-888-7828; www.search-institute.org. All rights reserved.

01 Screen-Free Activities." Reprinted with permission from Campaign for a Commercial Free Childhood (CFFC), 89 South
 et Suite 403, Boston, MA 02111. www.ccfc.org

apter 4: Navigating Friendships and Social Groups

ngredients of a Healthy Relationship." Originally printed as "A Recipe for Healthy Relationships." Reprinted with
 mission from Raphael House of Portland. "Take Care: A Guide to Safe Relationships" is a Raphael House project. www.
 haelhouse.com

Making a Plan for Success in Play: Extra Help for Children with Perspective-Taking Difficulties." Printed
 h permission from Deanne Nelson, MS, CCC/SLP and Katie Willis, MA, CCC/SLP.

lso's Choice Wheel is reprinted with permission from Cerebellum Corporation. Kelso's Choice Wheel is Copyright ©
 11 Barbara Clark, PhD, and Diane Hipp, CPS. Copyright © 2011 Design. Cerebellum Corporation. All rights reserved.
 lso's Character Wheel is reprinted by permission of Cerebellum Corporation. Copyright © 2012 Barbara Clark, PhD,
 d Diane Hipp, CPS. Copyright © 2012 Design. Cerebellum Corporation. All Rights Reserved.

When Our Kids Fight With Friends." Printed with permission from Glenda Montgomery.

irls' Cliques." Reprinted, with permission, from New Moon Girl Media, Duluth, MN. "Rosalind Wiseman on Cliques."
 w.newmoon.com

oy Groups." Excerpt from Rosalind Wiseman's *Masterminds & Wingmen: Helping Our Boys Cope with Schoolyard Power, Locker-
 om Tests, Girlfriends, and the New Rules of Boy World.* NY: Harmony Books, 2013. Pages 26, 38-45. Reprinted with permission
 m Random House Books. All rights reserved.

CyberbullyingNOT: Stopping Online Social Aggression." Reprinted with permission from Nancy Willard, MS, JD,
 rector of Embrace Civility in the Digital Age. www.embracecivility.org

hapter 5: Peer Mistreatment

Rights and Responsibilities." Reprinted with permission from Patricia Higgins, Principal of Thorndale Elementary
 hool, Quebec, Canada. http://thorndale.lbpsb.qc.ca/rights.htm

ip Sheet to Support Children Who Are Mistreated by Peers." Reprinted with permission from Stan Davis and
 arisse Nixon, PhD.

© 2014 FAMILY EMPOWERMENT NETWORK™ ALL RIGHTS RESERVED.

"**A Movement to Stand for Courage.**" Printed with permission from Nicole Jon Carroll, MSW, LCSW, founder and executive director of Stand for Courage. www.standforcourage.org

"**Empowerment Groups to Reduce Peer Mistreatment Among Girls.**" Reprinted with permission from Wendy Craig, PhD, Queen's University, Ontario, Canada.

Chapter 6: Fostering Resilience

Excerpt on 6:8 from ***Daring Greatly*** (p. 23) by Brené Brown, copyright © 2012 by Brené Brown. Used by permission of Gotham Books, an imprint of Penguin Group (USA) LLC.

Illustration of "**Steps to Resilience: Climbing the Staircase of Needs**" on 6:13. Reprinted with permission from JoAnne Nordling, MS, MEd. Adapted from *Taking Charge: Caring Discipline That Works at Home and at School*. Portland, OR: Parent Support Center, 2007.

"The Wholehearted Parenting Manifesto" from ***Daring Greatly*** (pp. 244-245) by Brené Brown, copyright © 2012 by Brené Brown. Used by permission of Gotham Books, an imprint of Penguin Group (USA) LLC.

Excerpt on 6:24, "**You're a Helicopter Parent If You . . .**" by Erin Wade from *The Dallas Morning News* (Aug. 15, 2005). Reprinted with permission from *The Dallas Morning News*.

"**Learning to be OK with Plan B: Helping Your Young Child Develop Resiliency.**" Printed with permission from Glenda Montgomery.

"**Developing Capable People Guidelines.**" Reprinted with permission from Jane Nelsen at Empowering People. From the book *Raising Self-Reliant Children in a Self-Indulgent World: Seven Building Blocks for Developing Capable Young People* by H. Stephen Glenn and Jane Nelsen, EdD. www.empoweringpeople.com

"**Understanding Resiliency in Kids.**" Reprinted with permission from Kelly Bartlett, writer, parent educator, and author of *Encouraging Words for Kids*. www.kellybartlett.net

"**Super Mom: Ditching the Cape.**" Reprinted with permission from Eryn Rodger, MA, Certified Positive Discipline Educator, Santa Cruz,CA.

"**Nature's Neurons: Do Early Experiences in the Natural World Help Shape Children's Brain Architecture?**" Reprinted by permission from Richard Louv. Originally posted July 26, 2012 on www.childrenand-nature.org.

"**Helping Kids Manage Anxiety: Ages and Stages.**" Reprinted with permission from Sue Campbell. Article originally appeared in the August 2012 issue of *Metro Parent*, Portland, Oregon.

Chapter 7: Courage to Act

Quote on mindfulness on 7:7 used with permission from Robert Slatford.

Story on 7:9 from "**Every Student a Star.**" Used with permission from Search Institute®. Copyright © 2000 Search Institute®. 615 First Ave. NE, Ste. 125, Minneapolis, MN 55413; 800-888-7828; www.search-institute.org. All rights reserved.

"**Visite Chez Grand-maman.**" Printed with permission of Lizanne Ryan, writer and grandmother, Outremont, Quebec.

 ALL RIGHTS RESERVED. © 2014 FAMILY EMPOWERMENT NETWORK™

About the Authors

KATHY MASARIE, MD, is a sought-after national speaker and facilitator specializing in empowering caring adults with communication and advocacy tools to enhance the lives of children from pre-school through high school. A pediatrician, Kathy served the medical needs of families in Pennsylvania and Oregon for over two decades. Out of her pediatric practice grew a special interest in preventing risky behavior in teens and the founding of Family Empowerment Network (www.family-empower.com). Through this organization, she offers one-on-one coaching, seminars, workshops, and classes on various topics on raising children. The culmination of her work has been the publication of *Raising Our Daughters, Raising Our Sons,* and *Face to Face: Cultivating Kids' Social Lives in Today's Digital World,* parenting discussion guides aimed at creating strong, healthy, and thriving families. Kathy lives in a cabin in Washington with her husband. She considers her son and daughter, and their partners, to be her greatest teachers and inspiration in life.

KATHY KELLER JONES, MA, is a developmental psychologist and licensed school counselor. For over three decades, she has supported elementary and middle schools by teaching social-emotional skills to students, conducting group and individual therapy, consulting with staff and parents, and creating school-community connections. She currently teaches parenting classes and consults with parents on the many challenges of doing their job well. In addition to working with children and families, Kathy has worked as a writer and a research psychologist. As a Jungian, she is interested in the individual's search for meaning and the importance of one's connection to nature. Kathy and her husband live in Oregon and share the joys of nature with their adult children, their partners, and their grandchildren.

JODY BELLANT SCHEER, MD, is a pediatrician whose dream is creating healthy relationships and peaceful co-existence within all families, institutions, and communities in the world. She has worked for over three decades with sick newborns, premature infants, and their families in Portland, OR. She is the co-founder of Medical and Educational Relief International Association (MERIA), Inc., a non-profit working to provide essential medical and educational services worldwide. As well, she regularly volunteers as a physician in developing countries, serves as a volunteer and board member of numerous non-profit organizations, is a foster parent, and teaches compassionate communication to medical, parent, and community groups. Jody lives with her husband on a houseboat in Oregon, where they enjoy frequent visits from their three adult children and large extended family.

CASSANDRA DICKSON, MA, is a writer and published poet. She is actively navigating the intersection of digital culture and childhood as she raises her two daughters, ages 10 and 13. With a long-standing interest in the connections between the human, animal, and natural worlds, Cassandra has worked for many years as both an environmental activist and an animal protection advocate. She has a B.A. in Modern Culture and Media from Brown University and an M.A. in English and Creative Writing from the University of Houston. She lives with her wonderful family, her husband and children, in Portland, Oregon.

© 2014 FAMILY EMPOWERMENT NETWORK™ ALL RIGHTS RESERVED.

RUTH MATINKO-WALD, MA, is a Positive Discipline-certified parent educator who brings decades of involvement with youth organizations to her work with Family Empowerment Network. She likes to consider herself a "human sparkler," one who brings out the best in everyone she encounters and sparks positive change. Along with Dr. Kathy Masarie, Ruthie offers talks to parenting groups and schools throughout the Portland, Oregon, area. She also facilitates parent discussion groups, using the *Raising Our Daughters*, *Raising Our Sons*, and *Face to Face* guides as the curriculum. Prior to working at Family Empowerment Network, Ruthie had a fun career in marketing, public relations, and book publishing in Oregon, in her home state of Pennsylvania, and in Florida. She was instrumental in making *Face to Face* a reality by bringing her writing, editing, and production skills to the task. Her professional work aside, Ruthie's most important job is being mom to two awe-inspiring daughters.

MONIQUE TERNER, MEd, RYT, is an educator, coach, and the owner of Creative Roots, LLC (www.creativerootspdx.com). She offers her clients over 20 years of experience working with children, parents, and educators in public, private, and alternative educational settings. As a certified YogaCalm® instructor, she also offers opportunities for children and adults to experience the benefits of yoga and mindfulness. In addition, she offers Academic Life Coaching® to teens; ARTbundance Creative Coaching® to teens and adults; advocacy and support for families of children with special needs; support and coaching for families who homeschool their children; as well as consultation and continuing education for professionals interested in learning about Interpersonal Neurobiology, Somatics, and Creativity. As a mom of three wonderful boys, Monique is most passionate about sharing ways in which we can empower children to lead happy and healthy lives and make a positive impact in our world.

© 2014 FAMILY EMPOWERMENT NETWORK™ ALL RIGHTS RESERVED.

Make Your Job Easier:
Use These Guides to Foster Strong, Healthy & Thriving Families

- **Compendiums of the best parenting information available**

- **Based on the 40 Developmental Assets**

- **Organized as guides for parent discussion groups**

By Kathy Masarie MD, Jody Bellant Scheer MD, and Kathy Keller Jones MA

"As a school counselor, I find the books an invaluable resource to use with parents. The information is solid, timely and relevant to raising kids in today's environment."

- Portland, OR, Counselor Tara Vargas

Go to www.family-empower.com to purchase your books and/or for a free Organizer's Guide for starting a *Raising Our Daughters/Sons* discussion group.

Family Empowerment Network®